CHILD SEXUAL ABUSE

CHILD SEXUAL ABUSE
ITS SCOPE AND OUR FAILURE

Rebecca M. Bolen

Boston University
Boston, Massachusetts

KLUWER ACADEMIC / PLENUM PUBLISHERS
NEW YORK, BOSTON, DORDRECHT, LONDON, MOSCOW

Library of Congress Cataloging-in-Publication Data

Bolen, Rebecca Morris.
    Child sexual abuse: its scope and our failure/Rebecca M. Bolen.
        p.   cm.
    Includes bibliographical references and index.
    ISBN 0-306-46576-0
        1. Child sexual abuse.   I. Title.

    HV6570 .B65 2001
    362.76—dc21
                                                                        2001016497

ISBN 0-306-46576-0

©2001 Kluwer Academic / Plenum Publishers, New York
233 Spring Street, New York, New York 10013

http://www.wkap.nl/

10 9 8 7 6 5 4 3 2

A C.I.P. record for this book is available from the Library of Congress

Printed in the United States of America

To my daughters,
Erin and Jenny,
with all my love

PREFACE

This book is the result of an intensive review of the professional literature on child sexual abuse that has occurred over an almost 10-year period. When I originally began this manuscript several years ago, I was struck by the dearth of scholarly books that reviewed the knowledge base as it related specifically to the scope of child sexual abuse. Existing books then and now were more likely either to be clinical in orientation or to focus upon a specific aspect of child sexual abuse. Often the books echoed the salient themes of their period. Thus, a number of books currently in print are concerned with recovered memories of childhood sexual abuse, whereas several books written in the mid to late 1980s were about purported false allegations made by children or their guardians.

On the other hand, only a few books in the last 20 years have had as their stated purpose a scholarly review of the empirical literature. Yet, these books are essential for providing easy reference to the extant knowledge base. Because the knowledge base is now voluminous, only the most ardent professionals in this field have the time to remain current across the breadth of the literature base. Thus, reviews of the child sexual abuse empirical literature serve important purposes. They allow these professionals to remain current in areas of child sexual abuse outside their primary knowledge area. Further, they provide concise reviews for other interested professionals.

While I never deviated from the purpose of providing an intensive review of this knowledge base, I also began to realize that this book would be strikingly incomplete if it were simply a review of the literature. Indeed, the more I delved into this literature base, the more I became struck by the inconsistencies between our empirical literature and our professional response to the problem of child sexual abuse. For example, I was (and remain) puzzled by the differences between the empirical literature and the response of some professionals regarding the issue of allegations of sexual abuse during divorce or custody disputes. If only a tiny percentage of these cases are falsely and maliciously filed, why do we retain such a skeptical view of them? I was also perplexed (and remain so) by the profession's narrow focus on nonoffending mothers when abuse by a father accounts for only a small percentage of all sexual abuse. Where is our literature base on nonoffending fathers? The answer is that it is nonexistent.

I finally began to realize that this book had to be more than a simple review of the literature. It also had to point out the discrepancies between our empirical knowledge base and our professional response to child sexual abuse while trying to offer some explanation for the often profound differences. This explanation appears to lie in our historical conceptualization of child sexual abuse, for our professional response to child sexual abuse only makes sense when framed within the assumptions deriving from this historical conceptualization. It surely does not make sense if we look only at the empirical knowledge base.

The book that emerged has three important sections. The first section sets the stage for this book by reviewing the historical context within which early theories of child sexual abuse were developed. The second section of the book then turns to the task of reviewing the empirical knowledge base that defines the scope of the problem of child sexual abuse. This section considers the prevalence and incidence of child sexual abuse, extrafamilial and intrafamilial abuse, factors associated with risk of abuse and of offending, and nonoffending guardians. It is argued throughout this section that child sexual abuse is an epidemic fueled by sociocultural structures and values. The final section considers the aftermath of child sexual abuse—the professional response to child sexual abuse.

In the important final chapter of this book, the scope of the problem of child sexual abuse—as illustrated in the empirical knowledge base—is compared to that of the professional response to child sexual abuse. This comparison provides striking evidence that society's response to child sexual abuse is failing profoundly. By reviewing the assumptions underlying society's response to child sexual abuse, I argue that the reason for such a complete system failure is that the systemic response is grounded in the historical and often myth-bound conceptualization of child sexual abuse rather than in the empirical literature.

It is my hope that this book will add momentum for restructuring the existing child welfare system. As the evidence put forth in this book clearly shows, a restructuring of society's response to child sexual abuse is an ethical and moral imperative. It is also my hope that this book can serve as an accessible reference for professionals in understanding the scope of the problem of child sexual abuse as explicated in the empirical knowledge base. Finally, it is my hope that this book will compel readers to advocate for those changes in society that will be necessary to reduce the epidemic of child sexual abuse. Until we are willing to look at the role of society (and thus its citizens) in maintaining child sexual abuse, this epidemic will continue.

ACKNOWLEDGMENTS

As my work on this book has spanned almost 10 years and three universities, many individuals I have known both professionally and personally have influenced me.

When this book first began to take shape, one of the professors at the School of Social Work at the University of Tennessee, Nashville Branch, Dr. Hia Rubenstein, was gracious enough to read portions of an early draft of this book. Others whom I knew personally also supported me in this early process. I would especially like to thank Theresa McRedmond, Beth Richardson, and Maryann McCue. My former husband, Larry Bolen, was also steadfastly supportive, and I am grateful for his encouragement during those years.

Many of the ideas for this book, spawned at the University of Tennessee, took shape while I was at the University of Texas at Arlington. Several professors had a major influence upon me, including Doreen Elliott, Charles Mindel, Maria Scannapieco, Dick Schoech, and Coleen Shannon. I would also like to acknowledge two friends and colleagues—Leah Lamb and Liz Hodges—with whom I have had rich and rewarding collaborations. Liz Hodges, as well as Jennifer Gradante, also offered excellent suggestions on selected chapters of the book. Other friends in the Dallas/Fort Worth metroplex also offered great support, especially Sue Gardner, Janice Garner, Jo Ann Stevenson, and Guillermina Garza Treviño.

During my time at the University of Texas at Arlington, I developed a working relationship with Diana Russell, with whom I recently wrote *The Epidemic of Rape and Child Sexual Abuse in the United States.* Her exceptional prevalence study profoundly influenced my development as a researcher. Other influential researchers who have contributed much to my understanding of child sexual abuse are John Briere, Jon Conte, David Finkelhor, Kathleen Faller, Judith Herman, Linda Williams, and Gail Wyatt, among many others.

My final stop with this book has been at my present affiliation, the Boston University School of Social Work. I am most grateful to a group of colleagues with whom I shared my ideas for this book. Their excellent feedback focused the final shape of this book. To Trudy Duffy, Christine Flynn Saulnier, Robert Hudson, Cynthia Poindexter, Betty Ruth, and Lee Staples I offer my thanks. Robert Hudson and Susan Fineran's advice and feedback on selected chapters were also invaluable. Likewise, I wish to acknowledge the support of the Dean, Wilma Peebles-Wilkins.

Dana Cooper, my copy editor for this book, was extremely helpful. She was an excellent resource as she read the book and made suggestions for consistency or clarification. Jayde Campbell also provided valuable and timely assistance. Further, I wish to thank the editor at Kluwer Academic/Plenum Publishers, Mariclaire Cloutier, who provided the forum for this book and who shepherded it through the final and critical steps.

My family has also been extremely supportive of my efforts, including my mother, Billie Morris, and brothers, Eric, Mike, and Jeff Morris. I would especially like to acknowledge my sister, Melani Jolly, who has believed in me and supported me through the many ups and downs in my life.

Finally, I wish to express my deep love for my children, Erin and Jenny, and I want them to know how grateful I am for their presence in my life. They are my inspiration, for I have seen in them the eyes of the child and the pristine future I wish not only for them, but for all children in our nation and in our world.

It is for my children and all children that I write, working toward the future they so deserve.

CONTENTS

LIST OF TABLES AND FIGURES

LIST OF TABLES

LIST OF FIGURES

PART I
SOCIOHISTORICAL CONTEXT

CHAPTER 1
INTRODUCTION

The scope of the problem of child sexual abuse within our society is an epidemic of such vast proportions that virtually all children are at risk of abuse. Children are abused by loved ones, friends, family friends, those in whom they place their trust, and those bound to care for them. They are abused by those they hardly know and even those they do not know. Children of all ages are at risk and vulnerable to sexual abuse, whether in their homes, their community, or even over the Internet. Society's response to this tragedy has been to develop programs that identify, assess, and treat the victims, treat or punish the offenders, and teach young children how to deflect approaches. Our failure as a society, however, has resulted in programs, however well-meaning, that fail to identify most victims, substantiate most identified abuse, identify most offenders, treat or punish most identified offenders, and prevent the approaches of offenders.

Why are our policies and programs failing? One premise of this book is that they are failing because they are grounded not in the available knowledge base that explicates the scope of the problem of child sexual abuse, but in historical and sometimes mythical perceptions of this abuse. The child sexual abuse knowledge base for many years had a history of introducing theories and hypotheses that often viewed the victim and even the victim's mother pejoratively. These theories then became a part of the accepted knowledge base on child sexual abuse even before they were rigorously analyzed and sometimes even though empirical findings disputed them. These value-laden, stubborn, and tenacious theories were then used to frame assumptions underlying policies and programs.

A second important premise of this book is that our development of and need to maintain these myth-bound policies and programs must be understood within a sociohistorical context. Only by understanding this sociohistorical context can we also understand why these theories are stubborn and tenacious and why they continue to assume priority over our empirical knowledge base in driving policies and programs. The primary purpose of this chapter is to briefly develop these premises and to relate them to the context of this book.

DEVELOPMENT OF PREMISES

Perhaps the single most influential person in the history of the professional literature on child sexual abuse is Sigmund Freud. Much has now been written about his effect on the developing knowledge base of child sexual abuse. Although he was the first to forward a formal theory of child sexual abuse, he also renounced that theory shortly afterwards. Freud's renunciation of his seduction theory profoundly and negatively influenced the study of child sexual abuse. The denial of the reality of child sexual abuse already entrenched in society was now given legitimacy by Freud's renunciation. This culture of denial shaped not only the manner in which our professional understanding of child sexual abuse unfolded, but also how we responded to the problem.

Resulting primarily from Freud's influence, child sexual abuse became a nonevent—a report of pure fantasy. In the few cases in which it was recognized to have occurred, it was rationalized as the daughter's seduction of her recalcitrant father. As a result of this unfortunate practice, child sexual abuse became almost synonymous with father-daughter incest. Both were deemed extremely rare events.

In the early 1980s, however, two seminal random surveys on the prevalence of child sexual abuse and its characteristics shattered the illusion that child sexual abuse was rare (Russell, 1983; Wyatt, 1985). Indeed, Russell found that 38% of females in her sample were victims of contact sexual abuse by the time they were 18. Using a similar definition, Wyatt found that 44% of women in her sample were abused. When the weight of this evidence exceeded society's ability to deny its reality, the child sexual abuse knowledge base burgeoned.

Researchers were now challenged to explain the phenomenon of child sexual abuse. Resulting at least in part from Freud's conceptualization of child sexual abuse as being synonymous with father-daughter incest, one of the next theories of child sexual abuse introduced was family systems theory. In this theory, all members of the family were implicated for their roles in initiating and maintaining the abuse. An issue for debate is whether the introduction of the theory guided, or was guided by, the sociohistorical conceptualization of child sexual abuse. Regardless, both psychoanalytic theory's emphasis on the culpability of the daughter and family systems theory's emphasis on the culpability of all family members had an important effect. Both allowed for the continued minimization of the role of society in the manifestation of this tragedy.

The knowledge base in the 1980s now revealed a curious paradox. On the one hand, rigorous random prevalence studies indicated that only approximately 30% of all abuse was intrafamilial and that 7% to 8% was father-daughter incest (Russell, 1984; Wyatt, 1985). On the other hand, the developing knowledge base focused almost exclusively on intrafamilial abuse, especially father-daughter incest. This bias was so extreme that papers indexed on father-daughter incest in a professional bibliographic database now number in the hundreds and those on intrafamilial abuse exceed 2,000, as compared to less than 15 papers indexed on extrafamilial abuse (Bolen, 2000a). Further, not a single known study exists on the most prevalent type of child sexual abuse—that by acquaintances—nor is there a single known study on nonoffending fathers, when 92% to 93% of all victims are not abused by their fathers. Yet, there is a plethora of literature, historically pejorative, on nonoffending mothers. Not surprisingly, some child sexual abuse professionals continue to believe that father-daughter incest is the most prevalent type of abuse.

Not only did biases that prioritized intrafamilial abuse and especially father-daughter incest persist in the developing knowledge base, but they also became codified in policies, programs, and statutes. Methods for identifying, assessing, and treating victims concentrated almost exclusively on intrafamilial abuse, whereas victims of extrafamilial abuse were largely forgotten—a policy that ensured that most victims of child sexual abuse remained unidentified. Another important impact of these biases was that mothers were assumed to be partially at fault for child sexual abuse. Thus, in the early 1980s (and even now) mothers were often charged as co-offenders in the abuse, even when they did not commit the abuse.[1] Further, nonoffending mothers were given the grave responsibility of protecting the victim from future abuse. The alternative was to lose their children to the system. Importantly, sexual abuse was the only major crime for which mothers—instead of law enforcement officials—had to assume this responsibility for protection of the victim. Further, policies and statutes ensured that, while victims could be removed from their homes, offenders could not. This is perhaps the strangest and most burdensome of all the policies designed to "protect" children.

Another example of how the sociohistorical context allowed myth-bound policies to prevail involves child sexual abuse prevention programs. Partially as a result of the insistence by feminists that children be empowered and partially because of our inability to identify potential offenders, early prevention programs targeted only the potential victim. Introduced in the 1980s, these programs were (and continue to be) designed to help children deflect approaches of offenders. While the effort is admirable, it is difficult to understand how they can be construed as prevention programs (i.e., programs that lower sexual abuse prevalence). For them to be prevention programs, children must not only have the power to deflect the approaches of potential offenders, but these deflections must also be of such magnitude that the prevalence of child sexual abuse is concomitantly lower (Bolen, in press). Both are somewhat unrealistic assumptions. Even today, when it seems obvious that prevention programs targeting potential victims instead of offenders are palliative at best, these remain the primary organized prevention programs.

Thus, policies and programs that developed in the early 1980s have simply gained momentum. We are today what we were 20 years ago—just more so. Seldom have conceptual shifts taken place, even as the developing empirical knowledge base has refuted many of the assumptions upon which these early policies and programs were based. Hence, policies, programs, and statutes on child sexual abuse remain myth-bound and myth-driven. As a result, they are sometimes unreasonable, unsuccessful, unsupported, and unconscionable.

This brief analysis demonstrates that the development of child sexual abuse policies and programs is best conceptualized as a shotgun approach. Our policies and programs are messy, inconsistent, and splotchy and have immense cracks through which many of our children fall. Yet, the analogy of cracks in these policies and programs gives too much credence to them, for it suggests continuity and coherence. Instead, a more appropriate analogy is of a partially completed jigsaw puzzle. In this puzzle, few of the exterior pieces are placed, and interior patterns are sparse. Those that are taking shape are so distorted as to be almost unrecognizable. The large number of pieces missing from the puzzle represents the vast numbers of victims unrecognized by our current system. These are our policies.

---

[1] In the first National Incidence Study (NIS), mothers were charged as perpetrators in 46% of the abuse committed. Finkelhor and Hotaling (1984) found, however, that the vast majority of these women had been charged because of their inability to protect the child and had never physically molested the child. In the latest NCANDS incidence study (U.S. Department of Health & Human Services, 2000c), 27% of all abuse was committed by mothers, a virtual impossibility given that retrospective studies indicate that less than 0.2% of all abuse is committed by mothers (Finkelhor, Hotaling, Lewis, & Smith, 1990; Russell, 1983; Wyatt, 1985).

What is surprising, however, is that the empirical knowledge base is such that if another puzzle represented it, the picture would be much better constructed. Certainly, there would still be significant gaps, but the puzzle would have coherence and continuity. It would have shape and meaning, and emergent patterns would be recognizable even with missing pieces.

Here lies our quandary. We have two puzzles—one representing the empirical knowledge base and one representing assumptions of child sexual abuse policies and programs—that should look identical. Instead, they bear little resemblance. Thus, while the extant knowledge base rather clearly defines the scope of the problem of child sexual abuse, the assumptions undergirding policies, programs, and statutes have little resemblance to that empirical knowledge base. As such, it is not surprising that these policies and programs often fail miserably. Only when the pictures do match—when policies and programs become empirically driven—will we be able to adequately intervene in the tragic problem of child sexual abuse.

The most important premises of this book are that society has a grave responsibility to create a safe environment for *all* children and that *all* victims have the right to appropriate intervention, treatment, and protection from further harm. Yet until history-driven policies, programs, and statutes become empirically driven, our best efforts will fail.

The purposes of this book are three-fold. The first purpose is to illustrate how the sociohistorical and theoretical context shaped the often myth-bound assumptions that drive child sexual abuse policies, programs, and statutes. The second purpose is to clearly explicate the scope of the problem of child sexual abuse—the empirical knowledge base. A final purpose is to make explicit the fallacies between the history-driven policies and the empirical knowledge base while also calling for new programs that are grounded in the available empirical literature.

Finally, it is important to emphasize the unit of analysis for this book. The emphasis in this book is on the implementation of societal-level policies, programs, and statutes that have patterned the identification and assessment of victims of child sexual abuse. Many professionals do exceptional work with victims or offenders of child sexual abuse. This book is not meant to question their clinical wisdom, gained through their years of experience. Instead, it is to suggest that the *types* of child victims, families, and offenders with whom clinicians work are shaped by the policies, programs, and statutes concerning child protection in the United States. Thus, this book is concerned with how the historical conceptualization of child sexual abuse shaped the policies, programs, and statutes that affected how our society identifies and assesses victims and offenders of child sexual abuse as well as nonoffending mothers.

ORGANIZATION OF THE BOOK

Chapters 2 and 3 develop the historical context of the knowledge base for child sexual abuse, with Chapter 2 illustrating how the sociohistorical context informed our socially constructed conceptualization of the problem of child sexual abuse. This chapter briefly reviews the work on child sexual abuse done prior to Freud, his original theory of trauma, its later renunciation, and the impact of its renunciation on the suppression of the developing knowledge base in child sexual abuse. The 1960s and 1970s enjoyed a resurgence in the awareness of child sexual abuse, with the late 1970s and early 1980s being a pivotal turning point in the knowledge base. The reasons for this resurgence in awareness, within a sociocultural context, are discussed. Moving into the 1990s, the current backlash is also conceptualized within a sociocultural context. The final section of this chapter looks ahead, suggesting how the current and future sociocultural context might affect the future professional response to child sexual abuse.

Chapter 3 attends to the sociohistorical context of the theoretical base for child sexual abuse. Early theories of child sexual abuse other than Freud's are developed and presented in order by how they assigned responsibility for the abuse. Those assigning culpability to the daughter are presented first, followed in order by those assigning culpability to the mother, the family, and the more recent theories that place the blame upon the offender. The importance of reviewing these early theories is to frame how this literature has skewed the developing knowledge base and social policies on child sexual abuse. This chapter concludes by suggesting an agenda for future theoretical development, research, and policy.

The next few chapters explicate the scope of the problem of child sexual abuse. To adequately review the empirical knowledge base of child sexual abuse, however, it is important to first define the parameters for methodologically rigorous research in child sexual abuse. This is the emphasis of Chapter 4. This chapter divides the research issues into those of validity—construct, internal, external, and statistical. Although this chapter is sectioned by terms most familiar to researchers, this chapter is also written for nonresearchers. Thus, technical jargon is avoided and concepts are simplified. Within these content areas, issues such as the definition, operationalization, and measurement of child sexual abuse are discussed.

Chapters 5, 6, and 7 explicate the scope of the problem of child sexual abuse. The purpose of Chapter 5 is to review both incidence studies on reported abuse and random prevalence studies that ascertain the problem of sexual abuse in the general population. Because methodology may critically impact the prevalence of abuse reported in these studies, a brief analysis of the effect of different methodologies on the stated prevalence is presented. Afterwards, incidence and prevalence studies are compared, thus providing some context for determining how well our society identifies actual cases of abuse. The final section of this chapter explicates the scope of the problem of child sexual abuse and delineates policy implications.

Continuing with the explication of the scope of the problem of child sexual abuse, Chapter 6 addresses extrafamilial abuse. Although extrafamilial abuse is the most prevalent type of abuse, its literature base is almost nonexistent. To address this paradox, the first section revisits historical reasons that extrafamilial abuse is minimized. The next section reviews the prevalence of extrafamilial abuse by type of perpetrator, comparing it to reported extrafamilial abuse. The empirical literature is then reviewed for each type of victim/perpetrator relationship. Although this literature is sparse, it is augmented by the author's recent case-by-case analysis of all extrafamilial abuse cases within Russell's (1983) community prevalence study. This literature review, by explicating how vast and unmanageable child sexual abuse is, illustrates the extent of the problem.

Chapter 7 addresses intrafamilial abuse. The first portion of this chapter discusses theories specific to incest. The format for the remainder of the chapter is similar to that of the preceding chapter except that the review of the literature is not inclusive. The reason is simple: the minimal literature on extrafamilial abuse represents new knowledge, whereas the voluminous literature on intrafamilial abuse represents old and mostly familiar knowledge. Instead, this chapter focuses on empirical support for dynamics purported by the various theories on intrafamilial abuse. This chapter also discusses the sociohistorical context for prioritizing intrafamilial abuse and how that context shaped our understanding of intrafamilial abuse. It is shown that many of our perceptions of intrafamilial abuse are indeed myth-bound. A final section discusses the important ramifications of our current conceptualization of intrafamilial abuse and its resultant policies.

The next two chapters then turn to a discussion of causality. The overriding question across these two chapters is why child sexual abuse occurs, with Chapter 8 focusing primarily on victims and Chapter 9 focusing on offending behavior. It is inappropriate, however, to discuss causality of child sexual abuse as it relates to victims, because to do so entertains a victim-blaming stance. Instead, the focus must be on how the environment in which children live contributes causally to child sexual abuse. In this perspective, children are at risk because their environment places them at risk. To develop causality, Chapter 8 presents an ecological, transactional, and developmental perspective of child sexual abuse victimization. If, as suggested, child sexual abuse is best explained as a sociocultural phenomenon, then causality is best understood as a function of societal factors, manifesting at the level of the society and community, that are then internalized by families and even the children themselves. As these sociocultural dynamics become internalized by children, they then manifest as vulnerabilities that place children at greater risk to be sexually abused. Understanding how those sociocultural vulnerabilities interact with the familial, developmental, and transactional history of the child is a secondary purpose of this chapter.

Chapter 9 then turns to a discussion of causality as it relates to perpetrators of child sexual abuse. To begin the chapter, the sparse literature on prevalence of abusive behaviors or the likelihood to abuse is presented. Because our literature on perpetrators derives almost exclusively from reported abuse cases, the next section delineates the steps that are required for offenders to become "identified" by the system. With few identified cases of child sexual abuse resulting in convictions, it is also important to compare characteristics of unidentified offenders (i.e., those reported by victims in random prevalence studies) to those of identified offenders. The next portion of the chapter moves to the question of why offenders abuse. The format for this portion of the chapter is similar to that of the previous chapter, with issues of causality being presented within an ecological perspective that emphasizes sociocultural factors. It is suggested that these sociocultural factors operate differently for offenders who are close in age to their victims versus those with greater age disparities. For offenders who are somewhat or much older than their victims, sociocultural values such as the inappropriateness of sex with young children may act as *inhibitors* that must be overcome. For peer offenders, sociocultural values such as entitlement towards sex may instead act as *disinhibitors*. While this chapter emphasizes the sociocultural context, issues such as previous victimization and social ineptness in the offender are also addressed. Finally, the important implications for primary prevention of child sexual abuse are discussed.

Chapter 10 then moves to a discussion of nonoffending parents. The available literature, however, almost exclusively refers to the nonoffending parent as the mother. This section starts by reviewing this literature within an historical context, analyzing why it has at times been so fiercely pejorative, and discussing how biased and pejorative assumptions have become enacted, formalized, and codified into policies, programs, and statutes. It is concluded that the biases in this literature contribute to expectations of mothers that are unrealistic, untenable, and unreasonable. The negative implications for these unrealistic expectations are also discussed. The final portion of the chapter offers two new models for better framing the reactions of nonoffending guardians to their child's disclosure of abuse. The first model borrows from Hobfoll's (1989, 1991) conservation of resources theory to conceptualize the disclosure of abuse as an extreme stressor for the victim's family. The second model then explicates a humanistic model of guardian support for nonoffending guardians of sexually abused children. This model, grounded in developmental and humanistic principles, conceptualizes the reactions of nonoffending guardians to the disclosure of their child's abuse as hierarchical, with progressively higher stages of guardian support. This chapter concludes with recommendations for changes in current policies that are more sensitive to nonoffending guardians and that are more grounded in the empirical literature.

Chapter 11 discusses the response of professionals to child sexual abuse. The focus of most of this chapter is on the various points of intervention with victims, families, and offenders. For each intervention, factors that influence decisions about that intervention are discussed. This chapter recognizes the efforts and successes of many excellent professionals, while recognizing the biases and failures of the system within which they work. The final section concludes with implications for having a policy-driven, versus an empirically-driven, professional response to child sexual abuse.

The purpose of the final chapter is to synthesize and integrate the important points made in the previous chapters. To do so, this chapter is presented in three parts. The first section compares two conceptualizations of child sexual abuse, one of which derives from the historical and theoretical literature and one that derives from the empirical knowledge base. Next, the basic premise of the book—that society's response to child sexual abuse is bound within its historical conceptualization—is considered by briefly analyzing society's response to child sexual abuse as represented by studies of identified cases. Comparing this response to the previous conceptualizations, it becomes clear that the assumptions grounding society's response to child sexual abuse are most similar to those that derive from the historical conceptualization of child sexual abuse. The next sections then present both short- and long-term recommendations for moving towards a response to child sexual abuse that is grounded within the empirical literature.

CHAPTER 2
HISTORICAL OVERVIEW

INTRODUCTION

Child sexual abuse is a social construction. It is surely a reality—a tragic reality—but the definition and scope of child sexual abuse, and its conceptualization, are socially constructed phenomena. As such, to understand child sexual abuse and society's response to it, the sociocultural context within which it is defined and conceptualized must also be understood. This book is therefore not only concerned with *what* we know about child sexual abuse, but also with *how* we frame what we know about child sexual abuse. While the empirical knowledge base largely frames *what* we know about child sexual abuse, how we conceptualize and make inferences from this knowledge base are impacted critically by the theories that guide our thinking.

The current knowledge base of child sexual abuse is largely atheoretical. In the absence of formal theories of child sexual abuse, however, we continue to frame ideas about the scope and impact of child sexual abuse. Where do these ideas originate? For lack of a better reference, that is, formalized and empirically supported theories of child sexual abuse, ideas may originate from our primary reference point—individuals such as ourselves. Major (1987), in a discussion of how men and women differentially view personal entitlement in issues of justice, states that expectations derive "from similarity biases in the acquisition of social comparison information" (p. 140). In other words, individuals define their expectations based upon the expectations of people like themselves, suggesting that the personal construction of a theoretical orientation is biased towards the sociocultural context of the individual.

With an atheoretical knowledge base, this personal construction of the reality of child sexual abuse is probably inevitable and has been an ongoing problem in the professional literature. In the absence of analyses of specific hypotheses concerning the origins of child sexual abuse, the conceptualization of its origins is left open to interpretation. Because interpretations are necessarily informed (a) by the persons' referents (i.e., individuals most like themselves) (Major, 1987), and (b) the sociocultural environment within which the individuals reside, these theories or hypotheses are often biased and, at best, reflect only a partial truth.

The purpose of this chapter is to discuss how the sociocultural context has informed the conceptualization of child sexual abuse. This chapter briefly reviews the work on child sexual abuse done prior to Freud, Freud's theory of child sexual abuse, its later renunciation, and the impact of Freud's renunciation upon the suppression of the developing knowledge base in child sexual abuse. The 1960s and 1970s enjoyed a resurgence in the awareness of child sexual abuse, with the late 1970s and early 1980s being a pivotal turning point in the knowledge base. The reasons for this resurgence in awareness, within a sociocultural context, are discussed. Moving into the 1990s, the current backlash is also conceptualized within a sociocultural context. The final section looks ahead, suggesting how the current and future sociocultural context might affect the future professional response to child sexual abuse.

THE PERIOD PRIOR TO FREUD

During the last 100 years, Freud has probably had a greater impact than any other person upon the professional knowledge base of child sexual abuse. While his influence fundamentally framed the profession's conceptualization of child sexual abuse prior to the 1960s, it continues to be felt even today. For this reason, the social context of the environment to which Freud was exposed is important to explore.

Child sexual abuse simply was not acknowledged prior to the late 1800s. While it would be reassuring to believe that child sexual abuse did not exist, it of course did. It simply was not labeled as such. Indeed, child sexual abuse has been documented throughout history, with Biblical references to child sexual abuse (Rush, 1980), and more extensive records of abuse in the Roman and Greek civilizations (Gray-Fow, 1987). Even in colonial America, records suggest that child abuse, including child sexual abuse, was widespread (deMause, 1988). DeMause, in *The History of Childhood* (1974), a classic analysis of childhoods in previous historical eras, states:

> *The history of childhood is a nightmare from which we have only begun to awaken. The further back in history one goes, the lower the level of child care, and the more likely children are to be killed, abandoned, beaten, terrorized, and sexually abused. (p. 1)*

This statement suggests that sexual abuse is certainly not a recent phenomenon—only its recognition.

Until the mid-1800s, then, sexual abuse was generally recognized only by its victims (Summit, 1989). Even then, the extreme belief in the ownership of children quite possibly influenced the victim's perception of whether abuse had occurred. Professionals also largely ignored the possibility that abuse had occurred. When faced with psychological trauma in victims of sexual abuse, professionals were likely to treat the victims pejoratively and to label them hysterical.

> *At the time, hysterical women were the target of contempt and indignation on the part of the physicians, the best of whom regarded the illness as a matter of simulation (manipulation) or "imagination." In the past, thinking it a particular disorder of the womb, they had treated it by extirpation of the clitoris...for some believed [it] would cure the wandering womb by "putting it in its place." (Brandcraft & Stolorow, 1984, p. 94)*

The first important work on child sexual abuse may be that of the Frenchman, Ampoise Tardieu (Cunningham, 1988). In 1862, as a forensic-medical expert, he documented 515 cases of sexual offenses, 420 of which were committed on children under the age of 15. During an 11-year period, he cited more than 11,000 cases of completed or attempted rape, 80% of which involved child victims (Masson, 1984). These cases, to be defined as assault, had to present with legal evidence of rape, including tearing of the hymen (Cunningham, 1988). Much of his work focused on how child sexual assault victims may not present with the requisite physical evidence. To a lesser extent, he acknowledged and wrote of the possible psychological effects of such sexual assaults and was the first professional to write of sexual abuse as a social problem.

Jean Martin Charcot, described by Masson (1984) as "France's most illustrious neurologist, defender of hypnosis, and physician of hysteria" (p. 14), was also influential in the views of child sexual abuse during this era. While Charcot did recognize that the sexual offenses occurred, he did not share the same compassionate view of the victims as Tardieu. Charcot's principal emphasis appeared to be on influencing officials to view offenders as mentally ill instead of "vicious" (Cunningham, 1988, p. 347), and he not only suggested that offenders were often "honest family" men (p. 347), but that up to 80% of accusations against them were false.

Another writer on child sexual abuse, Alfred Binet, suggested that all offenders had experienced a critical incident in childhood (Cunningham, 1988). Although he did not state that this critical incident was a history of child sexual abuse, he did make this connection in case studies. Binet also forwarded the idea that children were suggestible and that this suggestibility was related to situational and individual characteristics. His influence was especially felt in the courts, in which suggestibility came to be associated with pathology, thus offering a "rationale for disbelieving the testimony of children, especially those involved in sex crimes" (p. 349).

Other French authors, including Fournier, Bourdin, and Brouardel, also documented cases of rape. Regrettably, the works of these authors were fraught with misconceptions (Masson, 1984). Fournier was a proponent of the offender, whom he often considered "an excellent and perfectly honorable man" (Fournier, as cited by Masson, 1984, p. 43), and believed that children's assaults were "imaginary" (p. 44). Brouardel also believed that children lied about the sexual assault and that the genesis of these false accusations was hysteria. Bourdin reinforced the view that not only were victims lying, but that they also took pleasure in their lies because of "evil instincts" and "evil passions" (p. 48).

THE EARLY PERIOD: FREUD'S THEORY OF SEDUCTION

It was into this sociocultural environment that Freud moved. In 1885, while finishing his medical studies, he made a several-month study trip to Paris where he worked under Charcot (Masson, 1984), whom he admired. Masson, an expert on Freud, shows that during Freud's stay in Paris, he was not only exposed through Charcot's and Tardieu's writings to the reality and frequency of child sexual abuse, but also probably witnessed autopsies on some of its young victims. Freud also had in his possession the major French books on sexual violence against children and was familiar with the writings of Fournier, Bourdin, and Brouardel.

From Paris, Freud returned to Vienna, where he established his medical practice specializing in nervous disorders (Masson, 1984). Here he introduced a type of therapy that relied on the patient talking while the physician listened. This free association method of treatment allowed his patients to explore hidden emotions in an atmosphere free of judgment and censure (Rush, 1996) and opened for him a view into underlying issues of psychopathology. The most important turning point in Freud's career was when he began to understand the force called the unconscious, and he explored this realm not only in his patients, but also through his own self-analysis. This discovery set the stage for his work on child sexual abuse.

By 1896, Freud had formalized his theory on the etiology of hysteria, which he presented to his colleagues in a group of three papers entitled, "The Aetiology of Hysteria" (Rush, 1996). In these papers he presented a sample of 18 patients, labeled hysterical, who he concluded had been victims of childhood sexual assault by various caregivers (Joyce, 1995). In these three papers he further suggested that the abuse itself was responsible for the victims' significant psychopathology (neuroses). These papers, however, offered contradictory information concerning the identify of the perpetrators. He variously implicated teachers and female caretakers (but not mothers), and same-age, opposite-sex children such as brothers (Rush, 1996). Only later, in his private letters to Wilhelm Fliess, his good friend, did he suggest that fathers were most often the offenders.

Rejection of the Theory of Seduction

Freud's colleagues, including Charcot, who "found it preposterous that parents would molest their own children" (Joyce, 1995, p. 200), frankly rejected his theory, a rejection that continued as long as Freud embraced his seduction theory (Masson, 1984). As Masson states, "In accepting the reality of seduction, in believing his patients, Freud was at odds with the entire climate of German medical thinking" (p. 137). It is perhaps not surprising then, that by 1897 Freud had repudiated his own observations. In his now famous letter, he announced to Fliess, "I no longer believe in my *neurotica*" (Freud, as cited in Masson, 1985, p. 264). Freud now believed that most, but not all, of the assaults he reported had never occurred (Masson, 1984). He instead suggested that the young child, needing to release sexual tensions, wished for the sexual attention from her father. He believed that these tensions were universal and unfolded in developmental stages.

Having replaced his theory having a universal external etiology with a theory having a universal internal etiology (Masson, 1984), Freud then advanced his theory of the Oedipus complex, which became a "universal and intrapsychic rather than environmental hazard for emotional health" (Summit, 1989, pg. 414). According to the Oedipus complex, the female child initially takes her mother as her love object. When the child sees the male genitalia, however, she immediately recognizes it as superior and consequently falls victim to penis envy. Her father now becomes her new love object (Hall, 1954). It is during this stage, Freud hypothesized, that girls create incestuous fantasies of themselves with their fathers. Freud therefore came to believe that reported cases of incest were simply wishful fantasies for the love object. As Hare-Mustin (1987) states, "patients are made ill by their fantasies, not by what happens to them" (p. 19).

Rationale for Freud's Reversal

What could have caused Freud's complete reversal of thought in such a short time? As the impact of Freud's reversal has become recognized, different authors have forwarded rationales. This literature, however, often reflects the ideological background of the writer, with psychoanalytically trained professionals sometimes being more muted in their opinions and feminist writers being more provocative. Nonetheless, at least five rationales for his reversal have been forwarded.

The Effect of Professional Censure

When Freud first forwarded his seduction theory, he was young in his career, and the opinion of his colleagues probably mattered greatly (Masson, 1984). His theory of seduction was considered unpopular at the least and, more likely, outrageous. Perhaps an analogy of the pressure Freud might have felt to rescind his theory can be educed from the current environment. Even today, in an age far more enlightened than the one in which Freud lived, the backlash against a full knowledge of child sexual abuse is great. Professionals have been attacked, sometimes with serious repercussions. These attacks have occurred even though the scope of child sexual abuse is undeniable. Freud, however, was one of the few professionals of his era suggesting that "hysteria" was a result of actual incidents of sexual abuse. Because Freud's young professional reputation appeared to be at stake (Masson, 1984), he may have felt extreme pressure to rescind his theory.

Freud's Unresolved Issues

Another rationale for Freud's renunciation of his seduction theory was forwarded by Westerlund (1986). After analyzing Freud's letters and other historical writings, she suggested that Freud, after recognizing the existence of certain hysterical features in his brother and several sisters, was on the verge of discovering that his father might have sexually abused one or more of them. In the same letter to Fliess in which he recanted his theory, Freud stated, "In all cases, the *father*, not excluding my own, had to be accused of being perverse" (Freud, as cited in Masson, 1985, p. 264).

How can this statement be interpreted? Westerlund (1986) interprets it to mean that Freud's father may have been guilty of incest. The context within which this letter was written, however, must be considered. Freud had recently presented a theory in which most or all hysteria was reported to result from a childhood history of sexual abuse. It is especially obvious today that current symptomatology is not *always* the result of child sexual abuse. Perhaps because he had developed a theory of hysteria based only upon a history of child sexual abuse, Freud found himself in the awkward position of having to defend the position that *all* individuals with hysterical features were previously sexually abused. As Armstrong (1996) puts it, "Incest was the (sole) cause of female neurosis, thus female 'neurotics' must have experienced incest" (p. 302). Unable to reconcile this apparent conflict, Freud may instead have had impetus to abandon his theory (Rosenfeld, 1987).

It was also during this time that Freud experienced overly affectionate feelings towards his daughter and reported a dream to Fliess in which these feelings occurred (Westerlund, 1986). While Westerlund states that these were incestuous feelings, Freud suggested that as they were in a dream, they were symbolic of his need to suggest that the father was responsible for neurosis. There is some question whether Freud's "shocking" behavior towards his niece was also perhaps erotic in nature (p. 302). Westerlund cites Jones, Freud's biographer, as stating that it is likely that the cruel behavior with which Freud and his nephew treated his niece had some likely erotic component.

These three experiences, while equivocal, lend weight to Westerlund's (1986) argument that by endorsing a theory in which hysterical symptoms resulted from sexual abuse experiences, Freud may have come dangerously close to acknowledging a side of himself and his father with which he was most uncomfortable. Freud may have had significant personal issues with his original theory because of his own father's possible perpetration, his brother's and sisters' neurotic symptomatology, or his own possible erotic feelings. Westerlund hypothesizes that only by creating the Oedipus complex was Freud able to resolve the very personal nature of his original seduction theory.

Universality of Abuse

Another factor that may have contributed to Freud's renunciation of the seduction theory becomes apparent in one of his letters to Fliess, in which Freud struggles to accept that fathers—and not just a few—could commit acts of incest. As he stated, "The astonishing thing [was] that in every case blame was laid on perverse acts by the father...though it was hardly credible that perverted acts against children were so general" (Freud, as cited in Taubman, 1984, p. 35). As will be discussed later, Olafson, Corwin, and Summit (1993) suggest that the knowledge of the scope of the problem of child sexual abuse is so overwhelming that it is human nature, and the nature of society as a whole, to deny its existence or prevalence.

Theory of Periodicity

One of the more entertaining, although probably no less factual, rationales for Freud's renunciation pertains to a series of events involving Freud, one of his good friends, and one of his patients. While the following is not so much a rationale for rejecting his theory of seduction, it does give an interesting view of the process by which this reversal may have occurred. The following is a brief summary from Masson's (1984) book on Freud's renunciation of the seduction theory.

In the early years of his professional life, Freud worked with a patient, Emma Eckstein, who had been sexually abused as a child by her father (Masson, 1984). This trauma, Freud argued, was responsible for her hysteria. At the time, Freud was good friends with Wilhelm Fliess, a physician who was advancing a theory, perhaps not unusual for its time, that the nose was the center of sexual feelings and that an operation on the nose could correct sexual dysfunction, especially the desire to masturbate. Evidently, Ms. Eckstein may have had this desire, although it is not certain. Regardless, Fliess wanted to operate, and Freud consented.

Fliess had never performed this operation before and apparently made serious mistakes (Masson, 1984). After Ms. Eckstein had a severe and life-threatening hemorrhage, another physician reoperated on her nose and found that Fliess had inadvertently left a piece of gauze in her nose, causing the subsequent infection and hemorrhage. In Freud's first letter to Fliess after this second operation, Freud was obviously concerned about the error, but already appeared to be rationalizing it. In this letter, Freud said that Fliess had done the best he could and that it was an unfortunate accident. Although Freud expressed concern for his patient, he was "inconsolable" about Fliess' part in the affair (p. 69).

This incident markedly strained the relationship of the two men (Masson, 1984). Freud seemed to need to reconcile this experience so that the operation, and his approval of it, could be justified. The more letters that were written between the two, the softer the recriminations became.

Finally the men, relying on another of Fliess' theories—the theory of periodicity—began to alter the reality of the operation (Masson, 1984). This theory states that the numbers 28 (the female period) and 23 (the male period) are critical numbers and that all events in a person's life are determined by these numbers. Within 15 months of the operation, Freud and Fliess had begun to dismiss Fliess' culpability for the operation. Instead, they now believed that Ms. Eckstein would have bled anyway, as the operation fell on a critical date.

Nine months later, Freud dismissed the event further by stating that the bleeding was a result of Ms. Eckstein's "wish to have Freud by her side" (Masson, 1984, p. 102) and "her own perverse imagination" (p. 106). As Freud stated in his letter to Fliess, "As far as the blood is concerned, you are completely without blame!" (as cited in Masson, 1984, p. 105).

Freud now had reason to state that hysteria was not caused by real events, but by fantasized events. Perhaps it was a small step, then, to state not only that Ms. Eckstein's abuse was an incestuous fantasy, but that all female children have incestuous fantasies. As Masson (1984) states:

> From 1894 through 1897, no subjects so preoccupied Freud as the reality of seduction and the fate of Emma Eckstein. The two topics seemed bound together. It is, in my opinion, no coincidence that once Freud had determined that Emma Eckstein's hemorrhages were hysterical, the result of sexual fantasies, he was free to abandon the seduction hypothesis. (p. 107)

Psychoanalytic Perspective

All viewpoints discussed to this point are antagonistic to Freud's renunciation. Other viewpoints in the professional literature, mostly by psychoanalysts, are more sympathetic to Freud's renunciation. These viewpoints provide a balance to the literature presented thus far.

Both Powell and Boer (1994) and Tabin (1993), among others (see Rosenfeld, 1987, for example), take issue with the previous viewpoints, suggesting instead that Freud had important reasons for abandoning his seduction theory. Tabin first points out that only two of the 18 cases upon which the original seduction theory was based could be corroborated. The patients' disclosures themselves were often not willingly forthcoming, and Powell and Boer even suggest that the abuse memories were confabulations brought on by Freud's use of strongly suggestible statements. As

Tabin states, "His patients were not pleading from the couch that he accept their accounts of abuse in childhood. Furthermore, none of his cases showed any benefit from his interpretation that he could not otherwise explain in conventional terms. Indeed, these patients all fled from treatment" (p. 292). As reported in a letter to Fliess in 1897, Freud returned from vacation only to discover that he had no patients, after which he felt resigned to surrender "his dream that his theory would win him eternal fame" (p. 292).

The second major point of Tabin (1993) is that Freud continued throughout his lifetime to be aware not only of the childhood histories of sexual abuse in certain of his patients, but also its consequences. Thus, while he continued to attach greatest meaning to intrapsychic phenomena, he did not ignore the actual events.

Summary

Different authors have presented rationales for Freud's renunciation of his theory of seduction. One very possible rationale is that Freud advanced this theory in an era that was not amenable to its acceptance. Because of the response of his colleagues and the newness of his practice, he may have felt great pressure to rescind the theory. To accept the theory may also have meant his acceptance of his own father's "perverted" acts (Freud, as cited in Taubman, 1984, p. 35) and that he would have to look closer at his own possible sexual feelings towards his daughter and niece. Finally, to admit that so many of his hysterical patients were also victims of child sexual abuse would force him to accept a far greater prevalence of child sexual abuse than was comfortable.

The actual rationales for Freud's renunciation must be left for historians to decide. Awesome societal forces framed the environment in which Freud repudiated his theory. Given the sociocultural environment in which Freud lived, the far easier path was to renounce his theory of seduction and to embrace a theory that his colleagues and society could tolerate.

It is interesting to speculate how the professional response to child sexual abuse in the following decades might have differed had Freud strongly held to his original position. Perhaps the best way to frame what might have been is as a paradigm shift. Kuhn (1970) conceptualizes paradigm shifts as scientific revolutions initiated by the introduction of a theory that does not just rework what is already known, but requires a complete reconstruction and re-evaluation of prior knowledge. Because new paradigms confront the established paradigm, however, they are not readily accepted into the developing knowledge base. Indeed, many scientists who have introduced these paradigm shifts have been censured, and future generations have been left to resurrect their work.

Surely, with Freud's developing reputation, had he held to his theory of seduction, he might have initiated a scientific revolution of sorts in the understanding and conceptualization of child sexual abuse. Because of the societal forces already in place, however, even had Freud defended his theory of seduction, it might have been rejected by his colleagues for some time to come. Yet Freud did not choose this path, but instead bowed to pressure. By renouncing the seduction theory, he rationalized the perverted acts away, and they disappeared into thin air as the overactive imagination of a young child whose incestuous wish is played out through an incestuous fantasy.

The Effect of Freud's Renunciation

The renunciation of Freud's seduction theory and later, the forwarding of the Oedipus complex, profoundly affected the mental health profession. Psychoanalytic theory became the foundation for psychiatry for many years to come, with the Oedipus complex being the core of that theory. To use psychoanalytic theory, however, Freud's original theory of seduction had to be renounced. As Anna Freud wrote, "Keeping the seduction theory would mean to abandon the Oedipus complex, and with it the whole importance of phantasy life, conscious or unconscious phantasy. In fact, I think there would have been no psychoanalysis afterwards" (as cited in Masson, 1984, p. 113). The development of the knowledge base on child sexual abuse was thus effectively suppressed.

To accept psychoanalytic theory, however, was to negate the client's reality and to place the clinician in the role of expert. These experts, then, were thought to know more than the clients themselves about their clients' reality. Patients who disagreed with their clinicians' interpretations that their sexual abuse was simply a fantasy were said to be experiencing resistance (Lerman, 1988). Even when clinicians acknowledged the sexual abuse, victims were often blamed for seducing their fathers so that they might fulfill their incestuous fantasies (Rush, 1996).

This emphasis on intrapsychic versus extrapsychic phenomena in the etiology of the victim's psychopathology (Westerlund, 1986) also influenced the continued blaming of victims, effectively silencing them. As Rush (1996) states:

> Any attempt on the part of the child or her family to expose the violator also exposes her own alleged innate sexual motives and shames her more than the offender; concealment is the only recourse. The dilemma of the sexual abuse of children has provided a system of foolproof emotional blackmail: if the victim incriminates the abuser, she incriminates herself. (p. 275)

Finally, by blaming the victim, the social environment could then be held blameless. Westerlund (1986) states:

> When Freud relegated women's reports of sexual abuse by their fathers to fantasy, he...claimed a biological determinant rather than a sociocultural determinant for female neurosis. The incestuous wish for the father was to be seen as inherent in the daughter's nature, the result of her physical deficiency and intrinsic biological inferiority. Seduction fantasies were inevitable, they were representations of the innate female need to compensate themselves for their lack of a penis....Freud was seduced into and seduced others into protecting the sexual offender and thus betrayed the sexual victim. (pp. 307-308)

Freud advanced his original seduction theory after discovering that many of his "hysterical" female clients were reporting histories of incestuous abuse. He was then confronted with the knowledge that many fathers, possibly even his own, sexually abused their daughters. Given the opportunity to publicly identify this behavior in some fathers, he reneged, choosing instead to define "normal" behavior as girls having precocious sexual wishes that had to be fulfilled through vivid fantasy lives. He thus effectively colluded with a society that wished to deny the existence of child sexual abuse, while modeling a pattern of removing blame from the offender and placing it on the victim.

"With Freud's retraction of the seduction theory, he left behind at once the simple explanation for the trauma, his endorsement of the intrinsic strengths of the post-traumatic patient, and his intrepid strategies for undoing the traumatic effects" (Summit, 1989, p. 423). Possibly in no other clinical population has one person had such a significant and detrimental effect on the outcome of so many. With his reversal of the seduction theory, he colluded with a society not willing to know the truth.

THE MIDDLE PERIOD: 1900 THROUGH 1970

Most of Freud's many followers continued to embrace the Oedipus complex and its rationale for reports of child sexual abuse. Of note, however, two of the most distinguished of his followers, Carl Jung and Otto Rank, either broke with Freud or denounced his seduction theory. Interestingly, both men, as children, had probably been sexually abused (Goldwert, 1986). Goldwert suggests that their sexual abuse may have been one reason they came to resist Freud's emphasis on sexuality and the Oedipus complex.

Then in 1932, Sandor Ferenczi, one of Freud's most cherished colleagues, presented a paper even over the objections of Freud (Olafson et al., 1993) that suggested that children were being sexually abused (Summit, 1989). In his "Confusion of Tongues Between Adults and the Child," Ferenczi addressed not only the sexual abuse, but also the denial of this abuse by the adult world. Shortly thereafter, Freud and the professional community denounced Ferenczi for attempting to revive interest in the importance of childhood sexual assault (Summit, 1989) and after Ferenczi's death, with Freud's agreement, the publication was suppressed (Olafson et al., 1993). Although he may have been an early proponent of child sexual abuse victims, Ferenczi also had his own significant problems. Tabin (1993) suggests that these problems included "sexual play with his own medical patients" (p. 294) and "exchang[ing] kisses with his patients as a part of their treatment" (p. 295), although these incidents may have occurred earlier in his career. The confusing information again suggests that the exact historical events are unclear and are open to the interpretation of the presenter. Although Masson (1984) convincingly argues that Ferenczi was attempting to revive interest in child sexual abuse, even over the objections of Freud and other psychoanalysts, other viewpoints do exist.

For the next 30 years, hardly a word in the psychiatric community was said about sexual abuse. Typical of the few writings of this period were two studies by Bender, who recognized that the incest had occurred, but placed the blame for the abuse on the seductive nature of the daughter (Bender & Blau, 1937; Bender & Grugett, 1952). For example, in 1937, Bender and Blau wrote that they frequently considered "the possibility that the child might have been the actual seducer rather than the one innocently seduced" (p. 514). Even 15 years later, Bender and Grugett

(1952) concluded that "it was highly probable that the child had used his charm in the role of the seducer" (p. 826).

The next major event occurred in the 1950s when Kinsey, Pomeroy, Martin, and Gebhard (1953) published a survey reporting that 24% of the 4,441 female participants were, as children, sexually abused by adult men. Even though the large majority of these victims reported being frightened by this experience, Kinsey et al. stated instead, in a famous quote, "It is difficult to understand why a child, except for its cultural conditioning, should be disturbed at having its genitalia touched, or disturbed at seeing the genitalia of other persons, or disturbed at even more specific sexual contacts" (as cited in Olafson et al., 1993, p. 15). They suggested instead that the children were disturbed more by the reactions of the adults who discovered the contact than by the contact itself. Kinsey et al. were concerned, however, about the offenders who were often imprisoned for "accidental exposure of the genitalia while intoxicated, for nude swimming, and for the bestowal of 'grandfatherly affection'" (p. 15).

Between 1940 and 1965, three other nonrandom surveys reported that between 17% and 28% of respondents were sexually abused as children (Gagnon, 1965; Landis, 1940, 1956). Even after these surveys were published, however, the scope of the problem of child sexual abuse, although more clearly defined, was largely ignored by both the professional and lay communities (Herman, 1981). This era was thus largely marked by the suppression and distortion of information concerning the scope of child sexual abuse.

1970s AND 1980s

While no clear line divides this earlier era of suppression and distortion from the modern era in which the scope of child sexual abuse was acknowledged, it probably occurred sometime in the 1970s. During this period, several key events occurred. The C. Henry Kempe National Center for the Prevention and Treatment of Child Abuse and Neglect opened, the National Center on Child Abuse and Neglect (NCCAN) was established, and NCCAN funded the first comprehensive study on the incidence of child abuse and neglect (NIS-1) (Kinnear, 1995). Then in 1978, Russell (1983) conducted the first random community prevalence survey, consisting of a sample of 930 adult women in the San Francisco area and found that 38% of the respondents had experienced childhood contact sexual abuse. Because of the methodological rigor of her study (Bolen & Scannapieco, 1999), it was difficult to discount, even though it did generate considerable controversy. By the early 1980s, studies of child sexual abuse were beginning to proliferate, and the knowledge base began to develop rapidly.

What could account for this sudden interest in child sexual abuse? First may have been the impact of the Vietnam War and the political and social environment of the late 1960s and 1970s. This was a period of profound social consciousness-raising as society "grappled with the moral dilemmas posed by the Vietnam War" and all it represented (Vander Mey & Neff, 1986, p. 13). No longer was the status quo taken for granted, but it was often the impetus for controversy and rebellion. Social consciousness-raising and revolution in thought were rampant. Within this sociocultural context, it was probably far more difficult to suppress the "discovery" of child sexual abuse.

Another important factor was the developing feminist movement, which brought with it a heightened sensitivity to issues of females. Florence Rush's book, *The Best Kept Secret*, was published in 1980, followed in 1981 by Judith Herman's classic study on father-daughter incest. These and other feminist writings suggested that child sexual abuse was symptomatic and a direct derivative of living in a patriarchal society. Sexual abuse was conceptualized as a symptom of a greater problem—a male sense of entitlement to use females and children for sexual enjoyment (Herman, 1981). Sexual abuse of children and rape of females were thus conceptualized similarly. Consequently, while others were attempting to understand why child sexual abuse was so prevalent, feminists were instead attempting to understand why more children were not sexually abused. As Herman (1990) stated in a later feminist analysis of sexual assault,

> *If, as many feminists argue, the social definition of sexuality involves the erotization of male dominance and female submission, then the use of coercive means to achieve sexual conquest may represent a crude exaggeration of prevailing norms, but not a departure from them....The unanswered question posed by feminists is not why some men rape, but why most men do not. (pp. 177-178)*

By the end of the 1980s, the scope of the problem of child sexual abuse was more clearly defined. Several random community surveys (Russell, 1983; Wyatt, 1985) and even a national prevalence survey (Timnick, 1985) had now been conducted. While prevalence rates for child sexual abuse differed based upon the studies' methodologies, one fact was certain: Child sexual abuse, both for male and female children, was a substantial problem.

This knowledge brought with it a significant professional response, and numerous treatment centers were established for child and adult victims. Clinicians became sensitive to preventing what they termed "system-induced trauma" to victims (Conte, 1991, p. 12). Child sexual abuse also came to be viewed as a multidisciplinary problem. Treatment, evaluation, and assessment protocol were developed, and the response to child sexual abuse across all mental health professions burgeoned. While professionals were now trying to respond to the scope of the problem of child sexual abuse, however, empirical knowledge lagged. Studies in the 1980s were largely descriptive, answering broad questions about *who* and *how bad*. They were not yet sophisticated enough to answer questions about better treatment or assessment protocol. This lack of an empirical base for clinical protocols thus set the stage for the 1990s.

1990s

The climate of the 1990s can be framed by a single word—backlash. This backlash started as a series of controversies over the developing knowledge base, with two areas receiving particular attention. The first issue was whether females were being underidentified as offenders. The second issue was whether mothers involved in custody or divorce disputes were falsely and maliciously charging their ex-partners with sexually abusing their child. Shortly, however, controversies began erupting concerning the techniques used by clinicians. In probably the first major attack, clinicians were accused of leading young children to make false charges of ritual abuse. In the 1990s these attacks on clinicians gained in momentum and became more generalized so that clinicians working with both children and adults were now involved. Clinicians working with children were accused of using aggressive, suggestive, and leading techniques that placed the veracity of the child's disclosure into jeopardy. Clinicians working with adult clients were accused of leading their clients to falsely disclose histories of childhood sexual abuse. Regretfully, many of these attacks were hostile and even vicious.

While much has been written concerning this backlash, it is beyond the scope of this book to review this substantial literature. More salient to this book is the need to frame the backlash within the ideology of the 1980s and 1990s and to understand why the environment of the 1990s was ripe for a backlash.

The first reason that the climate was ripe for a backlash is the state of empirical research in the 1980s. In relation to the needs of clinicians and others directly involved in the assessment and identification of victims, the empirical knowledge base for child sexual abuse was clearly inadequate. The development of a knowledge base is complex, with the beginning phase marked by descriptive and exploratory research. Only then does research move to answering questions framed in a more sophisticated manner. Research in child sexual abuse is so new that there simply has not been enough time to develop an empirical base with sufficient breadth and depth. This problem has been inevitable given the short history of the empirical base.

Because of the seriousness of the issue of child sexual abuse, however, clinicians were forced to make clinical judgments beyond the limits of the empirical research base available. Inevitably, these judgments were questioned. One reason for the backlash, therefore, is to ask the important question: What is the basis for clinical judgments? Regretfully, however, this discussion has often been pointed and personal.

A second reason for the backlash was explored by Olafson, Corwin, and Summit (1993). It is their thesis that a cycle of discovery and suppression of child sexual abuse over time exists. In their view, the knowledge of child sexual abuse is so overwhelming that it must be denied. They state:

> If we were really to take into account the role sexual coercion and violence play in shaping human culture and personal identity, fundamental structures of thought could well be shaken and changed. Such great shifts in world view unsettle even those whose privileges and self-images are not directly threatened by them (Kuhn, 1970). Indeed, information about the prevalence and impact of sexual abuse may constitute unwelcome news on all shades of the political spectrum....The full realization that child sexual victimization is as common and as noxious as current research suggests would necessitate costly efforts to protect children from sexual assault.
>
> It remains to be seen whether the current backlash will succeed in resuppressing awareness of sexual abuse....If this occurs, it will not happen because child sexual abuse is peripheral to major social interests, but because it is so central that as a society we choose to reject our knowledge of it rather than make the changes in our thinking, our institutions, and our daily lives that sustained awareness of child sexual victimization demands. (p. 19)

A final reason for this backlash is similar, but framed within a feminist perspective. As Olafson et al. (1993) state, "It can be argued that the intensity of the current debate is fueled by the defense of gender and professional privilege and hierarchy" (p. 17). This quote speaks to one of the foremost statistics of child sexual abuse—that approximately 95% of offenders are male (Finkelhor, Hotaling, Lewis, & Smith, 1990; Russell, 1983; Wyatt, 1985), whereas approximately 70% of victims are female (Finkelhor & Baron, 1986). Further, with 30% to 40% of all girls being sexually abused prior to their 18th birthday (Bolen & Scannapieco, 1999), "common sense would suggest that some comparable percentage of the male population has been doing the victimizing" (Herman, 1990, p. 178). While Herman's statement may be somewhat of an exaggeration, as most offenders abuse multiple children (Abel et al., 1987, 1988a; Ballard et al., 1990), it is probable that a significant minority of men within society have committed, or are at risk to commit, sexual abuse (Bagley, Wood, & Young, 1994; Briere & Runtz, 1989).

To internalize this knowledge is paramount to a social revolution. One of the hallmarks of patriarchy is that it is founded upon the premise of the benevolent male taking care of the less-positioned female. History, however, suggests that the image of the benevolent patriarch is a myth. Instead, the prevalence of child sexual abuse suggests that the more likely reality may be one of male entitlement, male domination, and male subjugation of females and children. To truly understand the scope of child sexual abuse thus brings with it a responsibility to advocate, not only for the safety of children, but for the reform of basic tenets that undergird modern society and that may foster child sexual abuse—something the privileged majority do not willingly seek, as their power base would be disrupted. Instead, it becomes critical that the scope of the problem of child sexual abuse be suppressed.

In this context, the current backlash is about a far greater controversy than simply whether children and adults create or are implanted with false memories, whether leading questions influence victims, whether dissociative disorders can be induced, and all the other issues that have come to the fore in recent years. These controversies are better framed as screen issues for a far greater and underlying issue—that of the basic structure and privilege of members within society.

LOOKING FORWARD

Where will we be in 10 years? This is a difficult question for even those with crystal balls. What can be considered, however, is social forces that may shape the future agenda for child sexual abuse research, treatment, and policy decisions.

Perhaps the most important issue is the current environment of conservatism. This environment, and its concomitant political agenda, have already radically affected issues of children. While great gains for children's rights were made between 1960 and 1990, the country is experiencing a current reversal of these rights. As legitimized in the current welfare "reform" act, the federal government no longer views children as having innate rights to be fed, sheltered, and clothed. Guardians and more specifically, single mothers, are punished as well. Some of the most marginalized members of society are thus in grave danger of being completely without resources.

This environment of conservatism bodes poorly for the rights of children not to be sexually abused. If, as feminists contend, child sexual abuse is related to the abuse of power, then depowering the powerless and empowering the powerful may serve to tip the scales in favor of greater access to the sexual violation of children. When children are abused, the current conservative environment may also make it more difficult for the victims to be heard and especially, to be believed.

There is also grave concern that punishing the guardians of these children will increase the children's risk of abuse. Single mothers on welfare are now required to return to work, although the so-called welfare reform laws often exclude the resources these women need to find employment sufficient to afford safe child care. Although findings remain inconsistent, some community prevalence surveys suggest that children are at greater risk of abuse when their mothers work than when they do not, and this relationship is especially apparent for children living only with females (Bolen, 1998b). It may be that these findings reflect an issue of supervision as children lose the protective influence of their mothers and sometimes, safe alternative caretakers. *If* inadequate supervision is the issue, then the recent passage of the child welfare reform bill, which forces single mothers back into the work force without providing adequate funding for safe child care, may have ominous implications for the risk of their children to be sexually abused.

The current environment of political conservatism and the "reform" laws may thus have dire consequences for the protection of children. While the intended effects of these supposed reforms are chilling, the unintended effects may be even greater. In a climate that strengthens the disparity of power between adults and children, males and females, and whites and persons of color, the obvious losers are the less powerful. Whether this environment will contribute to an increased rate of sexual abuse of children remains to be seen. The possibility, however, cannot be discounted.

CHAPTER 3
THEORIES OF CHILD SEXUAL ABUSE: AN HISTORICAL AND SOCIOCULTURAL PERSPECTIVE

INTRODUCTION

Chapter 2 discussed the sociocultural context within which child sexual abuse was "discovered" and targeted. Chapter 3 now attends to the historical development of the theoretical base for child sexual abuse and how the sociocultural context influenced that development. Theories included in this chapter are therefore not intended to be inclusive, but are presented only within an historical context. Theories that are included are from the perspective of the victim. These theories have two important features: First, they suggest *why* sexual abuse occurs; second, they suggest *who* is at fault.

As discussed in Chapter 2, the theoretical base of knowledge for child sexual abuse began with Freud's seduction theory (Masson, 1984). After realizing that most of his hysterical clients were also victims of child sexual abuse, Freud forwarded a theory of seduction in which he posited an etiological link between child sexual abuse and later hysterical symptoms. This theory was met with rejection and scorn from the professional community, and he renounced the theory only a short time later. The import of this renunciation was so profound that little work to advance the knowledge base of child sexual abuse was done for many years to come. Even so, certain lines of thought, influenced by Freud's psychoanalytic theory, permeated the writings during this time. It is therefore not surprising that these writings, when they admitted to the occurrence of the sexual abuse, typically removed blame from the offender and placed fault for the sexual assault onto the victim, almost always assumed to be the daughter (Bender & Blau, 1937; Bender & Grugett, 1952).

The first formal theory of child sexual abuse, appearing in the professional literature in the 1960s and 1970s, may be family systems theory (Carper, 1979; Machotka, Pittman, & Flomenhaft, 1967). This theory, which derived from general systems theory, posited a systemic approach to father-daughter incest. All members of the family, including the mother and victim, were hypothesized not only to be responsible for the initiation of the incest, but also to collude in its maintenance (Kadushin & Martin, 1988). Like the earlier writings, family systems theory (a) applied primarily to father-daughter incest and (b) continued to remove blame from the offender.

Since the mid-1970s, several more sophisticated theories of child sexual abuse have been developed. Those that attempt to clarify why certain individuals might abuse a child include sociobiological theories (Williams & Finkelhor, 1995), feminist theory (Herman, 1990), attachment theory (Alexander, 1992; Marshall,

Hudson, & Hodkinson, 1993), and behavioral theories, including conditioning theory and social learning theory (Laws & Marshall, 1990). The primary theory that focuses on why certain children are at greater risk of abuse is feminist theory (Herman, 1981; Rush, 1980).

The following section briefly discusses the historical development of theories of child sexual abuse. Because the matter of culpability is central to this development, it is used to organize these next sections. Freud's theory was amply discussed in Chapter 2. Therefore, this chapter starts with the era following Freud.

THEORIES OF CULPABILITY

Seduction by the Daughter

As discussed in the previous chapter, certain important writers following Freud continued to acknowledge that child sexual abuse did occur. A few early studies also acknowledged its occurrence, but often rationalized that the daughter had seduced her father (Bender & Blau, 1937; Bender & Grugett, 1952). The import of Freud's Oedipus complex in these early studies is obvious. After rejecting his childhood seduction theory, Freud posited an internal etiology for child sexual abuse (Rush, 1996). As such, a victim reporting an abuse incident was said to be confusing the abuse memory with her fantasized desire as a child for her unavailable love object—the father. If abuse clearly did occur, it was therefore logical to place the blame on the daughter, who was said to be acting out her desire for her unavailable love object. The offender was then conceptualized as falling within the seducer's spell.

When placed within the perspective of Freud's influence, it is perhaps easier to understand why many writings of this early period blamed the victim. Regretfully, however, this trend of blaming the victim continued into more recent literature, and examples were fairly frequent even in literature published in the 1980s. For example, a study published in 1980 divided victims of incest into two groups—participant victims (those who had in some way encouraged the initiation or continuation of the sexual relationship) and accidental victims (those who had not done so) (Krieger, Rosenfeld, Gordon, & Bennett, 1980). One of the discriminating features of the groups was whether abuse had occurred more than once. If it had, the victim was assumed to have participated because she must have encouraged or initiated the abuse. The researchers commented on the "clearly seductive style" of one participant victim, a six-year-old girl who had been forced to masturbate her father since she was two years of age (p. 82).

In 1982, Yates also concluded that "the majority of youngsters have become not only victims but participants" (p. 482). These children purportedly did not report the abuse because of the "gratification that the incest provides" (p. 482). In his case study of an 18-month-old toddler who had been sexually abused since birth, Yates reported that the child's foster mother "could not lie down on the bed when he was awake, as he would crawl on top of her and attempt to burrow under her clothes" (p. 483). If a woman visited, he would "sit on her lap, wrap his arms about her neck, and deliver sensuous kisses. Then he would attempt to open her blouse or lift her skirt" (p. 483).

He went on to state that "eroticized preschool children...[are] readily orgasmic and also maintain a high level of arousal without orgasm" (p. 483).

Other permutations to the theory of seduction by the daughter are also found in the literature. For example, because not all girls were molested, Karl Abraham, an early follower of Freud, suggested that there must be something intrinsically wrong with those who were (Rush, 1996). On the other hand, Cohen (1983) suggested that the daughter initiated and participated in the incestuous relationship to keep the family together. The incipient guilt from having her incestuous fantasy realized, Cohen suggested, then enabled the daughter to recognize her responsibility for the abuse. Other historical literature suggested instead that the daughter was "seeking oral gratification from the father as a result of rejection by the mother" (Alexander, 1985, p. 79).

Occasional literature published in the 1990s also alludes to the daughter's culpability. For example, Lacey (1990) found that 18 of 112 female bulimic patients asked about a history of either incestuous abuse or incestuous fantasies reported experiencing incestuous feelings or fantasies and, "for two, the fantasies were in part acted out" (p. 400). The researchers suggested that "the relationship [between incestuous fantasies and actual abuse] can become blurred to the point of being indistinguishable, particularly if the patient has incorporated such thoughts into neurotic conflict" (p. 402). Another article published by Larson in 1993 presented a case study of an adolescent female abused by her father. This adolescent, "through continual reflection and discussion of the therapeutic relationship dynamics...was increasingly able to see the active role she'd played in her own incest" (p. 145).

Even though the professional literature has fewer examples of blaming the victim, some professionals continue to consider the victim partially culpable for the abuse. Many different studies have now assessed how professionals assign culpability for child sexual abuse. It is perhaps not surprising that early studies found that professionals attributed a substantial portion of the responsibility for the abuse to the victims themselves. For example, in an early survey, Galdston (1978) found that 52% of surveyed psychiatrists believed that daughters usually contributed to the incest. Studies published in the 1980s continued this pattern. In one of these studies (Wilk & McCarthy, 1986), 35% of law enforcement officers and 69% of child protective service workers considered teenage victims to be *as* guilty as the abusive father. Eisenberg, Owens, and Dewey (1987) also found that just more than half of medical personnel attached some blame to the victim. In other studies in which attribution of blame was measured on a scale from 1 (no blame) to 5 (high blame), the mean score for victim culpability ranged from 1.83 to 2.65 (Jackson & Sandberg, 1985; Saunders, 1988).

Even studies published in the 1990s, however, continue to find that 12% to 45% of professionals attribute some responsibility to the victim (Kalichman, Craig, & Folingstad, 1990; Kelley, 1990). One of these studies (Reidy & Hochstadt, 1993) concluded that mental health professionals do not blame victims. Yet, while the allocation of blame to the victim was low (below 30%), 37% of male respondents and 24% of female respondents did allocate some blame to the victim. Another study published in 1993 (Wagner, Aucoin, & Johnson, 1993) found that, on a scale of 0 (no responsibility) to 5 (very responsible), attribution of blame to the victim ranged from .12 to .25 for "resisting" victims and from .67 to 1.65 for "encouraging" victims (p. 64). Finally, Johnson et al. (1990) found that approximately half of the teachers and social workers queried said that there was some likelihood that an impetus for the abuse was the daughter's seductive behavior. This literature therefore suggests that professionals still do not, as a whole, endorse the opinion of child sexual abuse experts—that the victim is *never* to blame.

That any blame is assigned to the victim by professionals working with child sexual abuse victims has far-reaching implications.

> *The mere existence of a victim blame factor, however slight, reflects an apparent belief that incest victims may in some way be responsible for their own assault, and that children...may be held less than fully innocent in their actions in sexual matters when approached by adults who are most often family members, relatives, or people they know well and trust. (Jackson & Sandberg 1985, p. 54)*

Although the professional literature appears to be responding by reducing the number of published papers that suggest victim culpability, it is of concern that professional attribution of blame continues to some degree. While professionals may assign only a small amount of the blame to victims, some is too much.

Collusion by the Mother

The other person who has taken an historic beating in theories of child sexual abuse is the victim's mother. Several authors writing in the 1980s suggested that role reversal between the mother and daughter occurs in families of incest (Alexander, 1985; Cohen, 1983), and some empirical support for this dynamic exists (Herman, 1981; Salt, Myer, Coleman, & Sauzier, 1990). Role reversal purportedly occurred as the mother delegated more and more household tasks to her oldest daughter, while also withdrawing sexually from her husband (Kadushin & Martin, 1988). This abandonment by the mother of her duties was said to thrust the oldest daughter into that role, and sometimes the mother was even said to give her daughter as a sex object to her husband. As Kadushin and Martin stated, "The mother may overtly or covertly set the daughter up as her substitute in the marital relationship" (p. 304). Once the incest occurred, the mother was then said to collude in its maintenance because she had the most to gain.

Cohen (1983) described these mothers as weak, ineffectual, and dependent and believed they might have homosexual feelings towards their daughters. Swan (1985) also suggested that because mothers were increasingly employed outside the home, supervision of children decreased with a concomitant increase in the vulnerability of children. Implicit is the idea that mothers were to blame for not supervising their children at all times and thus for not protecting them.

Another typical response in early literature was to view sexual abuse as a symptom of family pathology, with the mother "as the cornerstone of the pathological family system" (Machotka et al., 1967, p. 100). In their presentation of incest as a symptom of family dysfunction, James and Nasjleti (1983) divided mothers into four groups: (a) the passive-child woman mother; (b) the intelligent, competent, distant mother; (c) the rejecting, vindictive mother; and (d) the psychotic or severely retarded mother. This list is unique for its absence of innocent or supportive mothers.

These hypotheses were not simply the products of a few unenlightened clinicians, but they may remain the norm. For example, an early study on attribution of blame found that 65% of child protective workers believed that the mother was as responsible for the incest as the father and that 85% of mothers gave their unconscious consent to the abuse (Dietz & Craft, 1980). Even in later studies, however, 70% to 86% of the respondents attributed partial responsibility to the mother for both father-daughter incest and sexual abuse by a neighbor (Johnson et al., 1990; Kelley, 1990; Reidy & Hochstadt, 1993). When studies apportioned responsibility for the abuse, 11% to 21% of the blame was attributed to the mother (Kalichman et al., 1990; Kelley, 1990). Another study by Conte, Fogarty, and Collins (1991) found that 59% of professional respondents agreed that mothers of incest victims should apologize to their daughters for their failure to protect them, thus implying attribution of blame.

It is of concern that little or no decrease in maternal attribution of blame by professionals is shown in the studies done in recent years. Another concern is exemplified in a study by Hanson and Slater (1993), who found, when comparing nine different motivations for abuse, that therapists and probation officers assigned the least culpability to the offender who stated that he and his wife were not getting along. Views such as these serve to propagate the myth that wives are responsible for the actions of their husbands.

How valid are these dynamics? Several authors, having examined the literature on nonoffending mothers, present views more compatible with empirical data (Gavey, Florence, Pezaro, & Tan, 1990; McIntyre, 1981; Myer, 1985; Wattenberg, 1985). This literature is discussed in greater detail in Chapter 10, "Nonoffending Guardians." As will be shown, in virtually all cases, the view of mothers as responsible for the sexual abuse is simply not supported in the empirical literature.

Incest As a Symptom of Family Pathology

Another repository for blame is the family itself. This conceptualization is most often found in the early literature on family systems theory in which incest was viewed as a homeostatic device that maintained equilibrium within the family (Carper, 1979). Central to this hypothesis was the concept of circular causality in which each member was said to contribute to the maintenance of the incestuous behavior and to join in a "conspiracy of silence" (Cohen, 1983, p. 155). The mother's abdication of her role as the father's sexual partner was generally implied as the crux of the family's problem, and some authors believed that the mother purposefully colluded to maintain the incestuous relationship (Kadushin & Martin, 1988). Others believed that incest was a dysfunctional attempt to ward off the fear of family annihilation or that it was an expression of the father's anger at his wife (Cohen, 1983; Hoorwitz, 1983). Kadushin and Martin (1988) forward this family systems theory perspective:

> *Father-daughter incest is a manifestation of a disturbed family equilibrium and occurs in response to an effort to establish an adaptation that is functional....The family in which incest occurs is likely to be an enmeshed, socially isolated, one in which intergenerational and parent-child role boundaries are vaguely defined and permeable....A family experiencing marital conflict is maintained intact by the*

reallocation of sexual-affectional role in incest. The female child is sacrificed...on the altar of family stability....Participants share the feeling that incest is preferable to family breakdown....[and] all participants have a vested interest in guarding against disclosure....Secondary gains experienced by the daughter reinforce any reluctance to discontinue the relationship....She has a special status...And, there is the secondary gain in sexual pleasure....A further secondary gain...is considerable enhancement of her power....Positive satisfactions in secondary gain increases [sic] the incentives to continue the relationship. (pp. 298-302)

Finally, Alexander (1985) contends that:

Much can be understood about the occurrence of incest if it is viewed in the context of a relatively closed system. Incest should not be viewed as an end in itself, but simply as a behavior symptomatic of a family that is isolated from the environment; that is avoidant of the differentiation of roles, functions, and individual members; and that uses the incest behavior as just one more means to avoid the growth and change that is inherent in adolescents seeking outside contacts and eventually leaving home. (p. 82)

The historical conceptualization of sexual abuse developed within family systems theory has little empirical support. Furthermore, families of incest cannot be clearly differentiated from other families in which victims of other types of child sexual abuse live or families with other types of dysfunction. Consequently, family systems theorists have yet to explain what is unique about families in which incest occurs compared to those in which it does not occur. This theory and its lack of supporting empirical data are evaluated further in Chapter 7, "Intrafamilial Abuse."

The Impact of Early Theories

These early theories have had a far-reaching impact on all areas of assessment, evaluation, and treatment. Perhaps the most important effect is that their concepts became codified in treatment philosophies and practices. For example, in the 1970s Giarretto (1982, 1989) established a treatment center based upon the family systems conceptualization of child sexual abuse. As with other treatment programs, mothers were held as central to the future welfare of their children. To ensure that sexual abuse by the father did not reoccur, mothers were counseled to improve their sexual lives with the offenders. Mothers were also made to apologize to their daughters for their inability to protect them, and families were not allowed to reunite until this apology occurred. This system thus effectively depowered mothers while empowering the offenders. This treatment model had a great influence on other developing treatment centers and by 1989, Giarretto reported that it was being used in more than 150 centers across the nation and internationally.

Another area of influence of these early theories is in the assessment of the nonoffending mother's ability to support her child. Given the sometimes hostile beliefs concerning mothers of child sexual abuse victims, it is not surprising that assessment tools used to determine maternal support often score her as unsupportive when she displays normative ambivalence and confusion. Various studies of maternal support, however, sometimes consider any display of ambivalence as indicative of a nonsupportive stance (Leifer, Shapiro, & Kassem, 1993). Yet, no known quantitative study has yet examined normal reactions to abuse by nonoffending mothers. Mothers are thus judged from perceptions originating from biased and historical theories rather than from an empirical knowledge base.

Another effect of these early theories is that the overemphasis on the role of the nonoffending mother has obscured a fundamental fact of child sexual abuse—that only approximately 7% to 8% of child sexual abuse is committed by father figures (Russell, 1984; Wyatt, 1985). In the other 92% to 93% of instances, therefore, a nonoffending father could as easily as the nonoffending mother have "protected" the child from the abuse. While numerous papers have been written on the role of the nonoffending mother, however, not a single known paper exists on the nonoffending father. These effects are discussed more fully in Chapter 10, "Nonoffending Guardians."

A final and lingering effect of these early theories is that child sexual abuse is often conceptualized as simply a family problem. This emphasis leads to an often delusional line of thinking that repairing the family dysfunction will reduce or eliminate the threat of sexual abuse for children. Consequently, if the mother were to have better sex with her husband, as Giarretto (1982, 1989) suggested, or if she were to better supervise her child, as Swan (1985) suggested, then the problem of child sexual abuse might disappear. Regretfully, nothing may be further from the truth, as 70% of all child sexual abuse is extrafamilial (Bolen, 2000a). Even with intrafamilial abuse, only approximately one-third of the abuse is committed by nuclear family members (Russell, 1983). An emphasis on father-daughter incest and family dynamics in incestuous abuse thus serves to obscure the scope of the problem of child sexual abuse (Bolen, 2000a). Perhaps the most important effect of blaming mothers, daughters, or families, then, is that doing so colludes with our societal need to deny the scope of the problem of child sexual abuse.

Feminist Theory

In the 1970s and 1980s, feminist writers began to discuss the relationship of child sexual abuse to the social environment (Herman, 1981; Rush, 1980). Feminists believed that child sexual abuse was symptomatic of a patriarchal society in which males had power over females. One of the ways in which males were said to abuse that power was through the sexual abuse of women and children. Abuse was thus conceptualized as an extension of socially normative behavior between males and females. As such, one of the striking questions posed by feminists was not why some men abused, but why all men did not (Herman, 1990).

Feminists were unwilling to consider rationalizations for abuse, regarding them as diluting the focus on the offender's behavior. Hence, their most important message to the developing knowledge base of child sexual abuse was that the offender was always 100% culpable and responsible for the abuse. As such, much of the early feminist literature was reactionary, attacking theories that suggested anything less than 100% culpability for the offender. Certain papers discussed Freud's retraction of the seduction theory and its effect on victims of abuse (Herman, 1981; Rush, 1980; Westerlund, 1986). Others were written in reaction to family systems literature and to reframe the role of the offender to the incest (Waldby, Clancy,

Emetchi, & Summerfield, 1989), whereas others reframed the pejorative literature on nonoffending mothers (Jacobs, 1990; McIntyre, 1981).

While experts on child sexual abuse have adopted the feminist position that the sexual abuse is totally the responsibility and culpability of the offender, not all mental health professionals so readily agree. Instead, most studies on attribution of blame find that culpability continues to be distributed among the child, offender, and nonoffending mother. Two different studies on professional attribution of blame published in the 1980s found that mean scores for offenders ranged from 2.7 to 4.3 on a five-point scale, with five designating full responsibility (Jackson & Sandberg, 1985; Saunders, 1988). In a study published in 1993 (Reidy & Hochstadt), mean offender blame was 5.4 on a six-point scale. Further, for studies published in the 1990s, only between 65% and 84% of blame is attributed by professionals to the offender (Johnson et al., 1990; Kalichman et al., 1990; Kelley, 1990; Reidy & Hochstadt, 1993). In one of these studies (Kelley, 1990), only 12% of the respondents held the offender entirely responsible for the abuse, although the offender was assigned the greatest amount of responsibility (70%) for the abuse. Of concern as well, professionals rate offenders as less culpable when they deny the abuse (Kalichman et al., 1990). Of particular concern is the finding by Kelley (1990) that professionals were more tolerant of, and recommended less severe sentences for, offenders who held a higher social status (a prominent attorney versus an unemployed alcoholic). Another study (Hanson & Slater, 1993) found that therapists and police officers attributed varying amounts of responsibility to the offender based on his motivation for the abuse. On a seven-point scale, responsibility ratings varied from 5.4 when the offender related a personal history of child sexual abuse or was not getting along with his wife to 6.2 when the offender admitted to the offense and said that his behavior was unacceptable. While these studies suggest that most of the blame is now being placed upon the offender, there are disquieting findings. Studies find that culpability is differentially related to characteristics of both the offender and the abuse situation, suggesting that professionals do not yet agree that the offender is fully responsible for the abuse. In this sense, feminists have failed to have the impact on the identification and conceptualization of child sexual abuse that they sought.

This failure to have the desired impact is acknowledged by feminists. When the feminist perspective of child sexual abuse was introduced in the 1970s, there was a sense of optimism for change. "It was heady stuff, then, the finding of *corroboration*; the high-energy dialogue; the sense of urgent purpose behind the research and analysis, the clear *naming* that signaled serious purpose" (Armstrong, 1996, p. 298). Feminists believed that change would come simply by naming child sexual abuse and by explicating and clarifying the societal factors they believed to be linked to child sexual abuse. Obviously, change did not come in the expected manner. As Armstrong stated of the past 20 years, "The point of feminists speaking out about incest in the first place seems all but irretrievably lost" (p. 299).

Why did the feminist movement not have the impact it expected? This is an intriguing question given the important advances in the knowledge base in other areas of child sexual abuse. There are probably several reasons, but perhaps the most important reason is that feminists were taking on awesome and deeply ingrained societal forces. The feminist analysis suggests that patriarchy is the most important contributor to sexual abuse. Yet patriarchy is deeply engrained and embedded within our culture. For the prevalence of sexual abuse to lessen, then, the very foundation of society, and the foundation representing the most powerful, would have to change. How could feminists expect the powerful majority to willingly give up that power?

Armstrong (1996) also advances another intriguing idea. She believes that the medical model has done extreme harm to the movement to conceptualize child sexual abuse as an abuse of power within society. By pathologizing victims, she suggests, the medical model brings the focus to bear upon the victims' psychopathology instead of why they are abused. Symptomatology in victims becomes paramount and the offender as the central figure disappears, becoming only a "passive spectre" (p. 300). In this shift in models, "there is an *acceptance of the wounding itself* that is both terrifying and dreadful. There is a profound pessimism in the implied tolerance" (p. 300). Within this perspective, she suggests that it is the degree of wounding, not the wrongfulness of that deed, that receives paramount interest. Of this paradox she states, "In allowing ourselves to be led from the understanding of incest as socially normative, supportive of male dominance, to the exclusive focus on florid symptoms, exotic behaviors, we have been led from the truth of agony to the brink of comedy" (p. 300).

Hers is an interesting perspective that may bear much truth. Perhaps though, the medical model is a first step towards accepting the scope of the problem of child sexual abuse. Society today is willing to concede the need to treat victims, although it in no way appears ready to concede the need to change the underlying societal structure that contributes to child sexual abuse. The medical model may therefore be a transitional model between what was and what will be. The danger, however, is in becoming lost in it and forgetting that a larger truth about child sexual abuse is being overlooked and largely forgotten.

SUMMARY

The historical development of theories of child sexual abuse has been affected by a variety of factors, perhaps the most important of which is the influence of Freud and his psychoanalytic theory. That he renounced his seduction theory and suggested that victims were fantasizing the assaults was perhaps the single most important factor in the developmental history of theories of child sexual abuse and directly impacted later writings that suggested that daughters seduce their fathers.

Possibly in reaction to the psychoanalytic influence on the profession's understanding of child sexual abuse, family systems theorists developed an alternative theory. While this theory made significant advances over those of recalled fantasies and seduction by the daughter, it had distinct disadvantages, the most important of which was that it continued to remove blame from the offender. The father, family, nonoffending mother, and even the victim had to share in the culpability for the abuse. It was not until feminists clearly began to state that offenders were always and completely responsible for their acts, regardless of the actions of others, that professionals began to move toward this possibility. The influence of feminists in recent years has thus been to bring the issue of culpability to the fore and to place it on the responsible party.

WHAT LIES IN THE FUTURE

Agenda for Theoretical Development

While the theoretical knowledge base of child sexual abuse has advanced considerably in the last 100 years, important problems remain, one of which is that the theoretical literature base relates primarily to incest. Seduction by the daughter, collusion by the mother, the influence of the dysfunctional family—all suggest a primary orientation towards father-daughter incest. Even much of the feminist literature has a primary orientation towards intrafamilial abuse. This emphasis in the theoretical literature on father-daughter incest and other types of intrafamilial abuse has also been reflected in the empirical literature. For example, of books and papers published between 1966 and 1998, 123 were indexed under father-daughter incest and almost 2,200 were indexed under intrafamilial abuse, whereas only 15 were indexed under extrafamilial abuse (Bolen, 2000a). This bias is also found in treatment centers in which the majority of victims have been abused by relatives, most often by father figures (Bolen, 1998a; English & Tosti-Lane, 1988). These statistics stand in stark contrast to findings in prevalence studies that report that approximately 70% of all child sexual abuse is extrafamilial (Bolen, 2000a).

The regrettable effect of this overemphasis on intrafamilial abuse is a concomitant de-emphasis on the full scope of the problem of child sexual abuse. If, for example, child sexual abuse is conceptualized as a problem of a few dysfunctional families, then the societal factors that allow sexual abuse to flourish can be ignored. From a standpoint of societal acceptance of the scope of child sexual abuse, it may be far less threatening to consider that a few deranged fathers may abuse their children than to accept that as many as 30% of girls and fewer males may be at risk of sexual abuse by someone other than a relative (Finkelhor et al., 1983).

Another important problem in the theoretical literature is that certain theories of child sexual abuse remain myth-bound, often even in the face of contradictory empirical literature. This is especially true of family systems theory, which developed when no empirical literature was available and surely reflected the mother-blaming, father-aggrandizing society of that era. Given the current state of knowledge, this biased view is no longer tenable. This is not to say that family systems theory has nothing to offer the understanding of child sexual abuse. Instead, intriguing findings in the literature suggest that family dynamics may be risk factors not only in intrafamilial abuse, but also in extrafamilial abuse (Alexander & Lupfer, 1987; Briere & Elliot, 1993; Ray, Jackson, & Townsley, 1991). As such, a reformulation of family systems theory that is concordant with the empirical literature and that expands its view to all child sexual abuse is surely overdue. To continue to advance the historical conceptualization of family systems theory and other myth-bound theories, even when the current empirical literature contradicts them, however, allows for the propagation of unsupported and biased literature.

Another important shortcoming in the theoretical literature is the failure to operationalize existing theories. Only a few theories of risk of abuse have been forwarded, and none has been operationalized sufficiently to be tested empirically, although the operationalization of theories of risk to offend has advanced further. Therefore, proponents of these theories need to clearly explicate testable hypotheses.

A final important shortcoming is the lack of an overall model of child sexual abuse. Current theories on child sexual abuse are typically unidimensional as, for example, family systems theory's unidimensional focus on families of father-daughter incest. Even feminist theory, as important as it is to the understanding of sexual violence, is unidimensional, focusing almost exclusively on societal factors that may affect the prevalence of sexual abuse. The same can be said for social learning theory, conditioning theory, and attachment theory. While these theories, properly operationalized, may be important to our eventual understanding of why certain individuals abuse children or why certain children are at greater risk of abuse, none alone is sufficient to understand the problem of child sexual abuse.

Just as Kendall-Tackett, Williams, and Finkelhor (1993) called for an overarching model to understand the development of symptoms after victimization, the same type of model is necessary for child sexual abuse as a whole. One of the most fundamental needs for this model is that it be theoretically and, as possible, empirically grounded. The grounding of the model in the current empirical knowledge base should reduce the serious biases currently found in the literature. For example, recognizing that studies concur that most nonoffending mothers are both supportive and noncollusive (Bolen, 2000b) would remove the temptation to include some of the early tenets of family systems theory that paint such a biased view of these women. Furthermore, this model must capture the important ecological framework of abuse, recognizing that factors at all systemic levels impinge upon risk to offend and to abuse. Finally, this model must capture the developmental trajectory of both the offender and victim. Work such as this has been done in the child maltreatment literature. For example, Belsky (1980) presented an ecological framework of child maltreatment, whereas Cicchetti and Rizley (1981) presented a transactional framework. More recently, Cicchetti and Lynch (1993) combined these frameworks to examine community violence. The purpose of Chapters 8 and 9 is, in part, to present a model such as this that is specific to child sexual abuse.

The course of theoretical development therefore needs to be four-fold: (a) to focus all theories upon all types of child sexual abuse (not just intrafamilial abuse); (b) to operationalize existing theories; (c) to refute or reformulate biased theoretical literature; and (d) to develop overarching models that synthesize the different levels of factors (individual, family and attachment, community, and societal) and that provide a transactional understanding of child sexual abuse.

Conclusion

When the development of the knowledge base of sexual abuse is considered from the perspective on an outsider, it must seem somewhat absurd. Surely it would make a smashing soap opera, with themes such as seduction, repression, suppression, false memories, mothers who collude, and fathers who are seduced—claims and counter-claims. This fiery development of the child sexual abuse knowledge base is a regrettable legacy of its history.

While other fields develop their knowledge base in a mostly linear manner, perhaps a suitable description of the historical development of the knowledge base of child sexual abuse is that it has been bipolar, reflecting the cyclical shifts between depressive phases (in which the knowledge base has been suppressed) and manic and euphoric phases (in which the developing knowledge has exhibited expansive thoughts and even a flight of ideas). This manic phase has inevitably been followed by the current depressive stage in which the field is suffering the consequences of its previous mania. It is an irritating and fatiguing depression.

The societal and professional response to child sexual abuse is equally cyclical (Olafson, Corwin, & Summit, 1993), with its phases of acceptance and suppression. Here, however, the more proper analogy may be one of posttraumatic stress disorder, with phases of intrusion and avoidance. The scope of the problem of child sexual abuse is, to a sophisticated society, an extreme threat to its self-perception. As such, the knowledge of the scope of child sexual abuse is proving exceptionally difficult to integrate. Just as the process of working through requires an acceptance of the shadow side of oneself, so does the societal process of accepting such an horrific shadow side. To expect and wish for an easy acceptance of this shadow side is idealistic. Those who watch their clients struggle to accept what they do not want to know about themselves, whether it is their victimization or their victimizing, know this truth. Being with clients who process knowledge about themselves, and sometimes about those they love, requires the proper respect for their defenses, allowing them to avoid the truth until they build the internal fortitude to return to it. Ultimately, as clients cycle between intrusive and avoidant stages, they also slowly integrate the knowledge into their being.

How can we expect anything less of a society that does not want to wear the label of a sexually violent society? Will it be accepted any more willingly? Perhaps feminists of the 1970s were naive to expect that hearing the truth would necessarily move the masses toward its acceptance. Yet these same feminists have benefited society by forcing a focus on knowledge that is not easily disavowed, although the battle to do so is mighty. This focus forces society to look at its shadow side. That it is to be denied and avoided is expected. Thus, while feminists symbolize the push towards an intrusive phase, the current backlash symbolizes the push towards avoidance. If so, perhaps the backlash is a necessary, albeit painful, process in society's struggle to integrate the scope of the problem of child sexual abuse.

What has become obvious during the last 100 years is that the development of the knowledge and theoretical base of child sexual abuse is immutably tied to society's willingness to know the truth about itself. While many researchers may wish to consider their research apolitical, it is also obvious that in an area of research so laden with societal values and societal self-perception, all research is political. Although few researchers probably enjoy the current fiery atmosphere surrounding the development of the knowledge base of child sexual abuse, it is a part of the inherited legacy and will probably remain so for some time to come. Each new advance in the knowledge base of child sexual abuse places a greater burden of truth upon society. This truth is distasteful and burdensome, requiring with its acceptance fundamental changes within society. As long as society reneges upon accepting its responsibility for the truth of child sexual abuse, the development of the empirical and theoretical knowledge base of child sexual abuse will surely remain contentious.

PART II
SCOPE OF THE PROBLEM

CHAPTER 4
METHODOLOGY

INTRODUCTION

The empirical literature on child sexual abuse has burgeoned in the last 15 years with a concomitant increase in the number of studies published. The plethora of studies available has led to predictable problems. First, not all studies are done to exacting, meticulous, and rigorous standards. Consequently, the reader of this literature should have an elemental, and preferably more sophisticated, knowledge of research methods and their potential effect on the study's outcome. A second problem is that many studies with similar focuses exist. How, then, does the reader compare and weigh the merits of similar studies? Why do similar studies sometimes have discrepant findings? When findings do differ, how does the reader compare the strength of the findings in the respective studies?

The purpose of this chapter is to provide the reader with a basic framework for comparing studies. The rubric within which this framework for comparison is framed is that of issues of validity. The definition of validity differs based upon the context within which it is used (Pedhazur & Schmelkin, 1991). Cook and Campbell (1976) recommend a classification scheme using four types of validity—statistical conclusion validity, construct validity, internal validity, and external validity, all of which refer to the validity, or strength, of inferences made. Statistical conclusion validity refers to the validity of inferences made based upon the statistical analyses used, whereas construct validity refers to the validity of inferences made based upon the measures employed. Internal validity refers to the validity of inferences made concerning the effect of the independent variable(s) on the dependent variable, after considering methodological features of the study. Finally, external validity refers to the validity of inferences made to a larger population (i.e., the generalizability of the study).

Each type of validity is critical to the eventual integrity of the study. When any type of validity suffers, the integrity of the study lessens. Research constraints sometimes predicate certain weaknesses in the study's design. For example, because of foreboding ethical issues, no known research has yet studied a randomly selected representative population of young child sexual abuse victims. Neither can sexual abuse be used as a manipulated variable in an experimental design—again for obvious ethical reasons. When constraints do occur, the challenge becomes to design the most rigorous study possible, given the constraints, and then to clearly state not only the methodology of the study, but also its weaknesses and limitations. The careful reader will then have the information necessary to make an informed decision concerning the strength of inferences made from the findings.

This chapter discusses types of validity as they relate to child sexual abuse research. The different types of validity are somewhat broadly interpreted. For example, all issues of measurement are discussed under construct validity, whereas all issues of research design are discussed under internal validity. This chapter is written for professionals with or without advanced training in research methods or statistics.

CONSTRUCT VALIDITY: MEASUREMENT ISSUES

Construct validity is the "appropriateness, meaningfulness, and usefulness of the specific inferences made from test scores" (American Psychological Association, 1985, p. 9). As such, construct validity is not so much concerned with the measure itself, but with the ability to infer from the measure (Pedhazur & Schmelkin, 1991). Obviously, poorly constructed measures increase the probability that inferences made from them are not valid.

While construct validity is primarily concerned with the already developed instrument and how well it captures what it was designed to measure, the measure's development is obviously critical to its later validity. For this reason, this section is concerned first with the definition, operationalization, and measurement of the constructs of interest, followed by a discussion of construct validity. Because many issues of construct validity can become extremely technical, this section provides only an overview of the issues.

Issues in Defining, Operationalizing, and Measuring Child Sexual Abuse

A construct is a concept that can be uniquely differentiated from another concept. Constructs are embedded within a theoretical framework from which they gain meaning. For example, the construct of depression, which can be differentiated from anxiety, assumes meaning when embedded within a theoretical framework. The construct most germane to the discussion in this book is child sexual abuse. As stated in Chapter 2, child sexual abuse, while a tragic reality, is also a social construction. Our understanding of child sexual abuse gains meaning within the definition that society provides for the act.

Because theory and constructs are inextricably woven, the researcher must always formulate a theoretical definition of the construct of interest. Only then can the researcher operationalize the construct by determining how it will be measured. Naturally, the operationalized definition must logically flow from the theoretical definition. For example, the researcher may operationalize the construct of child sexual abuse as sexual contact between a child under the age of 16 by a person at least five years that child's senior. Logically, the questions asked in the interview or questionnaire must then capture all criteria for this definition.

Definition of Child Sexual Abuse

Researchers have not yet reached a consensus on how inclusive the definition of child sexual abuse should be. "One of the major difficulties in assessing the extent of abuse and its effects is that the definition of sexual abuse is not consistent in the literature" (Craine, Henson, Colliver, & MacLean, 1988, p. 303), Across studies, variability is found in (a) the type of abuse allowed (i.e., contact versus noncontact abuse); (b) the age differential between victim and offender; (c) the age cutoff for adolescent victims; and (d) the type of victim/offender relationship.

Why does so much variability in the definition of child sexual abuse across studies exist? Why has no consensus been reached? A portion of the problem is in defining an event that has so much situational variability. As many writers are quick to point out (see, for example, Kelly, 1988), a too conservative definition of child sexual abuse invariably omits legitimate cases of child sexual abuse. On the other hand, a broad definition may allow for incidents of sexual contact that are difficult to classify as child sexual abuse. The difficulty is in creating an operationalized definition of child sexual abuse that is neither too broad nor too narrow. Perhaps the best method is that adopted by Russell (1983) and others in which respondents were asked to discuss all incidents of unwanted sexual contact. A research panel then made the decision regarding whether the incident was abusive. This latter method, although costly and time-consuming, appears to be an ideal method for assessing whether an incident is truly abusive. By doing so, the definition of child sexual abuse can also be modified later to be more or less inclusive (Wyatt & Peters, 1986).

Eventually the researcher must determine the study's criteria for child sexual abuse. Various factors enter into the researcher's decision to use a more narrow or broad definition. Sometimes the researcher's bias about what constitutes child sexual abuse may be the deciding factor. Alternately, the legal definition of child sexual abuse for that region may be used, or legal guidelines might predicate the criteria (Violato & Genuis, 1993). Another important concern may be the credibility of the study if a broad definition of child sexual abuse is used. Finally, researchers may choose to use a more narrow or broad definition based upon the needs for their study. Researchers attempting to ascertain the effect of child sexual abuse upon later psychopathology, for example, may choose to use only those victims with more extreme abuse. This use of a more restrictive population might obviate the problem of floor effects in which many victims may not exhibit clinical ranges of psychopathology (Berliner & Saunders, 1996).

While good reasons for making the definition of child sexual abuse more or less narrow exist, the problem is when comparing studies to each other. In all types of studies, differences in criteria for inclusion as a child sexual abuse incident have a significant effect upon rates of abuse. In Russell's (1983) community survey, for example, when noncontact sexual abuse was included, the prevalence of women sexually abused as children (i.e., under the age of 18) was 54%, but when noncontact abuse was excluded, the prevalence was 38%. It is therefore critical to assess how differences in the definition of child sexual abuse across studies might affect the outcome of the research. These next sections discuss the criteria for a definition of sexual abuse and their potential impact on the outcome of research.

Type of abuse allowed: The first issue is the type of abuse allowed (i.e., whether both contact and noncontact abuse should be included). With this issue, researchers may be concerned that including noncontact abuse may diminish the credibility of the study. For example, Haugaard and Emery (1989) found that victims of child sexual abuse could be divided into three subgroups. The first subgroup was primarily composed of those victims who experienced only noncontact abuse. This small subgroup included approximately 20% of all female victims and 38% of all male victims. Victims in this group were noteworthy for the limited effects of the abuse. The other extreme was a small clinical group (18% of all victims) in which victims had been penetrated vaginally, anally, or orally and had suffered the greatest deleterious effects of the abuse. The middle and largest group—victims experiencing other types of contact sexual abuse—comprised the bulk of the victims.

Using this study as a reference suggests that a broad definition of child sexual abuse might include victims of noncontact sexual abuse. A restrictive definition, on the other hand, might include the smaller portion of victims with the most severe abuse (i.e., penetration). This study also suggests, however, that any type of contact sexual abuse should be included unless there are specific reasons to restrict the definition to include only penetration.

Age differential between the victim and offender: Another controversial issue regarding the definition of child sexual abuse is whether to include sexual contact between same-age peers. It is now widely accepted that children in adult-child encounters cannot give informed consent. The issue is less clear, however, with child-child encounters, and there is concern that including same-age peer contact will allow for many cases of normal and mutual sexual exploration.

In a study on sibling incest, De Jong (1989) found that several factors discriminated abuse incidents from incidents of sexual play, including when (a) offenders were five or more years older; (b) children were at different developmental levels; (c) force, threat or the use of an authority position (e.g., in a babysitting situation) was applied; (d) penetration was attempted or completed; and (e) physical injury occurred. De Jong found that the age, developmental level, and force criteria distinguished most cases of sexual abuse. In the remaining cases, the two final criteria adequately discriminated abusive situations.

This is an interesting method of approaching the problem of distinguishing sex play from abusive events. This study suggests that the use of minimum inclusionary criteria might be the better approach. In this approach, events that meet certain criteria would automatically be included as abuse incidents. For the questionable incidents, another set of criteria could be established in which the event could be included if, for example, the event was unwanted, included penetration, or was injurious to the child. None of these three criteria are typical of developmentally appropriate sexual play between children.

Age cutoff for adolescents: There are two concerns about age cutoffs for adolescent victims of child sexual abuse. First, what is the upper age limit for child sexual abuse? Second, when is a sexual event involving an adolescent abusive?

Much dissension concerning the upper age limit for child sexual abuse exists. Especially in an era in which adolescents are exposed to sexual stimuli at a far quicker pace and become sexually active at a younger age, some may question whether 17-year-olds, for example, can be considered victims of child sexual abuse. Studies capture this controversy by sometimes limiting a sexual abuse event to adolescents as young as age 15 and below (Finkelhor, 1994).

The second issue for adolescents is whether a sexual event is abusive. One way in which researchers address this issue is by narrowing the sexual abuse criteria for older adolescents. For example, Wyatt (1985) included only unwanted experiences for adolescents over the age of 14, while allowing certain of these experiences for younger children. Another method is to widen the age limit between older adolescent victims and their offenders. For example, for children less than 14 years of age, Finkelhor (1979) used a five-year age differential between offender and victim, but a 10-year differential for victims ages 14 and over. Again, one solution is to allow the respondent to provide sufficient detail about the incident, after which a research panel decides whether the incident is abusive based upon criteria for inclusion.

The issues of the age differential between victim and offender and the upper age limit for adolescents are of great concern because of the potential, when setting arbitrary criteria, for missing valid cases of child sexual abuse. In a secondary analysis (Bolen, 2000a) of Russell's (1983) community prevalence study, peer abuse and abuse by dates and others in a romantic/sexual relationship with the victim were some of the most severe of all abuse incidents. Perpetrators in a romantic/sexual relationship were almost as likely as strangers to physically assault their victims. Penetration and the use of force or threat in both abuse by friends and those in a romantic/sexual relationship occurred more frequently than for any other extrafamilial abuse perpetrator type. Furthermore, multiple attacks occurred well above average for both of these groups. Criteria that exclude these cases therefore minimize the serious issue of sexual assault by same-age or near-age peers.

Victim/offender relationship: While child sexual abuse may be committed by a person of any filial or nonfilial relation to the victim, many clinical studies often restrict their samples to victims of intrafamilial abuse. This practice stems from a critical problem in the current assessment and treatment of child sexual abuse victims—that priority is given to victims of intrafamilial abuse, and especially victims of father-daughter incest. The available pool of child victims is therefore highly skewed toward populations of victims of incest.

Because much of the current literature derives primarily from samples of intrafamilial abuse, the definition of incest is an important consideration. The reader must know, for instance, whether the definition includes only father-daughter incest, incest by the nuclear family, or abuse by any relative. Even within father-daughter incest it is important to know what constitutes the relationship. For example, does the study include all father figures or just legally recognized fathers? Does the study include stepfathers? It is equally important that custody be specified. There is some indication that a significant amount of father-daughter incest may be committed by biological fathers who do not have custody of or who are not living with their children (Faller, 1990). Therefore, the reader must know exactly what type of relationship the sample constitutes. It is especially important not to generalize the findings beyond the limits of the sample. For example, it is inappropriate to draw conclusions for all victims of child sexual abuse from a study using only intrafamilial abuse victims.

Measuring Child Sexual Abuse

Once the criteria for the definition of child sexual abuse are determined, the next issue is how best to determine whether the respondent has been sexually abused. The issue concerning accurate disclosure can probably be subsumed within two categories—methodological and ideological concerns. From an ideological standpoint, the issue of accurate recall of abuse is heated and controversial. Because the focus of this chapter is methodology, the ideological nature of the debate is not addressed.

Methodologically, the issue is how best to garner accurate disclosures of abuse histories. Several methodological factors must be considered, including (a) the type of measurement used (e.g., interview format, self-administered questionnaire, or telephone survey), (b) the number of screen questions asked, (c) how behaviorally specific these questions are, and (d) characteristics of the interviewer. All may have a considerable impact on the accuracy of the disclosed abuse rate for that population. Needless to say, the accuracy of the disclosed abuse rate is often fundamental to the ability to infer findings from the study.

Mode of administration: Until the 1980s, self-administered questionnaires were assumed to be the mode of choice when asking questions about sensitive material. Yet in 1986, Peters, Wyatt, and Finkelhor found that studies employing self-administered questionnaires had lower prevalence rates of child sexual abuse than studies employing face-to-face interviews.

Two multivariate analyses of the effect of methodology of prevalence rates of child sexual abuse have now been conducted (Bolen & Scannapieco, 1999; Gorey & Leslie, 1997). In both, after controlling for other factors, no significant relationship between the mode of administration and prevalence was found. An Australian study (Martin, Anderson, Romans, Mullen, & O'Shea, 1993) that employed both a postal survey and a face-to-face interview format, however, found that the relationship between type of format and rate of disclosure was more complicated. While 25% of female respondents reported a history of contact sexual abuse prior to the age of 16, 10% of these cases were not reported during the face-to-face interview. Furthermore, 12% of women who reported no abuse on the postal questionnaire disclosed abuse during the interview. This study suggests that both methods have limitations and that multiple methods of assessment may be needed.

The mode of administering the measure may also be important in clinical studies. In reviewing studies of inpatient adult psychiatric or emergency room patients in which prevalence was noted, chart review was associated with the lowest prevalence rates of reported abuse. Prevalence ranged from 2% to 10% of all patients whose charts were reviewed (Briere & Zaidi, 1989; Carmen, Rieker, & Mills, 1984; Jacobsen, Koehler, & Jones-Brown, 1987). When the respondents were later asked directly about a past history of abuse, the prevalence of abuse reported in one of these studies went up to 70% (Briere & Zaidi, 1989). In studies using a questionnaire format, however, between 19% (Metcalfe, Oppenheimer, Dignon, & Palmer, 1990) and 24% (Goff, Brotman, Kindlon, Waites, & Amico, 1991) of all psychiatric inpatients, and 44% (Bryer, Nelson, Miller, & Krol, 1987) of female psychiatric inpatients reported a history of child sexual abuse. In other studies using face-to-face interviews, 46% (Beck & van der Kolk, 1987), 50% (Goodwin, Attias, McCarty, Chandler, & Romanik, 1988), and 51% (Craine et al., 1988) of patients reported histories of child sexual abuse. Finally, one study compared the disclosure of sexual abuse by adult female psychiatric patients during regular intake procedures to disclosure on a self-administered questionnaire (Dill, Chu, Grob, & Eisen, 1991). While 35% of patients disclosed at intake, 52% disclosed on the questionnaire; overall, 58% disclosed a history of child sexual abuse. These studies suggest that the method of eliciting disclosure affects the willingness of individuals to disclose a previous history of abuse.

Type of questions: Another crucial methodological characteristic is the type of questions used to elicit abuse disclosures (Peters et al., 1986). Studies typically use one or more screen questions to ask about the possibility of abuse. Screen questions can be either broad funnel questions or inverted funnel questions. In the former, if respondents answer "yes" to a broad question, it is followed by more restrictive questions. In the latter, a number of questions are asked, each pertaining to a narrowly delimited type of child sexual abuse. By clarifying the nature of the incident being solicited, this behaviorally specific format is thought to trigger memories that facilitate recollection of abuse incidents. This latter type appears to be the more effective method both in studies of rape (Koss, 1993) and child sexual abuse (Martin et al., 1993; Wyatt & Peters, 1986).

Number of questions: The number of screen questions potentially accounts for a great deal of the variation in reported abuse rates across studies. In an early review of community prevalence studies, Peters, Wyatt, and Finkelhor (1986) found that those using only one screen question had prevalence rates ranging from 6% to 22%. Prevalence rates in studies using two to four screen questions ranged from 11% to 34%, and studies using more than four questions had a range of 54% to 62% (including noncontact abuse). Peters et al. concluded that the number of screen questions was an important predictor of prevalence rate. Indeed, in a multivariate analysis of community, state, and national random prevalence studies done in North America (Bolen & Scannapieco, 1999), the number of screen questions was the strongest predictor of prevalence.

In another study, Williams, Siegel, and Jackson Pomeroy (2000) asked a series of 19 screen questions to a group of 136 women who, before the age of 13, had a documented case of child sexual abuse. This study reviewed the capability of the screen questions to elicit the respondents' histories of child sexual abuse. Although 80 percent of disclosing women were identified after four general gate questions, only after eight questions did 90 percent of the disclosing women report an initial incident of abuse. Fourteen questions were required to elicit all disclosures that were forthcoming in the interview. Even after 14 questions, however, more than a third of the index incidents were never disclosed and 12% of the women never disclosed any abuse incidents. These findings corroborate the findings by Bolen and Scannapieco (1999) that a large number of screen questions are necessary to elicit disclosures of child sexual abuse and that underdisclosure remains a significant issue even with the use of multiple screen questions.

Peters, Wyatt, and Finkelhor (1986) discuss factors involved in why multiple screen questions of an inverted funnel type (i.e., behaviorally specific format) coincide with higher prevalence rates. First, the way a survivor remembers the actual abuse might not match the manner in which the question is asked. Consequently, more questions are more likely to trigger a specific memory of abuse. Second, multiple screen questions may work better because they provide a longer period of time during which disclosure occurs, a factor that seems particularly important when dealing with sensitive material.

Characteristics of the interviewer and respondent: A final issue is the characteristics of interviewers and respondents. In their early review of methodologies of prevalence studies, Peters, Wyatt, and Finkelhor (1986) found that attention to the training of the interviewers might be an important methodological feature. They state:

> *It is probably not coincidence that in both of the higher prevalence sexual abuse [face-to-face interviewing] studies (Russell, 1983; Wyatt, 1985), interviewers were specially selected for the study and received extensive training designed to sensitize them to the*

issues involved in asking about sexual abuse. If [face-to-face interviewing] allows for the possibility of better reporting, it may be because of the possibility of using well-selected and trained interviewers to enhance candor. (p. 40)

Finally, matching the race or ethnicity of the interviewer with that of the respondent may be an important feature. In a secondary analysis (Bolen, 1998b) of Russell's (1983) community prevalence study, an interaction effect between race of the respondent and level of comfort with the interview was noted. Women of Asian descent who were uncomfortable with the interview disclosed far less abuse proportionally than those who felt more comfortable with the interview. This finding suggests that certain cohorts, especially if they do not feel comfortable with the interview, may be reticent to disclose actual abuse.[1]

Summary

How child sexual abuse is conceptualized, operationalized, and measured is fundamental to the validity of inferences made from the data and the ability to generalize beyond the given sample. When attempting to compare across studies, consider the following:

- How broad or narrow is the definition of child sexual abuse?
  - What are the criteria for the definition of child sexual abuse?
    - Does the definition include both intrafamilial and extrafamilial abuse?
    - Does it include contact and noncontact abuse?
    - What is the upper age cutoff for adolescents?
    - Is there an age differential between offender and child?
  - How were the disclosures obtained?
    - What was the mode of administering the measure for obtaining a disclosure of child sexual abuse?
    - How many questions were used to elicit disclosure?
    - What were the types of questions used? Were they behaviorally specific?
    - Were the interviewers matched on age and ethnicity?
- Were the interviewers trained and by whom?

For each of the answers to these questions, it is critically important to consider the effect of that methodological characteristic upon the disclosed abuse rate. Knowledge of the definition of child sexual abuse is thus essential in considering the validity, or strength, of findings resulting from the study.

Validity of Other Constructs

While the clear operationalization and definition of child sexual abuse is fundamental to the integrity of a study, other constructs measured within the study must be carefully defined, operationalized, and measured. The study's findings are only as

---

[1] Because Russell's (1983) study employed matching between the interviewer and respondent on race, it is possible that this finding reflects cultural differences in the respondents.

good as the measures employed. Regretfully, many measures employed in the social sciences have important limitations that fundamentally affect the findings of the study, and, thus, their inferences.

Two concepts—construct validity and reliability—are especially important when discussing measures. As mentioned earlier, construct validity refers to the meaningfulness that can be attached to inferences made from test scores (American Psychological Association, 1985). For example, a measure of depression should capably measure depression while being able to discriminate it from related constructs such as anxiety. Doing so increases the meaningfulness of the inferences made from the depression scores. Reliability, on the other hand, is concerned with "the degree to which test scores are free from errors of measurement" (p. 19). Reliability is most commonly measured in two different ways—as stability and internal consistency. The stability of the measure refers to the ability of the measure over repeated administrations to be scored in a consistent manner, whereas internal consistency refers to the ability of the instrument to measure the same phenomenon (Pedhazur & Schmelkin, 1991). If either the reliability or construct validity of the measure is weak, the integrity of the findings suffers. The following example illustrates the effect of measurement issues on the study of child sexual abuse.

An area of great interest is the relationship of family dynamics to child sexual abuse, especially incest. As a result, a variety of studies have now compared these constructs. Regretfully, many instruments developed to capture family dynamics still have significant problems with construct validity, including FACES (Olson, Sprenkle, & Russell, 1979; Olson, Russell, & Sprenkle, 1983), which has been used in some child sexual abuse research. (See, for example, Alexander & Lupfer, 1987, and Carson, Gertz, Donaldson, & Wonderlich, 1990.) This measure attempts to measure family dynamics across two primary dimensions—adaptability and cohesion. Adaptability is measured on a continuum of chaotic to rigidity; cohesion is measured on a continuum of disengagement to enmeshment. Both continua are curvilinear (i.e., healthier families are hypothesized to score at the midpoint on each continuum, whereas more dysfunctional families are hypothesized to score at either end of the continua). As such, healthier families should exhibit a balance between enmeshment and disengagement, and between rigidity and chaos. Dysfunctional families, on the other hand, should be either enmeshed or disengaged, and rigid or chaotic.

While this model may make intuitive sense, the cohesion continuum has serious issues with validity.[2] This problem with the validity of the measure leads to obvious problems with interpretation and treatment, as healthy families are assumed to be dysfunctional and, therefore, in need of treatment, whereas certain dysfunctional families are interpreted as healthy. While this is just one example, problems such as these can obviously skew the results of studies.

The issue of measurement error is potentially a serious problem in the professional literature. Regretfully, only readers familiar with the psychometric properties of the measures employed can critically analyze the findings for that study. This issue places a great responsibility upon the researcher not only for using measures with proven and strong psychometric properties, but also for reporting the known limitations of measures used. For the reader, the responsibility is in reading the

---

[2] See Cluff, Hicks, & Madsen, 1994, for a review.

methodology section sufficiently to be cognizant of the issues with the reliability and validity of the measures employed (if they are stated) and to consider how these issues might affect the findings.

INTERNAL VALIDITY: DESIGN ISSUES

"Internal validity refers to the validity of assertions regarding the effects of the independent variable(s) on the dependent variable(s)" (Pedhazur & Schmelkin, 1991, p. 224). In other words, is the relationship between the independent variable(s) and dependent variable a result of the independent variable(s) or something else? Obviously, the researcher wants to make the case that the effect is the result of the influence of the independent variable rather than a flaw in the study.

Internal validity can be improved using a variety of methods. First, certain types of designs that allow for greater control can be employed. Second, controls within the research procedures can be employed. These are discussed below, followed by a section on other general issues of internal validity.

Types of Designs Used

Study designs have four basic types: experimental, quasi-experimental, pre-experimental, or nonexperimental. First to be discussed are the experimental, quasi-experimental, and pre-experimental designs.

Experimental, Quasi-experimental, and Pre-experimental Designs

Experimental, quasi-experimental, and pre-experimental designs are characterized by the use of an intervention. Studies on treatment outcomes typically use one of these designs. In these studies, a prescribed treatment intervention for victims of child sexual abuse is often employed, after which measures to determine the efficacy of the treatment are administered. As White and Farmer (1992) state:

> A goal of such research is to draw causal inferences. Variables of primary interest are manipulated by the investigator, and their impact on target behaviors is assessed. The specific variables chosen for manipulation reflect an investigator's judgment of what is most important and will shape the nature of the interpretations subsequently made. (p. 48)

The primary difference among these designs is in their rigor. The most rigorous of these designs, an experimental design, employs random assignment of subjects to either experimental and control groups or across multiple treatment groups (Pedhazur & Schmelkin, 1991). Because subjects are randomly assigned to groups, they can be assumed to be equivalent. As such, and importantly, differences between groups after the intervention can then be causally attributed to the effect of the intervention. For example, at the posttest, if the treatment group has significantly less depression than the control group, the reduction in depression can be attributed to the effect of the treatment. Properly employed, significant results can thus be causally linked to the intervention.

Quasi-experimental designs do not use random assignment to groups. As a result, groups cannot be assumed to be equivalent and differences after treatment cannot be causally attributed to the effect of the treatment. Instead, it is possible that posttest differences between groups could be a result of pretest differences between groups. Consequently, when using quasi-experimental designs, researchers must employ other methods to determine the pretest equivalence, or lack, between or among groups. The classic method is to administer pretests (Pedhazur & Schmelkin, 1991). Using pretests, researchers can then statistically control for pretest differences between or among groups. Because quasi-experimental designs do not use random assignment, however, equivalence between or among groups can only be established statistically for the variables employed, allowing for the potential of the groups to differ in other unknown ways. As such, drawing causal inferences from the findings of quasi-experimental studies is inappropriate.

While experimental studies have obvious advantages over quasi-experimental studies, they are seldom used in child sexual abuse research. Because of the sensitive population involved, ethical issues in the design of research studies often arise. An issue of great concern when considering experimental designs is whether victims, by being randomly assigned to treatment and control groups, can ethically be denied treatment. As a result, subjects in control groups often receive a different, or sometimes, lesser treatment than the experimental group. For example, the control group may receive a behavioral treatment, whereas the experimental group may receive a cognitive-behavioral treatment. Another important issue is that many outcome studies use existing treatment populations (i.e., subjects are not randomly assigned). As such, the assignment to groups is often a matter of convenience or based upon some characteristic of the subject, thus requiring the use of the less rigorous quasi-experimental design.

Many child sexual abuse studies that employ an intervention do not fulfill the requirements for even a quasi-experimental design. These pre-experimental studies often use an existing sample and an intervention, but no control group. For example, a researcher may examine depression only in child sexual abuse victims. Without a control group, however, it is impossible to determine whether the treatment was responsible for any reduction in depression. These studies are thus fraught with issues of validity.

Nonexperimental Design

Few studies of child sexual abuse other than studies of the effects of interventions are appropriate for experimental or quasi-experimental designs. Instead, the research questions posed require nonexperimental, or survey, designs in which no intervention occurs. These studies are especially useful when attempting to determine the effects of abuse on victims. Studies such as these can be either cross-sectional or longitudinal.

The weaker design, but the one most widely used, is cross-sectional. In this design, measures are administered only the one time so that questions concerning a previous history of sexual abuse and current status are administered simultaneously.

As such, cause-and-effect relationships can become blurred (Briere, 1992). A few reasons for this blurring of cause and effect are as follows. First, the respondents' current status could impact their ability to recall the abuse, as, for example, with victims of severe abuse who exhibit extreme psychopathology. The perception of the abuse might also change given the victims' current status. Offenders, for example, may be motivated to embellish childhood trauma, whereas those whose victimization status is repugnant may minimize the abuse. Another issue is that the victims' reported psychological distress could actually have preceded the abuse, as, for example, depressed children who are then sexually abused. As a result, cross-sectional studies are not designed to determine causality, but only relationships.

The causal relationship between child sexual abuse and later adverse outcome is a compelling question in the literature, just as are the causal predecessors of child sexual abuse. Research that can address causal relationships, however, requires more sophisticated longitudinal designs that follow respondents over time. In these studies, measures are taken repeatedly over time. As such, after having controlled for alternative hypotheses, if the independent variable conclusively precedes the dependent variable in time and covaries with the dependent variable, it may have a causal effect upon the dependent variable. (See the section "Issues of Causality" later in this chapter for more information.) The strength of longitudinal studies is that they may allow for statements of causality. The weaknesses, however, are that they are much more difficult and costly to implement. For these reasons, only a small percentage of studies in the area of child sexual abuse are longitudinal, although more have been initiated in recent years.

Issues of Control

Use of a Control or Comparison Group

When attempting to determine whether some variable is related to child sexual abuse or eventual outcome, it is important to compare that variable in a nonabused group as well. Experimental and quasi-experimental designs do this by employing a control group (Pedhazur & Schmelkin, 1991). This control group, in comparison to the treatment group, does not have access to the manipulated variable (usually an intervention of some sort). As a result, for experimental designs the two groups can be compared at posttest and differences can be attributed to the effect of the manipulated variable (i.e., the intervention). Because quasi-experimental designs do not employ random assignment to groups, no causal statements can be made.

Nonexperimental studies also benefit by the use of control groups, often called comparison groups. As with experimental designs, these comparison groups are used as a basis for comparing differences on the variables of interest between the groups. In child sexual abuse studies, one of the most common nonexperimental designs employing a comparison group is when the victimized group is compared against a nonvictimized or other clinical group. When significant differences emerge, with other necessary controls, a case can then be made for attributing these differences to the victimization status of the respondent (although the effect can only be causally attributed if all conditions of causality are satisfied).

Several issues arise, however, in the use of comparison groups. A major concern is whether the comparison group is comprised of respondents who are also victims of sexual abuse. This problem may occur because researchers fail to screen the respondents in the comparison group for a history of sexual abuse, or may fail to use adequate methods to elicit disclosure of a previous history of sexual abuse. Even when rigorous screening occurs, however, traumatic amnesia, a primary defense of some victims of sexual abuse (Herman & Schatzow, 1987), may prohibit victims in the comparison group from disclosing their abuse history. Through the influence of the victims in the comparison group, this significant problem may obscure important relationships between the independent and dependent variables.

As an example, Dempster and Roberts (1991) used as a comparison group a population of children referred to a child psychiatric clinic for problems other than sexual abuse. (This type of comparison group is often used in studies of child victims of sexual abuse.) In 31% of subjects in the comparison group, however, sexual abuse could not be ruled out as a possibility. This finding suggests that studies that do not vigorously attend to childhood history of sexual abuse for respondents in the comparison group may be methodologically limited.

Another difficulty arises when studies using comparison groups analyze a specific type of sexual abuse, especially incest. Without proper screening procedures, victims of other types of child sexual abuse could easily be in the comparison group. Because victims of both intrafamilial and extrafamilial abuse suffer deleterious effects from their abuse (Gregory-Bills & Rhodeback, 1995), findings may be confounded, depending upon the purpose of the study. Conversely, some studies may wish to determine effects of incest over and above those of other types of sexual abuse. In this case, a comparison group of extrafamilial abuse victims is appropriate.

Even when it is clear that no known sexual abuse victims are in the comparison group, certain studies may choose to employ the method used by Hyland et al. (1993). This method creates a comparison group of individuals who have suffered no childhood *or adult* sexual trauma. Their rationale is that in any study of the long-term effects of child sexual abuse, the effects of adult rape and childhood sexual abuse cannot be readily separated. As such, the comparison group is confounded by the adult victims, thus lowering the strength of the discovered relationships, and possibly reducing meaningful relationships to nonsignificant relationships.

Another potential solution is matching each subject in the victimized group (or group of greatest interest) with an individual with similar characteristics, excluding abuse status, in the comparison group. As such, a one-to-one correspondence exists between subjects in the victimized and comparison groups.

Researchers are mixed in their support for using matching comparison groups. Kinard (1994) supports the use of a matched comparison group, suggesting that doing so can potentially "maximize similarities in life experiences and circumstances considered to influence the outcomes under investigation" (p. 649). Furthermore, Kinard suggests that unless groups are similar except for their abuse status, "group differences cannot reasonably be attributed to maltreatment" (p. 649). Briere (1992), however, suggests that matching may still be insufficient to provide the necessary level of comparison. Matching, he suggests, may also lead to lesser generalizability of the study, as the matched comparison group may represent an atypical population. He quotes Miller who states, "Matching cannot be used to make two groups equivalent when the groups are not in fact equivalent" (as cited in Briere, 1992, p. 199). Instead, Briere recommends that "it is usually best to draw representative abused and nonabused subjects from the same population" (p. 199). Differences between groups that do occur should be noted in the discussion section.

Other Issues of Internal Validity

A traditional discussion of internal validity usually begins with the stated threats to internal validity, including history, maturation, testing, instrumentation, regression toward the mean, selection, and mortality (Pedhazur & Schmelkin, 1991). A brief explanation of each of these follows.

- "*Selection* refers to the process used in assigning individuals (or other units) to different treatments or control groups" (p. 227). Selection is typically an issue when random assignment to groups is not possible.
- *History* refers to an event that occurs during the course of the study and that could affect its outcome.
- "*Mortality* refers to attrition of people or other units in the course of the study" (p. 227), such as when respondents drop out of the study.
- *Maturation* refers to changes in respondents that naturally may occur over time. Longitudinal studies are most prone to issues of maturation.
- *Testing* refers to any part of the testing process that may affect the study's outcome. For example, the process of being repeatedly tested on a given measure may affect its outcome.
- *Instrumentation* refers to aspects of the measure itself that may contribute to its outcome, as, for example, a measure that is not culturally sensitive.
- *Regression toward the mean* may occur in a group that has extremely elevated scores on a given construct (e.g., depression) being measured. The natural inclination, even without treatment, is for improvement to be noted (i.e., for the group to regress towards the mean of a normal population).

Because these issues have the potential to affect the outcome of the study, they can be interpreted as alternative explanations to the hypothesis in question.

All issues of internal validity should be addressed by the researcher *before* the inception of the research. When issues such as maturation and regression toward the mean are expected because of the nature of the study, researchers should have additional methods of ruling out these alternative explanations. Only when researchers can rule out all threats to internal validity can a sufficient case be made that significant relationships that emerge are the result of the effect of the independent variable(s) on the dependent variable.

In summary, a properly specified study will employ a research design that best answers the research question while using necessary controls to rule out alternative explanations. Experimental designs, the most rigorous designs that employ interventions, use random assignment to treatment and control groups. The most rigorous designs that do not employ interventions (i.e., survey or nonexperimental designs) are longitudinal. For all survey designs, rigor increases when comparison groups are employed. Especially for survey designs, issues of internal validity are extremely important.

EXTERNAL VALIDITY: SAMPLING ISSUES

Sampling is concerned with the method by which the sample is drawn from a larger population. Two methods—random and nonrandom sampling—exist. The most rigorous method by far, but also the most difficult to obtain, is random sampling.[3] In this type of sampling, every person in the population has an equal chance of being selected (Pedhazur & Schmelkin, 1991). Its advantage lies in the ability to generalize from its findings. If a sample is randomly drawn from a larger population, it can then be assumed to be representative, within a calculated margin of error, of the population from which it is drawn. Because it is representative, findings can then be generalized to the larger population, thus increasing the importance of the study.

Nonrandom sampling, on the other hand, is sampling of convenience. Because the representativeness of the sample to the larger population cannot be determined, generalizing the findings to the larger population is not appropriate (Pedhazur & Schmelkin, 1991). This section reviews issues that arise in sampling.

Generalizability

The primary goal of sampling procedures is to use a sample that is representative of the larger population so that findings can be generalized to that population. Studies of the prevalence of child sexual abuse must pay particular attention to this issue, as the purpose of these studies is to determine how many children are sexually abused. Unless the respondents sampled are representative of the larger community, be it a city, state, or nation, the study is significantly limited. While this methodological issue is critical for studies of prevalence, it is also important for other types of studies, as any sampling biases will necessarily limit the generalizability of the study. Indeed, only findings from studies using randomly drawn samples can be generalized, and even then the findings can only be generalized to the limits of the sample. For example, while many prevalence studies are random, they often sample a specific community. Generalizing these findings to the nation is therefore inappropriate.

The issue of sampling bias is equally important with clinical samples, as few clinical studies of randomly drawn samples exist. Most studies use only a single site. Even within that site, the subjects selected for the study are often drawn as a matter of convenience. Depending on the type of clinical setting, the sample could be biased towards a particular type of victim, as, for example, toward a certain socioeconomic stratum or race. Another concern with clinical populations of sexually abused individuals is whether the population is actually representative of all sexually abused individuals among clinical groups. Some studies, for example, use samples culled from hospital emergency rooms or child abuse community treatment programs. Studies that compare physically abused and neglected children find that children under six years of age are over-represented in these settings (Widom, 1988). It is possible that this same trend holds true for sexually abused children. Indeed, in the third National Incidence Study of Child Abuse and Neglect (NIS-3), Sedlak and Broadhurst (1996) found that

---

[3] Random sampling, which applies to survey designs, is different from random assignment to groups, which applies to experimental designs.

across age groups, three- to five-year-olds had the highest incidence rate. A secondary analysis (Bolen, 1998b) of Russell's (1983) retrospective community prevalence study, however, found that previously nonabused respondents were most likely to be abused between the ages of 11 and 13. The potential for the sample to be biased must therefore be considered.

Regretfully, a random sample of abuse victims is often difficult to achieve because doing so requires a knowledge of all abuse victims from which to draw. Short of prevalence studies in which the population is the larger community, such information is extremely difficult to obtain, suggesting that the majority of studies of victims of child sexual abuse cannot be generalized beyond the sample. As such, the replication of findings from nonrandom studies becomes extremely important. If a certain finding is replicated across several studies representing diverse populations, credibility is lent to the finding.

Replication of findings is best found in reviews of the literature and meta-analyses. For example, a review of effects of abuse on children (Kendall-Tackett, Williams, & Finkelhor, 1993) found that across several studies, posttraumatic stress disorder occurred in approximately one-third of all victims of sexual abuse. Because this finding was replicated across studies using diverse populations, it can be given greater weight.

In determining the limits of the generalizability of random samples, the following questions need to be asked. Is this a non-clinical or clinical sample? Does the sample include both male and female victims? Is the race or ethnicity of any group over- or under-represented or are any demographic variables clearly over- or under-represented? Finally, is the sample comprised of child or adult survivors of sexual abuse? One of the most important premises is that even in randomly drawn samples, the findings can only be generalized to the limits of the sample.

Response Rate

Even when samples are randomly drawn, an important issue is the response rate. Specifically, of those individuals contacted, how many actually consented to be interviewed or to complete the questionnaire? Another concern is how the response rate is defined. Researchers report response rates in different manners and sometimes report more than one response rate based upon different methods of calculation. For example, Wyatt (1985) reported three response rates—55%, 67%, and 73%—based upon different methods of calculation. Just as with the definition of child sexual abuse, comparisons of response rate across studies must use similar definitions.

When response rates are low, researchers usually compare demographics of the sample to those of the population as a whole. Significant differences between the drawn sample and population suggest that the sample is not representative of the larger population and that generalization must be done cautiously, if at all. To correct for this problem, researchers sometimes weight the data so that they reflect the larger population.

One study compared response rate in an original sample of 1,784 female and male undergraduates in which questionnaires were given to students in three different classes (Haugaard & Emery, 1989). From this original sample, 1,089 questionnaires were returned, for an overall response rate of 61% and a response rate in the three classes of 25%, 42%, and 74%. After the original questionnaires were returned, follow-up questionnaires were given to the original respondents, 98% of which were returned. The purpose of the follow-up questionnaire was to determine whether the abuse status of respondents affected the response rate.

In this study, the prevalence rate of child sexual abuse, as ascertained by comparing the original questionnaire to the follow-up questionnaire, was over-reported in classes with the lowest original response rate (25%) and under-reported in classes with the largest original response rate (74%) (Haugaard & Emery, 1989). A confounding factor, however, is that only the group with the largest response rate (74%) was given credit for returning the questionnaire. Haugaard and Emery conclude, "These data suggest that high participation rates may distort the estimates of the prevalence of child sexual abuse to the same extent, but in a different direction, as low participation rates" (p. 98).

Two recent multivariate analyses of prevalence studies have also examined the effect of response rate on disclosed abuse rates. Gorey and Leslie (1997) compared 16 random and nonrandom studies of the prevalence of child sexual abuse. In their study, response rate was significantly related to the study's prevalence rate for child sexual abuse, although the effect size ($\beta = .228$) was small. Another recent study, of all random community, national, and state prevalence studies of North American populations (Bolen & Scannapieco, 1999), however, found no relationship between response rate and prevalence rate, after controlling for other important factors.

What could account for the differences in these studies? First, Gorey and Leslie (1997) categorized studies by whether or not they had a "good" response rate, even though no research has ascertained what response rates are better for surveys of child sexual abuse prevalence. Their decision to convert this continuous variable into a dichotomous one also restricted the amount of information available in their analysis. Second, Gorey and Leslie failed to control for the number of screen questions. Because the number of screen questions is one of the most important predictors of prevalence (Bolen & Scannapieco, 1999), failure to include this variable potentially confounded their results. Regretfully, Gorey and Leslie did not articulate their definition for response rate, thus making it difficult to analyze their findings. Their inclusion of nonrandom studies and studies of limited populations (e.g., college students and clinicians) further weakens inferences drawn from their findings.

Thus, different studies on the effect of response rate on stated prevalence come to different conclusions. Haugaard and Emery (1989) and Gorey and Leslie (1997) suggest that prevalence studies with low response rates may lead to inflated estimates of child sexual abuse, although Haugaard and Emery also suggest that a high response rate may lead to underreporting. On the other hand, Bolen and Scannapieco's (1999) multivariate analysis of all random prevalence studies of community populations done in the United States found no relationship. Given that (a) the effect size in the study by Gorey and Leslie is small, and (b) Bolen and Scannapieco's findings are strengthened by their inclusion of all relevant studies, the effect of response rate upon prevalence rate appears to be negligible.

Sample Size and Issues of Power

When a study has sufficient power, it has a large enough sample size, given other constraints, to "detect relationships when they are, in fact, present in the population" (Briere, 1992, p. 201). While the size of the sample as a whole must be sufficient to test overall hypotheses, it is as important that the sample size of the smallest comparison group also be large enough. For example, a study comparing victimization status by gender must have an adequate sample size for each of the four cells (victimized males, victimized females, nonvictimized males, and nonvictimized females). Other issues such as unreliable measures, measures without adequate sensitivity, or unsuitable statistical analyses, may also affect the power of a study (Briere, 1992). When studies do not have sufficient power, meaningful findings may not reach significance. Because they are not significant, the possibility that they were a result of chance cannot be eliminated, and interpretations of the data are inappropriate.

As an example, Wyatt (1985) found that 40% of African American women and 51% of white women experienced contact sexual abuse in childhood. Even though this difference appears to be meaningful, it was not significant, most likely as a result of the smaller number of women in each group. Consequently, it is extremely important that researchers give adequate attention to the matter of sufficient power during the design phase of the study.

Issues in Sampling Child Victims

One of the most biased populations of victims of child sexual abuse is one that includes only child victims. For obvious reasons, only officially reported cases of child sexual abuse can be studied. Yet most reported and substantiated cases of child sexual abuse are of intrafamilial abuse, most often father-daughter incest. For example, in the NIS-3 (Sedlak & Broadhurst, 1996), a national incidence study of all cases of abuse coming to the attention of authorities, 54% of all abuse was committed by a parent or parent substitute, more than half of which was committed by a biological parent. This is a puzzling characteristic of reported cases. Whereas incest perpetrated by a parent accounts for only approximately 7% to 8% of all child sexual abuse (Russell, 1984; Wyatt, 1985), it accounts for more than half of all child sexual abuse coming to the attention of authorities.

Another concern with studies using populations of reported cases is that only approximately 5% to 12% of all abuse is reported (*Lexington, Herald Leader,* 1992; Russell, 1986; Saunders, Kilpatrick, Hanson, & Resnick, 1999). Because the vast majority of all abuse goes unreported, samples of reported and substantiated abuse cases can in no way be considered representative of all cases of child sexual abuse.

Issues in Sampling Adults Abused as Children

Retrospective studies of adult samples also have significant limitations, as they are only as good as the respondent's memory (Widom, 1988) or willingness to disclose. In studies using retrospective accounts of abuse, memories of abuse may be distorted by time or may be repressed, suppressed, or dissociated. For example, Williams (1994) found that 38% of 129 victims did not recall documented abuse that had occurred 17 years earlier. Forty-seven percent of those molested by family members did not recall that abuse, nor did more than half of victims whose abuse occurred prior to the age of seven. Briere and Conte (1983) also found that 59% of adult victims of childhood sexual abuse currently in treatment reported that at some time prior to the age of 18, they had not remembered their abuse. In at least two studies, a portion of women being interviewed about child sexual abuse reported incidents of abuse only after the initial interview (Kelly, 1988; Martin et al., 1993). Follow-up interviews may thus be necessary to better assess for abuse history.

Another consideration is that the recollection of past events is perceived and described from the perspective of the respondent's present situation (Widom, 1988). Respondents may, over time, redefine the abusive situation to resolve cognitive dissonance (Kilpatrick & Lockhart, 1991). Adult victims of childhood father-daughter incest, for example, must resolve both the abuse and their love for their fathers. How they do so may change the way in which they perceive the abuse.

It is also possible that respondents might reconstruct their own childhood histories to explain present behaviors. This is especially likely to occur in groups of people who have something to gain from being perceived as victims. Offenders, for example, might be more likely to embellish their histories if they think it might improve their present circumstances. Alternately, offenders might find it easier to live with their crimes if they perceive themselves as victims first. Conversely, victims whose abuse status is repugnant may minimize their abuse experiences. As such, retrospective accounts have their own potential biases that must be considered.

Summary

In summary, sampling issues may have a great impact upon the ability to generalize findings. The most rigorous methodology is to employ random sampling, which then allows the findings to be generalized to the population from which the sample was drawn. Making inferences beyond the stated population is not indicated.

Many studies, however, do not or cannot achieve random sampling. In these cases, generalization of findings beyond the sample is not indicated. For nonrandom samples, it is critical that the reader be absolutely clear about the limits and biases of the stated sample.

STATISTICAL CONCLUSION VALIDITY: ANALYTIC ISSUES

Statistical conclusion validity refers to the validity of inferences made based upon the statistical analyses used. To make appropriate inferences, (a) the correct analyses, given the independent and dependent variables, must be used; (b) the assumptions of the analyses must not be violated; and (c) the method must be properly employed. This next section overviews methods of analysis and their potential impact upon the inferences of findings.

Bivariate Versus Multivariate Analysis

Analyses of relationships can be either bivariate or multivariate. In the most basic type, bivariate analysis, two variables are analyzed to determine the strength of their relationship. Bivariate analysis is considered only a basic type of analysis because, unless using an experimental design, researchers cannot rule out the possibility that other factors may have contributed to the relationship (Briere, 1992). Neither can bivariate analysis by itself establish temporal ordering (i.e., whether the independent variable conclusively preceded the dependent variable in time). Yet examples of improper inferences being made from bivariate analyses were common in the early empirical literature on child sexual abuse.

Krieger, Rosenfeld, Gordon, and Bennett (1980), for example, noting the sexually seductive behavior of some child victims, concluded that the victims must actively participate when abuse occurred over time. Swan (1985) also suggested that children whose mothers work are at increased risk of abuse because they are not being properly supervised by their mothers. In the first example, the causal ordering of the independent variable and dependent variable was most likely reversed, whereas in the second example other factors that might contribute to the relationship were not ruled out.

To properly examine the relationship between maternal employment and risk of abuse, for example, multivariate analysis, in which more than two variables are analyzed at the same time, is indicated. Variables that might be theoretically important are marital status, income of the mother, total family income, the relationship of the caregiver to the child, gender of the child, and the location of the caregiving. By simultaneously analyzing several variables through multivariate analysis, the relationship of maternal employment to risk of sexual abuse, after controlling for other known relationships, can be determined. In other words, the analysis would remove the effects of the other variables while determining the unique relationship between maternal employment and increased risk of abuse. Only if a relationship remained and temporal ordering could be established (i.e., maternal employment conclusively preceded the abuse) could an interpretation of causality be warranted.

This point is important because of the number of studies of sexual abuse that employ only bivariate relationships. It is often tempting to infer more from the findings than is appropriate. Yet it is critically important that findings be conservatively reported. If the relationship is only bivariate, the researchers need to note this in their paper and to be clear about the limits of interpretation. As Briere (1992) states,

> The role of science in such endeavors is to as precisely as possible determine (1) the exact relationships between childhood sexual abuse and various types of psychological dysfunction; (2) which "effects" are likely to be epiphenomena of sexual abuse (i.e., arising from third variables, including other types of maltreatment); and (3) how preabuse functions, family-of-origin dynamics, and other variables moderate these relationships. Because correlational [bivariate] designs are, in and of themselves, insufficient to imply causation, the abuse researcher must use strategies that lessen the number of possible alternative explanations for their findings. (p. 199)

OTHER ISSUES

Issues of Causality

Although causality has been addressed throughout this chapter, it is important to specifically state the limits for deducing causality. While there is no consensus regarding the conditions of causality (Pedhazur & Schmelkin, 1991), for purposes of this discussion, three important factors—temporal priority, concomitant variation, and the elimination of alternate hypotheses—are considered.

First, temporal priority must be established (i.e., the independent variable must precede the dependent variable in time) (Cohen & Cohen, 1983). This is one of the most difficult of the conditions to achieve, simply because so many studies are cross-sectional. It is therefore difficult at best, and usually impossible, to determine whether the independent variable actually temporally preceded the dependent variable. Even in cases in which it appears to be self-evident, as when adults are asked about both a childhood history of sexual abuse and their current status, it is still difficult to exclude other possibilities. For example, as discussed earlier, the individual's current status might affect his or her perception, and therefore report of, previous abuse. It is also difficult to rule out the possibility that the person's current status was not already in place before the abuse. Two methods that do allow for establishing temporal priority are the use of an experimental design and the use of a longitudinal design.

The second condition that must apply is concomitant variation. This is the easiest condition to achieve and simply suggests that significant and substantive relationships between the independent variable and dependent variable exist (Cohen & Cohen, 1983). These conditions are established statistically, as with a significant and substantive correlation or beta coefficient.

The final condition is again difficult to achieve, and may never be fully achieved in nonexperimental research. This condition, the elimination of alternative hypotheses, requires that the relationship between the independent variable and dependent variable is not spurious (i.e., that the relationship is not caused by an unknown third variable) (Pedhazur & Schmelkin, 1991). This issue can never be ruled out in a bivariate relationship (unless within the scope of an experimental design), simply because it is entirely possible that some if not all of the shared variance (i.e., relationship between the independent variable and dependent variable) is a result of the effect of other variables.[4] For example, when a relationship between child sexual abuse and later depression is found, is this relationship a result of the child sexual abuse or a dysfunctional home life? Greater difficulty arises when only a small portion of the variance in the dependent variable is accounted for by the independent variable(s) (i.e., the R^2 is small).[5] It is entirely possible that another and

---

[4] Technically, variance is a measure of the dispersion of the scores around the mean and is the square of the standard deviation (Sirkin, 1995). Conceptually, it is how scores differ from each other or more specifically, how scores differ from the mean. Researchers are keenly interested in analyzing and explaining variance or how individuals differ. A far less interesting question is how individuals are the same, which is represented mathematically by the mean.

[5] R^2 is the percentage of variance explained in the dependent variable by the independent variables (Pedhazur & Schmelkin, 1991). A larger R^2 indicates that the researcher has better explained the variability within the dependent variable.

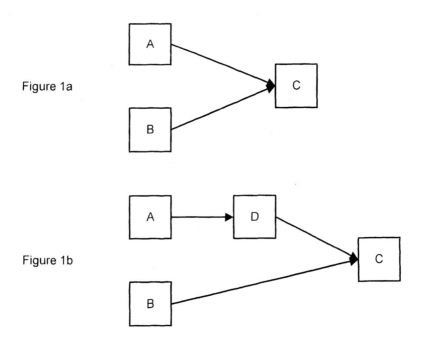

FIGURE 4-1. Example of a Spurious Relationship

unknown variable that was not analyzed might eliminate the relationship between the independent variable and dependent variable. Figure 4-1 attempts to illustrate this phenomenon.

As can be seen, when only independent variable *A* and *B* are analyzed (Figure 4-1a), the relationships between them and the dependent variable *(C)* are significant (as denoted by the line between the independent variables and the dependent variable). When variable *D* is added, however (Figure 4-1b), *A* no longer has a direct effect upon *C*, but is mediated by *D*, indicating that its purported effect on *C*, as shown in Figure 4-1b, was spurious. An example of such a relationship might be that between living with only a mother and risk of abuse. While Finkelhor (1984) found that living in a single-parent family was related to an increased risk of abuse, the important relationship may instead be the type of day care. Single mothers are not only more likely to be employed but also are more likely to be poor, suggesting that they might need to use informal methods of caring for their children while at work as opposed to the more expensive formal day care settings. Thus, the use of informal day care might mediate the relationship between having a single mother and risk of child sexual abuse.

All three conditions—temporal priority, concomitant variation, and the elimination of spurious causes—are required to make statements of causality between the independent and dependent variables. The elimination of any one of the three makes statements of causality inappropriate. It is of utmost importance that researchers and readers do not attribute causal relationships where they cannot be supported.

SUMMARY AND CONCLUSIONS

The purpose of this chapter was to explicate methodological issues that affect the eventual interpretation of a study's findings. This chapter was intended to leave the reader with the sober recognition that a simple reading of studies of child sexual abuse is not possible—and sometimes is not even ethical. There have been a vast number of studies on child sexual abuse. Some are extremely rigorous; some have so many methodological flaws that their findings are uninterpretable. It is of utmost importance that the reader consider the methodology before interpreting the findings.

White and Farmer (1992) state, "Research methods have the potential for shaping one's view of reality" (p. 45). This statement is an exceptionally important point for the reader of literature on child sexual abuse. Research methodology profoundly affects the results, and the results shape our view of the scope of the problem of child sexual abuse. As shown in Chapter 2, the historical literature on child sexual abuse, much of which did not rely on rigorous methodology, has significantly affected the current conceptualization of the problem of child sexual abuse. One of the regrettable side effects of this less-than-rigorous historical empirical base is that many myths and distorted views developed. One of the challenges of current research is to rebut these myths. Yet the effort to do so draws energy from the important task of advancing the knowledge base.

The implications for both researchers and readers of the literature are clear. Researchers have an ethical imperative to advance the knowledge base using only the most rigorous methodology possible. Study limitations that do exist, and their potential impact upon the inferences, must be clearly stated. Readers, especially those who professionally interact in any role with child sexual abuse victims, have an ethical imperative to analyze the literature they read. Taking any study at face value may have important negative consequences for the victims and the families with whom the professional works. Given the historical development of the literature on child sexual abuse, anything less may only perpetuate myths and add fire to existing controversies.

CHAPTER 5
INCIDENCE AND PREVALENCE OF CHILD SEXUAL ABUSE

INTRODUCTION

Since the late 1970s, much emphasis has been placed on determining the scope of the problem of child sexual abuse. These studies on the scope of the problem can be divided into two categories—studies of the incidence of child sexual abuse and studies of its prevalence. Prevalence studies, by retrospectively surveying a population of adolescents or adults, estimate the percentage of a population that has previously been sexually abused. Incidence studies instead estimate the number of new cases occurring within a given time period, usually within the previous year. These latter studies often query professionals or professional bodies concerning the number of cases coming to their attention in the previous year. Child protective services is most often surveyed, although law enforcement agencies, hospitals, schools, and mental health agencies are surveyed to a lesser extent.

While both incidence and prevalence studies are critical to clarifying the scope of child sexual abuse, they have significant limitations. The most prominent limitation of incidence studies is that they rely only upon reported abuse cases. The most prominent limitation of prevalence studies is that they rely upon the valid recall of abuse incidents that may have occurred many years previously.

The purpose of this chapter is to explicate the scope of the problem of child sexual abuse. To do so, incidence studies and random community-based prevalence studies are reviewed. For each incidence study, its methodology and findings are presented and the advantages and limitations of these studies are then reviewed. The next section is devoted to prevalence studies. Random community, state, and national prevalence studies conducted within the United States are reviewed and compared. Methodology may have a critical impact upon rates of abuse reported in these studies. As such, a brief analysis of the effects of different methodologies on the disclosure rate is presented. The final section explicates the scope of the problem of child sexual abuse and delineates policy implications.

INCIDENCE OF CHILD SEXUAL ABUSE

Incidence studies vary in their ability to capture the number of abuse cases that come to the attention of professionals. There are three primary, ongoing attempts to determine the incidence rate of child sexual abuse. The most comprehensive is the National Incidence Study of Child Abuse and Neglect, done every several years, and most recently conducted in 1993 (Sedlak & Broadhurst, 1996). It surveys not only all child protective services agencies, but also other community professionals who serve children and families. Two other important ongoing incidence studies use data only from state child protective services agencies. The Annual Fifty State Survey is collected by the National Committee to Prevent Child Abuse. The other survey is collected by the National Child Abuse and Neglect Data System (NCANDS).

Another potential source of child sexual abuse incidence is national crime data reported by the Bureau of Justice. The two primary surveys, the National Crime Victimization Survey and the Uniform Crime Report, however, do not uniformly distinguish between child and adult cases of sexual assault and rape. The Bureau of Crime Statistics, for example, only reports rape cases by age for certain states (Langan & Harlow, 1994). The National Crime Victimization Survey only gathers information for respondents ages 12 and older. Their data on child sexual abuse are therefore limited. A final unofficial survey of incidence rates done by the Gallup Poll in 1995 is also available. All studies are reviewed in the following sections.

Incidence Studies

Third National Incidence Study of Child Abuse and Neglect (NIS-3)

The most extensive survey of the incidence of child sexual abuse is the Third National Incidence Study (NIS-3) (Sedlak & Broadhurst, 1996). Data for this study were collected during a three-month period in 1993. In a nationally representative sample of 42 counties, child protective services agencies and selected community professionals were surveyed. Community professionals included the professional staff at schools, hospitals, law enforcement agencies, social service agencies, and public health departments.

Criteria for including a case of child abuse or neglect were as follows. The child had to be (a) a resident of the county surveyed, (b) under the age of 18 at the time of the incident, and (c) a noninstitutionalized dependent of parent(s) or parent substitute(s) at the time of the maltreatment. The maltreatment had to (a) occur during the study period and (b) be nonaccidental and avoidable. Incidents had to meet either the harm or endangerment standard. The more stringent harm standard required that the child (a) be abused by a parent or his or her substitute and (b) be moderately harmed by the incident. The endangerment standard included all children who met the harm criterion, but also included children who were in danger of being harmed. This standard also added adult caretakers who permitted sexual abuse and nonparental teenage caretakers who permitted or perpetrated sexual abuse (Sedlak & Broadhurst, 1996).

Three forms of sexual abuse were included. Intrusion required credible "evidence of oral, anal, or genital penile penetration" (Sedlak & Broadhurst, 1996, p. 2–10). Molestation with genital contact required that genital contact without intrusion occur. The other or unknown sexual abuse category involved other types of contact and noncontact abuse as well as "allegations concerning inadequate or inappropriate supervision of a child's voluntary sexual activities" (p. 2–14). Intrusive acts were assumed to cause injury, thus fulfilling a criterion for the harm standard. For any incident meeting the harm standard, evidence of "at least moderate physical or emotional injury/impairment" (p. 2–14) was required.

Based upon weighted estimates, 300,200 children were sexually abused during 1993, an incidence rate of 4.5/1,000 children. The incidence rate for males was 2.3/1,000 and for females was 6.8/1,000. Using only the harm standard, 217,700 children were sexually abused, representing a 3.2/1,000 incidence rate (Sedlak & Broadhurst, 1996). Comparable incidence rates for the 1986 NIS-2 (Sedlak, 1991) were 2.1/1,000 for the endangerment standard and 1.9/1,000 for the harm standard, an increase from 1986 to 1993 of 125% and 83% respectively. Whereas 75% of all cases of sexually abused children coming to the attention of professionals were investigated in 1986, only 44% were investigated in 1993.

When comparing rates of child sexual abuse between the 1986 and 1993 studies, it appears that the rate of sexual abuse might be increasing. Alternately, the increases could simply reflect improved recognition by professionals. Sedlak and Broadhurst (1996) suggest that both dynamics contributed to the increases in incidence rates. First, because cases meeting the harm standard are unlikely to escape the notice of professionals, Sedlak and Broadhurst suggest that cases of severe child abuse and neglect are likely to be increasing. Their remarks, however, refer to all types of child abuse and neglect. Because the wounds and scars from child sexual abuse are often hidden from view, this argument does not apply as strongly to cases of child sexual abuse. The researchers also suggest that professionals' improved recognition of more subtle cues may be responsible for the increase in the incidence rate, especially the increase over time in cases meeting the endangerment standard.

National Center on Child Abuse and Neglect Data System

The National Center on Child Abuse and Neglect (NCCAN), through a cooperative and voluntary federal and state partnership, developed the National Child Abuse and Neglect Data System (NCANDS) (U.S. Department of Health and Human Services, 1997). An annual report from these findings has been issued since 1990. The scope of the data collection is somewhat different from that of the NIS-3 (Sedlak & Broadhurst, 1996). Whereas the NIS-3 surveys child protective services agencies and other professionals, the NCANDS study gathers data only from child protective services agencies. Like the NIS-3, however, the NCANDS statistics are seriously biased towards perpetrators in a caretaking role. Indeed, only 5% of all perpetrators in this study were not caretakers. The NCANDS survey gathers two levels of information, the Summary Data Component (SDC), which "is a compilation of 15 key aggregate indicators of State child abuse and neglect statistics" (p. 1–1), and the Detailed Case Data Component, which is a compilation of information on case-level data. Incidence rates derive from the SDC collection effort.

Of 1,820,608 cases of alleged abuse or neglect screened in for investigation in 1998, 29% were substantiated or indicated.[1] Of all cases of child abuse and neglect, approximately 13% were cases of sexual abuse, for an incidence rate of 1.6/1,000 (U.S. Department of Health and Human Services, 2000c). This incidence rate has declined from 2.3/1,000 in 1990.

---

[1] "Indicated" was used by 11 states when cases did not have the level of evidence required by state law, but did have sufficient evidence to suspect abuse or neglect.

Fifty State Survey

The Annual Fifty State Survey is initiated by the National Committee to Prevent Child Abuse (NCPCA) (Wang & Daro, 1997). Like the data collected through the NCANDS (U.S. Department of Health and Human Services, 1997), NCPCA data are aggregated at the level of the state using data gathered from state child protective services agencies. The study provides the incidence and characteristics of child abuse reports, child fatalities, and interdepartmental changes regarding funding and the scope of services.

To obtain these data, a preliminary letter is sent to each state liaison, followed by telephone contact. For the 1996 data, 46 states provided at least partial data, 39 of which provided data for reported cases and 37 of which provided data for substantiated cases. Only 25 states were able to provide breakdowns by type of abuse (Wang & Daro, 1997).

Even for the responding states, methods of gathering data varied widely by state. For example, the method of categorizing reported abuse differed, with some states gathering data by family and others gathering data by incident (Wang & Daro, 1997). In addition, some states counted cases as reported only if they had been investigated. The level of initial screening done by child protective services thus impacted the number of cases reported. Other procedural variations in substantiated or indicated cases were noted. For example, standards for maltreatment varied by state, with some states requiring evidence of harm and other states requiring only evidence of potential harm. Substantiation rates also varied widely based upon whether they were reported as a percentage of (a) all cases investigated or (b) all cases reported. Because of this disparity among states, findings from the NCPCA data are based upon projections of estimated change from the previous year to the current year for those states reporting in the previous and current years.

The Fifty State Survey estimated that 3,126,000 cases of child abuse were reported to child protective services in 1996, 969,000 (31%) of which were substantiated. Of reported cases, 7% were of sexual abuse; of substantiated cases, 9% were of sexual abuse (Wang & Daro, 1997). Although numbers are not given, these data suggest that approximately 218,820 cases of child sexual abuse were reported, 87,210 of which were substantiated, for an incidence rate of 1.3/1,000 children.

Bureau of Justice Statistics on Child Rape

The Federal Bureau of Investigation (FBI) uses two sources to report annual rape data. The Uniform Crimes Report (UCR) includes incidents of sexual assault reported to law enforcement agencies, whereas the National Crime Victimization Survey (NCVS) includes incidents gathered in interviews of randomly selected individuals aged 12 and older. The latter survey contains both reported and unreported cases. Neither the UCR nor the NCVS consistently provides comprehensive data on all cases of child rape or sexual assault.

Because reporting techniques among states have recently become more sophisticated, some UCR statistics concerning the proportion of child rape to adult rape are now available. In the 1992 UCR (Bureau of Justice, 1994), 12 states, representing approximately 20% of the national total of rapes for that year, reported age breakdowns for rape victims. Of all rapes reported to law enforcement agencies for these 12 states, 16% of the victims were under the age of 12, at least 24% were under the age of 15, and 51% were under the age of 18.[2] In 1992, the incidence of committed rapes was .84/1,000 females. If 51% of all reported rapes occur to victims under the age of 18, the estimated rape incidence rate of child rape in 1992 was .43/1,000. These rates, however, are considered extreme underestimates of the actual number of rape incidents (Russell & Bolen, 2000).

Other Surveys

In 1995, the Gallup Poll conducted a telephone survey of 1,000 U.S. households chosen through random digit dialing. When a household was reached, queries were made to determine if children lived in the household and if parents were home. If so, an interview was conducted with the parent concerning his or her child.[3] Data were then weighted to reflect U.S. Census statistics. The overall response rate was 57.3%, with a refusal rate of 19%.

Parents were asked whether their child, as far as they knew, (a) had ever been forced to touch in a sexual way or been touched by an adult or older child or (b) had been forced to have sex. Within the year prior to the survey, 19/1,000 children were sexually abused. Lifetime prevalence rates for these children were 57/1,000.

Finally, the National Youth Victimization Prevention (NYVP) study conducted in 1992 and 1993 was a national random telephone survey of 2,000 children aged 10 through 16 (Finkelhor, 1998). Parents were initially asked for permission to interview their child. When they agreed, the child was then asked for consent to conduct the 30-minute to one-hour interview. The participation rate for households was 72%.

Sexual abuse was categorized as either serious noncontact incidents or contact incidents. Serious noncontact incidents "included a perpetrator touching the child in a sexual way (but without contact to the private parts) or exposing himself or herself to the child" (Finkelhor, 1998, p. 380). Also included were attempts by parents to have the child "do something sexual." Contact incidents could be clothed or unclothed. Violence to genitals was described as someone intentionally trying to hurt the child's private parts by kicking them or trying to hit them with an object. Using these definitions, Finkelhor found that 6.7% of all children related an incidence of sexual abuse occurring within the last year, for an incidence rate of 67/1,000. Of children aged 12 to 16, 7.5% related an incidence of contact or noncontact sexual abuse, 2.1% experienced contact abuse only, and 0.5% experienced a completed rape within the last year. Five percent of children also experienced nonsexual violence to the genitals. The latter group had a higher representation of boys, whereas the sexual abuse group had a higher representation of girls.

---

[2] Certain of these figures were computed based upon the UCR table provided. The data are estimates because not all states provided data for each age.

[3] When more than one child was in the household, one child was randomly selected. If more than one parent was home, one parent was randomly selected to be interviewed.

Analysis of Incidence Rates

Limitations of Incidence Studies

Incidence studies are necessarily limited. As stated earlier, their greatest limitation is that they include only cases of sexual abuse that come to the attention of authorities or, in the Gallup Poll, parents. Several studies, however, suggest that sexual abuse cases that come to the attention of authorities or parents represent only a small minority of all child sexual abuse. For example, in Russell's (1983) prevalence study of child sexual abuse, only 2% of intrafamilial abuse cases and 6% of extrafamilial abuse cases were officially reported. A later random prevalence study by Saunders et al. (1999) found that 12% of all abuse was officially reported. Conversely, 7% of victims in a state prevalence study had officially reported their abuse (*Lexington Herald-Leader*, 1992), whereas Arroyo, Simpson, and Aragon (1997) found that only 27% of a college sample indicated that their abuse had been disclosed to *anyone*. The disclosures in the latter study, however, included official and unofficial sources. Because these studies are retrospective, they include victims whose abuse occurred many years ago, so may not accurately reflect current disclosure patterns.

Another serious flaw in incidence studies is that they primarily target abuse by caretakers. In the NIS-3 (Sedlak & Broadhurst, 1996), for example, 29% of sexual abuse was committed by birth parents, 25% was committed by other parental figures, and another 45% was committed by other caretakers, including relatives other than parents. The majority of child sexual abuse, however, is committed by someone other than a caretaker (Finkelhor, Hotaling, Lewis, & Smith, 1990; Russell, 1983; Wyatt, 1985). Russell's (1983) study (as reanalyzed by Bolen) is one of two random prevalence surveys to gather information on all incidents of child sexual abuse for each respondent. Of the 648 incidents of abuse reported by the 930 female respondents, only 74 to 103 of the perpetrators could be considered caretakers.[4] Even using the broader estimate, this total represents only 15.9% of all child sexual abuse. Using the more narrow estimate, this total represents 11.6% of all abuse.

Limiting the definition of child sexual abuse to that by caretakers necessarily affects the incidence rate. If, for example, the NIS-3 included only 16% of all abuse that occurred in 1993, the corrected incidence rate would be 28.3/1,000 for all children and 42.8/1,000 for female children (Sedlak & Broadhurst, 1996).[5]

The effects of a restricted definition of child sexual abuse and a low disclosure rate can be more fully analyzed by comparing incidence rates using official sources to those using unofficial sources (i.e., the Gallup Poll and the NYVP). It was striking that the incidence rate in even the most encompassing official survey, the NIS-3 (Sedlak & Broadhurst, 1996), was much lower than those for the Gallup Poll (1995) and NYVP (Finkelhor, 1998). While the NIS-3 had an incidence rate of 4.5/1,000,

---

[4] The conservative number includes 45 parental figures, 16 teachers, four clergy, and nine babysitters. The broader estimate adds to this figure 11 grandparents (not all of whom were in a caretaking role at the time of the abuse), 12 employers/supervisors, and six household employees (not all of whom were caregivers).

[5] The formula divided the incidence rate by 15.9% (e.g., 4.5/.159 = 28.3/1,000 incidence rate for all children). The rate for females was based upon an incidence rate of 6.8/1,000.

the Gallup Poll reported an incidence rate of 19/1,000 and the NYVP reported an incidence rate of 67/1,000 for all sexual abuse and approximately 21/1,000 for contact sexual abuse. Importantly, both the Gallup Poll and the NYVP had broader definitions of child sexual abuse, allowing abuse by noncaretaking perpetrators. The discrepancy in incidence rates among these studies suggests that the official response to child sexual abuse is not adequate to address even child sexual abuse of which parents are aware or of which children are willing to disclose. It must be emphasized, however, that much abuse that occurs in childhood is never disclosed. For example, as stated earlier, Arroyo, Simpson, and Aragon (1997) found that only 27% of childhood victims currently in college ever disclosed to anyone.

In summary, national incidence studies cannot represent the true scope of the problem of child sexual abuse. Instead, they only represent the scope of the problem that comes to the attention of authorities. Even for abuse coming to the attention of authorities, incidence rates only represent cases of investigated and substantiated abuse of primarily caregivers. Thus, incidence rates grossly underestimate the true incidence of child sexual abuse.

Advantages of Incidence Studies

While incidence rates cannot accurately reflect the scope of the problem of child sexual abuse, they do serve important purposes. First, they give some indication of the response by government and state agencies to the problem of child sexual abuse. In this regard, the current response is clearly inadequate. For example, only perhaps a quarter of abuse that occurs is disclosed to anyone, and less than that comes to the attention of authorities. Yet, less than half of all abuse coming to the attention of authorities and meeting the narrow criteria as defined by child protective services (i.e., caretaker abuse) is investigated and substantiated. As Sedlak and Broadhurst (1996) suggest, substantiated abuse is only the very tip of the iceberg, indicating that the current response to child sexual abuse is extremely poor.

If a role of child protective services is to protect children at risk as well as the victim, the large number of cases of child sexual abuse that fail to qualify for investigation is clearly problematic. Offenders often abuse more than one victim (Abel, Becker, Cunningham-Rathner, Mittleman, & Rouleau, 1988a; Ballard et al., 1990). For each legitimate abuse case that does not qualify for investigation, multiple children may be placed at unnecessary risk. Another role of child protective services is to offer resources needed by victimized children. Numerous studies have now shown that abuse by noncaretaking perpetrators also has deleterious consequences, sometimes severe (Feinauer, 1988; Gregory-Bills & Rhodeback, 1995). Federal and state policies that effectively exclude these cases of child sexual abuse not only deny the victim's access to needed resources, but also place other children at risk for abuse and clearly undermine the scope of the problem of child sexual abuse.

A second purpose of studies of incidence rates, deriving from the first, is to use the knowledge gained as an impetus to make policy decisions about how to adequately intervene. In their conclusions about the NIS-3 data, Sedlak and Broadhurst (1996) state:

The number of NIS-countable children who are investigated by child protective services has remained fairly stable, or risen slightly, since the last national incidence study in 1986. As a result, CPS investigation has not kept up with the dramatic rise in the incidence of these children, so the percentages who receive CPS investigation of their maltreatment have fallen significantly. The low rates of CPS investigation of the maltreated children, especially of those already seriously injured by maltreatment, warrant immediate attention. (p. 18, executive summary)

In other words, even in the small minority of sexual abuse cases meeting the criteria for investigation, child protective services cannot adequately respond and, in fact, its response rate is decreasing. One is left to wonder what would be required if the government adequately addressed the entire scope of the problem of sexual abuse.

PREVALENCE OF CHILD SEXUAL ABUSE

Several studies have attempted to determine the prevalence of child sexual abuse within specific populations. These studies are far different from incidence studies as they represent not only victims of child sexual abuse coming to the attention of authorities, but also those whose abuse was never reported and substantiated. As mentioned earlier, *unreported* abuse represents the vast majority of all child sexual abuse cases. By asking adolescent or adult respondents whether they were victims of child sexual abuse, these retrospective prevalence studies give a much different, and more realistic, picture of the scope of the problem of child sexual abuse.

Prevalence studies of child sexual abuse represent a variety of populations and methodological rigor. Prevalence studies can be random or nonrandom, with the most rigorous studies being random. Within random studies, an important objective is to representatively sample a larger population so that the findings can be generalized to that population. The most important random surveys are those that sample an unbiased community, state, or national population. If random studies lack sufficient methodological rigor, however, their ability to generalize becomes somewhat meaningless. Another important objective of studies, therefore, is to be of sufficient methodological rigor that valid estimates of prevalence within a clearly defined margin of error can be obtained.

The purpose of the following sections is to review random studies of the prevalence of child sexual abuse, noting their methodological variations. For ease of presentation, random surveys in the United States are presented in Table A5-1 (at the end of the chapter). These tables are divided by type of survey, including adolescent, community, state, and national populations. The following sections review these studies and then present brief analyses of the effects of methodology on reported prevalence. (A fuller explication of methodology can be found in Chapter 4, "Methodology.")

Studies Representing Adolescent Populations

At least four studies have surveyed random populations of adolescents (see Table A5-1 at the end of the chapter). Two studies were of adolescent populations within a specific community, one was of a state population, and one was national in scope. All studies addressed their questions to the adolescents themselves. The study by Erickson and Rapkin (1991) sampled the youngest cohort—middle-schoolers—and also included older adolescents. Hernandez (1992) sampled only ninth graders, whereas the other two studies sampled mostly high school students. Modes of administration varied across studies, but all used only a few screen questions. Two studies were directed primarily at dating experiences (Ageton, 1983, 1988; Hall & Flannery, 1984).[6] The Ageton study was further restricted to incidents occurring within the last year (thus being more similar to an incidence than a prevalence study). Further, Hernandez required that the perpetrator be older than the victim.

Based upon self-reported lifetime prevalence of abuse (which excludes the Ageton study), prevalence of child sexual abuse ranged from 12% to 18% for females and from 2% to 12% for males. Mean prevalence was 7% for males and 16% for females.

National Prevalence Studies

Hypothetically, studies that provide the best estimates of the prevalence of child sexual abuse are national in scope. Seven known national studies of the prevalence of child sexual abuse have been done, as shown in Table A5-1.

One of the most important features of a random national prevalence study is how well it samples the larger population, ideally representing all individuals within the United States. The easiest method of sampling a national population is by using random digit dialing. This method, however, naturally excludes those without a private telephone. Using another method of sampling, such as a self-administered questionnaire, generally requires that the population be more narrowly focused. For example, using a self-administered mailed questionnaire, Elliott and Briere (1992) sampled women represented in 12 different professions. Their study cannot then be considered representative of all women in the United States. As would be expected, all national prevalence studies sampled a large number of respondents, ranging from 1,000 to 10,847.

An important consideration in the comparison of prevalence across studies is the definition of child sexual abuse employed. Whereas two national prevalence studies used the more conventional definition of contact sexual abuse, the three studies with the lowest prevalence estimates confined their definitions to rape (Abma, Chandra, Mosher, Peterson, & Piccinino, 1997; Moore, Nord, & Peterson, 1989; Saunders, Kilpatrick, Hanson, Resnick, & Walker, 1999). Conversely, the *Los Angeles Times* Poll survey (Finkelhor et al., 1990) and Vogeltanz et al. (1999) defined child sexual abuse as including both contact and noncontact. Another facet

---

[6] For the Ageton (1983, 1988) study, one of the two screen questions asked about sexual pressure from someone such as a date or friend to do more than the respondent wanted, whereas the other asked about a completed or attempted sexual attack or rape, but did not specify a relationship. In the Hall and Flannery (1984) study, the sexual abuse questions were embedded in a questionnaire concerned with sex roles and male-female relationships. The screen question asked if a "guy" (p. 400) had used physical force or threat to make the respondent have unwanted sex.

of the definition of child sexual abuse is the age limits for both the victim and perpetrator. By this standard, the study by Elliott and Briere (1992) had the most restrictive definition, requiring that the abuse occur prior to the age of 16 by a perpetrator at least five years older. Another crucial feature of studies is the number of screen questions employed. Studies have now confirmed that multiple screen questions are required to elicit more accurate disclosures of sexual abuse (Bolen & Scannapieco, 1999; Williams, Siegel, & Jackson Pomeroy, 2000).

The age of the respondents might also impact the reported prevalence of child sexual abuse. For example, Russell (1986) and Vogeltanz et al. (1999), among others, found that reporting of a childhood history of sexual abuse differed based upon the current age of the respondent. Studies representing all ages of respondents are naturally considered more informative. In national studies, Moore et al. (1989) limited their sample to respondents 17 to 23 years of age, Elliott and Briere (1992) limited their sample to professional women, and the Gallup Poll (1995) limited its sample to parents of children.

Prevalence of child sexual abuse for these national surveys ranged from 2% to 16% for males and from 8% to 30% for females. The mean prevalence of sexual abuse across studies was 19% for females and 9% for males. When the definition of abuse was restricted to rape, the mean prevalence was 10% for females. After excluding studies that examined only rape, the mean prevalence of sexual abuse for females was 25%.

State Prevalence Studies

Four studies of the prevalence of child sexual abuse in a state population have been done (see Table A5-1). These studies represent the states of Texas, Kentucky, portions of North Carolina, and portions of Minnesota. They also incorporate larger samples. The smallest sample utilized ($N = 637$) was in the Kentucky study (*Lexington Herald-Leader*, 1992), and the largest ($N = 1,157$) was in the North Carolina study (Winfield, George, Swartz, & Blazer, 1990). This latter study, however, contained an over-representation of the elderly, although weights were applied. All studies used only a single screen question, which might account for the lower estimates of the prevalence of child sexual abuse in these studies.

The mean prevalence ranged from 1% to 9% for males and from 2% to 28% for females. The mean prevalence was 6% for males and 14% for females.

Community Prevalence Studies

Seven studies using a community population have been done, six of which originated in California communities (see Table A5-1). Sample sizes tended to be smaller in these studies, although Russell (1983) had 930 respondents and Siegel et al. (1987) had 3,125 respondents. Three studies had somewhat restrictive populations. Essock-Vitale and McGuire (1985) surveyed the most restrictive sample, using Caucasian middle-class women raised by at least one natural parent. Springs and Friedrich (1992) surveyed female patients ages 18 to 50 who, within the previous year, had been seen at a specific family practice clinic, whereas Finkelhor (1984) surveyed Boston area parents of children ages 6 to 14 living at home. Therefore, these studies cannot be considered representative of the larger community.

The number of screen questions ranged from 1 to 14, whereas the definition of child sexual abuse was almost uniformly contact sexual abuse. Two studies had broader definitions, requiring only sexual experiences (Finkelhor, 1984; Springs & Friedrich, 1992). Three other studies gathered information on both contact and noncontact abuse (Russell, 1983; Wyatt, 1985; Wyatt et al., 1999). Studies also varied in the age range of the victim and the age differential between victim and perpetrator. In Siegel et al.'s (1987) study, the victim had to be younger than the age of 16, whereas the victim had to be younger than the age of 17 in the study by Finkelhor (1984). Both Russell (1983) and Wyatt (1985; Wyatt et al., 1999) also had certain conditions in which the perpetrator had to be five or more years older.

Across studies, the prevalence of child sexual abuse for females ranged from 7% to 45%; the comparable prevalence for males was 4% to 7%.[7] The mean prevalence was 6% for males and 24% for females. The studies reporting the lowest prevalences for both males and females used only one or two screen questions.

Studies by Wyatt, Russell, and Vogeltanz et al.

Three of the most methodologically rigorous prevalence studies of child sexual abuse ever done—Russell (1983), Wyatt (1985), and a replication study by Wyatt et al. done in 1999—employed similar methodologies. All studies randomly sampled community populations and employed face-to-face interviews that lasted up to several hours in length. By employing numerous behaviorally and relationship-specific screen questions (eight for Wyatt and 14 for Russell), these studies were specifically designed to capture the extent of female victimization. Further, respondents were asked to describe all abuse incidents that had occurred to them, after which the researchers categorized the incidents as either contact or noncontact abuse or nonabuse. One limitation of Wyatt's studies, however, was that her sample sizes were extremely small for studies of this nature. Generalizations from her samples to the larger community must therefore be done cautiously.

One of the benefits of Russell's (1983) and Wyatt's (1985; Wyatt et al., 1999) studies is that they allow comparisons of the prevalence of contact and noncontact abuse. For contact abuse, the prevalence for female child sexual abuse was 38% in Russell's study and 45% in Wyatt's 1985 study. Prevalence went up to 54% and 62%, respectively, when noncontact abuse was included. In her replication study done in 1999, Wyatt et al.'s prevalence for contact sexual abuse was 34%.

Another rigorous study done by Vogeltanz et al. (1999) was national in scope and employed similar definitions and methodology as those used by Russell (1983) and Wyatt (1985; Wyatt et al., 1999). In the Vogeltanz et al. study, the face-to-face private interviews were approximately 90 minutes in length. Eight behaviorally specific questions were asked by research center interviewers trained in interviewing

---

[7] When studies reported both contact and noncontact abuse, the percentage for contact abuse was used.

techniques as well as sensitive issues. Overall, 17% to 26% of respondents acknowledged a history of contact and noncontact child sexual abuse using Russell's broad definition and 24% to 32% did so using Wyatt's broad definition.[8]

Why are Russell's and Wyatt's prevalence estimates so much higher than those for other studies done to date and even for the study by Vogeltanz et al. (1999), which employed similar methodology? Because their prevalence estimates are so much higher than those of other studies, the validity of their estimates must be considered. First to be explored is the possibility that their prevalence estimates are inflated.

One possible reason that prevalence estimates in the studies by Russell (1983) and Wyatt (1985; Wyatt et al., 1999) seem unusually high is that there may be regional differences in the United States in the prevalence of child sexual abuse. In Finkelhor et al.'s (1990) analysis of the *Los Angeles Times* Poll Survey (LATP), a regional difference was noted. In this study's analysis, the United States was divided into eight regions, six of which had sexual abuse prevalence estimates for females between 25% and 27%. The Mountain/Desert region, however, reported a prevalence rate of 35% for females, whereas the Pacific region (which includes California) reported a prevalence of 40%. Finkelhor et al. offer possible reasons for this regional variation in prevalence, including that (a) individuals in the Pacific region are more candid about sexual abuse experiences, (b) abuse may occur more frequently in this region, or (c) a disproportionate number of victims may choose to live in this region.

By comparing those respondents who had spent the majority of their childhood inside versus outside of California, Peters, Wyatt, and Finkelhor (1986) attempted to determine whether regional differences in the Wyatt (1985) survey affected prevalence rates in that study. The prevalence rates of these two groups were almost identical, however, suggesting that the prevalence of child sexual abuse in California is no higher than elsewhere.

Another analysis of all random community, state, or national prevalence surveys (discussed at greater length later in this chapter) analyzed regional differences. In this analysis (Bolen & Scannapieco, 1999), after controlling for other relationships, the California studies did not report significantly higher prevalences than those done in other parts of the United States, including national studies. While the sample of available prevalence studies was small ($N = 22$), this finding does suggest that, with the current knowledge base, regional differences in the United States cannot be assumed to account for the differences in prevalence among studies. This issue is far from clear, however, and future research must resolve it.

Another consideration is why the prevalence in Vogeltanz et al.'s (1999) study is so much different from those found in Russell's (1983) and Wyatt's (1985; Wyatt et al., 1999) studies. Even though these studies employed similar methodology, there are reasons to suspect that minor methodological variations might account for the discrepancies in prevalence across studies. First, the primary purpose of the study by Vogeltanz et al. was to determine alcohol use and its abuse in women. The importance of the questions concerning child sexual abuse could, therefore, have been downplayed. Second, it was not clear whether interviewers prompted for all

---

[8] The larger figures for both Wyatt's and Russell's definition include all women who reported childhood sexual activity, but without enough information to determine if an incident qualified as a case of child sexual abuse.

incidents of abuse, although this issue should not have affected prevalence. Third, Russell suggests that interviewers who are part of a survey firm, as was used in the study by Vogeltanz et al., may not be as well trained to handle sensitive topics or may hold misperceptions about child sexual abuse that introduce interviewer bias (Russell & Bolen, 2000). Finally, a total of 130 women in this sample did not provide enough information about their sexual experiences to determine if they qualified for an incident of sexual abuse. Overall, 12% of the sample (and 18% of the weighted sample) did not provide sufficient information, suggesting that the interview format was insufficient to accurately assess a previous history of child sexual abuse. This is a methodological issue of particular concern and one that jeopardizes the validity of their findings.

In summary, because of the methodological rigor of the studies by Russell (1983) and Wyatt (1985; Wyatt et al. 1999), it is important to consider their prevalence estimates when attempting to determine the more realistic scope of the problem of child sexual abuse. Because the prevalence figures of Russell and Wyatt are higher than those of other studies, it is perhaps easy to discount them as biased. It must be emphasized, however, that these studies had exceptional methodological rigor. While it is easy to explain the lower estimates of other studies as a result of methodological weaknesses, it is much more difficult to identify methodology in the studies by Russell and Wyatt as biasing prevalence estimates.

Effect of Methodology on Prevalence

Given the number of prevalence studies and their confusing array of methodologies, how can one safely describe the scope of the problem of child sexual abuse? The most conservative method is to report the range of prevalence estimates across studies and to let the reader make the decision. This method has the detriments of (a) relying upon the reader's level of expertise in this area, and (b) allowing the readers' personal biases to affect their judgement. Another method is to use the mean prevalence across studies. This method is also extremely limited, because it applies equal weight to studies with lesser and greater methodological rigor.

Another important method is to rely upon qualitative reviews of the prevalence of child sexual abuse, several of which now exist (for example, see Finkelhor, 1994; Leventhal, 1988; Salter, 1992). Most of these reviews are written by experts, and thus have great import. Still another method is to rely upon quantitative meta-analyses of studies of the prevalence of child sexual abuse. Studies of this type have the advantage of using objective statistical techniques. Two such studies have now been done (Bolen & Scannapieco, 1999; Gorey & Leslie, 1997). Both use the prevalence of child sexual abuse reported by each study as the dependent variable, while using methodological features of studies as the predictors.

Study by Gorey and Leslie (1997)

The study by Gorey and Leslie (1997), discussed in the previous chapter, is only summarized here. In their empirical analysis of 16 random and nonrandom studies of the prevalence of child sexual abuse, the definition of child sexual abuse employed (β = .631) and response rate of the study (β = .228) accounted for 50% of the variance in prevalence. Stated another way, they found that approximately half of the variation in prevalence across studies was primarily a result of the definition of child sexual abuse employed and, to a much lesser extent, the response rate. Whereas the response rate accounted for only approximately 5% of the variance in prevalence, however, they relied only upon this information when suggesting estimates of child sexual abuse.[9] Specifically, they suggested that a reasonable estimate of the prevalence of child sexual abuse for females was 12% to 17% and for males was 5% to 8%. It is interesting to note, however, that these estimates were subjective and did not rely on the analytic techniques available within the analysis.

Several limitations to this study were noted in the previous chapter. The method of operationalizing their variables of interest, including response rate, was not clearly articulated, and the dependent variable appeared to be confounded by placing undue emphasis upon the methodology of studies reporting on the prevalence of child sexual abuse for males.[10] As important, when deriving estimates of the prevalence of child sexual abuse, Gorey and Leslie (1997) used the response rate as the sole basis for their estimates, even though it was only marginally significant and accounted for only a small portion of the variation among prevalence rates across studies. Other limitations are that they (a) combined random and nonrandom studies, (b) combined special populations with community populations, (c) did not adequately represent the range of prevalence studies, (d) dichotomized critical variables, which resulted in a loss of information, and (e) did not include the number of screen questions in their analysis.

Study by Bolen and Scannapieco

Another more recent study (Bolen & Scannapieco, 1999) included in its sample 22 random studies of the prevalence of child sexual abuse. These studies represented all known random prevalence studies of national, state, and community populations done in North America. To correct for limitations in the Gorey and Leslie (1997) study, the dependent variable was limited to the prevalence, across studies, of child sexual abuse by gender. Thus, separate models were developed for male and female child sexual abuse. In this manner, missing data could not adversely impact the findings. Variables were not arbitrarily dichotomized and the number of screen questions was included as a predictor.

Using stepwise regression, this study found that the log of the number of screen questions (β = .756), log of the number of female respondents (β = -.727), and log of the year in which the study was reported (β = .320) accounted for 58% of the variance

---

[9]These estimates were the attenuated average prevalence for studies considered to have "good" response rates (i.e., response rates higher than 60%) (p. 393).

[10] Only nine of the 16 studies had populations of males. To determine the predictors of child sexual abuse for the seven studies without males, Gorey and Leslie computed the mean prevalence for male child sexual abuse and then used it to compute the dependent variable. This technique unduly weighted the methodology of those studies surveying males.

in the dependent variable (Bolen & Scannapieco, 1999). A lesser number of respondents and a greater number of screen questions were related to higher prevalence. Studies done in more recent years also had higher prevalences after controlling for other relationships. Importantly, neither the definition of child sexual abuse nor the response rate contributed significantly as predictors of prevalence, after controlling for other known relationships.

In this study, the number of screen questions proved to be the most critical predictor of the stated prevalence of child sexual abuse for both males and females (Bolen & Scannapieco, 1999). This finding suggests that surveys with a small number of screen questions significantly under-report the prevalence of child sexual abuse. Indeed, in a study in which childhood victims of sexual abuse were interviewed 17 years later, Williams et al. (2000) found that a minimum of eight screen questions were necessary to capture 90% of the forthcoming disclosures of child sexual abuse. Fourteen questions were required to capture all forthcoming disclosures.

Another important predictor of prevalence in the study by Bolen and Scannapieco (1999) was the number of female respondents, with larger studies having the smaller prevalences after controlling for other relationships. Historically, it has been assumed that larger sample sizes more accurately reflect the prevalence of a given characteristic within a population. The finding reported in the analysis by Bolen and Scannapieco suggests otherwise, at least for females. A possible reason for this finding is that the time spent with each respondent probably decreases as the sample size increases. For example, in smaller samples, respondents may be more likely to be personally interviewed. It could be that this increased attention is responsible for the higher prevalence estimates reported in smaller studies.

One of the disturbing findings of the study by Bolen and Scannapieco (1999) was that, after controlling for other known methodological factors, the prevalence of abuse of females increased logarithmically as the year of the study increased.[11] This logarithmic increase has at least two potential explanations. First, it could be that the prevalence of female child sexual abuse is actually increasing. Alternately, it could be that the relationship between year of the study and prevalence was confounded by a third unknown variable. It is possible, for example, that overall methodologies of studies in recent years are more capable of assessing for child sexual abuse, reflecting a learning curve based upon gained knowledge. It is therefore possible that this third unknown variable could be the gained knowledge of the profession. In this case, a logarithmic, rather than linear, increase would be expected.

It is likely that both explanations are implicated. It is probable that methodologies have improved in more recent years. It might also be that no single variable can capture this improvement. Yet, the year in which the study was reported accounted for approximately 10% of the variance in female prevalence.[12] Given the influence of this variable, it is entirely possible that at least a portion of the relationship between year of the study and stated prevalence can be attributed to an actual increase in prevalence of abuse of females over time.

---

[11] In a logarithmic increase, the rate of increase slows over time.
[12] This variance estimate is based upon the square of the partial correlation reported in the stepwise regression.

SCOPE OF THE PROBLEM OF CHILD SEXUAL ABUSE

Estimated Prevalence of Child Sexual Abuse

The purpose of this chapter was to provide an estimate of the scope of the problem of child sexual abuse. The scope of child sexual abuse is traditionally defined by its incidence rate or prevalence. Incidence rates give an estimate of the cases of child sexual abuse that, on a yearly basis, come to the attention of authorities. Prevalence, on the other hand, is an estimate of the number of lifetime victims of child sexual abuse. Because of their reliance upon cases coming to the attention of authorities, incidence rates are considerably less accurate than prevalence estimates. Even prevalence figures must be considered underestimates, however, because of the known issue of traumatic amnesia of child sexual abuse events (Williams, 1994). Respondents cannot report what they do not remember.

This section presented many different methods for estimating the prevalence of child sexual abuse. Of the studies reported, prevalence estimates of female child sexual abuse range from 2% to 62%, including noncontact abuse. Qualitative reviews generally suggest that 20% or more of the female population is sexually abused by the age of 18 and that 5% to 10% of the male population is sexually abused (Finkelhor, 1994). Estimates provided by Gorey and Leslie (1997) are 12% to 17% for female child sexual abuse and 5% to 8% for male child sexual abuse. All estimates provided so far, however, are at least partially subjective.

The final method of estimating the prevalence of child sexual abuse was included in the meta-analysis done by Bolen and Scannapieco (1999). One of the strengths of the multiple regression analysis done in this study is that empirically derived prevalence estimates of child sexual abuse can be computed based on derivations of the independent variables (i.e., number of screen questions, sample size, and year of study). Using this information, Bolen and Scannapieco developed predictions of the prevalence of female child sexual abuse based upon a survey done in 1997. Estimates of the prevalence of female child sexual abuse were 30% to 40% for studies using a moderate level of rigor (i.e., 8 to 14 screen questions and 1,000 to 2,000 respondents) and were 23% to 29% for studies using only four screen questions. For males, the empirically derived prevalence estimate for comparable studies was 3% to 13%, although it was suggested that the higher number probably was a low estimate for male child sexual abuse.[13]

In summary, the most reliable estimates of child sexual abuse currently available suggest that 30% to 40% of female children and 13% or more of male children are sexually abused in childhood. Because these estimates are empirically derived from all available random community-based prevalence studies done in North America (Bolen & Scannapieco, 1999), they provide unmistakable evidence that child sexual abuse is of epidemic proportions, especially for female children.

As discussed in the paper by Bolen and Scannapieco (1999), these high prevalence estimates have at least three important implications. First, the debate

---

[13] The most methodologically rigorous study of male child sexual abuse employed only four screen questions. It is almost certain that studies utilizing more screen questions would have identified more victims of abuse.

TABLE 5-1. Estimated Incidence Rates of Females Based upon Sexual Abuse Prevalence Estimates of 25%, 33%, and 40%

	Prevalence of Female Victims			Incidence with 1.8 Incidents/Victim[a]		
	25%	33%	40%	25%	33%	40%
Lifetime total of victims	8,275,000[b]	10,923,000[b]	13,240,000[b]	14,895,000[c]	19,661,000[c]	23,832,000[c]
Total each year	460,000[d]	607,000[d]	736,000[d]	827,500	1,092,000	1,324,000
Rate/1,000[d]	13.9[e]	18.4[e]	22.2[e]	25.0	33.0	40.0

[a] The incidence rate was computed based upon a population estimate of 33,100,000 females under the age of 18. [b] Computed by multiplying 33,100,000 females by .25, .33, and .40. [c] Computed by multiplying the lifetime total of victims by 1.8 (e.g., 8,275,000 × 1.8 = 14,895,000). [d] Lifetime total ÷ 18. [e] Computed by dividing the total each year by 33,100,000.

concerning child sexual abuse "can now move from minimizing the social problem to addressing its causes and treatment" (p. 299). Continued denial of the magnitude of the problem is now irresponsible. Second, only the most methodologically rigorous studies of prevalence of child sexual abuse should now be undertaken. Because methodological rigor was shown to affect the stated prevalence across studies, "poorly designed studies will only contribute to confusion" (p. 300). Finally, rigorous analyses are needed to examine child sexual abuse trends over time. If child sexual abuse is increasing, then the development of effective prevention programs becomes even more compelling.

Comparison of Incidence Rates to Prevalence

Prevalence estimates are now compared to incidence rates to determine how well society is responding to the scope of the problem of child sexual abuse. Tables 5-1 and 5-2 provide information for this section and are based upon U.S. Census data utilized by the NIS-3 (Sedlak & Broadhurst, 1996).

The first table (Table 5-1) presents estimates of the number of females sexually abused each year and the number of yearly incidents of abuse, based upon an estimated prevalence of 25%, 33%, and 40%. These estimates represent the lower, middle, and upper bounds in the Bolen and Scannapieco analysis (1999). If the prevalence of child sexual abuse is 25%, for example, then 8,275,000 females will be sexually abused prior to their 18th birthday. Many victims, however, are abused multiple times. In Russell's (1984) random community prevalence study, for example, victims had an average of 1.8 incidents. Translating the above numbers of victims into incidents, at 1.8 incidents for each victim the 8,275,000 victims represent 14,895,000 incidents over 18 years. To obtain yearly estimates, these totals are divided by 18 to derive 460,000 female victims for each year and 827,500 incidents for each year. If this latter number were divided by the total number of female children in the population (i.e., 33,100,000), the yearly incidence rate for female children would be 25/1,000 at

TABLE 5-2. Incidence Rates of Female Child Sexual Abuse in Incidence Studies as Compared to Estimated Incidence Rates Derived in Table 5-1

Actual Incidence Rates			Percent of All Abuse Known to Professionals at Prevalence Rates of		
Incidence Studies	Number of Incidents	Incidence Rate	25.0%	33.0%	40.0%
NIS-3	225,000	6.8/1,000	27.2%[a]	20.6%[b]	17.0%[c]
NCPCA	65,407[d]	2.0/1,000[e]	8.0%[a]	6.1%[b]	5.0%[c]
NCANDS	94,571[d]	2.9/1,000[e]	11.6%[a]	8.8%[b]	7.3%[c]

[a] Percentages are derived by dividing the actual incidence rate by 25.0 (e.g., 6.8 ÷ 25 = 27.2).
[b] Percentages are derived by dividing the actual incidence rate by 33.0 (e.g., 6.8 ÷ 33 = 20.6).
[c] Percentages are derived by dividing the actual incidence rate by 40.0 (e.g., 6.8 ÷ 40 = 17.0).
[d] The number of incidents was computed by multiplying the total number of incidents by 75% (the proportion of female to male abuse in the NIS-3). For the NCPCA, the total number of incidents was 87,210 and the total number of incidents for the NCANDS was 126,095. [e] The estimated incidence rate was computed by dividing the number of incidents by the 33,100,000 females under the age of 18 in the population.

a prevalence of 25%. Comparable estimates of incidence rates for prevalence estimates of 33% and 40% are 33/1,000 and 40/1,000 respectively.

Table 5-2 then compares the incidence of *identified* abuse to the *estimated* incidence of child sexual abuse occurring in the population, based upon prevalence estimates of 25%, 33%, and 40%. To compare *identified* abuse (Table 5-2) to *estimated* abuse (Table 5-1), compare the columns between tables with similar prevalence estimates (e.g., 25% for both tables). For example, the 6.8/1,000 incidence rate reported in the NIS-3 is 27.2% (Table 5-2) of the predicted incidence rate of 25.0/1,000 based upon a prevalence of 25.0% (Table 5-1). In other words, if 25% of the female population is sexually abused and victims are abused an average of 1.8 times each, then only 27.2% of all abuse of females is being identified by authorities. For a prevalence estimate of 33%, only 21% of all abuse of females is coming to the attention of authorities. For a prevalence of 40%, only 17% is coming to the attention of authorities. Further, based upon incidence rates reported by the NCPCA and NCANDS, only approximately 5.0% to 11.6% of all abuse that occurs is substantiated by child protective services.

These tables are provided to indicate the weakness of the current system in identifying and assessing sexually abused children. Even though these figures are estimates, they do suggest that the current response to the problem of child sexual abuse remains limited and the response by child protective services is even poorer.

POLICY IMPLICATIONS

One of the overriding themes of this book is that the current response to the scope of the problem of child sexual abuse remains inadequate. The estimated prevalence of female child sexual abuse, within some margin of error as a result of the small number of studies, appears to fall within 30% to 40%. The estimate for males is 13% or more (Bolen & Scannapieco, 1999).

The analyses in this section, however, suggest that the large majority of this abuse does not come to the attention of authorities or does not present with enough evidence to pursue an investigation or substantiation of the abuse by child protective services. Even the most liberal estimate suggests that only about one-fourth of all committed abuse is recognized and substantiated. More likely, 20% or less of all abuse is recognized and substantiated.

These analyses thus suggest that the official response to child sexual abuse is seriously inadequate. In this regard, the analysis by Wang and Daro (1997) in the Annual Fifty State Survey of trends across time is not reasonable. In their analysis, Wang and Daro suggested that the reason for a decrease in the proportion of substantiated child sexual abuse during the last few years is because child protective services is less burdened with such cases. They state:

> To a certain extent, the rapid increase in the number of reported cases of child sexual abuse observed in the mid to late 1980's reflected the increased awareness and attention to a form of maltreatment which had been virtually ignored prior to this time. Child welfare agencies across the country were inundated with cases, many of which had involved several years of ongoing abuse. After over ten years of attention to this problem, it is possible that the reservoir of cases involving years of abuse have [sic] been so reduced such that child welfare is less burdened with such cases. (pp. 7-10)

This analysis instead suggests that child protective services is not keeping up with the current cases of child sexual abuse and is continuing to fall behind.

What can be done to stem the tide of this horrendous problem? It is suggested that the most important step in responding to the extreme threat of child sexual abuse is that the government needs to assume *full* responsibility for the protection of its youngest members. The government not only needs to put into place a mechanism for protecting its young, but also must provide adequate funding for the mechanism to work. Providing a mechanism without adequate funding almost guarantees that it will fail. The latest NIS-3 report found as much (Sedlak & Broadhurst, 1996).

Protection of our young should proceed simultaneously along two paths. Without both, the process is destined to fail. First, victims of child sexual abuse need to be adequately identified and assessed. Second, primary prevention of child sexual abuse needs to become a national priority. This section addresses the issue of assessment and identification, whereas Chapters 8 and 9, "Risk Factors for Child Sexual Abuse Victimization" and "Offenders," discuss implications for prevention.

Analyses presented in this chapter suggest that the large majority of sexually abused children are not identified. As the NIS-3 suggests, one reason for this may be that the mechanisms in place to do so are inadequate (Sedlak & Broadhurst, 1996). The current system is significantly overtaxed. While professionals in the community may be more capable of assessing subtle cues of abuse, as Sedlak and Broadhurst suggest, child protective services cannot handle the cases referred to it. Even in cases with potentially serious injuries, most are not currently investigated. The problem appears to be worsening, as the ability of the system to handle the load of cases declined substantially between 1986 and 1993.

The decline has been evident even as child protective services has employed creative strategies. For example, in some states clerical staff have been cut while the number of frontline workers has increased. While this strategy has possibly increased the number of workers, it has also added clerical tasks to the already burdened caseloads of workers. Another strategy has been to make changes in centralized intake and intake assessment (Wang & Daro, 1997). Changes have also been made to narrow the definition of child abuse and neglect so that fewer cases of reported abuse are investigated.

In spite of these strategies, child protective services appears to be falling further behind in its ability to identify and assess victims of child sexual abuse. The financial support is simply not available. While a few states have experienced increases in budgets in recent years, they "were relatively small and may well be offset by the decline in funding expected from Federal sources" (Wang & Daro, 1997, p. 17). Until a massive infusion of money into the system is available, the current system is destined to fail, as it is currently doing. When the system fails, so does the societal obligation to protect its young.

To adequately identify and assess victims of child sexual abuse, government and society should first and foremost endorse a national policy that *all* children have the *right* to be protected. This responsibility should be shared by local, state, and federal governments. When this occurs, the necessary monetary and other resources also need to be made available.

After a national commitment to the protection of our young is made, other steps to ensure that children do not fall through the cracks are necessary. First, the definition of an incident of child sexual abuse that can be investigated by child protective services needs to be widened to include all perpetrators. Limiting the investigation of child sexual abuse incidents to those involving caretakers increases the likelihood that known perpetrators will remain undetected and untreated, thus placing potentially hundreds of thousands of children at increased risk of sexual abuse each year.

Second, criteria for investigation need to be broadened so that no probable cases of child sexual abuse are left uninvestigated. While this is a difficult and complex issue because of the infringement upon the rights of those in which the abuse is clearly unfounded, an overemphasis on the protection of the rights of these adults will leave many more children unprotected. One method of approaching this issue is to develop a working commission of experts to propose alternate solutions.

Next, a decision concerning appropriate standards for assessment and treatment needs to be considered. It is suggested that all identified victims be assessed by licensed graduate-level mental health professionals to determine their current clinical status. Victims in need of treatment should have access to it whether or not they can afford it. Further, all child protective services workers investigating child sexual abuse should be required to have graduate-level mental health degrees.

In order to adequately protect children, offenders should be removed from their victims'—and other children's—environment. Responsibility for protecting victims from their assailants needs to be that of law enforcement agencies. Requiring that nonoffending mothers be held responsible for the protection of their children from a known offender defies all logic. When society fails in its duty to protect, it is unconscionable to hold the mother responsible for further contact between the perpetrator and victim. Law enforcement agencies, instead of mothers, should be held accountable for their inability to protect known victims from known perpetrators. (This issue is discussed further in Chapter 10, "Nonoffending Guardians" and Chapter 12, "Conclusions.")

It is also suggested that an enormous infusion of money be invested in preventive research and programs. Much of this money should be earmarked for research and primary prevention programs whose purposes are to prevent abuse, as opposed to preparing children for how to handle abuse situations or approaches that do occur.

Funding also needs to increase for research. The General Accounting Office (GAO) 1997 report recently concluded that there is insufficient funding of research ("GAO Calls For," 1997). It also suggests, however, that "focuses on such topics as the causes and effects of sexual abuse" and other topics are "not relevant to "most local agencies' attempts to reform their services" (p. 132). It is argued instead that primary research such as that of causality of child sexual abuse *should* impact these agencies. Optimal strategies of identification, assessment, treatment, and prevention cannot be attained in an empirical void. That child protective services does not target all child sexual abuse nor its victims suggests that the scope of the problem of child sexual abuse is not yet clearly understood. Primary research about the scope of the problem should therefore *drive* efforts to reform agencies.

Finally, if there is one set of unsolved and even unresearched questions that begs for analysis it is this: How can such an advanced society allow so many of its children to be sexually abused? *Why* do 30% to 40% of girls and 13% or more of boys (Bolen & Scannapieco, 1999) fall victim to child sexual abuse? Until we can answer these questions, there is no reason to expect that the prevalence of child sexual abuse will diminish. The best identification and assessment strategies in the world may not lessen the scope of the problem of child sexual abuse.

TABLE A5-1. Random Prevalence Studies of Child Sexual Abuse

Study	Sampling Frame	Sample Size	Sampling Technique	RR	Mode	SQ	Definition	Age Limit	Female Prev	Male Prev
Adolescents										
Ageton, 1983 National Youth Survey	National	1,725 males & females ages 11-21	Multistage cluster sampling	73%		2	Sexual attack; rape or its attempt or pressured; pushed to do more than wanted		7% to 9%; for the oldest group 8% to 15%	
Erickson & Rapkin, 1991	Los Angeles middle class school district	543 male & 627 female middle & high school students	Random sample stratified by school	84%[1]	SAQ	1	Unwanted sexual experience		18%	12%
Hall & Flannery, 1984	Milwaukee area	508 adolescents ages 14-17	Random digit dialing	56%	FTF	1	Guy used force or threat to have unwanted sex		12%	2%
Hernandez, 1992	Minnesota public school system	1,643 male & 1,535 female ninth graders	Computer generated random sample	94% of school districts	SAQ	2	Unwanted contact for IA; forced contact for EA	Offender had to be older	10% (2% IA) (6% EA) (3% both)	
National										
Abma et al., 1997 (National Survey of Growth)	National	10,847 females; oversampled African Americans and Latinos	Probability subsample of 1993 sample	79%	FTF SAQ CASI	8	Forced or nonvoluntary intercourse	<18	12%	—
Elliott & Briere, 1992	National	2,963 professional women	Stratified random sample of 12 professions	55%	SAQ	9[2]	Contact	<16 & offender ≤5 years older	27%	—
Gallup Poll, 1995	National	1,000 parents	Random digit dialing	57%; 19% refused	TEL	2	Forcible/unwanted contact by adult or older child	As a child	30%	9%

Study	Location	Sample	Sampling	Response	Method	No.	Definition	Age	%	%
Moore et al., 1989	Larger national survey	565 women & 556 men ages 17-23	National probability sample	71%[3]	TEL	1	Forced to have sex against will or raped	<18	8%[4]	2%[4]
Saunders et al., 1999[5]	National	4,008 women; oversampled ages 18-34	Two-stage probability sample; random digit dialing	85%	TEL	4	Completed non-consensual penetration	< 18	9%	—
Timnick, 1985[6]	National	1,145 men & 1,481 women	Random digit dialing	76%	TEL	4	Respondent's perception of sexual abuse; contact and noncontact	<18	27%	16%
Vogeltanz et al., 1999	National	1,099 women; 696 previously interviewed in 1981; oversampled heavy drinkers[7]	Stratified to include heavy drinkers	85% 91%[8]	FTF	8	Used Russell's and Wyatt's definitions	Same as Russell and Wyatt	17% (R)	23% (W)
State										
George & Winfield-Laird, 1986[9]	Piedmont of N. Carolina	1,157 women ages 18-64; oversampled elderly		77% of original sample	FTF	1	Forced contact	<16	2%[2]	
Kercher & McShane, 1984	Valid Texas driver's license	593 women & 461 men	Systematic random sampling	53%	SAQ	1	Sexual abuse as a child	As a child	11%	3%
Murphy, 1987[10]	Central Minnesota	415 women & 403 men	Random digit dialing	65%	TEL	1[3]	Exposure, nude photographs, rape	<18; by an adult	8%[2]	1%[2]
Nance, 1992[11]	Kentucky	354 women & 283 men		73%	TEL	1[3]	Respondents' perception of abuse	< 16	28%	9%

Study	Sampling Frame	Sample Size	Sampling Technique	RR	Mode	SQ	Definition	Age Limit	Female Prev	Male Prev
Community										
Essock-Vitale & McGuire, 1985	Los Angeles	300 Caucasian women ages 35-45 raised by a natural parent	Random digit dialing	66%	FTF	1	Raped or molested	< 18	17%	
Finkelhor, 1984	Boston parents of children 6-14 living at home	334 women & 187 men	Area probability sample	74%	FTF SAQ	2	Sexual things done or attempted they defined as abuse	< 17; offender ≤5 years older	15%	6%
Keckley Market Research, 1984	Nashville area[2]	603 adults[2]		61%[2]	TEL[2]	1[2]	Any unwanted sexual activity that felt uncomfortable[2]	<18; excludes peers or dates[2]	11%[2]	7%[2]
Russell, 1983[12]	San Francisco	930 women	Probability Sample	65%[13]	FTF	14	IA - exploitative; EA - unwanted	<18	38% C 54% NC	
Siegel et al., 1987	Los Angeles	1,645 women & 1,480 men	Two-stage probability by census block & household	68%	FTF	1	Pressured or forced sexual contact	< 16	7%	4%
Springs & Friedrich, 1992	Rural midwestern community	511 female patients ages 18-50 at family practice clinic	Simple random sample	39%	SAQ	1	Sexual experience	< 18; offender ≤5 years older	22%	
Wyatt, 1985	Los Angeles	126 African Americans & 122 white Americans	Multistage stratified probability sampling using quotas; random digit dialing	67%[14]	FTF	8	Ranged from non-bodily contact to rape; >12 had to be unwanted or involving coercion	<18; offender ≤5 years older unless unwanted	45% C; 62% NC	

| Wyatt et al., 1999 | Los Angeles | 182 African Americans & 156 white Americans | Multi-stage stratified probability sampling using quotas; random digit dialing | 71% | FTF | 8 | Ranged from bodily contact to rape; >12 had to be unwanted or involving coercion | Offender 5+ years older unless co-ercion | 34% C |

Note: RR = response rate; SQ = number of screen questions; FTF = face-to face; SAQ = self-administered questionnaire; TEL = telephone; CASI = audio computer-assisted self-interviewing; IA = intrafamilial abuse; EA = extrafamilial abuse; C = contact; NC = noncontact; R = Russell; W = Wyatt;

[1] The study reported that half of the total enrollment sample (2,840) was asked to participate, and 21 parents refused. However, only 1,197 students participated, suggesting a response rate of 84%. [2] As reported by the original researcher. [3] Eighty-two percent of second wave, which was 82% of first wave. [4] Computed based upon figures provided in report. [5] Also see Resnick, Kilpatrick, Dansky, Saunders, & Best, 1993; Saunders et al., 1992. [6] Also see Finkelhor et al., 1990. [7] The weighted N was 654 when cases with insufficient data were excluded. [8] Eighty-five percent for 1981 follow-up survey; 91% for newer survey. [9] Derived in part from Finkelhor, 1994; also see Winfield, George, Swartz, & Blazer, 1990. [10] Also see Murphy, 1991. [11] Also see Wolf, 1992 and Lexington Herald-Leader. [12] Russell has written numerous papers and books that refer to this study. The most comprehensive are Sexual Exploitation (1984) and The Secret Trauma (1986). [13] Eighty-one percent if including only refusals; 65% if excluding those refusing to list members in house; 50% if excluding those not home. [14] Seventy-three percent if include all who terminated but whose eligibility could not be determined; 67% if including those not contacted before eligibility; and 55% with all who could not be contacted.

CHAPTER 6
EXTRAFAMILIAL ABUSE

INTRODUCTION

Extrafamilial abuse is sexual abuse by anyone other than a relative. Although much has been written about intrafamilial abuse, especially father-daughter incest, almost nothing has been written about specific types of extrafamilial abuse. Little more is known about certain types of extrafamilial abuse than simply how prevalent they are, even though extrafamilial abuse comprises the majority of all child sexual abuse (see Table 6-1). Most of the scant empirical literature available has focused on substitute caregivers, either unrelated (Margolin, 1991), in day care (Faller, 1988), or children in foster care or alternate settings (Rosenthal, Motz, Edmonson, & Groze, 1991; Zuravin, Benedict, & Somerfield, 1993)—categories that are sometimes defined as intrafamilial abuse. Other studies have focused on child-child sexual encounters (Haugaard & Tilly, 1988) and date rape (Muehlenhard & Linton, 1987; Rouse, 1988), although the latter studies usually include both adolescent and adult victims. Yet, all studies done to date (other than those on date rape) are of reported populations. Because only approximately 6% to 12% of all abuse is reported (Russell, 1983; Saunders, Villeponteaux, Lipovsky, Kilpatrick, & Veronen, 1992), these studies represent an extremely biased population. Thus, little is known about extrafamilial sexual abuse, even though it is the most prevalent type of abuse.

The first portion of this chapter provides estimates of extrafamilial abuse based on random retrospective surveys and compares these estimates with reported cases of abuse. The chapter then turns to historical reasons that the literature base on extrafamilial abuse has been virtually ignored and that extrafamilial abuse remains vastly underidentified. Next, the primary types of extrafamilial abuse are presented, including abuse by acquaintances, strangers, authority figures, friends of the family, friends, and dates. The final section presents a summary of findings as well as recommendations for moving forward in identifying, assessing, and treating this abuse.

PREVALENCE AND INCIDENCE OF EXTRAFAMILIAL ABUSE

Prevalence

Because random prevalence studies of child sexual abuse attempt to capture all adults in a given sample who were sexually abused as children, they probably remain the best sources for developing information concerning the scope of the problem of extrafamilial abuse. Yet, methodological variations contribute to inconsistent information across studies. Differences in rigor affect their stated prevalence, with more rigorous studies generally having the higher prevalence estimates (Bolen & Scannapieco, 1999). Further, some studies report only on females. A more tedious

TABLE 6-1. Percentage of Extrafamilial Abuse Incidents to All Child Sexual Abuse by Relationship of Perpetrator to Victim*

Relationship	Russell, 1983[a] F	LATP, 1985[b] M	LATP, 1985[b] F	Saunders et al., 1992 F	Siegel et al., 1987[c] M	Siegel et al., 1987[c] F	Wyatt, 1985 Cauc. F	Wyatt, 1985 A/A F
Stranger	11	40	21	14	28	21	51	37
Acquaintance	30	31	33	50	16	30	26	32
Friend	8	13	8		32	23		
Friend of family	10				10	8		
Authority figure	1						4	2
Date, etc.	11				8	10		
Other		5[d]	9[d]					
Total	71	84–89	62–71	65[e]	94	92	81	71
Prevalence	31	12–13	17–20					

Note. F = female; M = male; A/A = African American.
*Adapted from Bolen (2000a) with permission by Sage Publications.
[a] Based on all respondents. [b] Reanalyzed by Finkelhor, Hotaling, Lewis, & Smith, 1990. [c] These columns are not directly comparable to those of other researchers because Siegel et al. reported multiple assailants for respondents; hence, their figures add up to more than 100%. [d] The "Other" group may include some distant nonrelatives. [e] Does not add up due to rounding.

problem is the lack of uniformity in how the studies report the relationship of the offender to the victim, making the comparison across studies problematic. Finally, studies differ in how many incidents they gather and whether they report extrafamilial abuse data by incident or respondent. Even with these challenges, it is beneficial to compare information on extrafamilial abuse across prevalence studies (see Tables 6-1 and 6-2).

As shown in Tables 6-1 and 6-2, studies have yet to agree on the prevalence of extrafamilial abuse. Russell (1983) found that 31% of female respondents reported at least one incident of extrafamilial abuse. Wyatt et al. (1999), in a more recent study, found that 22% of females were victims of extrafamilial abuse (not included in Table 6-1 or 6-2). Yet, Vogeltanz et al. (1999) found that only 9% to 16% of females were abused extrafamilially (Table 6-2). This finding is more remarkable because this study employed Russell's and Wyatt's broad definition of child sexual abuse which included noncontact abuse.[1]

The only other study for which extrafamilial abuse prevalence can be estimated, although not precisely as a result of a nebulous "other" category, is the *Los Angeles Times* Poll survey (LATP) (analyzed by Finkelhor et al., 1990) (see Table 6-1). For males, 12% to 13% experienced extrafamilial abuse, whereas 17% to 20% of females experienced extrafamilial abuse. Because only a single incident of abuse was reported for this study (as compared to all incidents in Russell's study), and only four screen

---

[1] Please refer to the previous chapter for a discussion of why Vogeltanz et al.'s figures might be lower than Russell's and Wyatt's, even though they used similar criteria.

TABLE 6-2. Prevalence (Percentage) of All Respondents Abused by Type of Extrafamilial Abuse

Relationship	Russell, 1983[a] F	LATP, 1985[b] M	F	Siegel et al., 1987 M	F	Vogeltanz et al., 1999[c] F
Stranger	7.3	5.9	5.9	1.0	1.4	
Acquaintance	8.9	4.5	11.3	0.6	2.0	3.5 – 4.6[d]
Neighbor	2.2	1.9	2.2			
Minor role	2.7					
Friend	4.2			1.2	1.6	3.2 – 4.7
Friend of family	5.9					
Authority figure	5.6	7.2[e]	13.8[e]			1.7 – 2.1
Date, lover, spouse	6.9			0.2	0.7	4.2 – 8.1
Other		0.7[f]	2.5[f]	0.5	3.7	
Total prevalence	31	12 – 13	17 – 20			9 – 16

[a] Russell's data were reanalyzed in a qualitative analysis by Bolen (2000a). The figures presented are a result of that analysis. [b] Reanalyzed by Finkelhor et al., 1990. [c] This study used the definitions for contact abuse employed by Russell (1983) and Wyatt (1985). The left figure is based on Russell's definition and the right is based on Wyatt's definition. [d] Other adults not in family (includes strangers). [e] This category overlaps with other categories. [f] This "Other" category might also include distant relatives.

questions were used (as compared to 14 for Russell), it is likely that that these estimates are low.

Studies also have yet to agree on how much of all sexual abuse is extrafamilial, with ranges from 62% to 81% for females and 84% to 94% for males (Table 6-1). Regardless, these numbers are high enough to suggest that the preponderance of all abuse is extrafamilial. A further area of disagreement is how to categorize extrafamilial abuse. Researchers divide it into as few as two and as many as six categories. Differences even appear across studies *within* perpetrator categories; discrepancies are most obvious in stranger and acquaintance categories.

Prevalence by type of extrafamilial abuse is also an important question (Table 6-2). Again, the numbers vary considerably by study. It is likely, however, that Russell's (1983) and Vogeltanz et al.'s (1999) studies have the more accurate figures. First, because Siegel et al. (1987) used only a single screen question to elicit disclosures, they probably had unreliably low estimates by type of abuse. Further, the LATP (Timnick, 1985), reanalyzed by Finkelhor et al. (1990), used only four screen questions and reported only a single incident of abuse. Again, it would be expected that these estimates are low. These two studies do, however, allow a comparison of abuse trends between males and females.

First, the LATP (Finkelhor et al., 1990) and the study by Siegel et al. (1987) agree that stranger abuse is approximately as prevalent among females as males. This is an interesting finding because females are usually at much greater risk than males to be sexually abused. Yet, while 21% of all abuse of females was by strangers in the LATP survey, for a prevalence of 6%, 40% of abuse of males was by strangers, for a prevalence of 6% (see Tables 6-1 and 6-2). Hence, the same percentages of males and females were abused by strangers, a finding similar to that of Siegel et al. (1987). The only other type of abuse in which males and females are at approximately the same risk is abuse by friends (Siegel et al., 1987). Again, given the limitations of the LATP and Siegel et al. studies, these findings certainly have to be considered tentative.

Turning to Russell's (1983) and Vogeltanz et al.'s studies (Table 6-2), the prevalence estimates must be described as phenomenal.[1] Female respondents in their samples were at exceptional risk for all types of extrafamilial abuse. The only category in which risk was low in Vogeltanz et al.'s study was for abuse by authorities. In Russell's study, the only types of abuse that posed even a marginal risk to females were those by neighbors and individuals in a minor role with the victim. (This latter type of abuse included victims who were approached by someone they knew and who had some minor role in their lives, e.g., a gardener, boarder, co-worker, etc.) When these categories were collapsed into the more general category of acquaintances, however, 13% of all respondents were sexually abused by an acquaintance—an extraordinary risk. Further, more than 5% of the respondents in Russell's survey were abused by a stranger, friend of the family, authority figure, or date. The risk of being abused by friends was only slightly less (4%). These are incredible figures, suggesting a profound risk of female sexual abuse by nonrelatives representing virtually every type of relationship with the victim.

Regretfully, the latest detailed data for extrafamilial abuse available from prevalence studies were gathered in 1985 by the LATP (Finkelhor et al., 1990). Yet, this study has important methodological issues. Not only did it use only four screen questions, but it also used a broad definition of sexual abuse that included noncontact abuse. While its findings are important, difficulty arises when comparing its findings to those of studies using the more rigorous definition of contact sexual abuse.

A further problem is that the random prevalence study with the greatest amount of information concerning extrafamilial abuse is that by Russell (1983), which is also the oldest of the random prevalence studies. While Wyatt et al.'s (1999) more recent random prevalence study confirms that extrafamilial abuse remains more prevalent than intrafamilial abuse, only minimal information by perpetrator type is available within this study.

Because detailed information on type of perpetrator is dated, it is difficult to ascertain trends over time. There are indications, however, that certain types of extrafamilial abuse were increasing in the recent past. A trend analysis of Russell's (1983) study is shown in Table 6-3. In this analysis, the actual year of abuse was compared to determine trends across time. Types of abuse were entered in descending order in the table based upon mean year of the abuse. Hence, abuse at the top of the table was increasing in frequency in more recent years, whereas abuse at the bottom of the table was decreasing in frequency. What is striking about this table is that the

---

[1] In the study by Vogeltanz et al., 18% of the weighted sample did not give enough information to determine whether abuse occurred. This rather large percentage suggests that problems occurred with the format of the face-to-face interviews which may have lowered the prevalence of abuse.

TABLE 6-3. Trend Analysis of Russell's (1983) Survey as Reanalyzed by Bolen

Relationship	N	Mean Year of Abuse	Mean Age of Offender
Friend	48	1960	17
Date, lover, or husband	73	1960	19
Brother/male cousin[1]	50	1957	18
Stranger	73	1956	30
Father/step-father	43	1954	40
Other male relative	32	1953	37
Authority figure	59	1952	41
Acquaintance	141	1950	23
Friend of family	66	1949	34
Uncle	48	1948	42
Female relative	8	1948	19
All extrafamilial	460	1954	28
All intrafamilial	181	1952	33

Note: Intrafamilial abuse is in italics.
[1]Brothers and male cousins were collapsed into a single category because their mean years of abuse and age were virtually identical.

top three categories included predominantly juvenile offenders. Of these, abuse by friends and dates had the most recent increase in abuse prevalence.

What could account for this change in abuse patterns over time? One plausible explanation is that this pattern represents the greater availability of children and adolescents to younger males. One of the important trends in the last half of the 20th Century has been for a younger age of first dates as well as for more heterogeneous friendship groups. The increase in prevalence of abuse by friends and dates in the years preceding Russell's (1983) survey could thus represent the greater amount of unsupervised time female children and adolescents spent with these young men.

Comparison of Prevalence to Incidence

As shown in Table 6-1, prevalence studies indicate that extrafamilial abuse is by far the most prevalent type of abuse. A comparison of these studies to incidence studies, however, points up sharp discrepancies between abuse that occurs in the general population and abuse that is identified. For example, in the latest National Incidence Study (NIS-3) of abuse identified by authorities, including child protective services, the majority of substantiated abuse was by a parent (29%) or parental figure (25%) (Sedlak & Broadhurst, 1996). In the other incidence study in which data on the relationship of the perpetrator are provided—the NCANDS (U.S. Department of Health and Human Services, 1997)—only 5% of all perpetrators identified by child protective services were not in a caretaking role. These findings suggest that whereas the majority of all abuse that occurs is extrafamilial, the vast majority of identified abuse is intrafamilial.

Underemphasis of Extrafamilial Abuse

These analyses indicate that extrafamilial abuse is easily the most prevalent type of abuse, even though intrafamilial abuse is the abuse most often identified. Yet, while only approximately 5% of all *committed* child sexual abuse is by a biological father or stepfather and approximately 30% of *committed* abuse is intrafamilial (Finkelhor et al., 1990; Russell, 1983; Siegel et al., 1987; Wyatt, 1985), much of the current knowledge base focuses on intrafamilial abuse. Indeed, in October 1998, 123 entries published since 1966 and indexed under father-daughter incest were listed on PsychLit and almost 2,200 entries were indexed by incest. Conversely, only 15 studies were indexed under extrafamilial abuse (Bolen, 2000a). What can be responsible for this lapse in the literature base?

To understand this problem, we must first return to the historical and theoretical formulation of the problem of child sexual abuse, starting with Freud. Although Freud's theory of seduction and later renunciation were discussed fully in Chapter 2, an important point needs emphasis in this chapter. When Freud repudiated his theory of seduction, he posited instead that females relating histories of child sexual abuse were not actually abused but were simply recalling incestuous fantasies of themselves with their fathers (Masson, 1984). Thus, by the early 1900s, child sexual abuse and father-daughter incest were immutably bound.

It eventually became apparent that some children (girls) were sexually abused, but because of Freud's influence, it was assumed that most of these abuse victims were sexually abused by their fathers. Deriving from psychoanalytic explanations, these girls were said to be acting out their incestuous wishes by seducing their fathers (Rush, 1996). This psychoanalytic interpretation predominated well into the second half of the century.

Other important theoretical developments prior to the 1980s centered on the culpability of the mother (Machotka, Pittman, & Flomenhaft, 1967) and family dynamics (Carper, 1979) in the maintenance of father-daughter incest. These themes were typical of much of the writings on child sexual abuse prior to 1980, with an important exception being that of feminist theory. Yet, even much of the early feminist literature on child sexual abuse, by reacting to this biased literature, also targeted father-daughter incest (see Herman, 1981, for example). Thus, this point/counterpoint literature maintained an important focus on father-daughter incest. This historical emphasis on incest not only set the stage for how the problem of child sexual abuse was conceptualized in more recent eras, but also had a dramatic effect on policies and intervention strategies.

By the time the first rigorous random prevalence study on child sexual abuse was published by Russell (1983) in the early 1980s, the stage was set. Even though Russell's study showed convincingly that sexual abuse was also, and predominately, about types of abuse other than incest, the professional literature maintained a primary focus on father-daughter incest. Literature that did focus on extrafamilial abuse was not so much concerned with blending the types of abuse for the purpose of developing overarching theories of child sexual abuse, but with explaining how incest and extrafamilial abuse (child molestation or pedophilia) were conceptually different.

The understanding of offenders at that time was that they were either fixated, having a primary sexual orientation towards children, or regressed, having a primary sexual orientation towards adults (Groth, 1982; Groth, Longo, & McFadin, 1982). Not surprisingly, incest offenders were typically considered to be regressed, whereas pedophiles were considered to be fixated. With this in mind, it was assumed that incest offenders could be rehabilitated by targeting the problems that had made them regressed in the first place. Groth believed that the largest precipitant of abuse for this group of offenders was stress. Much writing at the time also considered that these offenders were socially inadequate and isolated (Araji & Finkelhor, 1986; Panton, 1978, 1979). Another body of literature suggested that family dynamics, and especially the mother's withdrawal from the sexual relationship, were responsible for the abuse (Kadushin & Martin, 1988). Interventions thus targeted the development of appropriate social skills while also employing family and marital therapies (see Giarretto 1982, 1989, for example).

Concomitantly, victims were considered to have the worst outcomes if they were abused by their fathers. The belief was that the extraordinary betrayal of trust that occurred in incest was responsible for many of the serious and deleterious effects of abuse (Gelinas, 1983). Victims of pedophiles and other child molesters, while they were recognized to suffer from the abuse, did not experience the same betrayal of trust so could be expected to have fewer negative outcomes.

The systems that intervene in child sexual abuse cases, although they vary by state, also developed differently for incest and extrafamilial abuse. Not only were laws developed that protected children from statutory rape and other sexual acts, but concomitantly most states passed laws that prohibited incest (Russell & Bolen, 2000). Thus, incest and child molestation were conceptualized as two different types of crimes. While the laws prohibited both incest and extrafamilial abuse, however, the implementation of these statutes appears to provide differential protection to victims of intrafamilial and extrafamilial abuse. For example, although incest victims are always routed through child protective services, extrafamilial abuse victims may be routed through law enforcement (Faller, 1994).

This disparity has serious implications. First, it suggests that victims of extrafamilial abuse may not have the same availability of services given to intrafamilial abuse victims. Second, it biases the perception of abuse frequency. Because child protective services is the agency to which most mandated reporting occurs, official reports of abuse are heavily weighted towards intrafamilial abuse (see the NIS-3, for example).

This trend is especially intriguing because children and parents may report extrafamilial abuse more often than they report intrafamilial abuse. For example, in a survey of 521 parents of children 6 to 14 years of age living in the Boston metropolitan area, none of the known abuse committed by relatives was reported (Finkelhor, 1984). On the other hand, 23% of known abuse perpetrated by an acquaintance and 73% of known abuse perpetrated by a stranger was reported by parents (Finkelhor, 1984). Sauzier (1989) also found that children were more reticent to disclose abuse by a natural parent. While 39% of victims of extrafamilial abuse disclosed immediately, only 17% of victims of abuse by a natural parent did so. Another 32% of victims of extrafamilial abuse never disclosed, whereas 53% of victims of abuse by a natural parent never disclosed.

Similarly, treatment populations of victims are heavily weighted towards victims of intrafamilial abuse (see Bolen, 1998a; English & Tosti-Lane, 1988, for example). Because clinicians may use observation to establish what they consider normal, it is not unusual for clinicians to conclude that most abuse is intrafamilial, and most often father-daughter incest.

A similar problem is scarce resources. When only a finite and inadequate amount of resources exists, they must be prioritized. Based on the assumption that intrafamilial abuse is worse for the victim, and because the father is often living with the victim, father-daughter incest has historically been prioritized as the "worst" type of abuse. Victims of extrafamilial abuse, on the other hand, are more often assumed to be in no, or little, danger of revictimization. As such, their cases may go unreported or uninvestigated. Scarce resources are thus targeted heavily towards intrafamilial abuse.

In summary, the historical emphasis on intrafamilial abuse has led to biases in laws and policies designed to protect victims, the treatment of offenders and victims, the allocation of scarce resources, and the theoretical and empirical literature. This profound minimization of the problem of extrafamilial abuse has created a number of problems. First, extrafamilial abuse victims do not have equal access to protection and treatment.[2] Further, as evidenced by the data in the NIS-3 (Sedlak & Broadhurst, 1996), extrafamilial abuse cases are also less often reported and investigated. Incest offenders are also treated as less of a threat, even though a large body of literature now exists that suggests that they indeed pose an important risk to other children (Abel et al., 1987, 1988a; Ballard et al, 1990). The prioritization of intrafamilial abuse also leads to the continuing myth that this type of abuse is actually more prevalent and that extrafamilial abuse is not as much of a threat to children.

Finally, a focus on intrafamilial abuse logically leads to a discourse on family dynamics and issues central to the victim. This type of discourse, however, impedes the more critical level of discourse on societal factors and issues more removed from the victim that are implicated in the extrafamilial abuse of children. When intrafamilial abuse is prioritized, issues of primary concern center on those of dysfunctional families. When extrafamilial abuse is prioritized, however, and it is realized that children are at significant risk of abuse by virtually any type of nonfilial male relationship within their environment, then the level of discourse must move to a higher level. This level of discourse necessitates a focus upon the societal structure that contributes to this problem. Now simply targeting dysfunctional families no longer suffices. Instead, strategies that target the sociocultural structure are necessary. This latter level of discourse is essential for addressing the scope of the problem of child sexual abuse. Hence, the most important effect of minimizing extrafamilial abuse is that the scope of the problem of child sexual abuse is obscured.

TYPES OF EXTRAFAMILIAL ABUSE

This next section furthers the discussion of risk of extrafamilial abuse by reviewing the different groups of perpetrators. In the following section the major types of extrafamilial abuse, including abuse by strangers, acquaintances, authority figures

---

[2] Since intrafamilial abuse is the less common type of abuse but has a greater representation in treatment populations, it can be concluded that extrafamilial abuse victims are more often left untreated.

(including abuse by unrelated caregivers), friends of the family, friends, and dates are presented. As discussed earlier, there is virtually no literature available on the dynamics of many of these types of abuse, but that which is available is presented. Because of the dearth of literature, the sections discussing the different types of abuse often rely primarily on the author's secondary analysis of Russell's (1983) community prevalence study of female violence.[4] Because much of the following sections derive of necessity from this analysis, the methodology for this study is introduced briefly.

Of 463 incidents of extrafamilial abuse reported in Russell's (1983) study, incident reports were gathered for 360 incidents. These incident reports comprise the primary sample for the reanalysis. To analyze the data, the 360 incident reports, grouped by perpetrator, were first reviewed in detail. Based on similarities among dynamics and characteristics of the abuse, incidents were then placed into like categories within perpetrator groups. The process of coding proceeded iteratively as the incident reports were read and codes were assigned. Incident reports were placed, and sometimes replaced, into congruent categories. As categories gained shape and context, the incident reports and categories continued to be re-evaluated until the "best fit" was gained. The final result was an analysis not only of the overall types of abuse, but also of subgroups within each.

The important limitations of this study are that (a) it applies only to females, and (b) it is dated. Regretfully, no comparable studies of male victims have been done, nor is there a more recent random retrospective study that contains similar data. Because studies of offenders are biased by those who have gotten caught, neither can they be relied upon to provide representative data.

Strangers

One of the most frightening of all types of abuse is that by strangers. The fear, of course, is that children will be accosted by strangers in the children's neighborhoods and will be abused, raped, and sometimes even murdered. The public seems to be most concerned about this type of abuse, and prevention programs are often targeted at this type of approach. The question is whether this stereotype of stranger abuse is correct.

The answer is yes—and no. First, it is generally agreed that the vast majority of abuse is perpetrated by a known other. Thus, while stranger abuse is a type to be feared, as more than 7% of all female respondents in Russell's (1983) sample were victimized by strangers, it is only one of many types of abuse to be feared. As shown in Table 6-2, both males and females are at approximately equal risk of abuse by a stranger, a finding that is born out by the percentage of offenders who have a primary sexual orientation towards young males (Frenzl & Lang, 1989). As such, stranger abuse is definitely a prevalent form of abuse that deserves great concern.

The offender literature on this type of abuse bears out what is known historically and through common sense. Offenders purposefully move into areas with children to

---

[4] Some of this information has previously been published (Bolen, 2000a), whereas other is presented for the first time in this chapter.

target them for perpetration (Elliott, Browne, & Kolcoyne, 1995). Sometimes victims are groomed; sometimes they are picked up off the street. Victims are targeted based upon physical appearance, availability, and a sense of vulnerability (Conte, Wolf, & Smith, 1989; Elliott et al., 1995).

The findings resulting from the author's reanalysis of Russell's (1983) data appear to corroborate this literature. Girls abused by strangers were likely to be approached in a number of ways, the most popular of which was while the child was walking around or to or from school. A second popular type of approach was targeting the child who was in a safe place (usually somewhere in her neighborhood). Indeed, only 18% of stranger abuse was committed outside the child's neighborhood. Also of interest, even though we consider the youngest children to be at greatest danger from abuse by a stranger, especially when walking around, almost half of the victims of stranger abuse who were accosted while walking around were over the age of 13. Hence, this type of abuse represents a significant risk even to adolescents. Further, it is often a more severe type of abuse, as approximately half of all abuse included penetration, and force or threat was used in 70% of all cases. A weapon was used in 11% of cases and physical assault occurred in 24% of cases.

The primary methods by which strangers approach children are discussed briefly next. Categories are listed in order by their prevalence, from most to least prevalent as found in Russell's (1983) study.

Walking to or from locations other than school: In the majority of incidents in this category, most of which involved some type of penetration or its attempt, victims were approached on foot. One-third of these incidents involved multiple perpetrators. Most perpetrators simply grabbed their victims while they walked on the street, most often after sunset, whereas another smaller group of victims was actively followed. A few victims were approached by perpetrators in cars. In those instances in which the victims refused the ride, they were physically dragged into the car.

Walking to or from school: Of the children abused while walking either to or from school, most were approached on foot. Perpetrators who approached by car either asked for directions or asked the children if they wanted a ride. If the children did not agree to the ride, they were forcibly dragged into the car. Older adolescents were almost as likely as younger children to be at risk of this type of abuse.

Safe place: Children in this group were abused in what could be considered a safe place—in their own yard, in the park, at the beach, at the community pool, and in the countryside. None of these instances involved penetration or its attempt, although one was life-threatening. Most incidents involved children under the age of eight and most perpetrators were much older than their victims.

Movies: A small number of victims were approached in a movie theater. Perpetrators either purposefully sat beside their victims and fondled them or simply placed the children on their laps. This type of abuse was typically less severe, but the victims were uniformly young, ranging in age from six to nine.

Hitchhiking: A particularly dangerous type of abuse occurred when the victims hitchhiked. In all instances some type of penetration occurred or was attempted, and victims were often physically assaulted, even by multiple perpetrators.

Other: The final group of stranger abuse is the inevitable "other" group. Victims in this group were approached by a taxi driver, Santa Claus, while standing in a crowd, on a subway, while sitting in a parked car waiting for mother to return, during military invasions, and by fake officials.

Acquaintances

Sexual abuse by acquaintances is the single largest category of child sexual abuse, accounting for 16% to 50% of all abuse, depending on how this category is defined (Table 6-1). Although acquaintance rape is now the subject of intensive investigation, the same cannot be said of acquaintance child sexual abuse. Indeed, although this is the most prevalent type of child sexual abuse, not a single study focuses on it. This is a distressing oversight. Of necessity, therefore, the information on acquaintance abuse must again derive from the author's reanalysis of Russell's (1983) community prevalence study.

In this study, abuse by acquaintances was in some ways different from that by strangers, as more than half of all abuse occurred outside the neighborhood, a figure matched only by abuse by authority figures. The mean age of the victim at the time of abuse was 12, although only 9% of this abuse occurred to children younger than 10 years of age. Distribution of age of the perpetrator was bimodal, with one large segment under the age of 15 and another large group between the ages of 41 and 50. This group had the second highest number of multiple perpetrators and one of the higher rates of penetration (61%). Nine percent of perpetrators in this category used a weapon, 13% physically assaulted the victim, and 75% used force or threat. The following categories give more complete descriptions of the types of approaches of acquaintances, again in order by prevalence.

Neighbor: Neighbors marginally represented the largest group of acquaintance abuse. Most of these instances of abuse occurred at the perpetrator's house, more than one-third of which occurred multiple times. Children were enticed with candy, with money, or with activities. Some children were advised not to go, but went anyway out of curiosity. A smaller number of children were abused at a location other than the neighbor's house. In most of these incidents, children were molested by someone in the apartment complex in which the victims lived, and in one-third of these instances, perpetrators simply grabbed the victims in the hall. Most victims were between the ages of five and 10.

House of known person: Another large group of abuse occurred when the victims went to the houses of those they knew. Most of this abuse involved penetration or its attempt. Younger girls were at greatest risk when visiting a girlfriend, where they were abused by one of the girlfriend's relatives (e.g., brother, stepfather, uncle). Adolescent victims, who were at greater risk, typically went with someone else to the house of a male acquaintance. How did these older adolescent girls find themselves in these situations? First, most of the victims were considerably younger than the perpetrators, most of whom were in their twenties or thirties. Another pattern that frequently emerged in the interviews was victims in this, and other, categories describing how young and naive they were. As one victim said, "It was my first awareness that some men are like that, and I shouldn't be so naive—trusting."

Minor role: Another large group of victims was abused by someone in a minor role. Perpetrators included coworkers, customers, shoemakers, recreation center aides, a maid, photographer, person collecting for newspaper money, barber, janitor, delivery man, jeweler, boarder, and ice-cream man. These men used their casual relationships with the victims to gain access.

Safe place: Victims abused in what could be considered a safe place also comprised a large group within acquaintance abuse. Only one of the perpetrators was older than 18 years of age and the average difference between the victims' and perpetrators' ages was three years. Among victims abused in safe places, most were abused while playing in the neighborhood, including at school or at a park. This type of abuse was typically by an older adolescent who either abused the girl "for the sport of it" (see discussion in Chapter 9, "Offenders") or as a deliberate attempt.

Walking: Similar to stranger abuse, several children were abused while walking around or coming home from school. Most often these children were approached by perpetrators who were not in cars. Unlike stranger abuse, however, most assaults did not occur at night, and most of these perpetrators were adolescents. Most incidents occurred during innocuous situations, such as walking on a beach, to church, or to work. This category was particularly severe, as most of the incidents resulted in penetration or its attempt. In a minority of cases, there were multiple abusers, guns were involved, or the victims were physically assaulted.

Parties: A smaller group of abuse occurred when victims went to parties. This abuse was particularly severe, as all involved rape or its attempt. Almost half of the victims were abused by multiple perpetrators, and half of all incidents involved alcohol or drugs. Most perpetrators were in their twenties.

Farm worker: A smaller number of victims were abused by a worker on a farm where the child lived, visited, or was working. Workers on a farm were most likely to fondle their victims on repeated occasions and were usually considerably older.

Other: In the miscellaneous situations, most of which resulted in rape or attempted rape, victims were abused in a car by someone at least 10 years their senior, went for rides with groups of young adult men, were "picked up" at a club or dance, or were so drunk or high that they were incapable of resisting.

Friends of the Family

Six percent of the female respondents in Russell's (1983) survey were abused by friends of the family. Victims were fairly equally distributed in age, and perpetrators were either older adult friends of the victims' parents or younger adolescent friends of a member of the family, usually a sibling. Approximately one-fourth of these incidents resulted in penetration and 40% involved force or threat.

Adult friends—while visiting: About 40% of victims in this group, most of whom were between the ages of eight and 13, were abused while either visiting or being visited by the perpetrator. Dynamics were similar in both situations. Some men had special nonfilial (e.g., godfather) relationships with their victims. Yet, all perpetrators used their special positioning within the family to approach the child.

Adult friend—other location: Another 40% of abuse involved adult family friends who approached young victims at other locations. Victims were approached while attending a funeral, in a barn, at a store, the perpetrator's woodshop, a university, the playground, on a farm, while bicycling, fishing, riding in a car, on a date with the older person, and on a hike.

Adolescent friends of the family or of siblings: A few victims were abused by friends of siblings or adolescent friends of the family. Most victims were young, and perpetrators were usually seven to 10 years older than their victims. Penetration or its attempt was rare and approaches were diverse.

Mother's boyfriend: In this final group, abuse was sometimes very severe. This type of abuse would almost definitely be more prevalent today because of the larger number of divorcees.

Friends

The focus of child sexual abuse is seldom on abuse by friends, perhaps because of the issue of how to separate normal sexual play among peers and abuse. Even though abuse by friends was one of the less prevalent types of abuse in Russell's (1983) study, more than 4% of all respondents in her sample reported a history of this type of abuse. Trend analyses suggested, however, that this abuse was increasing in prevalence at the time of her survey in 1978. While the victim and perpetrator were usually within three years of age of each other, incidents in this category were often as severe as, or more severe than, other types of abuse. Indeed, 61% involved penetration, 11% involved the use of a weapon, and 75% involved force or threat. Abuse by friends was categorized by ages of the victims and perpetrators, as follows.

Victims younger than 14 and perpetrators close in age: Of the incidents of abuse that occurred among victims who were less than 14 years of age and perpetrators who were within three years of the victim's age, a few occurred within the context of some type of contact play situation between the friends (e.g., using wrestling as a method of fondling the victim). More often, however, boys took advantage of more innocuous play situations to fondle their victims.

Wide age disparity: Another prevalent category was abuse by friends more than three years older than the victim. Most of these victims were under the age of 14, and three-fourths of all abuse resulted in penetration or its attempt.

Victims aged 14 or older and perpetrators close in age: In a few cases of abuse, the victims were older than the age of 14, and the perpetrators were within three years of age of the victim. All cases included rape or its attempt, and all were particularly severe.

Romantic/Sexual Partners

Another type of sexual abuse that is more widely discussed in the literature on rape than in child sexual abuse is that of abuse by a romantic or sexual partner. Yet, it remains a significant problem for adolescents, as 7% of all females in Russell's (1983) study were victims of this type of abuse. Further, this abuse (along with abuse by friends) was increasing in the 20 years prior to her survey. This abuse is of great concern because of its severity. Almost every incident involved penetration (as a result of the definition of abuse), and in only one incident was no force used.

Needless to say, this group also included some of the youngest perpetrators and oldest victims.

These cases represent the border between child sexual abuse and adult rape, and the dynamics were often similar to date rape experienced on college campuses. The categories in which the relationships were particularly violent, involving both sexual and physical violence, were also very similar to adult battering relationships. These cases allow us to recognize that child sexual abuse is on a continuum that, in a very gray area, moves into adult rape, sexual assault, and domestic violence. The different types of this abuse, in order by prevalence, are discussed next.

Parking: The most prevalent type of abuse in this category occurred when victims and their dates parked in cars or under similar circumstances. In a third of these cases, perpetrators were significantly older than their victims. Many incidents in this and the following categories were petting situations that went further than the victims wanted. The males forced themselves on their victims, sometimes pinning their hands behind their back or dragging them back into the car when they tried to escape. In many of these cases the perpetrators acted entitled to the sex. Other males raped their victims and then bragged about it at school, which led to further humiliation and degradation of the girls.

Perpetrator's house: A smaller number of victims, most of whom were within three years of age of the perpetrators, were raped when they went to the perpetrators' houses. Often the reasons to visit seemed innocent to the victim, such as to eat lunch or to listen to records.

Husband: Another category of abuse of adolescents younger than the age of 18 is that by husbands. In this small category, relationships were very similar to battering relationships with considerable sexual violence in addition to significant physical violence. In some cases the victims were significantly younger than the perpetrator.

Violent relationship: A few victims were in violent nonmarital relationships in which abuse occurred on multiple occasions. These incidents were similar in dynamics to battering relationships and often included the use of weapons and physical assault. In all incidents the perpetrators were within three years of age of their victim.

Other: Other victims were raped in more diverse situations, including visiting the victim while she was home alone, getting the victim drunk before raping her, attacking her at a friend's house, at or before a party, or deceiving the victim to get her alone. All were violent, and a few involved the purposeful ingestion of drugs or alcohol to render the victim unable to resist.

Authority Figures

Russell's Study

The last category of extrafamilial abuse in Russell's (1983) survey was abuse by authority figures. Overall, 6% of respondents in her study were abused by an authority figure. There is much confusion about what this category means, as exhibited by the conflicting findings in Table 6-2. For the reanalysis of Russell's data, however, it was taken to mean abuse in which the perpetrator had either a specific caretaking, supervisory, or caregiving role with the victim. This category included medical personnel, teachers, clergy, employers, and babysitters. This type of abuse had very different dynamics than many of the other categories of abuse. It was the most likely category to have multiple attacks, but the least likely to have the abuse reported to the police (0%). It was also the least likely to involve penetration or force, and it also had the oldest offenders.

Teachers and tutors: A few teachers abused their students. Although one student was six years of age, the remaining victims were between the ages of 11 and 17. While schoolteachers represented the largest group of perpetrators, other children were abused during private lessons, and one child was abused during summer camp. Much of this abuse occurred multiple times. Teachers gained access to their victims by asking them to stay after school, asking for help cleaning the office, threatening to lower the victim's grades, during daily tickling sessions (for the youngest victim), and when the victim was sent to the office. These situations are all graphic examples of the betrayal of those who should be protecting their charges.

Employers: Of the employers, a fourth were also physicians. Other victims working as babysitters were sleeping over when the father came into the victim's room. Other situations were more diverse.

Medical personnel: Victims abused by medical personnel were typically in their late teens and, as expected, perpetrators were considerably older. Perpetrators included physicians, dentists, and a male nurse. Of the doctors, one gave the victim a pelvic examination inappropriately, one rubbed up against her with an erection when the victim was naked, one used a vibrator inappropriately on the victim, and two fondled the victims during the examination. Two dentists fondled victims during appointments, and one male nurse molested an older adolescent while tending to her when she was gravely ill in a hospital. In no cases did penetration occur or was it attempted.

Babysitters: A few abusers were babysitters, half of whom were female. (Overall, nine of the 462 perpetrators of extrafamilial abuse were female.) The male perpetrators (both adolescent and adult) inflicted severe abuse.

Clergy: In situations in which the victims were abused by officials of the church, they were at greatest risk when they were being transported by the perpetrator, most often to or from church-related activities.

Other Studies on Abuse by Authority Figures

While the reanalysis of Russell's (1983) data provides the only representative sample of abuse by authority figures, some studies on reported abuse by nonrelated caretakers and abuse in day care centers have been done. One of the limitations of retrospective studies such as Russell's is that it is impossible to gather large samples of the rarer types of abuse. Studies of reported abuse, on the other hand, are sometimes able to compile large samples of even a single type of abuse. It must be remembered, however, that reported abuse is in no way representative of all abuse. Regretfully, it is impossible to determine the nature of the bias. With these qualifications, it still remains important to review this literature.

Abuse by Unrelated Caregivers

Margolin and Craft (1989) analyzed a sample of 2,372 substantiated cases of children sexually abused by caregivers, 832 of which were committed by unrelated caregivers. In a later study, Margolin (1991) analyzed those 325 cases of abuse that were not committed by partners of the parent or child care providers working in a licensed day care center. These cases represented 34% of all substantiated abuse committed by nonparental caregivers and 18% of all substantiated abuse.

Abuse by nonparental caregivers was divided into seven separate categories depending on the type of caregiving relationship (Margolin, 1991). These are discussed briefly below.

Regular caregivers (31%): These children were sexually abused by nonrelated caregivers, selected by the parents, who routinely cared for the child for pay, often in the child's home. This was the only caregiving arrangement in which female caregivers had substantial representation among the offenders, accounting for 36% of the abuse. Female caregiver offenders tended to abuse male children more often (55%), whereas male offenders abused female children more often (69%). A second distinctive characteristic of this abuse was the youth of the caregiver, with a mean age of 17 years.

Ad hoc caregivers (8%): These caregivers were used to help out in single, pressing situations. While this person was occasionally engaged because the parent was in a crisis situation, the caregiver was used more often for more mundane reasons. Often the children were not watched in their home. In this category, 88% of the offenders were male and 60% of the victims were female.

Sleep-over (6%): Sexual abuse in this category occurred during a sleep-over at a friend's house. All but one of the offenders were male, most of whom were father figures or hired caregivers. In no instance was a mother figure present.

Friends and relatives of regular caregivers (16%): This category included children abused by friends or relatives of the regular caregiver. Because of their relation to the caregiver, they were often in contact with the victim, even helping out with caregiving tasks. Most were husbands, sons, or boyfriends of the caregiver. In almost a quarter of these cases, the caregivers were aware of a previous history of child abuse, although they did not tell the parents.

Family friend (9%): In abuse by family friends, parents were often instrumental in arranging visits because the adult friend was seen as a positive role model for the child. Caregivers were usually not paid for their caregiving, but instead were assumed to be motivated by their affection for the child. Children often agreed to the contact because they received gifts or engaged in enjoyable activities.

Live-in caregiver (8%): These offenders, who were most often the parents' friend, were living at the victim's house. Parents in many of these houses were either aware of the offender's prior criminal record or knew that he had previously made a sexual advance towards the child.

Child's adult friend (6%)[4]: These offenders had befriended the child without the parent's assistance, often by offering some type of reward or pleasurable activity to the child.

---

[4]   Another 16% of children were abused in other situations.

In this study, abuse by female caretakers was typically confined to a single caregiving arrangement—that of regular caregiving (Margolin, 1991), whereas abuse by males occurred in a variety of situations. It is of significance that in a field where female caregivers predominate, males were responsible for 84% of the abuse. There was a small percentage (17%) of cases, however, in which female caregivers were indirectly responsible for the abuse by allowing their relatives and friends who were known to be at risk to sexually offend to be in contact with the child. Parents were also partially responsible in some cases for ignoring their child's disclosure of sexual abuse (in 3% of the cases), or by knowingly allowing a caregiver with a history of child molestation to care for the child (in 11% of the cases). This final finding at first glance speaks of gross negligence on the part of the parents. Margolin, however, suggests another alternative:

> While it is possible that parents' failure to protect their children stemmed from complacency or indifference, a second possibility is that parents had no one else with whom to leave their children. This implies that efforts to combat sexual abuse by nonrelated caregivers must not only consider the importance of alerting parents to the contingencies of this abuse... but also, that more resources need to be devoted to making safe and affordable child care alternatives available to them. (p. 220)

Finally, a related study of reported abuse found that children were at an exceptionally high risk with adolescent nonfamilial male caretakers (Margolin & Craft, 1990). Male nonrelated babysitters abused children three times more often than male siblings and five times more often than female babysitters. Further, adolescents accounted for 44% of all cases of child sexual abuse among nonparental caregivers. More importantly, male nonrelated adolescents accounted for 14% of *all* cases of child sexual abuse by caregivers (including abuse by parents). As has been found in other types of abuse, the younger abusers also committed the more severe abuse (Margolin & Craft, 1989, 1990). If one considers the number of male babysitters used versus female babysitters and the amount of time a babysitter takes care of children versus the time a parental figure watches the children, one can understand the significant threat that male adolescent caregivers pose to children.

Sexual Abuse in Day Care Centers and Homes

A small number of studies have analyzed reported abuse occurring in day care centers. The largest is by Finkelhor, Williams, and Burns (1988), who attempted to identify all cases of sexual abuse reported nationwide for a three-year period. In 270 different facilities nationwide, sexual abuse was substantiated for a total of 1,639 victims. They estimated that, over a three-year period, approximately 2,500 children were abused in daycare centers.

Cases were classified into four major types according to the number and identity of perpetrators (Finkelhor et al., 1988), including abuse by child-care workers alone (35%), abuse by peripheral staff or outsiders (13%), abuse by families of staff alone (25%), and multiple perpetrators (17%). The remainder were unclassifiable. In 38% of these facilities, the perpetrators were not child-care workers. As with most abuse, males were the primary offenders, and females were the primary victims. Female offenders abused primarily when accompanied by a male.

The most serious cases were those that involved multiple perpetrators and multiple children (Finkelhor el al., 1988). These cases also had the youngest children, the most serious sexual activities, and the highest likelihood of pornographic production, drug use, or ritual abuse. Abuse was quite severe with at least one child being raped in 93% of the facilities. Interestingly, two-thirds of the abuse occurred around toileting. The overall impression of the authors was that victims of abuse in day care centers were more threatened, coerced, and terrorized than victims of other types of sexual abuse.

Most abuse had been going on for six months before the child told, with immediate disclosure occurring in only 20% of cases (Finkelhor et al., 1988). Instead, parents' questions about suspicious behavior most often led to disclosure. As is typical of other populations, few characteristics of the child, excluding gender, appeared to be related to risk of abuse other than possibly how attractive the child was. Certain factors were associated, however, with less severity of abuse, including being in a high-crime, inner-city neighborhood and having a large staff. Facilities in which parents had more ready access to their child also had less risk of severe abuse.

Another study of 48 children abused in day care settings divided the sites into day care centers (which accounted for 75% of the abuse) and day care homes (Faller, 1988). Day care centers were further divided into multi-perpetrator centers (61% of all centers) and single-perpetrator centers. Boys and girls in day care centers with multiple offenders had approximately an equal chance of being victimized, almost always by more than one offender (often male and female). In these centers, numerous serious threats were made to the children. Boys and girls in centers with only one perpetrator were equally likely to be victims, but they were always abused by only one man who usually provided a peripheral service to the center. There were seldom threats. Children abused in day care homes were almost always female and experienced the least number of forms of sexual abuse.

In comparing these studies, males accounted for 60% of the offenders in Finkelhor et al.'s study (1988), whereas males were involved in 98% of all abuse in Faller's study (1988) (although females were listed as co-offenders in approximately half of the abuse).[6] Considering that male caretakers comprised only about 5% of the staff in one study (Finkelhor et al., 1988), it is remarkable that males are responsible for so much of the abuse. Conversely, most victims were female (Faller, 1988; Finkelhor et al., 1988), with girls being at greatest risk in day care homes (Faller, 1988). Most victims experienced multiple types of abuse (e.g., fondling, intercourse, etc.), more than half were involved in group sex, and just less than half were involved in exploitation (usually photography for pornographic purposes) (Faller, 1988). Threats were common and were used most frequently at the sites with multiple offenders (Faller, 1988; Finkelhor et al., 1988).

In summary, while reported cases of abuse in day care situations are rarely reported, this abuse is often more severe than in other types of sexual abuse, with a

---

[6]   In the final chapter, "Conclusions," however, it is shown that child protective services frequently charges female caregivers as co-offenders even when they never physically perpetrate the abuse.

small portion of these victims being subjected to heinous abuse. As these children are so young, this is a particularly difficult type of abuse to comprehend.

Abuse by Teachers

Two recent studies have considered the issue of abuse by teachers. One study, which surveyed 494 teachers in New York, found that 24% of teachers were aware that an allegation of sexual abuse had been made against a teacher in their school district within the previous year (Anderson & Levine, 1999). Fifty-six percent of teachers reported that they were aware that a *false* allegation of abuse had been made against a teacher in their school district in the last few years. This is an interesting wording of the question asked of respondents, because these researchers never asked whether teachers were aware of *true* allegations of abuse—only *false* allegations. Further, more than half of the teachers believed that it was probable or somewhat probable that students make allegations against teachers and that allegations might even be brought against themselves. A primary focus of the paper by Anderson and Levine was whether teachers might limit contact with students based upon fears of false allegations of abuse.

The other recent study surveyed affiliates of the Ontario Teachers' Federation to determine their knowledge of abuse allegations (Dolmage, 1995). A total of 47 incidents involving elementary schoolteachers, only one of which involved a female teacher, were known to these affiliates over a five-year period. Of the 38 cases that had gone to court, only 16 resulted in convictions. While the researchers argue that the acquittal rates are far in excess of what would be expected, it is shown in Chapter 9, "Offenders," that less than 20% of *substantiated* abuse in the United States leads to convictions and that 2% or less of abuse known to or suspected by professionals leads to conviction. That this study found a conviction rate of 42% of alleged abuse is instead quite remarkable. Even so, Dolmage concludes from this study that "a number of teachers are falsely accused each year" (p. 137).

While the issue of false allegations by children cannot be dismissed, a review of the literature on false disclosures in Chapter 11, "Professional Response to Child Sexual Abuse," indicates that only approximately 1% to 5% of all disclosures made by children are false. Thus, it is of concern that both studies instead appear to assume that false disclosures are prevalent. Further, ignoring his finding that 95% of allegations were made against male teachers—which is exactly the proportion of male offenders in the general population (Finkelhor et al., 1990; Russell, 1983; Wyatt, 1985)—Dolmage (1995) instead calls for procedures to "protect innocent [*male and female*] teachers from character assassination" (p. 138). Yet, he fails to question why 95% of those needing such protection are male. Again, this is not to ignore the troubling issue of occasional false disclosures, but it is instead to suggest that a logical alternative hypothesis in both of these studies is that most allegations of sexual abuse against teachers are probably true, regardless of whether the teachers are convicted.

SUMMARY AND CONCLUSIONS

One of the most outstanding findings of this analysis of extrafamilial abuse is of the pervasiveness and omnipresence of the threat of extrafamilial abuse. Seventy-one percent to 89% of all child sexual abuse is by nonrelatives, the most common type of which is abuse by an acquaintance. Yet, virtually every type of extrafamilial relationship is amply represented in offender populations, including abuse by friends, dates, strangers, authority figures, and friends of the family. Further, approximately 95% of all extrafamilial abuse perpetrators are male (Finkelhor et al., 1990; Russell, 1983; Wyatt, 1985). Thus, female and male children remain at high risk of abuse in virtually every category of nonfilial male relationship. This multiplicity of relationships complicates the ability of programs to adequately protect children from these diverse offenders.

Yet, the pervasiveness of the threat of extrafamilial abuse can only be fully understood when also recognizing its diversity of location and dynamics. For example, a population of identified offenders (Elliott et al., 1995) approached children in each of the following (and often multiple) locations: offender's home (39%), child's home (51%), outdoors (56%), friend's house (87%), child's neighborhood (94%), and vehicle (96%). These findings are confined to populations of identified offenders. In random population surveys reporting on unidentified offenders, Wyatt (1985) found that approximately a fourth of all abuse occurred at the victim's home. Yet, both Russell (as analyzed by Bolen, 2000a) and Wyatt found that victims were at high risk in each of the following locations: walking in the neighborhood or to or from school, in public locations within and outside of the neighborhood, at the perpetrator's house (usually a known other), and in a vehicle. Thus, no location appears to be safe.

Another indication of the pervasiveness of the threat of extrafamilial abuse is the multitude of approaches of the offenders. In the study of identified offenders by Elliott et al. (1995), the following strategies were commonly employed: using play or teaching activities (47%); babysitting (52%); transportation (54%); bribes, outings, or providing affection, understanding, and love (70%); gaining trust of the whole family (80%); stories, lies, magic, or treasure hunts (86%); and asking the child for help (91%). These findings are corroborated by prevalence-level data. In the author's (Bolen, 2000a) secondary analysis of Russell's (1983) survey, 66 methods of approach by extrafamilial abuse offenders were categorized. All attempts to collapse these dynamics into coherent groups were unsuccessful. Types of approaches in which 10 or more cases were involved included approaching the child while alone, while playing, while walking, when visiting the perpetrator, while parking in a car, asking if the child wanted a ride, coming into the child's room, and taking the child to the offender's house. On the other hand, these cases accounted for only 40% of the extrafamilial abuse cases, and most cases defied categorization.

As extraordinary as the pervasiveness and threat of extrafamilial abuse are, another equally extraordinary finding is that we know so little about this type of abuse. No studies focus specifically on the most prevalent type of abuse—that by an acquaintance—nor do any studies address other prevalent types of extrafamilial abuse, including abuse by friends, dates (specific to minors), family friends, and authority figures. Indeed, the available literature on extrafamilial abuse pertains to ritual abuse, abuse of children in day care centers, child pornography or prostitution, and abuse of institutionalized children, some of whom are abused intrafamilially. Yet, these types of abuse account for only a tiny fraction of extrafamilial abuse.

It is phenomenal that, 20 years into the serious study of child sexual abuse, we have so little literature on extrafamilial abuse. The only information available on the dynamics of this type of abuse, other than that in Russell's (1983) now dated study, is that which derives from identified victim and offender populations. Certainly, this is an important knowledge base, and it deserves recognition for its contributions. Yet, because this literature base utilizes nonrandom identified populations, it has to be considered fundamentally biased. Further, the literature on offenders seldom attempts to account for the different types of extrafamilial abuse, instead dividing offenders by motivation or other characteristics that designate the typologies. Again, these typologies are essential to our understanding of identified offender populations, but they focus primarily on identified offenders with known pedophilic arousal patterns for children. Yet, as argued in Chapter 9, "Offenders," there is likely a large population of extrafamilial abuse offenders these typologies do not recognize—offenders who abuse as extremes of socialization patterns. This substantial group of offenders in Russell's (1983) survey abused for sport, as a means of conquest, and through a sense of entitlement. It is certain that our literature resulting from identified offender populations maintains other biases as well, such as focusing on the worst and most prolific offenders.

Further, this literature does not explain, for example, the differences between the approaches of neighbors versus acquaintances versus dates. As with intrafamilial abuse, a literature base that explicates the dynamics of different types of extrafamilial abuse is essential to understand the varied approaches. Further, these types of studies are a necessary prerequisite for developing adequate prevention programs. Until we recognize that we identify and incarcerate only a tiny and extremely unrepresentative fraction of extrafamilial abuse offenders, we will not have the national urgency to address the challenging prevention issues brought forth by this still undeveloped knowledge base. Hence, the most critical problem in the area of extrafamilial abuse is still the lack of information, which not surprisingly contributes to misconceptions, biased policies, ineffective primary prevention programs, and unrealistic optimism.

RECOMMENDATIONS

Recommendations are threefold. First, we need to improve the knowledge base on extrafamilial abuse. This chapter has stressed the weakness of our knowledge base in the area of extrafamilial abuse, especially given that it is the most prevalent type of child sexual abuse. Research is needed to fill this void. We also need to develop a better understanding of the different motivations and modus operandi for the different types of offenders for both male and female victims. Professionals cannot be expected to develop adequate prevention programs until this knowledge base is available. We also cannot rely on literature on adult rape by acquaintances and dates to understand the unique dynamics that apply to approaches of children and adolescents. This lack of an adequate knowledge base of extrafamilial abuse is one of the most striking weaknesses of the literature base and is profoundly related to society's inability to adequately identify, assess, and treat victims of extrafamilial abuse. This type of research needs to become a national funding priority.

Second, we need a better method of identifying, assessing, and treating victims of extrafamilial abuse. In a child protection system beset with perhaps insolvable funding problems, calling for more seems somewhat foolhardy. On the other hand, calling for anything less than a system designed to protect *all* children from child sexual abuse is untenable. The addition of extrafamilial abuse cases will almost definitely require a complete overhaul of the already overburdened child protection system. Yet, extrafamilial abuse victims deserve the same accessibility to services that identify, assess, treat, and protect victims.

Third, we need to define risk factors at the level of society that clarify why so many children are abused extrafamilially. As discussed in this chapter, a focus on intrafamilial abuse leads primarily to a discourse on family dynamics, whereas a focus on extrafamilial abuse leads to a discourse on societal factors that place so many children at risk of abuse. This change in focal point is absolutely critical to adequately protect *all* children.

In sum, professionals must recognize extrafamilial abuse for what it is—the most prevalent type of child sexual abuse. Recognizing it as such, professionals then need to attend to it with the same vigor and passion—through research and policy decisions—as we attend to intrafamilial abuse. In short, we need to insist that *all* victims of child sexual abuse have equal access to the identification of the abuse, assessment, and treatment. To make this available, research should target extrafamilial abuse, and policies should be redefined to be inclusive of victims of extrafamilial abuse.

CHAPTER 7
INTRAFAMILIAL ABUSE

INTRODUCTION

Intrafamilial abuse, or incest, is abuse by a relative.[1] Most often when we consider incest, we think about fathers as the offenders. Siblings, uncles, and cousins also abuse with some regularity, however, with lesser levels of abuse by grandfathers and other male relatives. Of all types of incest, abuse by a female perpetrator is the least common (Finkelhor, Hotaling, Lewis, & Smith, 1990; Russell, 1983; Wyatt, 1985).

The purpose of this chapter is to introduce these types of child sexual abuse, discuss their dynamics, and compare prevailing notions about incest to the empirical literature. One of the most common misconceptions is that incest is more prevalent than extrafamilial abuse. The previous chapter argued instead that extrafamilial abuse accounts for approximately 70% of abuse. This chapter continues this discussion by comparing prevalence-level data to incidence-level data, that is, all committed intrafamilial abuse is compared to only that intrafamilial abuse that is reported and substantiated. Doing so provides an analysis of how well professionals are identifying, assessing, and treating victims of intrafamilial abuse. This section also continues to highlight society's preoccupation with and prioritization of incest.

The next sections turn to developing a deeper understanding of intrafamilial abuse. First, the important theories that help to frame our understanding of incest are discussed, followed by an explication of the dynamics of families in which incest occurs. Because of the societal emphasis on father-daughter incest, these sections are disproportionately represented by the empirical and theoretical literature discussing father-daughter incest. The final sections then evaluate the literature base on intrafamilial abuse. The primary question addressed in these sections is whether what we think we know about intrafamilial abuse (i.e., theories of incest) is adequately supported by what we really know (i.e., the empirical literature). In addressing this question, some of the prevailing notions about intrafamilial abuse are compared to the empirical literature. This section suggests that some of what we think we know still bears little resemblance to what we do know. The final section discusses the implications for major findings in this chapter.

INCIDENCE AND PREVALENCE: A COMPARISON

Tables 7-1 and 7-2 provide information on the scope of the problem of intrafamilial abuse. Table 7-1 compares the percentage of intrafamilial abuse incidents by perpetrator to all incidents of abuse, whereas Table 7-2 provides prevalence estimates by type of intrafamilial abuse perpetrators. Both tables utilize the minimal data available from random community, state, and national prevalence studies.

---

[1] Incest and intrafamilial abuse are used interchangeably in this chapter.

TABLE 7-1. Percentage of Intrafamilial Abuse Incidents to All Child Sexual Abuse by Relationship of Perpetrator to Victim

Relationship	Russell, 1983 F	LATP, 1985[a] M	LATP, 1985[a] F	Saunders et al., 1992 F	Siegel et al., 1987 M	Siegel et al., 1987 F	Wyatt, 1985 Cauc. F	Wyatt, 1985 A/A F
Natural parent	4%[b]		3%	8%[c]		11%[c]	2%	1%
Step-parent	3%		3%				4%	9%
Grandparent	1%		2%					1%
Sibling	4%	1%	2%				3%	3%
Uncle	7%	5%	14%				6%	7%
Cousin	4%	5%	5%				4%	8%
Other	4%			32%	12%	9%		
Female	1%							
Total	29%[d]	11%	29%	40%	12%	20%	19%	29%

Note. F = female; M = male; A/A = African American.
[a] The LATP (*Los Angeles Times* Poll survey) was reanalyzed by Finkelhor et al., 1990. [b] Both an adoptive and a foster father were also included in this category. [c] Includes all father figures. [d] Does not add up due to rounding.

    As shown in Table 7-1, intrafamilial abuse accounts for only a minority (11% to 40%) of all child sexual abuse. What is more informative about this table, however, is its comparison of the percentages of abuse by types of intrafamilial offenders. Abuse by uncles is most prevalent, accounting for approximately 25% to 50% of all intrafamilial abuse. The only exception is African Americans in Wyatt's (1985) study, in which the primary type of abuse was by step-parents. Cousins and father figures are the second most prevalent offenders, followed by more distant relatives and siblings. Abuse by a grandfather is more rare, but the rarest type is abuse by a female perpetrator of any relationship. Finally, this table suggests that intrafamilial abuse of males accounts for only 11% to 12% of all abuse, which is lower than the comparable percentages for females (24% to 40%). Although males remain at risk of abuse by uncles and cousins, the risk of abuse by a parental figure diminishes perceptibly.

    Table 7-2 compares the prevalence of abuse, by type of perpetrator, for the two random prevalence studies reporting this information (or for which it could be computed), and provides summary information for Wyatt et al.'s (1999) study. Because Russell (1986) captured all incidents of abuse, as compared to only a single incident in the *Los Angeles Times* Poll survey (LATP), her data are probably more accurate. In her study, the threat of abuse by uncles, male cousins, and father figures is obvious, as 3% or more of all respondents were abused by each of these types of perpetrators. Abuse by siblings and more distant relatives represented a somewhat lesser risk. Overall, approximately 2% of males and 8% to 16% of females experience intrafamilial abuse as children (Finkelhor et al., 1990; Russell, 1983; Wyatt, 1985; Wyatt et al., 1999). In sum, these tables indicate that, while intrafamilial abuse is not as prevalent as extrafamilial abuse, that by uncles, cousins, fathers, siblings, and more distant relatives remains a significant risk for children, especially females.

TABLE 7-2. Prevalence (Percentage) of All Respondents Abused by Type of Intrafamilial Abuse

Relationship	Wyatt et al., 1999	Russell, 1986 Female	LATP, 1985[a] Male	LATP, 1985[a] Female
Natural parent		3.0		.8
Step-parent		1.7		.8
Grandparent		.9		.5
Sibling		2.2	.2	.5
Uncle		4.9	.7	3.9
Cousin		3.0	.7	1.4
Other		2.7		
Female		.4		
Total prevalence	12	16	1.6	8.0

[a] The *Los Angeles Times* Poll survey was reanalyzed by Finkelhor et al., 1990.

By comparing prevalence-level data shown in the previous two tables to incidence-level data reported in the NIS-3 (Sedlak & Broadhurst, 1996), we also gain a perspective of how well professionals are identifying cases of intrafamilial abuse. Prevalence-level data suggest that 7% to 8% of all abuse is committed by parental figures (Russell, 1984; Wyatt, 1985).[2] Yet in 1993, 29% of all cases of child sexual abuse identified by authorities were perpetrated by a natural parent, and 25% of all cases were perpetrated by step-parents.

There are at least two explanations for the enormous discrepancies between incidence-level and prevalence-level data. First, although it defies credibility, it is conceivable that abuse by natural parents has increased astronomically since the mid-1980s when the last prevalence-level data for intrafamilial abuse are available. An increase of such proportions over such a short period of time, however, seems entirely implausible. The second, more logical explanation is that these differences reflect systemic biases that prioritize parental incest. As discussed in previous chapters, it is likely that historic patterns of prioritizing intrafamilial abuse—and especially father-daughter incest—have led to these systemic biases.

THEORIES OF INTRAFAMILIAL ABUSE

This section now turns to a discussion of theories that frame our understanding of intrafamilial abuse. One of the interesting aspects of theories of intrafamilial abuse is that they exist at all. That they exist suggests that there is an entrenched belief that incest is qualitatively different from child sexual abuse as a whole. Otherwise, theories that discuss the etiology of child sexual abuse would be sufficient to explain incest.

---

[2] This range is more accurate than that in Table 7-1 because it is based upon all *incidents* of abuse (as compared to all *victims* of abuse as shown in Table 7-1).

Theories pertaining to child sexual abuse as a whole typically target reasons that motivate potential offenders to actually engage in an offense. In contrast, theories that address intrafamilial abuse are far more likely to focus on family dynamics, often suggesting that family dysfunction contributes to the intrafamilial abuse. This important shift in focus thus tends to minimize the responsibility of the incest offender. Even today the dynamics of the family in which incest occurs sometimes receive as much focus as does the behavior of the offender, and papers continue to be published about the "incestuous family" (Alexander & Schaeffer, 1994; Greenspun, 1994), as if the family itself were incestuous rather than just the offender. Another negative effect of emphasizing family dynamics in intrafamilial abuse is that the offending behavior is then set apart from other types of child sexual abuse. Conte (1991) expresses this opinion:

> One erroneous idea about the nature of sexual abuse it that incest is a unique clinical problem. Incest offenders have long been believed to represent a clinical problem distinct from and different from nonincestuous offenders (i.e., pedophiles). This belief is at the foundation of current social policy, which tends to support community-based treatment for the incest offender who is not regarded as dangerous to society as a whole...all family views of the problem rest on two key assumptions: Incestuous fathers and stepfathers do not act out sexually outside of the home, and incest is the sexual expression of non-sexual needs. (p. 6)

This chapter argues instead that intrafamilial abuse is simply one type of sexual abuse. As will be shown, the dynamics of father-daughter incest are not substantially different from those of abuse by siblings or uncles, which are not substantially different from dynamics of abuse by other intrafamilial offenders. Perhaps the most delimiting characteristic of intrafamilial abuse is simply that the child is more accessible. The following sections discuss the leading theories of intrafamilial abuse, primarily father-daughter incest, followed by a review of the empirical literature for the different types of intrafamilial abuse. A final section then briefly assesses the validity of the various theories of intrafamilial abuse.

Sociobiological Theory

Westermarck was the first to develop a biological hypothesis for incest avoidance (Erickson, 1993; Wolf, 1993). In the late 1800s, he proposed that individuals who lived in close proximity during childhood developed an innate aversion to sexual intercourse with those persons. Freud, on the other hand, believed that humans had inherent incestuous tendencies and that the repression of these impulses led to a universal neurosis which he labeled the Oedipus complex (Erickson, 1993). In more recent work, both Parker and Parker (1986) and Erickson (1993) have advanced an approach to incest avoidance that considers the quality of the attachment bond in intrafamilial relationships. Specifically, Erickson suggests that secure attachment among family members is "the foundation of adaptive kin-directed behavior, including incest avoidance" (p. 413). Conversely, individuals with more insecure familial bonds are hypothesized to be more likely to engage in incestuous behaviors. Further, incest is hypothesized to be most likely between individuals with no familial bond. Parker and Parker, in applying this theory to father-daughter incest, suggest that fathers who are more involved in the early care of their daughters are less likely to commit incest.

Family Systems Theory/Functional Theory

Family systems theory is most concerned with dynamics of families in which incest occurs. This theory proposes that incest begins because of the dysfunctional dynamics within this family (Alexander, 1985) and that incest is a symptom of the more pervasive pathology within the family (Coleman & Collins, 1990). Once incest begins, it is then maintained by the family in a circular and reciprocal process (Larson & Maddock, 1986) as a homeostatic device (Levang, 1989). Thus, incest is assumed to serve some type of function within the family setting (Greenspun, 1994). (See Chapter 3 for a more lengthy discussion of this theory.)

Larson and Maddock (1986) have proposed a series of four different types of patterns in intrafamilial abuse, all of which serve some type of family function. The affection-exchange family has a high need for expression and nurturance, and the sexual abuse is hypothesized to serve the function of providing this need for affection. This family system is considered to be the most prevalent for families of intrafamilial abuse (Trepper & Niedner, 1996). The second group, the erotic-exchange family, is one in which interactions among various family members are sexualized, and the sexual abuse is simply an extension of family norms. The aggression-exchange family instead interacts in a negative and hostile manner, with abuse often occurring as a form of punishment or humiliation. The final rage-expression family has the most dramatic cases of abuse in which physical and sadistic abuses occur. Trepper and Niedner state that "this type of abuse never appears to be consensual" (p. 397). Yet, it is hard to imagine a case in which a child could conceivably consent to the abuse. Even children who agree to participate are not assumed to have given consent, simply because they do not have that power.

The functional model of intrafamilial abuse has a number of drawbacks. First, as will be shown throughout this chapter, it has only minimal empirical support. Second, it does not adequately explain why intrafamilial abuse occurs in only some families in which these dynamics are present. Third, while more recent writings in family systems theory are careful to state that the offender is responsible for the incest, theories that continue to attribute the instigation of the abuse to family dynamics simply dilute that statement of responsibility. Finally, this functional model ignores the fact that approximately 95% of intrafamilial abuse is perpetrated by males (Finkelhor et al., 1990; Russell, 1983; Wyatt, 1985). Why only males act out the dysfunction in families is never addressed by family systems theory.

Attachment Theory

Attachment may also be an important factor that places children at greater or lesser risk of child sexual abuse. Alexander (1992) was the first to discuss the relevance of attachment to intrafamilial sexual abuse, specifically father-daughter incest. She believes that insecure attachment is a general risk factor that places children at greater risk of sexual abuse (Alexander & Anderson, 1998). Further, she believes that the type of insecure attachment is related to specific dynamics within the "incestuous" family (p. 347). She categorizes families in which incest occurs by type of attachment, either dismissing/avoidant, anxious/ambivalent, or disorganized.

In families whose members are dismissing/avoidant, she suggests that the incestuous father is more authoritarian and that the mother is neither available nor empathetic to the child (Alexander & Anderson, 1998). The rejection the child experiences in this family sets the stage for the initiation of the abuse and the interference with its termination. In families whose members are anxious/ambivalent, Alexander believes that role reversal is an important dynamic. Thus, offenders have an expectation that their sexual and emotional needs will be met. Nonoffending guardians, because of their excessive dependency and problems with self-protection, are less able to attend to their children's needs. These children, in turn, may be more vulnerable to abuse because of their coyness that characterizes their attempts to coerce or control others. Finally, disorganized offenders may have minimal impulse control, whereas disorganized nonoffending mothers may be inaccessible to their children because of their mothers' tendency to flee the alarmed child. Alexander also recognizes that securely attached children might be abused intrafamilially, although she suggests that the circumstances would be extenuating.

Alexander's work (1992; Alexander & Anderson, 1998) is important because it provides a theoretical rationale for incest that is far less biased than family systems theory. As the presentation of her hypotheses currently stand, however, they are not yet complex enough to capture what is known about child sexual abuse and attachment. First, the attachment literature acknowledges that parents can have different attachment styles (Fox, Kimmerley, & Schafer, 1991). Thus, a mother may be dismissing, whereas the father may be avoidant. The second important weakness in the presentation of her current hypotheses is that the theory continues to pathologize the nonoffending mother. In all categories, Alexander discusses how nonoffending mothers, by nature of their insecure attachments, are not supportive of their abused children. Instead, the empirical literature finds that the majority of nonoffending guardians are supportive (Bolen, 2000a). Thus, it is of concern that this literature continues the pejorative emphasis on nonoffending guardians. Finally, attachment theory does not adequately explain why some insecurely attached fathers succumb to incest whereas others do not, nor why some insecurely attached fathers succumb, whereas insecurely attached mothers do not.

Feminist Theory of Male Dominance

The final theory to be discussed is feminist theory. This theory proposes that incest, as well as all child sexual abuse, is symptomatic of a society in which patriarchal norms are the standard (Coleman & Collins, 1990). As Waldby et al. (1989) state, "patriarchy is the world view that seeks to create and maintain male control over females—it is a system of male supremacy" (p. 97). Thus, feminists believe that sexual assault, one form of which is child sexual abuse, is intrinsic to and derivative of a system of male supremacy (Dominelli, 1989; Herman, 1990). As Herman (1981) states:

Whereas male supremacy creates the social conditions that favor the development of father-daughter incest, the sexual division of labor creates the psychological conditions that lead to the same result. Male supremacy invests fathers with immense powers over their children, especially their daughters. The sexual division of labor, in which women nurture children and men do not, produces fathers who are predisposed to use their powers exploitatively. The rearing of children by subordinate women ensures the reproduction in each generation of the psychology of male supremacy. It produces sexually aggressive men with little capacity to nurture, nurturant women with undeveloped sexual capacities, and children of both sexes who stand in awe of the power of fathers. (p. 62)

Because the family in a patriarchal society is defined as private space under the rule of male control, the powerless and dependent position of the members of the family is exacerbated (Dinsmore, 1991). Access to information is also controlled largely by the father, which results in an increase in paternal power. The father's exercise of power, however, is supposedly tempered by trust, with a resultant expectation by the powerless members of the family that they will be protected by the powerful father (Dominelli, 1989). When incest occurs, the failure of the father to live up to this expectation is a betrayal of that trust and an abuse of that power.

Within families, rigid delineations of gender structured along traditional lines are posited (Herman, 1981). As a result, "mothers are usually rendered powerless" (Coleman & Collins, 1990, p. 340) through any of several means, including having a higher than average number of children, being less educated than average, being economically dependent on their spouses, or being controlled by husbands through isolation or physical force. Once incest ensues, it then becomes an organizing force behind the family's pattern of interaction (Carter, Papp, Silverstein, & Walters, 1986). Thus, feminists believe that incest is a result of the power imbalance within the family and the misuse of that power.

Finally, feminists believe that the offender "is not the product of a disturbed or dysfunctional family and may be as normal or abnormal as the rest of the so-called normal population" (Rush, 1980, p. 2). Hence, incest is conceptualized as an exaggerated result of normative behaviors and beliefs for males within society (Dinsmore, 1991). The question posed by feminists is not why some men abuse, but why all men do not (Herman, 1990).

Summary

These four theories suggest different dynamics that lead to abuse. Sociobiological theory suggests that a lack of intimate connection when the child is very young places that child at greater risk of abuse. Family systems theory instead suggests that an environment of dysfunction is necessary—and causal—to incest, which is then conceptualized as a dynamic meeting some function within the family. Alternately, attachment theory posits that insecure attachment and the resultant family dynamics set the stage for the incest. Finally, feminist theory suggests that incest remains an issue of patriarchal power, with males given entitlement over females.

The next sections review the dynamics of abuse by different family members. One purpose of this review is to investigate empirical support for these theories. After presenting these types of abuse, a later section compares the empirical literature with the theoretical literature.

TYPES OF INCEST

Parental Abuse

Parental abuse, especially father-daughter incest, has received more attention than any other type of child sexual abuse, partially as a result of its historical emphasis and more recently as a result of its prioritization in systems designed to identify and assess child sexual abuse. Consequently, the literature base on parental abuse is so extensive that it cannot be reviewed comprehensively in the short space available. Instead, this review focuses on some of the most important assumptions of the theories presented.

Physical Environment of the Family

The most outstanding characteristic of parental sexual abuse is that approximately 99% is perpetrated by fathers or father figures (Finkelhor et al., 1990; Russell, 1983; Wyatt, 1985). The second most outstanding characteristic is that females are at greatly increased risk of sexual abuse. Indeed, in a study of 1,145 adult men and 1,481 women randomly sampled from a national population, not a single male was abused in childhood by a father or father figure, whereas approximately 25 females were abused (Finkelhor et al., 1990). Further, no males or females were abused by a mother or mother figure. Racial differences also exist. African American females appear to be especially vulnerable to stepfather abuse (Wyatt, 1985), a finding that may simply represent their greater likelihood of having a stepfather.

While it is now well known that primarily males abuse primarily females, it is important to stress the theoretical implications of this finding. A close inspection of the theories of father-daughter incest indicates that most of these theories are nongendered. As an example, although family systems theory states that dysfunctional dynamics within the family are causal to incest, it never specifically addresses why these dysfunctional dynamics manifest in abuse by the father instead of the mother. What deters mothers in these same dysfunctional families from abusing? That parental abuse is almost exclusively committed by fathers requires some justification. Yet, the only theory that does so is feminist theory. This theory proposes that the unequal power structures favoring males explains why parental incest is almost exclusively committed by fathers.

Power, Control, and Domination

Feminist theory also posits that incest is an abuse not only of power, but of a powerful, dominant, and controlling patriarch (Herman, 1981). A large body of empirical literature supports this dynamic, as other types of violence frequently co-exist with the incest. Indeed, many victims are also physically abused (Herman, 1981;

Sirles, Smith, & Kusama, 1989), and domestic violence also occurs in many of these families (Sirles & Franke, 1989; Williams & Finkelhor, 1990). For example, Alexander and Schaeffer (1994) found high levels of physical violence in more than half of the families of origin of adult survivors of intrafamilial abuse. In 90% of these high-violence families, the father was the primary perpetrator of violence. In some families, an older son might also be sexually abusing the victim or another sister. Indeed, one study found that abuse by a brother was preceded by father-daughter incest in one-third of the families in which sibling abuse occurred (Smith & Israel, 1987). High levels of domination and control are also found in families in which father-daughter incest occurs (Dadds, Smith, Webber, & Robinson, 1991; Herman, 1981). Thus, father-daughter incest is only one type of violence and control perpetrated by the male members of these families.

Stressors within the Family

Feminist theory also suggests that power imbalances within the family contribute to an unduly large number of stressors. Indeed, families of father-daughter incest have greater than the national norm of children (Anderson & Shafer, 1979; Herman, 1981; Owen & Steele, 1991), and the pregnancies are not always the choice of the mother (Herman, 1981). Traditional divisions of labor are also typical (Herman, 1981), with families having structured and even rigid roles and responsibilities (Dadds et al., 1991). As such, mothers in these families are the primary caregivers and maintain primary responsibility for household tasks. Yet, they are often emotionally and socially isolated (Herman, 1981; Williams & Finkelhor, 1990), thus decreasing available family resources.

Families in which father-daughter incest occurs experience other psychosocial stressors as well, including financial concerns (Wright, 1991), criminality (Gordon & Creighton, 1988; Williams & Finkelhor, 1990), unemployment (Anderson & Shafer, 1979; Gordon & Creighton, 1988), and psychiatric illness (Ballard et al., 1990). While some researchers have also found high levels of alcoholism in these families (Ballard et al., 1990; Gordon, 1989), other studies suggest that the use of alcohol is not unusually high (Groff & Hubble, 1984; Herman, 1981) and that alcoholism is not a factor for the majority of incest offenders (Williams & Finkelhor, 1990). In sum, increased psychosocial stressors, large families, traditional divisions of labor, and restricted resources coalesce to ensure that nonoffending mothers are overwhelmed.

Caregiving of the Father

Sociobiological theory suggests that early patterns of caregiving are related to the risk of abusing one's child. Parker and Parker (1986), who were the first to test this theory, compared incestuous fathers and stepfathers to controls matched on age. They found that incestuous fathers were significantly less likely to be involved in childcare during the first three years of the child's life and to be less likely to have been in the home during that time. To adjust for some of the methodological weaknesses of this study, Williams and Finkelhor (1995) later compared offending fathers and a closely matched control group on their involvement in caregiving. In this carefully constructed study, they found that after controlling for other possible explanations, fathers who were actively involved with their daughters during a portion of the first six years of their daughters' lives were at lower risk to commit incest. The types of caregiving that provided the most dampening effect were nonbodily caregiving activities, as compared to bodily caregiving activities. They also found that predisposing risk factors such as a previous abuse history were independently related to greater risk to abuse. Thus, early caregiving was not a fail-safe mechanism. Indeed, a small group of men engaged in early caregiving as a part of the grooming process for later victimization. Finally, they found that early caregiving was not related to a reduction in sexual arousal.

This study offers weak but mixed support for the sociobiological explanation of incest. Early caregiving did appear to provide an inhibitory mechanism for incest, but only when other predisposing factors were not present. Further, in some cases children were actually at greater risk when their fathers were closely involved in early caregiving. Finally, the mechanism of inhibition (i.e., decreased sexual arousal) was not supported.

Another indicator of support for the sociobiological theory is that children are at greater risk of abuse by stepfathers, who are typically less involved in early caregiving than biological fathers. Indeed, Russell (1986) found that children were seven times more likely to be abused by a stepfather than a biological father and that 17% of female children living with a stepfather prior to the age of 14 were abused by him prior to that age. Margolin and Craft (1989) also found that stepfathers and adoptive fathers were disproportionately likely to abuse their children. These studies suggest that sociobiological theory has some empirical support, although the specific mechanism for the increased risk is not yet clearly explicated.

Dysfunctional Dynamics within Families

Several studies have assessed general dynamics within families in which fathers abuse their children. These studies almost uniformly agree that these families exhibit high levels of overall family dysfunction, even more so than families with victims of other types of intrafamilial and extrafamilial abuse (Briere & Elliott, 1993; Draucker, 1996). These families are low in community involvement and are often socially isolated (Herman, 1981; Williams & Finkelhor, 1990). In addition, they exhibit a lack of openness, empathy, and expression of feeling (Madonna, Van Scoyk, & Jones, 1991). The overall tone of these families is described as cynical and hopeless.

Other studies have found that fathers appear to have less insight into the structure of these families than mothers and children. Indeed, Milner and Robertson (1990) found that offenders viewed their children (including the victim) in a positive manner and reported few problems with them. Another study found that while fathers thought their relationship with the daughter they abused was good, mothers and daughters thought it was poor (Sagatun & Prince, 1989). This difference held up even after treatment. In fact, fathers rated the father-daughter relationship as the best within the family and the mother-father relationship as the worst, whereas victims perceived the father-daughter relationship as worst.

These studies support a family systems theory interpretation that incest occurs within a dysfunctional environment. Given the nature of the studies, however, it is not certain whether the dysfunction actually precedes the abuse. Even if it were to precede the abuse, there are some important cautions concerning the dynamics. First, family systems theory posits that these dynamics are causal to incest, and no such link is as yet supported by this literature. No known prospective studies of high-risk families have been done to determine whether these dysfunctional dynamics are present before the abuse is initiated. Also, as mentioned earlier, why does only the father act out sexually? Why don't these same dysfunctional dynamics place the mother at increased risk to commit incest? Finally, as discussed in a later section, many of these same dynamics are found to lesser degrees in families in which other types of intrafamilial abuse occurs and even in families of victims of extrafamilial abuse. Family systems theory has as yet offered no explanation for why these dynamics are also found in families with victims of other types of abuse.

Relationship between Parents

According to family systems theory, the relationship between the parents is often marked by discord as well as emotional and sexual withdrawal by the mother (Cohen, 1983). In partial support, one study found that families with marital discord had a seven times greater risk of father-daughter incest (Paveza, 1988). Conversely, in a review of the literature on incest offenders, Williams and Finkelhor (1990) concluded that marriages in the families were no worse than those of men who had other social or psychological problems. Further, it is important to recognize that these studies assess the marital discord after the abuse is disclosed and may not adequately represent marital relationships prior to the incest. Indeed, it would seem that marital discord would be the norm once incest was disclosed.

Family systems theory also suggests that the husband's lack of sexual satisfaction may be a causal agent for the incest (Cohen, 1983; Frude, 1982), and some researchers have confirmed a lack of sexual satisfaction in these marriages (Kirkland & Bauer, 1982). Herman (1981), however, found that many offenders had sex upon demand with their wives. Another study compared a small sample of families in which father-daughter incest occurred with families with no history of sexual abuse (Maddock, Larson, & Lally, 1991). Interestingly, before treatment for the incest, offenders indicated more satisfaction in their sexual relationship than those in the post-treatment group. Indeed, the offender's report of sexual satisfaction prior to treatment exceeded even that of the control group. After treatment, however, incest offenders reported high levels of sexual dissatisfaction.

Finally, sexual dissatisfaction must be viewed within the context of the incest. As Faller (1990) states of fathers in her study, "when there were sexual difficulties, they were as likely to be the consequence of the husband's sexual preference for children as to be the wife's lack of desire or lack of desirability" (p. 67).

Offending Behavior of the Father

Another assumption of family systems theory is that the incest serves a function within the family (Larson & Maddock, 1986). As such, it was historically assumed that incest offenders abused only within the family (Conte, 1991). Instead, a large number of studies now indicate that many fathers do not restrict their offending behavior to only a single child. Russell (1986), for example, found that 32% of fathers had abused another relative. In Herman's study (1981), 41% of the families with more than one daughter had multiple victims of incest. In another 37% of families, multiple victims were suspected. Phelan (1986) also found that 82% of available daughters in families with biological father incest were sexually abused, whereas 70% of available daughters in families with stepfather incest were abused. In still another study, Ballard et al. (1990) found that incest offenders attending Parents United reported that they perpetrated intrafamilial abuse against an average of 4.5 children. Nor do incest offenders restrict themselves to children within the family, as 49% of incest offenders in one study sexually abused children outside of the family (Abel, Becker, Cunningham-Rathner, Mittleman, & Rouleau, 1988a).

Two important assumptions of family systems theory are that (a) incestuous fathers do not abuse outside the home; and (b) incest is the sexual expression of nonsexual needs (Conte, 1991). Both assumptions are repudiated by these data. Incest offenders frequently abuse nonrelated children as well. As such, it is impossible for the abuse to serve simply a family function.

Summary

Theories of incest have only mixed support. Perhaps the theory with the greatest support is feminist theory. Much of the empirical literature does suggest that abuse is a manifestation of a powerful and dominant father abusing his privilege. The finding that 99% of all parental offenders are male is most supportive of this theory (Finkelhor et al., 1990; Russell, 1986; Wyatt, 1985). Further, only feminist theory addresses reasons for this gender disparity. Feminist theory also provides an explanation for the other violence perpetrated by these fathers, suggesting that fathers are exploiting their power (Herman, 1981).

Feminist theory's emphasis on the dominant male, however, cannot by itself explain the inception of father-daughter incest. While it would be expected that a family focused around patriarchal norms would have some unifying characteristics, this theory cannot explain the extreme levels of dysfunction in many of these families. The theories that best explain this dysfunction are family systems and attachment theories. Family systems theory, however, suffers from many weaknesses. First, many of its dated hypotheses are value- and myth-laden, as shown in the previous sections. For example, its emphasis on the mother as central to the inception of incest is clearly repudiated by the data. (See Chapter 10 for a more detailed discussion of nonoffending mothers.) Indeed, the only hypothesis with consistent support is that these families exhibit high levels of dysfunction, although its role as causal to the incest has not as yet been supported empirically. Questions that remain to be answered are: (a) Why do these same dynamics occur in families in which incest does not occur? and (b) Why does the father instead of the mother act out this family dysfunction by abusing?

Attachment theory proposes instead that the type of insecure attachment, and its concomitant behavioral patterns within the family, are the factors that not only place families at greater risk for the inception of incest but that also define the characteristics of the incest once it occurs. While there are still weaknesses to certain of the hypotheses put forward by Alexander (1992), this theory appears to hold greater promise than family systems theory for explaining not only the family dynamics observed in families in which father-daughter incest occurs, but also one mechanism of transmission.

Finally, sociobiological theory offers an explanation for the relationship between caregiving and risk of abuse. Specifically, it suggests that fathers who do not involve themselves in the early caregiving of their children are at greater risk to abuse them. Partial support for this theory exists (Parker & Parker, 1986; Williams & Finkelhor, 1990).

Taken together, it is suggested that a combination of attachment theory, feminist theory, and sociobiological theory offers the best explanations advanced thus far for the inception of father-daughter incest. On the other hand, family systems theory's historical hypotheses and conceptualizations are so myth-bound and value-laden that they need to be abandoned. While further versions of this theory might help to clarify the maintenance of family dynamics, its use as a causal theory is not indicated at this time.

Finally, it is again important to acknowledge that father-daughter incest is only one of many types of child sexual abuse. Indeed, it accounts for only approximately 7% to 8% of all child sexual abuse (Russell, 1984; Wyatt, 1985). It is intriguing to speculate why, given its rarity, professionals and society continue to focus upon it. Obviously, many people think of father-daughter incest as the most heinous of the commonly known types of sexual abuse. It does seem easier to understand how someone can abuse a stranger, even if that stranger is a child, than to understand how a father can abuse his child. There may be another more subtle reason, however, for its focus. It may be that our current heightened concern with father-daughter incest might actually be a smoke screen. By focusing on this type of abuse, we do not have to recognize how prevalent and significant are the other types of abuse. As long as society continues its focus on father-daughter incest, the societal and gendered focus necessary and pertinent to informing assessment, treatment, and prevention for all types of abuse will not occur.

Abuse by Grandfathers

Abuse by a grandparent accounts for approximately 11% of all substantiated abuse by nonparental caretakers (Margolin & Craft, 1989) but only 1% to 2% of all child sexual abuse (Russell, 1983; Wyatt, 1985). Of grandparents who abuse, grandmothers account for 0% to 7% of that abuse (Cupoli & Sewell, 1988; Margolin, 1992; Margolin & Craft, 1989; Russell, 1986). Children are at greatest risk when they are in the temporary care of their grandparents. In a study by Margolin (1992), of the grandchildren with a substantiated case of abuse, 10% were in the custody of their grandparents at the time of the abuse, and another 64% were in the temporary care of the grandparent (almost always an overnight visit). As expected, 88% of the victims were female.

There are two historic views of abuse by a grandfather: (a) These men are compensating for physiological impotence and are, therefore, unlikely to repeat the offenses; and (b) There is multigenerational incest in the family in which the offender abuses children across generations (Goodwin, Cormier, & Owen, 1983). The minimal literature on this type of abuse supports the second hypothesis. In one dated study of a small sample of children abused by grandfathers, 80% of the mothers were also victims of child sexual abuse, and all had been sexually abused by their fathers (Goodwin et al., 1983). The offenders abused an average of 3.3 children each, almost all of whom were relatives. In Russell's (1986) random community prevalence study of female respondents, 44% of the grandfather perpetrators had also sexually abused another relative. Margolin (1992) also found indications of tri-generational abuse, as 34% of the grandfathers had also sexually abused their own daughters. Margolin states, "these differences suggest that individuals from families with a history of trigenerational sexual abuse may either feel inured to these violations or feel there is little likelihood of successful intervention" (p. 740).

In Russell's (1986) retrospective accounts of abuse, grandfathers abused more frequently (82% of victims were abused more than one time) and longer (70% were abused more than a year) than other incest perpetrators. Yet, grandfathers were significantly more likely to abuse their victims at the least severe level, although they were not significantly less likely to use force. Margolin (1992) instead found mixed results concerning severity of the abuse. Although the most common type of substantiated sexual abuse was fondling without penetration (45%), 31% of victims experienced digital penetration, and intercourse was attempted or completed in 24% of all cases. Seventy percent of the victims were abused three or more times, and 35% were abused for more than a year. Another interesting finding in Russell's study was that 55% of victims were also abused by other incest perpetrators, as compared to 13% of other incest victims. This finding was corroborated in Goodwin et al.'s (1983) study, in which almost half of the victims were abused by another offender. A final interesting characteristic of abuse by grandfathers is the preponderance of step-grandfathers who abuse (35% in Margolin's study). In her study, abuse by step-grandparents was more severe than abuse by biological grandfathers, as 18% of the victims experienced intercourse (as compared to 8% of biological grandfathers), 55% experienced digital penetration (versus 35%), and 24% experienced threats and physical violence (versus 10%).

Thus, abuse by grandparents is almost always committed by the grandfather, who most likely also abused his own daughter. Step-grandfathers also appear to be at increased risk to offend. While this abuse is more frequent than most other types of intrafamilial abuse, it may be less severe.

Sibling Incest

Approximately 1% to 2% of all women are victims of sibling abuse. This abuse accounts for approximately 7% to 14% of all intrafamilial abuse and 1% to 4% of all child sexual abuse (Tables 7-1 and 7-2).

Professionals once thought that sibling abuse was a lesser form of sexual abuse, assuming that it involved little more than sex play by children close in age. Empirical evidence, however, has disputed this claim. First, age disparity between victims and offenders is often great, and a series of studies have found that the offender is often more than five years older than the victim (Adler & Schutz, 1995; Russell, 1986). Further, not all offenders are juveniles. For example, Russell (1986) found that only 70% of sibling offenders were juveniles. Siblings also perpetrate more severe abuse. In studies on sibling abuse, 28% to 83% of incidents involve some type of oral, vaginal, or anal penetration (Laviola, 1992; Margolin & Craft, 1989; O'Brien, 1991; Smith & Israel, 1987). In 33% to 64% of the abuse, force or threat is also involved (De Jong, 1989; Gilbert, 1992; Rudd & Herzberger, 1999; Russell, 1986), and 17% to 29% of all abuse involves physical injury (De Jong, 1989; Margolin & Craft, 1989). Often the offenders seem to have little consideration for the pain the victims are experiencing (Laviola, 1992). Much sibling abuse is also of long duration (O'Brien, 1991; Rudd & Herzberger, 1999). For example, Cantwell (1981) found that abuse lasted from one to nine years in 40% of the cases, whereas Adler and Schutz (1995) found that the abuse lasted an average of 22 months. Conversely, in the only study of sibling abuse that derives from a random community sample, Russell (1986) found that it was significantly less likely than other types of incest to last longer than a year.

There may be a heightened sexual climate in families in which sibling abuse occurs. For example, Smith and Israel (1987) found that 48% of the sibling offenders in their study had observed sexual activity between parents or with one parent and another party. In 76% of these families, at least one parent was having an extramarital affair, and in 32% of the families, father-daughter incest had preceded the brother's participation. Laviola (1992) also found that there were other incestuous relations in 71% of families in which sibling abuse occurred. Further, a third to a half of victims of sibling abuse are also abused by others (Cantwell, 1981; Gilbert, 1992; Laviola, 1992), often by other brothers or fathers (Cantwell, 1981). Additionally, some offenders abuse more than one child. Across studies, 8% (Smith & Israel, 1987), 27% (Gilbert, 1992), and 53% (O'Brien, 1991) of offenders had multiple victims, and the average number of victims (not necessarily siblings) per offender was 1.8 in O'Brien's study. In comparison to other adolescent sex offenders, sibling offenders in O'Brien's study had also committed the most offenses (an average of 18 separate incidents each) and had longer careers as offenders.

Several characteristics of sibling incest are similar to dynamics of father-daughter incest. First, most offenders are male (approximately 80%) (De Jong, 1989; Smith & Israel, 1987), often the oldest son (Adler & Schutz, 1995), and most victims are female (86% to 94%) (Margolin & Craft, 1989; Smith & Israel, 1987). As such, most abuse (68% to 74%) is heterosexual (Finkelhor, 1980; Smith & Israel, 1987). Stepchildren also appear to be at heightened risk both to offend and to be victimized (Pierce & Pierce, 1990; Smith & Israel, 1987). Further, families in which sibling abuse occurs may have larger families. Laviola (1992) found that more than half of the families in which sibling abuse occurred had four or more children, and the average number of siblings in a small study was 6.2 (Rudd & Herzberger, 1999). Russell (1986) also found that 77% of the victims came from families where six or more members depended on the family income (as compared to 32% of victims of other incest perpetrators). Further, Worling (1995) found that one of the discriminating factors between sibling offenders and other adolescent sex offenders was that sibling offenders had more available younger children in their families. Often there is physical abuse in these families as well (Laviola, 1992; Wiehe, 1990), even more so than in families of other adolescent offenders (O'Brien, 1991) and other adolescent sex offenders (Worling, 1995).

Dynamics within families in which sibling incest occurs also appear to be dysfunctional (Laviola, 1992). Studies on sibling abuse have found that parents are often absent, emotionally neglectful, or unavailable (Laviola, 1992; Smith & Israel, 1987). For example, Rudd and Herzberger (1999) found that mothers were often overwhelmed by life circumstances, ill, or alcohol abusers. Fathers were uniformly described as absent through death, alcoholism, mental illness, or extreme emotional distance. Families often experience other stressors as well, including illness or disability of a family member, parental depression, and financial hardship (Adler & Schutz, 1995; Laviola, 1992; Pierce & Pierce, 1987; Rudd & Herzberger, 1999), and responses to these stressors are often maladaptive (Laviola, 1992). For the offenders, the sexual offending is usually one of multiple problems, including prior involvement with the justice system (O'Brien, 1991), school problems, and a variety of behavior problems (Adler & Schutz, 1995; O'Brien, 1991; Pierce & Pierce, 1987). These families also have rigid rules against expressing feelings and deny that problems exist (Laviola, 1992). They have heightened negativity and argumentativeness, heightened marital discord, and low satisfaction within family relations. Findings such as these led O'Brien (1991) to conclude that existing family culture was a contributing factor to the abuse, whereas Smith and Israel (1987) concluded that approximately half of the families were severely disturbed.

Not unexpectedly, parents of sibling offenders often have a personal history of sexual abuse. Three different studies found that between 36% and 63% of mothers and 8% to 10% of fathers were victims of childhood sexual abuse (Adler & Schutz, 1995; O'Brien, 1991; Worling, 1995). Another study found that 72% of mothers or fathers of the victim had been sexually abused as children (Smith & Israel, 1987). A large percentage (42% to 52%) of adolescent sibling offenders also have a history of sexual abuse victimization (Longo, 1982; O'Brien, 1991; Smith & Israel, 1987) as well as physical abuse and neglect (Longo, 1982). In one study, offenders were sexually abused most often by their father or another family member (O'Brien, 1991).

Finally, O'Brien (1991) found an interesting intergenerational pattern. Those sibling offenders who were previously abused by males most often went on to victimize boys (68%), whereas only 7% of those offenders victimized by females chose boys as victims. These data support a psychodynamic interpretation that the offender may be attempting to achieve symbolic mastery over his own victimization by identifying with the aggressor. Alternatively, sexual arousal and pleasure may become paired with a specific gender via the process of conditioning.

In summary, there are numerous ways in which sibling abuse replicates the dynamics of other sexual abuse. Most of the abusers (brothers) are older males (Cantwell, 1981; Finkelhor, 1980; Smith & Israel, 1987), and most of the victims (sisters) are younger females (Finkelhor, 1980). Thus, most of the abuse is heterosexual (Finkelhor, 1980; Smith & Israel, 1987). Family dynamics are also similar to those in father-daughter incest. Families are described as patriarchal, with fathers dominating and controlling other members (Laviola, 1992). There is often physical abuse in these families (Laviola, 1992; Wiehe, 1990) as well as other psychosocial stressors (Laviola, 1992; Pierce & Pierce, 1990). Further, there are often a large number of children and dependents (Laviola, 1992; Russell, 1986), as well as dysfunctional dynamics (Laviola, 1992).

Finally, sibling offenders are less likely to be adjudicated than other adolescent sex and nonsex offenders (O'Brien, 1991), and even child protective services appears to minimize this abuse (Adler & Schutz, 1995). O'Brien states that the implication is that society does not see this behavior as serious. He concludes that society must send a stronger message. Russell (1986) also writes of this abuse, "The notion that brother-sister incest is usually a harmless, mutual interaction is seriously wrong" (p. 289).

Other Relatives

Uncles and male cousins are the other relatives who frequently commit sexual abuse. While uncles and cousins abuse at approximately the same rate as fathers (Russell, 1986), there is almost nothing in the literature about abuse by these extended family members. There are only two known studies on abuse by cousins (De Jong, 1989; Russell, 1986) and two on abuse by uncles (Margolin, 1994; Russell, 1986). Yet, approximately 4% to 5% of all women and 1% of all men have been abused by uncles, whereas 1% to 3% of all women and 1% of all men have been abused by cousins (Table 7-2). African American females are abused by male cousins approximately twice as often as Caucasian females (Wyatt, 1985).

Russell (1986) was the first to investigate sexual abuse by uncles. In her random retrospective community sample of 930 females, there were 48 incidents of childhood sexual abuse by an uncle and none by an aunt. Uncles, like grandfathers, were more prone to abuse at the least severe level, and only 23% used physical force. Most of the incidents of sexual abuse occurred around the rituals of greetings and farewells. Interestingly, some of the uncles also behaved in a sexually predatory fashion with adult relatives, and 41% were known to have sexually abused another child.

Margolin (1994) assessed characteristics of substantiated abuse by uncles or aunts. Of the 151 perpetrators, only three were aunts. Yet, aunts were 28 times more likely than uncles to provide childcare, whereas uncles perpetrated 48 times more abuse than aunts. Thus, while uncles provided only about 3% of the childcare given by aunts or uncles, they perpetrated 98% of the abuse. These findings again highlight the striking gender bias in child sexual abuse.

In Margolin's (1994) study, uncles obtained access to the children in several ways. In the most prevalent type of abuse, 24% of uncles abused the children when they visited in the uncles' homes, the vast majority of whom were spending the night, usually to have more time with their cousins. Another 21% of uncles were providing temporary childcare at the time of the abuse. Of interest, almost half of the perpetrators in this group were less than 21 years of age. Still another 19% of uncles were living with the nieces or nephews they abused. These men often had a history of drinking problems as well as a criminal or psychiatric history. The final larger category of abuse (14%) occurred when children visited their grandparent's homes. Uncles were either visiting or were living there. Again, approximately half of these offenders were less than 21 years of age. In a minority of cases, abuse included penetration (17%), lasted for more than a year (28%), or included force or threat (22%). In approximately one-quarter of cases, the perpetrator was known to have a previous history of sexual abuse, and in 11% of these cases parents were aware of the previous record. Indeed, 6% of parents knew about their children's abuse but continued to allow them to visit the uncle.

Abuse by cousins is also prevalent, accounting for 4% to 8% of all abuse. Overall, 1% to 3% of the population is abused by cousins (Tables 7-1 and 7-2). Although victims are predominantly female, boys are also at risk for abuse by cousins, as shown in Table 7-2. Not surprisingly, approximately 80% of this abuse is committed by cousins within 10 years of age of the victim. In Russell's (1986) community prevalence study, cousin offenders were 16 to 18 years old on average, whereas victims were seven to 11 years old. De Jong (1989) also found that most abuse occurred only one time (59% to 84%), although Russell found that 22% of the victims were abused for more than two years. Further, this abuse is typically severe. In De Jong's study, penetration was attempted or completed in 69% of the cases, and physical injury occurred in 33% of cases. Almost half of the victims reported being threatened or of having been forced to participate. Approximately half of the abuse incidents occurred in the victim's home, with the other half occurring in the offender's home. Of the victims, 76% lived in single-parent homes.

In summary, abuse by uncles and cousins is also similar to that of other types of child sexual abuse in that perpetrators are primarily male, whereas victims are primarily female. Access to the child is usually gained while providing childcare (uncles) or while visiting (uncles and cousins).

DYNAMICS OF FAMILIES WITH INTRAFAMILIAL ABUSE

One final method of understanding intrafamilial abuse is to compare dynamics of families in which incest occurs to dynamics in other types of families. Various studies have now compared families with nuclear abuse to those with other intrafamilial abuse (Alexander & Lupfer, 1987; Ray, Jackson, & Townsley, 1991), or have compared families with intrafamilial abuse to families without intrafamilial abuse (Alexander & Lupfer, 1987; Harter, Alexander, & Neimeyer, 1988; Jackson, Calhoun, Amick, Maddever, & Habif, 1990; Madonna et al., 1991; Ray et al., 1991). Most of these studies are retrospective.

One study compared families with nuclear abuse (most often the father) to families of abuse by an extended family member and to families without abuse (Alexander & Lupfer, 1987). In this study, families with nuclear abuse had more traditional relationships between husband and wife, parent and child, and male and female than victims abused by an extended family member. On the other hand, scores for cohesiveness and adaptability in all families with intrafamilial abuse were similar, but differed significantly from those families who had no victims of sexual abuse. The authors concluded that characteristics described by Herman (1981) regarding traditional family values were also found to a lesser degree in families with non-nuclear intrafamilial abuse.

A second group of studies compared families with intrafamilial abuse to families with no abuse. As compared to families with no abuse, families with any type of intrafamilial abuse were less cohesive (Alexander & Lupfer, 1987; Harter et al., 1988; Jackson et al., 1990) and less adaptable (Alexander & Lupfer, 1987). These families were also more controlling (Jackson et al., 1990) and traditional, and fathers were more powerful (Maddock et al., 1991). Individual members had less autonomy (Madonna et al., 1991), were less able to support autonomy or intimacy of family members (Madonna et al., 1991), and were more socially isolated (Harter et al., 1988). Further, they exhibited less empathy and trust, their range of feelings was more constricted and masked (Carson, Gertz, Donaldson, & Wonderlich, 1990; Madonna et al., 1991), and family members often had distorted and incongruous beliefs about themselves and the family (Madonna et al., 1991). Finally, families with intrafamilial abuse also have a higher number of psychosocial stressors than families without victims of sexual abuse (Levitt, Owen, & Truchsess, 1991). This review suggests that families in which intrafamilial abuse occurs have many of the same characteristics of those families in which father-daughter incest occurs, including more stressors, more powerful fathers, greater traditionality, and greater dysfunction.

Another study compared dynamics in families with intrafamilial abuse to families of victims of extrafamilial abuse as well as to families with no abuse victims (Ray et al., 1991). The general hypothesis of this study was that dynamics found in families in which incest occurred would be found to a lesser extent in families with extrafamilial abuse, an hypothesis that was partially supported. Indeed, characteristics found in both intrafamilial and extrafamilial abuse included a lack of involvement of family members with each other, especially as this involvement related to closeness, emotional support, and activities that would promote a child's development. Compared to families with no abused members, those with abused members were less cohesive, less likely to encourage independence, and less organized around responsibilities, activities, and rules. In general, families of intrafamilial abuse had the greatest pathology, families with extrafamilial abuse had less pathology, and families with no abuse victims had the least.

A final study compared families with nuclear family abuse to those with extended family abuse, extrafamilial abuse, and families with no abuse victims (Alexander & Lupfer, 1987). In this study, the same progression was found, with scores typically stepping down from nuclear family abuse, whose scores indicated the most pathology, to extended family abuse, to extrafamilial abuse, and finally to no abuse. The largest difference was most often between nuclear family incest and extended family incest. The exception is that cohesion scores in all families with abuse victims were somewhat uniform but were significantly higher, indicating more pathology, than those for families with no abuse victims.

In summary, it appears that many of the dynamics found in father-daughter incest and other intrafamilial abuse are also exhibited in families with extrafamilial abuse. The differences appear to be in the level of intensity of these dynamics.

SUMMARY

Intrafamilial abuse accounts for 11% to 29% of all child sexual abuse (Finkelhor et al., 1990; Russell, 1983; Wyatt, 1985). African American females are more likely to be abused by a family member, especially a non-natal father, uncle, or male cousin

(Russell, 1983; Wyatt, 1985). Caucasian females are more likely to be abused (in descending order) by uncles, fathers, male cousins, and brothers, followed by all female relatives (Russell, 1986). For Latinas, however, fathers, uncles, and male cousins abuse equally, followed by brothers. Latinos are at greatest risk of abuse by uncles and cousins (Finkelhor et al., 1990).

The most fundamental conclusion of this section is that families in which intrafamilial or extrafamilial abuse occurs have similar dynamics, with the primary difference being the level of pathology. Specifically, pathology decreases progressively in the following order: families of father-daughter incest, families of nuclear family incest, families with extended family incest, families with victims of extrafamilial abuse, and finally, families with no victims of abuse.

Intrafamilial abuse replicates father-daughter incest in other ways as well. In families of both father-daughter incest and sibling abuse there are often multiple victims of abuse within the family as well as other violence. The victims often have multiple perpetrators, and offenders regularly abuse multiple victims. As with father-daughter incest, the majority of sibling abuse is by an older male against a younger female and is often long-standing. Sibling abuse is also marked by forceful and severe abuse. Similarly, grandfathers and uncles abuse multiple victims, and victims are often abused by multiple perpetrators. In all types of intrafamilial abuse, the most prevalent pattern by far is that older males abuse younger females.

Families of victims of extrafamilial abuse also have many of the same characteristics as families in which father-daughter incest or intrafamilial abuse occurs. These include lack of involvement, low cohesion, low organization, low independence, and low adaptability, but more traditional relationships. As would be expected, however, the dynamics are more severe, indicating more pathology, in families with intrafamilial abuse.

Thus, characteristics of families of victims of intrafamilial and extrafamilial abuse are often a replay of the dynamics of father-daughter incest. Older males abuse younger females, and power, control, and violence are often used to dominate the members of the household. Multiple victims and multiple perpetrators are typical of all types of intrafamilial abuse. Characteristics that would indicate a patriarchal home are seemingly present in most cases of intrafamilial abuse, but especially in abuse within the nuclear family. The point is not that these types of abuse replicate dynamics of father-daughter incest, however, but that dynamics of all types of child sexual abuse are similar.

IMPLICATIONS

This final section considers the implications of the two primary findings of this chapter: (a) that the dynamics of father-daughter incest are *not* unique, but are similar to those in families with other intrafamilial and extrafamilial abuse victims; and (b) that intrafamilial abuse, and especially father-daughter incest, is vastly over-represented in identified populations of abuse.

What is the significance of the finding that the dynamics of father-daughter incest are not unique? First, it shatters a primary assumption of a more recent conceptualization of family systems theory. This conceptualization suggests that dysfunctional family dynamics contribute to the incest, which then serves a function within the family (Larson & Maddock, 1986). Although they vary in severity, the dysfunctional dynamics are instead similar across families with victims of abuse, including father-daughter incest, other intrafamilial abuse, and even extrafamilial abuse. Thus, if family dysfunction contributed to the inception of father-daughter incest, we would also have to assume that family dysfunction contributed to the inception of other types of intrafamilial as well as extrafamilial abuse. Further, if father-daughter incest served some type of function within the family, we would also have to assume that other types of intrafamilial and extrafamilial abuse served some type of function within the family. While family dysfunction in any family may increase risk of abuse for children within the family, it is absurd to assume that the abuse of a child by a distant relative, neighbor, family friend, or stranger would serve some function within the family.

Second, family systems theory posits that family dynamics are causal to father-daughter incest. Yet if so, then these same family dynamics would also have to be considered causal to other types of intrafamilial and extrafamilial abuse. While dysfunction within families might place children at *increased* risk of sexual abuse, it is again somewhat absurd to consider that family dysfunction *causes* abuse by strangers, neighbors, or family friends. Instead, the more likely hypothesis is that family dysfunction acts only as a potentiator to increase risk of abuse for father-daughter incest, other intrafamilial abuse, and extrafamilial abuse.

The final and most important implication of recognizing that father-daughter incest is not unique is that we must also look *outside* the family to understand factors that explain the abuse. Feminist theory articulates the most logical causal agent—male entitlement that results from living within a patriarchal society. This factor best explains why far more female children are sexually abused than male children and why almost all offenders, including parents who abuse, are male. It also offers a better explanation than family systems theory for the dynamics of families in which incest occurs, including violence, domination, and control by the father and other male members of the family. Thus, father-daughter incest, as well as other types of intrafamilial abuse, are simply a part of a greater truth—that of all child sexual abuse. As Cole (1982) states, "Incest will stop when males, of any age, are no longer more powerful and more privileged than females" (p. 88).

The second important finding of this chapter, and indeed this book, is that intrafamilial abuse, especially father-daughter incest, is vastly over-represented in identified populations of abuse. As a result, extrafamilial abuse continues to be minimized by current child sexual abuse policies.

What are the advantages of prioritizing abuse by caregivers, especially abuse by a father figure? The most obvious and important advantage is that scarce resources are prioritized for those children who are in the greatest danger of continued victimization. This has been the underlying philosophy of child protective services, especially as budgets have been cut. Another advantage is that this focus has led to a sophisticated knowledge base—especially for father-daughter incest—during a short period of time.

There are a number of disadvantages, however, to prioritizing intrafamilial abuse and abuse by caregivers. Perhaps the most important and global disadvantage is that a narrow focus on one type of abuse, especially when it constitutes a small minority of all abuse, removes attention from other more prevalent and sometimes equally severe types of abuse. Thus, we have neither the studies nor much interest in extrafamilial abuse; neither do we have studies or much interest in societal factors that contribute to abuse. For example, no known study has considered how a sense of male entitlement to sex or ownership of women and children contributes to risk to offend. Yet, theoretical literature on this dynamic is now well more than 20 years old. What we do have, however, is numerous studies that analyze family dynamics and the role of the nonoffending mother in abuse (although we have no studies on the role of the nonoffending father). In other words, our policies and our historical emphasis on father-daughter incest have profoundly shaped and biased our views of child sexual abuse, its causal factors, its scope, our knowledge base, and even our perception of the culpability of nonoffending mothers. Thus, our literature today provides an intensely biased view of the scope of the problem of child sexual abuse, with a concomitant, intensely biased response to the problem of child sexual abuse. This is one of the gravest consequences of prioritizing intrafamilial abuse, especially father-daughter incest.

There is yet, however, an even more grave consequence. Because abuse by caregivers is prioritized, the vast majority of offenders are at less risk of identification, apprehension, and treatment. As such, our society is profoundly failing in its responsibility to protect its young. Given that perhaps as many as 30% of females are sexually abused extrafamilially during childhood (Russell, 1983) and that most male victims are abused extrafamilially (Finkelhor et al., 1990), we do not provide adequate protection to a huge number of victims. That these victims may not have access to treatment is a moral and an ethical issue of almost as much concern. These are extremely important issues, all of which need immediate attention.

As we eventually move beyond our myopic focus on intrafamilial abuse, we will also naturally devote more resources to victims of extrafamilial abuse, more research dollars to the study of extrafamilial abuse, more resources for protecting these young victims, and will move away from our pejorative literature and fascination with the nonoffending mother. Until then, our response to the scope of the problem of child sexual abuse will remain grossly insufficient, failing totally in its responsibility to many victims of abuse.

CHAPTER 8
RISK FACTORS FOR
CHILD SEXUAL ABUSE VICTIMIZATION

INTRODUCTION

This chapter discusses factors associated with risk of sexual abuse. In keeping with the emphasis of this book on framing child sexual abuse within a theoretical perspective, this chapter provides a theoretically grounded model of risk for abuse. Unless otherwise stated, the definition of child sexual abuse employed in this chapter is unwanted sexual contact of someone under the age of 18. If the contact is consensual, it is considered sexual abuse if the offender is in a position of authority or power by virtue of age or position. For example, sexual contact by a father or teacher is always considered sexual abuse, even if the child considers it consensual.

Previous work on risk of abuse has focused almost solely on *which* children are at greater risk of sexual abuse. An equally compelling question is *why* these children are at greater risk of abuse. The movement in questions from *who* to *why* is an important strategy with both prevention and policy implications. From a prevention standpoint, a more targeted prevention approach can be developed when professionals know *why* certain factors increase risk. Implications for moving from *who* to *why* are also important in considering policy recommendations. It is the thesis of this chapter that children's risk of sexual abuse is best explained using sociocultural factors, followed by factors within the family. If sociocultural factors in risk of sexual abuse are implicated, then a reduction in the scope of the problem of sexual abuse entails changes—formalized in policies—at the level of the greater society. An additional implication is that prevention efforts targeted at potential victims cannot effectively address the scope of the problem of abuse.

The focus of this chapter is twofold. The first purpose is to present an ecological, transactional, and developmental perspective of child sexual abuse victimization. The second is to develop known risk factors at each systemic level of influence within this framework.

Review of Existing Literature

Before presenting a theoretical framework for ecological influences on risk of sexual abuse, the existing literature on known risk factors is briefly reviewed in Table 8-1. Only the random community, state, and national prevalence studies reviewed in Chapter 5, "Incidence and Prevalence of Child Sexual Abuse," are used as the basis for this table. Relying upon studies that are not random in nature or that have an artificially restricted population would simply muddy the already dirty waters.

TABLE 8-1. Risk Factors for Child Sexual Abuse

	Results	Conclusion
Race/ethnicity	No significant differences (3, 7, 14). Males and females: One study found that Asians had the lowest prevalence (4). Another found that Caucasians had a greater prevalence than Latinos (13). Females only: In one study, Caucasians had a greater prevalence than African Americans (11). In another, Latinas had a greater prevalence than Caucasians (10). Another study found that Caucasians had a greater prevalence before age 11, but that African Americans and Latinas had a greater prevalence after age 11 (2b). Males only: Males of English and Scandinavian descent had a higher prevalence in one study (5). Another study found that African American males had a higher prevalence than Caucasian males (11).	Findings are too diverse to form a conclusion. The complexity of findings suggests differential and complex pathways to abuse based upon race/ethnicity.
Gender	All studies found that females are at substantially greater risk of sexual abuse (4, 5, 6, 9, 10, 11, 12, 13).	Females are at greater risk than males of sexual abuse.
Age of respondent	Three studies found that older women report less abuse (1, 2a, 5). No contradictory findings are reported.	While it is probable that older women *report* less abuse, it is not known whether they also *experience* less abuse.
Age of child	The most sophisticated analysis of age (2b) found that female children were at greatly increased risk of sexual abuse during their preteen and early teen years. African American females and Latinas were at much greater risk in later adolescence, whereas the risk for Caucasian females increased almost linearly over time, with a slight increase during preadolescence and early adolescence. Other studies reported that the age of greatest risk was between seven and 13.	Ages 11 through 13 may be a time of particular risk for female children, although the consensus is that risk remains high from age seven on. Very early abuse, however, may not be easily remembered. Incidence studies suggest that much abuse does occur when children are very young.
Limitations of child	One study found that having a physical, emotional, or mental limitation placed the child at greater risk (11).	Further research is required before conclusions can be drawn.
Problems within the family	Two surveys found that alcohol use in the family was related to greater risk of abuse among adolescents (8, 11). One of these surveys found that higher drug use or smoking was also related to greater risk (11).	Further research is required before conclusions can be drawn.

Maternal employment	Only one study found a relationship, and it was complex (2b). Female children were only at increased risk when their mothers worked part-time or when their mothers worked full-time and they were living with only females. In two studies, the relationship was nonsignificant (7,11).	Maternal employment does not appear to be a risk factor, although the complexity of the finding suggests that childcare may be an issue. Future research should consider factors such as formal/informal care situations.
Separation of parents	Six different studies reported that some type of parental absence (emotional or physical) is related to greater risk of abuse, including a single-parent family (6), separation prior to the age of 16 (11), a single or reconstructed family (9), and having unprotective parents (7). One study found that males were at increased risk when living with only their mothers or with no natural parent and that females were at increased risk when living with only their fathers or no natural parent (5). Another study found that females were only at increased risk when living with a male in the household after separation (2b).	The more complex analyses suggest that family structure is more complicated than simply assessing for some type of separation. It may be that separation by itself is not the issue, but that the type of family structure interacts with the gender of the child to determine risk.
Religion	Only two studies found a relationship (2b, 7). One study found that children not brought up in an organized religion were at increased risk (7). The other study found that children whose parents did not belong to an organized religion were at increased risk before the age of nine, after which Protestant children were at increased risk (2b).	Because few studies have reported findings for this variable, it is too early to draw conclusions.
Income	One study reported that poverty was a risk factor (11).	Income is difficult to measure because of the retrospective nature of the surveys. While it is generally considered that a relationship does not exist, further research using well-operationalized questions is required.

1. Bagley & Ramsay, 1986. 2a. Russell, 1983. 2b. Bolen, 1998b. 3. Elliott & Briere, 1992. 4. Erickson & Rapkin, 1991. 5. Finkelhor, Hotaling, Lewis, & Smith, 1990. 6. Gallup Poll, 1995. 7. Hall & Flannery, 1984. 8. Hernandez, 1992. 9. Hibbard, Ingersoll, & Orr, 1990. 10. Kercher & McShane, 984. 11. Moore, Nord, & Peterson, 1989. 12. Siegel, Sorenson, Golding, Burnam, & Stein, 1987. 13. Nance, 1992. 14. Wyatt, 1985.

A careful study of this table suggests that the current knowledge base is quite limited. Of the potential factors listed, only gender is unequivocally a factor that places children (females) at greater risk of sexual abuse. For certain of these factors, previous reviews have suggested that there is no relationship, whereas this table suggests that there may be a relationship. For example, previous reviews (Finkelhor & Baron, 1986; Finkelhor, 1994) have suggested that race is not a risk factor for child sexual abuse. On the other hand, this table suggests evidence of a relationship, although it is probably complex. Conversely, previous reviews have suggested that separation of the parents, in various forms, is a risk factor for child sexual abuse. While most studies certainly agree with this conclusion, Bolen's (1998b) reanalysis of Russell's (1983) data suggests that separation is not a risk factor in every case and that it may only increase risk if other factors are also present.

The complexity of these findings suggests that risk of sexual abuse must move to a higher level of conceptualization. A primary intent of this chapter is to do so.

ECOLOGICAL AND TRANSACTIONAL FRAMEWORK

Characteristics of an Ecological and Transactional Model

In 1980, Belsky developed an ecological model of child abuse and neglect. This paper was followed by Cicchetti and Rizley's 1981 paper in which a transactional model of child abuse and neglect was developed. In more recent years, Cicchetti and Lynch (1993) combined these approaches to develop an ecological and transactional model of community violence. The model presented in this chapter applies the literature on child sexual abuse to the work done by these researchers.

An ecological and transactional model suggests that, when attempting to develop a comprehensive model of a social problem, ecological/systemic influences and transactional/developmental influences must be considered. Inspired by Bronfenbrenner's (1977) general systems theory, Belsky (1980) suggested that four systemic levels had to be considered when conceptualizing the problem of child abuse and neglect within an ecological context, as follows.

- Macrosystem—the beliefs and values within the culture that contribute to the problem
- Exosystem—the community within which the individual lives
- Microsystem—the family
- Ontogenic system—the individual

For each level, Belsky explicated factors related to risk of child maltreatment.

An ecological approach is insufficient, however, to explain the complex interactions among risk factors, especially when considering the developmental trajectory of the child. For capturing the dynamic nature of abuse development, Cicchetti and Rizley's (1981) transactional model is more appropriate. "In a transactional model, environmental forces, caregiver characteristics, and child characteristics all influence each other and make reciprocal contributions to the events and outcomes" (Cicchetti & Lynch, 1993, p. 97). Their model focuses primarily upon transactions among risk factors, which are divided into two broad categories. Potentiating factors increase the probability of abuse, whereas compensatory (protective) factors decrease the risk of abuse. Both can be enduring (more permanent or chronic conditions) or transient (temporary conditions) (Cicchetti & Rizley, 1981), and proximal (those that impinge directly upon the child) or distal (those that are not experienced directly by the child, such as social class) (Baldwin, Baldwin, & Cole, 1990). Examples of proximal factors are inadequate nutrition, discord between parents, unsafe living conditions, or specific life stressors. Importantly, abuse is hypothesized to occur when "potentiating factors outweigh compensatory factors" (Cicchetti & Lynch, 1993, p. 97). For example, children with supportive families (a compensatory factor) might only be at increased risk for abuse when there are numerous stressors (potentiators).

An advantage of applying an ecological and transactional approach to the understanding of child sexual abuse is its breadth. Many previous theories and models of child sexual abuse have either focused upon only a single dynamic or are atheoretical. While single-focus theories may make critical contributions to the literature, by themselves they do not adequately explain the scope of the problem of child sexual abuse. Similarly, the problem with atheoretical models is that they do not explicate theoretical pathways to abuse. Instead, an encompassing model that subsumes other theories and that explicates pathways to abuse is needed.

Ecological, Transactional, and Developmental Model of Child Sexual Abuse Victimization

Ecological Influences

Risk of sexual abuse can be conceptualized as a result of various external influences that are experienced by children internally as potentiating or protective factors. In other words, children are at risk of sexual abuse because of factors that occur outside the child (i.e., at the level of the macrosystem, exosystem, and microsystem). Although level of causation is external to the child, however, these causative factors, via systemic dynamics, manifest at the level of the child. Thus, they act at the level of the child as potentiating or protective factors. Figure 8-1 elaborates this process. As can be seen, stressors at each hierarchical level impact all lesser levels. The macrosystem, for example, impacts the exosystem (community) and microsystem (family) both directly and indirectly. The macrosystem, exosystem, and microsystem all influence the ontogenic (child) system level, again both directly and indirectly. This model thus suggests that risk at the level of the child is influenced by all levels of the system.

An important purpose of the ecological and transactional model of child sexual abuse is to clarify levels at which risk factors originate. Historically, literature has focused most heavily on the level of the child (ontogenic) and secondarily on the family (microsystem). For example, historical conceptualizations of family systems theory sometimes blamed the child for initiating father-daughter incest because of the power the child gained (Kadushin & Martin, 1988). Yet, the issue of power is better

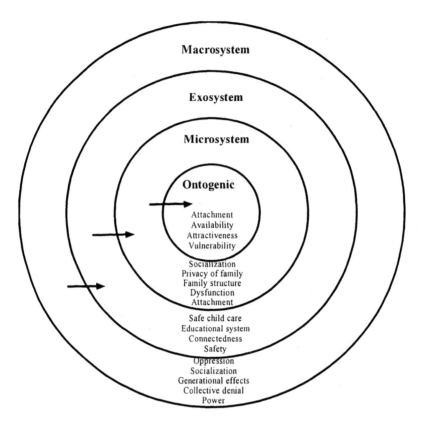

FIGURE 8-1. Ecological Model of Child Sexual Abuse

see p. 138 for def.

explained at the level of the macrosystem. In this conceptualization, because of societal norms, fathers have the majority of power within the family which they may then choose to abuse by targeting their children for abuse. Power originates, then, at the macrosystem (society) but is manifested at the microsystem (family).

Because of this confusion between the level at which risk factors originate and then later manifest, the literature has historically focused upon the lower levels of the systemic level influences, specifically the level of the child or family, for dynamics leading to the abuse. Yet, strong cultural influences impinge upon the child and family. Many risk factors, while historically conceptualized as ontogenic or microsystem risk factors, are probably better conceptualized as macrosystem or exosystem influences.

A theory proposed by Reiss (1981) has important implications for this conceptualization. Reiss suggested that families develop paradigms that represent a set of beliefs and assumptions about their environment and that these paradigms affect how families process information about their environment. Cicchetti and Lynch (1993) expanded this conceptualization by suggesting that these family paradigms are actually the "family's representational model of the community in which they reside" (p. 113). These representational models, by shaping the family's viewpoints and expectations, then become mechanisms for the perpetuation of violence within communities.

This theory provides an impetus for understanding how factors that manifest at one level are better conceptualized as originating at a higher hierarchical level. Both the family and community may internalize a representational model of the cultural beliefs and values of the greater society. This representational model appears to be mostly stable, but also dynamic, changing slowly over time as the social climate changes. Because it develops as a result of the transaction among the family or community and the greater society, it is a dyadic property, reflecting the confluence between the family or community and the greater society. Through the inculcation of cultural beliefs and values via the family and its members, children may manifest risk factors that are better conceptualized as societal in origin.

The importance of the greater society when conceptualizing the problem of child sexual abuse is also suggested by the fact that it is pervasive within the fabric of society. The chapter on incidence and prevalence of sexual abuse suggested that approximately 30% to 40% of female children and 13% or more of male children are sexually abused (Bolen & Scannapieco, 1999). Because of the pervasiveness of the problem of child sexual abuse, no model that focuses solely on deficits in children and families to explain it will suffice. Adequate explanations of child sexual abuse must begin at the level of the macrosystem and exosystem. While these levels will not explain all factors that place children at risk of sexual abuse, it is suggested that these two levels will explain the majority.

Transactional and Developmental Influences

A model that relies solely on systemic level influences, however, is not sufficient to explain risk of abuse because it does not consider the developmental and transactional trajectory of the child. The addition of this trajectory to the model of risk is illustrated in Figure 8-2.

This model now has three parts. First, the model carries forward from the previous model the concentric circles representing the ecological influences that impinge upon the child. Added to this ecological model are the developmental growth of the child, represented by the cone, and the interaction of risk factors, represented by the heavy line through the center of the cone.

The addition of time to the model implies that risk of sexual abuse can only be understood within the context of the developmental stage of the child. The child's developmental stage might impinge upon risk of abuse in at least two ways. First, the child's developmental maturity (cognitive, affective, or physiological) may be related to an increase or decrease in risk of abuse. For example, very young children may not be cognitively mature enough to understand potentially dangerous situations. Second, children may be differentially accessible or vulnerable to potential offenders based upon their age.

The transactional framework of the model (the heavy line that runs through the cone and that represents risk) suggests that systemic influences and the developmental stage of the child, acting individually as potentiating or protective factors, then complexly combine and are carried forward as the child's level of risk. Specifically,

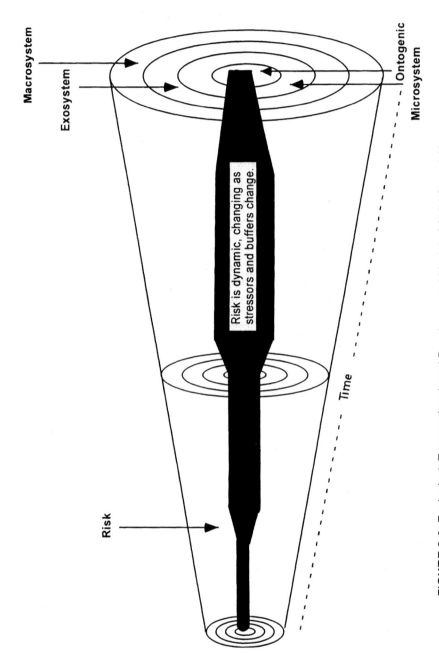

FIGURE 8-2. Ecological, Transactional, and Developmental Model of Child Sexual Abuse

this model suggests that, at any point in time, risk factors at varying systemic levels interact transactionally with the developmental stage of the child and previous history to determine the child's current level of risk. Because of this complex interaction, risk of abuse may increase or decrease over time as the environmental context and developmental stage of the child change. Thus, the heavy line that runs through the middle of the cone represents risk—a dynamic property—that can increase or decrease in magnitude over time.

Summary

In summary, it is proposed that the macrosystem, and secondarily, the exosystem are most critical to understanding risk of sexual abuse. The less important risk factors at the level of the family are best conceptualized as primarily representing the influence of the macrosystem and exosystem on the family. This influence is expressed through the family's internalized representational model of its expectations for living within the greater community and society. Ecologically, the least important level is that of the child. Like the level of the family, factors at the level of the child are best understood as the confluence of ontogenic factors (child) as they converge with the expectations of the greater society. These ecological influences then combine complexly and interact with the developmental trajectory of the child to explain risk of abuse. While risk factors eventually manifest as internally mediated at the level of the child, they are causally external to the child, operating at higher ecological levels.

Finally, while this chapter focuses solely upon factors that place children at risk of sexual abuse, it is only half, and the less important part, of the story. Victims are abused, not because they possess factors that place them at greater risk, but because these factors place them at greater risk to be targeted by offenders. Some children with numerous risk factors escape abuse, whereas some children with no risk factors are abused. They are abused because offenders target them for abuse. While this chapter develops risk of abuse, the following chapter develops risk to offend. Both aspects of abuse—risk to commit abuse and risk of abuse—critically inform our understanding of child sexual abuse.

ECOLOGICAL INFLUENCES

Macrosystem

As conceptualized by Belsky (1980), the macrosystem is the "larger cultural fabric in which the individual, the family, and the community are inextricably interwoven." Belsky describes "society's attitudes toward violence, corporal punishment, and children" (p. 328) as one of the most important factors in fostering child abuse and neglect. Similarly, when discussing child sexual abuse, the most important factor may be society's attitudes towards male privilege and sexuality.

When a problem is as pervasive as that of child sexual abuse, it must be assumed that certain societal conditions coalesce to maintain it. For instance, it is absurd to consider the problem of violence in the United States without considering society's tolerance for violence. It is therefore logical to assume that certain societal-level conditions foster a culture in which child sexual abuse is allowed to thrive. This section focuses on cultural beliefs, values, and dynamics that may foster child sexual abuse.

Power

Experts now agree that child sexual abuse is primarily an abuse of power. The most classic conceptualization of abuse is that of more powerful adults abusing less powerful children. Yet, the issue of power is more complex, for three reasons. First, up to 40% of all offenders are juveniles (Davis & Leitenberg, 1987; Fehrenbach, Smith, Monastersky, & Deisher, 1986) and approximately 70% are under the age of 25 (Wyatt et al., 1999). Second, approximately 95% of offenders are male (Finkelhor et al., 1990; Russell, 1983; Wyatt, 1985; Wyatt et al., 1999). Finally, approximately 70% of victims are female (Finkelhor & Baron, 1986). Therefore, a simple analysis of the power of adults over children is insufficient.

Instead, power must be considered in some type of interaction with gender. That 95% of offenders are male suggests that adult males are far more likely than adult females to abuse their power over children. Because the power structure within the United States is, as most would agree, patriarchal, the vast over-representation of male to female offenders is easily explained. This power structure also probably explains why the large majority of victims are female, as females have less power than males. Indeed, the patriarchal power structure also explains the high number of juvenile male offenders, as they are certainly growing into their adulthood. In line to take their place within the hierarchical structure of the United States, they thus have power over female children. As such, a trickle-down theory of power centered on male privilege may explain the important gender and age differences in both offenders and victims. In this system, males are most likely to abuse females; further, older males target younger victims. The one exception is abuse in which juvenile males, because of their greater power and strength, abuse girls close in age.

A thorough analysis of power, however, must take not only age and gender into consideration, but also race and ethnicity. Because patterns of power by age and gender reside within each race, it logically follows that within-race abuse will follow the lines of patriarchal power. For example, abuse patterns within each race will be similar to those established for the United States as a whole, with minor variations. Because physical attraction is an important characteristic when offenders target potential victims (Conte, Wolf, & Smith, 1989; Elliott, Browne, & Kolcoyne, 1995) and because of the more segregated nature of communities in the United States, it would appear likely—and empirical research supports (Wyatt, 1985)—that abuse is primarily same-race.

Finally, it is suggested that there may be diverse pathways by which power leads to child sexual abuse. First, some males may be so assured of their power that they have an inculcated sense of male privilege. These individuals might have a keen sense of ownership of individuals within their environment, perhaps manifesting in intrafamilial abuse, but also placing them at risk to commit sexual abuse against a nonrelative. Second, abuse may be a reaction to a male's need to feel more powerful.

A review of incest offenders (Williams & Finkelhor, 1990), for example, found that they tended to have inadequate masculine identities rather than hypermasculine characteristics. In other words, men who sense they are not sufficiently masculine may also be at greater risk to commit abuse.

Oppression

Another important societal dynamic that is probably implicated in risk of sexual abuse is oppression of minorities. The United States has a long history of oppression and institutionalized racism. Oppression and discrimination result in a variety of problems within minority communities, including less access to resources, income, and wealth. The lesser resources coalesce to place a greater burden upon minority communities by increasing stressors. These stressors, in turn, may increase risk of abuse.

All minorities may not be at equal risk of sexual abuse, however. Blauner (1972) has suggested that minorities can be divided into those who are colonized peoples (e.g., Mexican Americans, African Americans, and Native Americans) versus those who choose to immigrate. Further, they suggest that oppression and discrimination are greatest for those who are forcibly colonized. If this is the case, then Mexican Americans, African Americans, and Native Americans are at increased risk of abuse because they are the most oppressed groups and thus suffer greater stressors. Asian Americans and other immigrants, because they neither represent the most oppressed nor the most powerful groups, are at lesser risk of abuse. Finally, Caucasian children, because they represent the most powerful race, may be at increased risk of abuse by the most powerful members of society—Caucasian males. These complex pathways may partially explain the diverse findings in Table 8-1 concerning race.

Socialization

Another macrosystem factor that is probably implicated in the high prevalence of child sexual abuse is the socialization of both males and females, the standards of which are bound within the sociocultural norms of society. As such, beginning at even a very young age, males are socialized to be more aggressive than their female counterparts. By adolescence not only are males socialized to be more sexually aggressive than females (Orenstein, 1994), but they are also inculcated into a system of male entitlement that extends to the distribution of family labor (Major, 1993), pay within the work force (Moore, 1994), marriage (Steil, 1994), and romantic relationships (Attridge & Berscheid, 1994). The model used for presenting this inculcated sense of male entitlement as it reflects on the level of the community and family is shown in Figure 8-3.

This model suggests that socialization of cultural norms primarily occurs through the community and familial environment, through which individuals internalize sex role stereotypes to a greater or lesser extent. Male entitlement both informs and is informed by the socialization process. Thus, the large majority of males in American

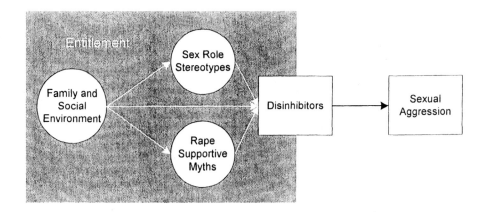

FIGURE 8-3. Relationship of Socialization to Sexual Aggression

culture develop a sense of male entitlement to the world around them, including entitlement to sex. This same environment is responsible for the formation of sex role stereotypes and attitudes towards sexuality of females and children which vary in strength depending upon the person's environment. The combined influences of a social environment of male entitlement, gendered stereotypes, and hostile attitudes towards females decrease disinhibitors for sexual abuse that then make the act of sexual aggression more likely. Indeed, much research, especially that on rape, has found that males subscribing to traditional values, including more hostile views of females, have less egalitarian models of relationships between males and females (Greendlinger & Byrne, 1987), have more sexual partners (Pleck, Sonenstein, & Ku, 1993), are more sexually aggressive, are more likely to rape females (Mosher & Anderson, 1986; Muehlenhard & Linton, 1987), and express a greater likelihood of sexually abusing children (Briere & Runtz, 1989).

While males develop a sense of entitlement, females conversely develop a sense of their lack of entitlement and vulnerability to the more powerful members of society. Females internalize this message especially within their preteen years (Orenstein, 1994) so that, by the time they move into high school, they have more fully internalized socially proscribed roles for females. While female children are surely not willing victims of child sexual abuse, they are socialized to be less powerful than, and to defer to, the more powerful and more entitled males. These dynamics can only exacerbate the physical power differential between males and females and help to explain the gross disproportion of male to female offenders.

Generational Effects

Another factor that can be conceptualized at the level of the macrosystem is the generation into which the child is born. Some studies have found that older females, especially those above the age of 50, report less abuse (Russell, 1984; Saunders, Villeponteaux, Lipovsky, Kilpatrick, & Veronen, 1992). Potential explanations have been proposed. First, it could be that older women are less comfortable with the interview process and may, therefore, under-report. When an interaction effect between level of comfort with the interview and age was explored in Bolen's (1998b) reanalysis of Russell's (1983) data, however, this hypothesis was not supported. Other possibilities are that older women may not remember abuse that occurred to them, may be less willing to report abuse they experienced, or that abuse may be increasing in more recent years. Indeed, a recent meta-analysis of random prevalence studies in North American community populations (Bolen & Scannapieco, 1999) supported the latter hypothesis. In this study, after controlling for other relationships, prevalence of abuse was found to increase with the chronological year of the study. While a portion of this relationship may be a result of a general improvement in the methodology of more recent studies or a greater willingness of younger generations to disclose, it could also indicate an increase in prevalence of abuse in more recent years. Because of the gravity of this finding, it is certainly one that cannot be dismissed summarily.

It is also possible that *patterns* of abuse may be changing and that these changing patterns account for fluctuations in abuse prevalence. An analysis by Bolen (2000a) of Russell's (1983) extrafamilial abuse data supports this contention, as prevalence by type of perpetrator had changed over time. Specifically, abuse by dates and friends of females increased in the years preceding the survey, whereas abuse by individuals in a minor role to the victim (e.g., barbers, ice cream men, etc.) decreased. A recent random retrospective survey by Wyatt et al. (1999) also found that offenders in this survey, as compared to those in a comparable survey published in 1985, were significantly younger.

That a pattern of change might exist suggests that abuse is contingent upon social factors. For example, after the sexual revolution of the 1960s, children and adolescents started dating earlier and also had more unsupervised interaction with opposite-sex friends. Increasing availability of children in these relationships may have contributed to changing patterns of abuse in more recent years.

Collective Denial

The final sociocultural dynamic to be discussed is society's willingness to deny the scope of the problem of child sexual abuse. In Chapter 2, child sexual abuse as a social construction was discussed. In this view, while a physical reality to child sexual abuse exists, the social construction of the problem informs society's willingness to recognize and respond to it.

Although child sexual abuse has occurred throughout history, it was not recognized as a social problem in this country until the mid-1970s and early 1980s. Society's willingness to define child sexual abuse as a problem allowed a burgeoning of identified victims, beginning in the 1980s. This trend has continued somewhat, but has been affected by society's tolerance for child sexual abuse. Because the prevalence of child sexual abuse may be anathema to a society that prefers to view itself as technologically advanced and compassionate, society as a whole may try to defend against and deny this reality.

This environment of denial then sets the stage for what Beckett (1996) refers to as sponsors, or those who represent interest groups. For example, Beckett describes how, between 1985 and 1990, one sponsor group supported the view that many children make false accusations, and since 1990 sponsor groups have suggested that many victims are recounting false memories. Importantly, the social construction of child sexual abuse has been purposefully molded by the sponsors of the respective schools of thought. These social constructions of the problem of sexual abuse have also been inflamed by media exposure of dramatic cases and the novelty they provide. Because these schools of thought "resonate with salient cultural themes" (p. 73), they gain support. Cultural themes are themselves ambiguous, however, as on the one hand, society maintains a view of the child as victim, but on the other, maintains "a darker, more suspicious view of children as 'insidious, practiced liars'" (p. 74).

In the end, these themes of the victim as actively lying about purported abuse resulted in a more suspicious and cautious approach to the identification and assessment of child sexual abuse in the 1990s. While no known macro-level studies have explored how these socially constructed themes have affected reported rates of child sexual abuse, it is possible that the entrenchment of these themes is related to the lower investigation and substantiation rates of child sexual abuse found nationally in more recent years (Sedlak & Broadhurst, 1996). For example, Wyatt et al. found that Caucasian (but not African American) women in their 1999 random retrospective survey were significantly less likely than women in Wyatt's comparable 1985 study to disclose their abuse to anyone. It is also highly probable that while the actual prevalence of child sexual abuse only slowly changes over time, society's tolerance for the knowledge of such a heinous act has a profound effect on the patterns of reported abuse. Society's unwillingness to accept the full scope of the problem of child sexual abuse nonetheless allows for a culture in which child sexual abuse thrives by its secrecy.

Summary

In summary, risk factors originating at the level of the greater society are conceptualized as crucial to understanding the scope of the problem of child sexual abuse within the United States. It is suggested that dynamics of power, oppression, and socialization are central causal factors that allow child sexual abuse to thrive. Changing patterns of socialization may also be implicated in changing patterns of abuse. Finally, a culture of denial and incipient backlashes may profoundly affect patterns of reported abuse.

Exosystem

The exosystem is the group of formal and informal social structures available within the immediate community of the child and his or her family. Important among these structures are the neighborhood in which the family lives, the school, the workplace, and the availability of needed resources (Belsky, 1980; Cicchetti & Lynch, 1993). Indeed, all informal social networks and formal support groups are included at the level of the exosystem.

Although this level has been strongly implicated in research on child abuse and neglect, the link between the exosystem and child sexual abuse remains more elusive. Indeed, no factor at the level of the exosystem has consistently been found to predict a history of child sexual abuse. While the obvious statement is that exosystem factors do not relate to risk of sexual abuse, this statement is probably premature until more sophisticated investigation takes place. The following sections investigate exosystem factors that may be related to risk of sexual abuse.

Availability of Appropriate and Safe Childcare

Increasingly, mothers with children are returning to the work force. Currently, 64% of mothers of preschoolers work, increasing to 71% during school age.[1] The obvious question, then, is who is tending the children? A more salient question to this chapter is whether the childcare structure is related to risk of abuse.

There are reasons to suggest that differences in childcare settings may be related to risk. In Bolen's (1998b) reanalysis of Russell's (1983) community prevalence study of females, a complex relationship between maternal employment and family structure emerged. In this relationship, female children living with both natural parents were only at increased risk of sexual abuse when their mothers worked part-time. On the other hand, children living with only females after their parents separated were at increased risk of sexual abuse when their mothers worked either part-time or full-time. It is possible that the intact families were most likely to use informal care situations only when the mothers worked part-time since, when both parents work, permanent formal childcare arrangements for their child were almost a necessity. Because they have decreased financial resources, divorced families with no resident male may have been more likely to rely upon informal care situations regardless of how much the mother worked. While other possibilities certainly exist, the potential for informal childcare to be a risk factor cannot be ruled out. Certainly, a more formal test of this hypothesis should be done before conclusions are drawn.

Educational System

Another important institution in which children spend a large portion of their time is the school system. While school systems may strive to be gender neutral, they have historically not been successful. Indeed, by the time they graduate from high school, females have significantly lower self esteem than their male counterparts and score significantly lower on math proficiency tests (American Association of University Women, 1991; Greenberger, 2000). This institutional discrimination of females may have an indirect link to females' greater risk of sexual abuse. Orenstein (1994), in her analysis of two middle schools, convincingly argues that female students suffer great sexual oppression and harassment and that the schools, often unintentionally, encourage traditional gender roles and role expectations of students. Especially in this middle-school environment, Orenstein shows that males appear to become more

---

[1] *www.census/gov/popullation/socdemo/nf-fam/htabMC-1.txt*; Nov. 16, 1998.

aggressive while females, especially those in predominantly Caucasian upper-middle-class suburban schools, become increasingly passive. This developmental stage may thus represent a time of increased risk for girls. Indeed, Bolen's (1998) reanalysis of Russell's (1983) community prevalence study found that females were at greatest risk of sexual abuse during their preteen and early adolescent years. While other factors may contribute to increased risk during this developmental stage (to be explored in a later section), the traditional gendered roles learned in this educational environment may be an important contributor.

Connectedness

Garbarino, in his ecological model of child abuse and neglect (Garbarino, 1977), discusses how individuals who do not experience a feeling of connectedness to their environment are less likely to avail themselves of a social network of resources. This isolation has, in turn, been found to be a risk factor in other types of child abuse and neglect. The relationship between a sense of connectedness and risk of sexual abuse has received some interest in the child sexual abuse literature. Among factors studied have been connectedness to a formal religion, physical isolation, and connectedness to a friendship network.

The findings, though limited, have been mostly disappointing. For example, findings do not support a relationship between living in an isolated area and increased risk of abuse (Finkelhor & Baron, 1986). Another factor with only inconsistent support is the social network of friends and other social resources available to children and their families. In a bivariate analysis, Hall and Flannery (1984) found that girls whose friends were more likely to report having had sex were also more likely to have been sexually abused. The causal direction of this relationship, however, might be reversed. Instead, it may be that sexually abused girls are more likely to make friends who are sexually active. Another concern is whether children who have fewer friends are at greater risk of sexual abuse. When Finkelhor et al. (1990) investigated this relationship retrospectively in the *Los Angeles Times* Poll (LATP) survey, however, they found no relationship.

A final area of analysis has been the relationship of risk to belonging to an organized religion. Two different studies have found such a relationship. Hall and Flannery (1984), in a bivariate analysis, found that respondents brought up in a religion and who as adults had a religious preference were significantly less likely to have been sexually abused as children. Bolen's (1998b) reanalysis of Russell's (1983) study, however, found that this relationship was more complex. Only females under the age of nine whose parents did not endorse a particular religion were at increased risk of sexual abuse. On the other hand, these same children were significantly less likely than Protestants to be sexually abused in adolescence. For Protestants, risk of abuse increased in almost a linear fashion over the age of the child.

These findings do not lend a great deal of support to the hypothesis that children whose families are not well connected or who themselves have fewer social supports are at greater risk of abuse. On the other hand, this hypothesis has not been well operationalized in prevalence studies. Until further studies are done, interpretations from these data are certainly premature. Perhaps the best conceptualization of connectedness, however, is as a protective factor instead of as a potentiator of risk. Instead of the lack of connectedness increasing risk, being connected to social supports may instead act to buffer risk when in the presence of another risk factor.

Safety within the Community

The final risk factor to be discussed within the exosystem is the overall safety of the community and safety precautions children take within the community. This section starts with an important premise: No community is safe. In the reanalysis of Russell's (1983) community prevalence study (Bolen, 2000a), extrafamilially abused females were molested in every conceivable location. While all locations were amply represented, 34% of children were abused in their neighborhood (but not at their house), almost half of whom were abused while walking around, including walking to or from school. Only a few incidents occurred at night, and almost all of the incidents occurred when the child was close to home. For this reason, how the child is typically transported may be an important risk factor. Children who routinely walk to or from school may be at increased risk. Children who walk alone in their neighborhoods may also be at increased risk.

The age at which adolescent females are allowed to start dating and whether they are allowed to have unsupervised access to male friends may also be related to risk of abuse. As discussed in Chapter 6, "Extrafamilial Abuse," sexual abuse of adolescent females by friends and dates is prevalent. Thus, early dating and unsupervised access to male friends may place children at greater risk simply because they are exposed at younger ages to more risky situations. Finally, for the same reasons, another risk factor may be whether children are allowed to be alone with nonparental adult males, regardless of the closeness of the relationship.

Summary

The exosystem is probably not as critical as the macrosystem in determining risk of abuse, but most likely continues to play an essential role. Its most important role may be as the transmitter of cultural values and beliefs through the institutions at this level, primarily the school and church. Through their roles in the socialization of children, they may inadvertently maintain dynamics that allow child sexual abuse to thrive. Another important, but less formal, institution is that of childcare. Because children have unequal access to safe childcare in America, children living in poverty may be less likely to be placed in safe childcare situations, thus inadvertently increasing their risk of sexual abuse. Finally, the children's and their families' connectedness to social networks may act as a buffer against child sexual abuse.

Microsystem

The microsystem is the level at which the children interact with their families. This level includes family dynamics, parenting styles, psychological resources of the parents, and the developmental histories of the parents (Belsky, 1980; Cicchetti & Lynch, 1993).

The traditional focus upon risk factors has been at the level of the family (microsystem) and child (ontogenic). Family dysfunction (i.e., unhealthy patterns of relating) as a risk factor for intrafamilial abuse has received special notice, whereas probably a more important risk factor at the level of the microsystem—the family as the transmitter of social norms—has remained unresearched. This section focuses upon the processes by which family dynamics might be implicated in risk of sexual abuse.

Task of Socialization

Much as the community was conceptualized as important in the transmission of societal norms, so too are parents. Previously, family paradigms were conceptualized as the "set of core assumptions, beliefs, or convictions that families hold about their environments" (Cicchetti & Lynch, 1993, p. 113) that become internalized into representational models of one's world. Parents thus internalize a model of their environment most often based upon acceptable and traditional norms. These norms are then passed onto their children through socialization, one of the primary tasks of families (Duvall, 1985). Inevitably, children come to internalize the socially sanctioned norms as their own.

Other tasks of the family are also bound within traditional social norms. These tasks include the allocation of resources, division of labor, maintenance of order (i.e., the hierarchy of the family structure), the placement of members in the larger society, and the maintenance of motivation and morale (Duvall, 1985). Within each of these tasks, social norms may affect the way in which these tasks are performed. For example, male members of the families may be regarded more highly than female members, may receive greater resources within the family, and may be assigned fewer household responsibilities. Males might also be given greater access to external resources and may be taught that they are more highly favored within the greater society. Through the socialization of females and males into gendered roles and role expectations within families, females may be socialized into patterns that increase their risk of sexual abuse, whereas males may be socialized into patterns that increase their risk to commit sexual abuse.

Privacy and Primacy of Family

Another risk factor at the level of the family is the socially prescribed privacy and primacy of the family. Within American culture, families are construed as essential systems that are clearly bounded within the larger community. Within broad social limits, families are allowed to maintain their own rules and roles with minimal interference from larger social institutions. The privacy that families are allowed to maintain is critical for maintaining the dynamics of incest. Further, this assumption of privacy within the family makes the process of disclosure of known abuse to authorities and the collaboration of family members with authorities more unlikely and more difficult.

Family Structure

Family structure, specifically the relationship between parental separation and increased risk of sexual abuse, has received a great deal of attention. Historically, children living with both natural parents have been considered at less risk of sexual abuse. Indeed, several different random prevalence studies have found that parental separation is a risk factor for sexual abuse (Finkelhor et al., 1990; Hall & Flannery, 1984; Moore et al., 1989; Russell, 1983).

The issue appears to be more complex, however. Certain studies suggest that the relationship between family structure and risk of abuse can only be understood when considering the structure of divorced or separated families. In Finkelhor et al.'s (1990) reanalysis of the LATP survey (Timneck, 1985), for example, males were at greatest risk of abuse when they lived with both non-natural parents or when they lived with only their mothers. Females were at greatest risk when they lived with both non-natural parents or with only their fathers. Similarly, in Bolen's (1998b) reanalysis of Russell's (1983) data, females were at greatly increased risk of sexual abuse when they lived with any male in the household after their parents' separation. Of all groups, the girls with the least risk of abuse were those who lived with only females after separation and whose mothers did not work. These analyses suggest that living with the same-sex biological parent may be a protective factor and that separation by itself is not a risk factor. Stated another way, living with both natural parents is not necessarily a buffer against abuse. Instead, the protective factor may be the presence of the natural same-sex parent.

Family Dysfunction

The relationship between family dysfunction and abuse risk has received much interest. Regretfully, much of this literature has had clearly pejorative connotations. Without wanting to contribute to this pejorative literature, it is possible that families with unhealthy ways of relating may have increased levels of child sexual abuse victimization within members of the family. First, families with less healthy ways of relating may involve their children in more high-risk situations. Second, these families may have children who themselves have less healthy ways of relating. These children may be less capable of assessing dangerous situations, thus being at greater risk of sexual abuse. Third, less healthy families may be less connected to their communities, thus indirectly increasing their risk of abuse.

Several random prevalence studies have found that problems within the family are related to a greater prevalence of sexual abuse. In a random sample of ninth graders, Hernandez (1992) found that adolescents reported significantly more abuse if any of their relatives or nonfamily members living in the home had substance abuse problems. Moore et al. (1989) also found that children of parents who drank heavily, used drugs, or who smoked were at greater risk of sexual abuse. Other nonrandom studies comparing families of victims of intrafamilial abuse, extrafamilial abuse, and no abuse also find that families of abuse victims have greater levels of dysfunction, with families of intrafamilial abuse victims having the greatest levels of dysfunction (Alexander & Lupfer, 1987; Ray, Jackson, & Townsley, 1991). These studies suggest that family dysfunction may be a generalized potentiator of sexual abuse risk for children.

Attachment to Parents

Attachment to parents may be an important risk factor and may explain better than family systems theory the relationship between family dysfunction and child sexual abuse. Attachment theory was developed by Bowlby (1969, 1973, 1980) to explain relationship patterns between parents and their children. Attachment is the internal representational model of the relationship between children and their parents or attachment figures that derives from the early relationship between infant and attachment figure (Bowlby, 1988). Attachment relationships can be more or less secure, and the presence of a less secure attachment relationship has been found to be an important risk factor for child physical abuse and neglect. Indeed, almost all physically abused children and their parents are insecurely attached (Carlson, Cicchetti, Barnett, & Braunwald, 1989).

The importance of attachment traverses both the microsystem and the ontogenic system. At the level of the microsystem, insecure attachment of parents may be a risk factor—for two reasons. First, parents may transmit that insecure attachment to their children, which then places their children at greater risk of sexual abuse (to be discussed in the next section). Second, insecurely attached parents may be less capable of accurately assessing dangerous situations. (See Alexander, 1992 and Bolen, 2000c for more on attachment and child sexual abuse.)

Summary

Perhaps the most important influence at the level of the family is the task of socialization in which males are socialized to receive preferential treatment and to be more sexually aggressive, whereas females are socialized to be more deferential to authority and more passive. The socialization of children within the family may be one of the most important factors related not only to risk of abuse but also to risk to offend. Another essential factor may be the attachment relationship between the child and parents, with children of insecurely attached parents being at greater risk of sexual abuse. Although family dysfunction has been found to be a risk factor for child sexual abuse, it may be that the relationship of dysfunction to risk is better conceptualized as related to insecure attachment. For example, one study documented a relationship between family dysfunction and insecure attachment (Hadley, Holloway, & Mallinckrodt, 1993). It is possible that the insecure attachment of dysfunctional family members may account for any greater level of risk of abuse. Finally, family structure may be closely related to risk of abuse. Findings suggest that living with a same-sex natural parent may be a protective factor and that separation itself may not be a risk factor.

Ontogenic

The final type of risk in Belsky's (1980) typology is ontogenic, or those characteristics intrinsic to the child. Processes such as the children's negotiation of developmental periods, the nature of their internal representational models of self and other, their ability to regulate emotions, cope with stressors, develop autonomous selves, form effective peer relations, and successfully adapt at school are included in this level. In other words, the ontogenic level is the one at which mostly external processes coalesce internally. For example, the child's attachment pattern is externally mediated by the attachment figure's representational model. Similarly, children's coping mechanisms are partially shaped by external socialization processes. This model thus conceptualizes risk factors at the ontogenic level not as those innate to the child, but as those that develop mostly through external processes. This is an extremely important conceptualization, because recognition that external factors affect internal processes removes the tendency to focus on deficits in the child that might contribute to the abuse.

Attachment of Victim

At the level of the child, the child's attachment status is probably a risk factor, although it is obviously affected by the caregiver's attachment status. Securely attached children have internal representational models of positive images of both self and other (Bowlby, 1988; Paterson & Moran, 1988). These children are most likely to seek out attachment figures upon stress (Main, Kaplan, & Cassidy, 1985) and, because of their representational models, may be most likely to accurately assess cues. As a result, these children may be at less risk of sexual abuse. Insecurely attached children, however, may be at increased risk of sexual abuse. Because insecurely attached individuals have negative self or other internal representational models (Bowlby, 1988), they may be less likely to accurately assess cues for dangerous situations or individuals within their environment.

The type of attachment status might also be important. Ambivalently attached individuals have negative self models but positive other models (Bartholomew & Horowitz, 1991). These children tend to be needy and clingy with their attachment figures (Bowlby, 1988; Sroufe & Fleeson, 1986). As such, they may be at greater risk of abuse by offenders who purposefully entice them into relationships in which some of their relational needs are met. Avoidantly attached individuals, on the other hand, have positive self models but negative models of others. Their tendency to identify with aggressive behavior (Bowlby, 1988; Renken, Egeland, Marvinney, Mangelsdorf, & Sroufe, 1989) may place them at greater risk of abuse in which the offender entices the child through his or her perceived power. Disorganized children, who as adults have negative self and other models (Bartholomew & Horowitz, 1991), may be at greater risk for all types of approaches.

While no known studies have examined these issues in children who are sexually abused, some studies in the area of child abuse and neglect have been completed. An interesting study by Troy and Sroufe (1987) found that relational patterns among children had implications for understanding relationships. In this study, children ages four and five with different attachment patterns were paired. Children with secure attachments were least likely to be bullied or victimized by other children. When victimization occurred, however, ambivalently attached children were most likely to be victimized, whereas avoidantly attached children were most likely to be the aggressors. To better understand the relationship between attachment and risk of sexual abuse, prospective studies are necessary.

Availability, Attractiveness, and Vulnerability

The most important risk factors at the ontogenic level may be whether the children are available, attractive to potential offenders, and vulnerable. In studies that ask offenders why they abused a particular child, these three themes emerged (Ballard et al., 1990; Budin & Johnson, 1989; Conte et al., 1989; Elliott et al., 1995). Elliott et al. found that 42% of offenders were attracted to a female victim because she was pretty. Availability was just that. Was the child in the wrong location at the right time? Needless to say, many of these locations were deemed safe by the child and parents. Indeed, the offender had purposefully moved into that location because the offender thought it would be a place in which to find a potential target.

The final motivational factor—vulnerability—is intriguing. In two different studies (Conte et al., 1989; Elliott et al., 1995), offenders stated that they could sense when a child was vulnerable. Perhaps the child was standing off to the side or for other reasons appeared to be excluded from the larger group. Regardless, offenders believed that they could sense which children were especially vulnerable. This factor might also explain why previously abused children are at greater risk to be reabused.[2]

Summary

Only a few factors at the ontogenic level may be related to increased risk of sexual abuse. First, insecurely attached children may be at greater risk of abuse. On the other hand, however, the children's attachment must be understood as being directly affected by their parents' attachment. Thus, attachment of the child actually originates at the level of the microsystem. The other important factors at the ontogenic level must be conceptualized as relating to what the offender is looking for, specifically whether the child is attractive, available, or vulnerable.

---

[2] For example, whereas 38% of all children in Russell's (1983) sample were sexually abused, 56% of abused children were reabused (computation by author).

DEVELOPMENTAL STAGE OF THE CHILD

The second portion of the model of risk is the developmental stage of the child. This portion of the model encompasses two areas. The first is how risk of abuse changes with the age of the child. From this perspective, it is not necessarily developmental changes within children that place them at inherently greater or lesser risk for abuse, but changes that occur and that make them more or less attractive to potential offenders. The second area is the developmental history of the child. Both are explored in this section.

Changes in Risk Based upon Developmental Age

Children appear to be at greater risk of sexual abuse at different times during childhood. Whether this is a result of or coincidental to their developmental stage is currently unclear. Most studies, when examining risk of abuse by age, have concluded that risk is greatest between the ages of seven and 13 (Finkelhor, 1994). To determine this risk, researchers have divided the number of children abused at any given age by the total number of respondents, giving an estimate of risk at any given age. A slightly different method of computing risk is to consider the number of children abused at any given age by those who have not previously been abused. This method controls for a previous history of abuse and gives a somewhat different picture of risk. In Russell's (1983) community prevalence study, greatest risk for the first experience of abuse peaked between the ages of 11 and 13, with a somewhat smaller peak in later adolescence (Bolen, 1998b). As noted earlier, age of greatest risk may also vary by race. In this same secondary analysis of Russell's data, African American females and Latinas were at greatest risk of abuse throughout early and middle adolescence, whereas Caucasian females had a somewhat linear increase in risk of abuse over the age of the child, with a slight increase in the preteen years. Previously it was suggested that these differential pathways were best explained at the level of the macrosystem.

All retrospective studies on child sexual abuse report a very low prevalence of abuse during the first five years of life. This finding contradicts incidence studies that find that the greatest incidence of reported abuse occurs between the ages of three and five and then decreases over time (Sedlak & Broadhurst, 1996). Issues of infantile and early amnesia probably account for the lower report of early abuse in retrospective prevalence studies (Williams, 1994). While the incidence studies represent a very biased population (i.e., only those cases for which abuse has been disclosed or discovered and substantiated), the incidence of abuse at these early ages does suggest that even very young children are attractive to offenders. At this age, the extreme discrepancy in power and reliance of the children upon their caregivers may place these very young children at increased risk of abuse.

Elementary school-age children may also be at increased risk of sexual abuse because of their reliance upon caregivers and the extreme discrepancy in power between an adult male and young child. Because these children are becoming increasingly independent, new risk factors emerge as they are allowed to move into their immediate environment with somewhat less supervision. The greater independence and relative naivete of these children may be the more important risk factors for this age group, especially because they assume that these locations are safe.

Preteen children, because they are moving into and through puberty, have a greater awareness of their own sexuality. Combined with their continued naivete, they may remain especially susceptible to abuse. Again, their increasing independence may be a contributing risk factor. Further, as discussed earlier, the socialization of preteens appears to be much more heavily focused upon gendered norms, thus potentially increasing risk for preteen females of sexual abuse.

Teenagers, because they are now more fully developed, may become more attractive to certain potential offenders. Only those pedophiles with explicit tastes for younger children will now be eliminated as potential offenders. The adolescents' increased independence allows them to move unsupervised into areas beyond their immediate environment, thus making them accessible to more potential offenders. The female adolescents' interest in developing romantic heterosexual relationships makes them especially susceptible to certain types of approaches such as date rape.

This developmental approach, as can be seen, emphasizes not what can be considered as negative attributes, but normal attributes of children that make them more susceptible to potential offenders. This framework is not only intentional but imperative because it allows the emphasis to be placed upon those characteristics of the child that are most attractive to potential offenders. It thus removes the potential for victim blaming.

Developmental History

An important component of the model presented in this chapter is the recognition that stressors are cumulative (Masten, Best, & Garmezy, 1990; O'Grady & Metz, 1987; Rutter, 1979; Rutter, Cox, Tupling, Berger, & Yule, 1975). Not only do current stressors impinge upon risk of abuse, but so do past stressors. For example, children with a history of multiple losses or hardships would be considered at greater risk of sexual abuse than children with no such history, even when the number of current stressors is the same. Similarly, children with a previous history of sexual abuse would be considered at greater risk than nonvictims, all other factors being equal. Even distant stressors may critically impact on risk of abuse except when those stressors have been satisfactorily resolved psychologically. Thus, risk is dynamic, changing as stressors in the child's life change and as previous stressors mount or eventually lose their power.

TRANSACTIONAL INFLUENCES

The transactional portion of the model is perhaps the most critical, for it represents the juncture among risk factors. This juncture can only be described as a complex process by which factors come together and crystallize into some level of risk.

Risk factors are protective or potentiating, enduring or transient (Cicchetti & Rizley, 1981), and proximal or distal (Baldwin et al., 1990). While Cicchetti and

Lynch (1993) suggest that abuse might occur when potentiating factors outweigh protective factors, such a simple summative procedure does not appear to adequately explain the relationship among risk factors. Certain researchers have instead found that risk factors have a compounding or synergistic effect. For example, Rutter (1979; Rutter et al., 1975) found that in a sample of 10-year-old children, those with only one risk factor did not have an appreciably greater chance of developing a psychiatric disorder. With two risk factors, however, children were at a fourfold increase, and with four risk factors children were at a 10-fold increase. Moore et al. (1989) also found a synergistic relationship between risk factors and a history of child sexual abuse. Only 6% of children with no risk factors were sexually abused; 9% of children with one risk factor, 26% of children with two risk factors, and 68% of children with three or more risk factors were abused.

Other literature has found that protective factors work only in the presence of a potentiating factor. In other words, the effect of the protective factor is indirect, operating only in interaction with a potentiating factor (Rutter, 1987). Being dependent upon some type of interaction, the effect is not apparent in the absence of a risk factor. One such protective factor is good parenting. Parker and Parker (1991), for example, found that victims of child sexual abuse who were treated poorly by their parents had greater impairment than victims who experienced good treatment by their parents. In the nonabused control group, however, scores measuring adjustment did not differ between groups having poor and good parenting. Only when the risk factor of abuse was added to the protective factor of good parenting did the buffering influence of good parenting become apparent. O'Grady and Metz (1987) conclude of research on protection factors, "the general pattern of results suggests that multiple risk factors may combine complexly and potentiate each other, and protective factors...may powerfully buffer the adverse effects of risk and stress" (p. 17).

In summary, while certain risk factors may independently contribute to increased risk of sexual abuse, they also complexly and synergistically combine at the level of the child to increase or decrease risk of sexual abuse. As discussed earlier, Cicchetti and Rizley (1981) suggest that abuse may occur when potentiating factors outweigh protective factors. Because risk factors are often time-dependent, the child's risk of sexual abuse is dynamic, changing as the child's circumstances change. While an early risk factor (e.g., loss of a parent early in the child's life) may have an ongoing effect, it is likely that its effect decreases as distance is gained from the event. From this perspective, while cumulative factors are hypothesized to impinge upon risk of sexual abuse, more current risk factors are expected to have a greater effect than more historic risk factors.

A simple formula of adding all potentiating factors and subtracting all protective factors, however, is probably not sufficient. This formula ignores the complex interactions that occur among risk factors, as well as the possible synergistic effect of multiple risk factors. To fully understand risk, then, requires a complex analysis of (a) the number of potentiating and protective factors, (b) the timing of the events, and (c) the nature of the risk (i.e., whether it is enduring or transient, and distal or proximal).

SUMMARY, CONCLUSIONS, AND IMPLICATIONS

A primary thesis of this book is that child sexual abuse is a sociocultural problem. This chapter extends this thesis by framing risk of abuse within an ecological perspective. Within this perspective it is suggested that the most important risk factors for child sexual abuse originate at the macrosystem. The macrosystem, in turn, has a critical impact upon the exosystem. Risk at the level of the exosystem is primarily a result of the inculcation within its systems (e.g., the church and schools) of cultural values and beliefs. It is only at the level of the family (microsystem) that some of the factors can be conceptualized as not being directly related to the internalization of cultural mores. Even so, because one of the primary tasks of the family is socialization of its children, cultural norms continue to profoundly affect risk even at the level of the microsystem (family).

This ecological approach to risk of abuse is critical for examining factors that may causally contribute not only to risk of abuse, but also to the widespread and continuing problem of child sexual abuse in the United States. The contribution of this ecological approach is that it targets the level at which causal influences occur instead of the level at which they are exacerbated. This has been a continuing problem as child sexual abuse literature has focused upon those issues inherent within children that place them at greater or lesser risk of abuse. Instead, the ecological model recognizes the critical function of societal beliefs, values, and norms in the manifestation of abuse.

This ecological model suggests that these external and causal factors are then internalized at the level of the child as risk of abuse. Even though the risk factors may actually be manifested at the level of the child, however, the ecological model serves to remind us that they originate causally at higher levels. Because children internalize these factors as their own, risk of abuse historically has been studied as an attribute of the child instead of recognizing its critical social derivation. Instead, risk of abuse is more properly conceptualized as a social phenomenon that becomes inculcated, much in the same way as the socialization of cultural mores, into the child.

The drawback to a purely ecological approach, however, is that it is less capable of explaining how these causal factors that originate at higher levels come to be manifested in the children themselves as internalized level of risk of abuse. For this analysis, developmental and transactional approaches are necessitated. A developmental approach reminds us that risk is cumulative and is informed by historical events. Thus, developmental history, both positive and negative, informs current risk of abuse by making children more or less vulnerable. Second, children's risk of abuse may change depending upon their age, primarily because they may become more or less attractive or available to potential offenders.

The transactional portion of the model frames the method by which these risk factors, developmental age, and history of the child coalesce into level of risk. Risk factors can be either potentiating or protective, enduring or transient (Cicchetti & Rizley, 1981), and proximal or distal (Baldwin et al., 1990). All characteristics must be taken into account when considering risk of abuse. Because of its complexity, risk of abuse may not be quantifiable in the foreseeable future.

Implications are clear, however. The study of risk of abuse must move from the conceptualization of risk originating at the level of the child to that of a social construction. It must be recognized that simply living in this country places an extreme and unacceptable risk for abuse upon all children. That 30% to 40% of female children and 13% or more of male children are sexually abused (Bolen & Scannapieco, 1999) suggests as much.

Framing risk of sexual abuse as a social construction reframes the entire perspective of prevention. Because risk of sexual abuse is much more about the society in which the child lives than about the child, to be effective, prevention efforts must target the society in which these children live. Surely targeting the child will do some good, especially age-appropriate prevention strategies (Bolen, in press). On the other hand, targeting children is like targeting needles in the middle of the proverbial haystack to protect the needles from the haystack. Protecting our children from child sexual abuse requires that we target society first, the communities in which the children live second, the families third, and the children last. Instead, our focus is exactly backwards.

How do we go about targeting society? To address this question requires first that the knowledge base on offenders be reviewed within the context of why these (mostly) men abuse. This knowledge base is reviewed in the next chapter. The final section then discusses prevention strategies that target society.

CHAPTER 9
OFFENDERS

INTRODUCTION

This chapter focuses on perpetrators of child sexual abuse. A large body of research on perpetrators now exists, almost all of which necessarily refers to populations of *identified* offenders, or those who have been caught. The previous chapters have suggested that most child sexual abuse victims are never identified. Therefore, it is safe to assume that the literature on offenders is biased towards that small proportion of offenders coming to the attention of authorities. Part of the purpose of this chapter is thus to compare what we know about *identified* offenders to what we know about *unidentified* offenders.

This chapter will not attempt to review all literature on offenders, for two reasons. As indicated, we are currently not sure whether this literature accurately reflects all offenders or only those who come to the attention of authorities. Second, the literature is now voluminous. What this chapter will instead attempt to do is to provide an overview of the prevalence and characteristics of perpetrators and to discuss possible rationales for their offending behavior. This discussion follows that in the previous chapter, which in part presented an ecological model of child sexual abuse. That discussion was focused not so much on risk factors inherent in the victims themselves, but on those within the larger sociocultural context. Special emphasis was given to sociocultural factors that foster conditions in which child sexual abuse can thrive. An overriding theme was that females are at increased risk of sexual abuse, and males are at increased risk to offend simply by virtue of living in a male-dominated society.

Certainly, most males do not sexually abuse children. Thus, a simple sociocultural explanation is insufficient to understand propensity to abuse. It is suggested, however, that the culture within this society sets the stage for abuse to occur. That is, certain sociocultural values such as the idealization of sex with younger females and tolerance for the sexualization of female children act as social *disinhibitors* for abuse. Although other preconditions are usually necessary to allow a potential offender to abuse (Finkelhor, 1984), it will be argued that no *disinhibitor* other than sociocultural norms is necessary in certain cases. Yet, sociocultural values present a paradox since values such as the inappropriateness of child-adult sex may instead act as *inhibitors* to abuse. This paradox is also addressed. Other disinhibitors to be discussed are more properly explained at the level of the microsystem, or the individual and family. Finally, important implications and recommendations for the primary prevention of child sexual abuse are discussed. First, however, the scope of the problem of offending behavior is analyzed.

LIKELIHOOD OF ABUSE[1]

How many males are at risk to purposefully sexually abuse a child? It has long been of concern that far more offenders exist in the general population than come to the attention of authorities. That 30% to 40% of girls, and as many as 13% or more of boys, are sexually abused (Bolen & Scannapieco, 1990) suggests as much. Herman (1990) probably stated this rationale best when she said, "When one-third of the female population has been sexually victimized, common sense would suggest that some comparable percentage of the male population has been doing the victimizing" (p. 178). Even though her statement may be somewhat exaggerated, the minimal literature does suggest that a significant minority of all males have the potential to purposefully abuse a child.

In the earliest studies of likelihood of abuse, Freund et al. (1972) showed slides of naked children to nondeviant men (mostly psychology students). From this study they concluded that nondeviant males had "clearly sexual reactions to female children" (p. 132) as young as six to eight years of age. Further, when Malamuth asked male college students, "If you could be assured of not being caught or punished, how likely would you be to engage in pedophilia, that is, sexual activity with a child" (as cited in Finkelhor & Lewis, 1988, p. 65), 15% agreed to some likelihood. This finding is all the more remarkable because the activity was defined as pedophilia, an illegal event.

In a later random community study using sophisticated techniques to ensure the anonymity of respondents, 4% to 17% of males agreed that they *had* sexually abused a child at some time in their lives (Finkelhor & Lewis, 1988).[2] In a college male population, however, only 1% of males admitted to having had sexual activities with a child under the age of 13 when they were 18 years or older, although the average age of the respondent was only between 22 and 23 (Bagley, Wood, & Young, 1994). Another 5% admitted to some interest in sexual activity with a child under the age of 13. Only slightly more men targeted female than male children. Another 3% indicated that they had experienced sexual activity with an adolescent aged 13 to 15 when they were 18 years or older. Three percent admitted to some interest in sexual activity with a male between 13 and 15 years of age, and 9% admitted to some interest in sexual activity with a female between 13 and 15 years of age. A final study found that 21% of college males reported some sexual attraction to small children, 9% reported fantasies of having sex with a child, 5% reported masturbating to fantasies of sex with a child, and 7% reported some likelihood of having sex with a child (Briere & Runtz, 1989).

A limitation of these studies is that they address only abuse by adults who are physically attracted to younger children. Yet, approximately 40% of all child sexual abuse incidents occur with children 14 years of age and older.[3] Another reason to believe that these studies may underestimate the prevalence of abusive behavior is

---

[1] Portions of this section are also found in Bolen, in press.

[2] The method utilized precluded an exact number of respondents. Of the two samples, however, 4% and 17% stated that they had sexually abused a child. Given confidence limits, the range was between 1% and 21% of all men.

[3] Computed by the author from Russell's (1983) community prevalence study.

that many offenders appear to abuse for reasons other than sexual attraction to children. (This thesis is explored further in the section, "Motivations to Abuse: Unidentified Offenders.") While it is premature to suggest the percentage of males at risk to abuse a child or adolescent, these arguments suggest that the 4% to 21% of men in these studies professing some likelihood to abuse may be an underestimate. Even that 6% to 21% of males may be at significant risk to abuse a child, however, is an amazing statistic. The risk of males within this society to abuse children surely warrants great concern.

WHO ARE THE PERPETRATORS?

Because the empirical knowledge base on offenders is necessarily on *identified* offenders, one of the unanswered questions is whether *identified* offenders accurately represent *unidentified* offenders, a question that is addressed in the following sections. The first section, by discussing the process by which offenders are identified, acknowledges the vast number of offenders who do not come to the attention of authorities. The second section presents the minimal literature on *unidentified* offenders and then compares this literature to that on *identified* offenders. The final section presents models and typologies of offenders that attempt to categorize characteristics of these offenders and their motivations for offending.

How Many Offenders Are Identified?

Identified and unidentified populations of offenders may be very different. Perhaps the most important reasons for these differences are that social policies prioritize certain types of abuse, especially intrafamilial abuse, and most offenders are not caught. Because the first issue has been discussed throughout the early chapters of this book, this section addresses only the second issue.

Becoming an identified offender requires a myriad of steps. First, the child must disclose the abuse, or abuse must be suspected. Second, the person who observed the abuse or to whom the abuse was disclosed must report the abuse to the proper authorities. The official reporting body must then deem the complaint serious enough to warrant an investigation. If the investigation leads to a substantiation of the abuse, it can be referred for prosecution. If sufficient evidence exists, the case can then be prosecuted. Finally, the perpetrator must be convicted.

Disclosure: First, the child or perpetrator must be willing to disclose the abuse, or the abuse must be observed. It is safe to say that the vast majority of all abuse is not observed. Perpetrators obviously do not want to get caught and, therefore, usually go to great lengths to hide their actions. For the same reason, perpetrators do not admit to having sexually abused a child. Children are also reluctant disclosers. Few children tell, and most who do so delay their disclosure (Russell, 1983; *Lexington Herald-Leader*, 1992; Saunders, Villeponteaux, Lipovsky, Kilpatrick, & Veronen, 1992; Sauzier, 1989).

The third party who is told about the abuse then has the responsibility of deciding how to handle the disclosure. This is not an easy task because child reporting mechanisms differ by state. This task may be especially ominous for a lay person unfamiliar with state policies. Regardless, lay people often do report known abuse, accounting for 27% of all child abuse cases in 1993 known to child protective services (Sedlak & Broadhurst, 1996). The process for mandated reporters is clearer, and every state now has formal child abuse reporting laws (Pence & Wilson, 1994). Legally, those who report are not required to have proof of their suspicions—only reasonable suspicion. Even so, only 40% of all maltreatment and 35% of serious maltreatment was reported to or identified by child protective services in 1986 (Finkelhor, 1990a). Zellman and Antler (1990) also found that only 44% of surveyed mandated reporters said that they consistently reported suspicious abuse. A more recent study found that only 69% of suspected abuse was officially reported by professionals (King, Reece, Bendel, & Patel, 1998). Thus, only a fraction of all abuse is disclosed or suspected, and only a fraction of known abuse comes to the attention of authorities.

Investigation: The next step is that child protective services or law enforcement agencies must be willing to investigate the offense. The most recent figures indicate that child protective services investigated only 42% to 44% of all cases of child sexual abuse known to professionals in 1993, down from 72% to 75% in 1986 (Sedlak & Broadhurst, 1996).[4]

Substantiation: Not only does the case have to be investigated, but it also has to be substantiated. As would be expected, not all investigated cases are substantiated. In 1997, substantiation rates were 34% for all cases of child abuse and neglect, down from 38% in 1990 (U.S. Department of Health and Human Services, 1998, 1999). There are various reasons that cases are not substantiated, the most logical of which is that abuse did not occur. The recent trend in which fewer cases of abuse are investigated, however, is very disturbing. Certainly, a case that is not investigated cannot be substantiated, nor for that matter, can abuse be definitively ruled out. Further, it is extremely disturbing that only about 10 of every 100 cases of child sexual abuse known to professionals are substantiated.[5] It is illogical to assume that 90% of cases of suspected or disclosed abuse did not occur.

Prosecution and sentencing: Finally, the majority of substantiated cases of sexual abuse are not prosecuted. While studies vary in the percentage of cases that are prosecuted, all agree that the percentage is low. In the study with the lowest percentage, Tjaden and Thoennes (1992) found that criminal charges were filed in only 17% of all cases of child sexual abuse. A poll by the *Lexington Herald-Leader* (1992) of abuse occurring over a period of three years in 10 counties in the state of Kentucky also found that charges were filed in only 19% of substantiated cases. The first National Incidence Study (NIS-1) (Finkelhor, 1983) also found that criminal action was taken in only 24% of substantiated cases, a finding replicated in a study by Sauzier (1989). Still another study found that although criminal charges were filed in 42% of all cases of probable abuse, felony charges were filed in only 24% of

---

[4] The first figure in each set (42% and 72%) applies to those cases meeting the more rigorous harm standard in which abuse was committed by a parent or parental substitute. The second figure in each set applies to the more relaxed endangerment standard that broadens the relationship of the perpetrator and harm criteria (Sedlak & Broadhurst, 1996).

[5] Of 100 cases of suspected abuse known to professionals, 69% are reported, of which 44% are investigated, and of which 34% are substantiated ($100 \times .69 \times .44 \times .34 = 10$).

all cases (Martone, Jaudes, & Carvins, 1996). A final study found that 39% of substantiated cases were prosecuted (Brewer, Rowe, & Brewer, 1997).

Further, of those cases sent to prosecutors, only a small percentage of offenders are actually sentenced. Sauzier (1989) found that of 156 victims of sexual abuse, only 10% of all offenders were incarcerated. Martone et al. (1996) also found that convictions occurred in only 15% of all cases of probable abuse, although 85% of those convicted were incarcerated. Finally, the *Lexington Herald-Leader* (1992) found that of the 19% of cases of sexual abuse that were prosecuted, 91% of offenders were convicted or pled guilty, only 65% of which were incarcerated.

Two other studies consider cases of child sexual abuse referred for prosecution. In one study of all child sexual abuse cases referred for prosecution over an eight-year period, 30% of perpetrators pled guilty prior to the trial, and less than 5% were convicted at trail (Bradshaw & Marks, 1990). In a more recent analysis, only 60% of cases submitted for prosecution over a one-year period were accepted, although 85% of the cases accepted for prosecution were convicted (Cross, Whitcomb, & De Vos, 1995). Of those convicted, 38% were incarcerated for more than a year, 40% were incarcerated for one year or less, and 22% were not incarcerated. Cross et al. conclude that child sexual abuse trials are rare, with cases being four times more likely to be declined than accepted by prosecutors.

Because of the different ways in which these studies are reported, they are difficult to compare. For certain of these studies, however, the total percentage of offenders who were incarcerated can be computed. The *Lexington Herald-Leader* (1992) found that offenders were incarcerated in only 10% of all cases of substantiated abuse, whereas Martone et al. (1996) found that offenders were incarcerated in only 13% of all cases of probable abuse. Sauzier (1989) found that offenders were incarcerated in only 10% of all cases that were referred for evaluation, whereas Cross et al. (1995) found that offenders were incarcerated in 40% of all cases submitted for prosecution, although only 19% of all offenders were incarcerated for over one year.

Summary: Given the current knowledge base, we cannot at this time estimate the percentage of offenders known to authorities. This analysis suggests, however, that most cases of sexual abuse are not disclosed. Even in disclosed cases that are then reported to child protective services by professionals, most are not investigated. Of those cases that are investigated, most are not substantiated. Of those cases that are substantiated, most offenders are not prosecuted. Only if the case is prosecuted does the offender have a better-than-average chance of conviction. Even then, however, most convicted offenders spend less than one year in jail. In the end, offenders may be convicted in only one or two of every 100 cases of suspected abuse known to professionals. Of substantiated abuse, only about 7% of offenders will spend more than one year in jail.[6] Yet in Chapter 5, "Incidence and Prevalence," it was noted that using even the most optimistic estimates, only about one-fourth of all abuse that occurs is known to authorities. Thus, the population of *identified* offenders

---

[6] Of 100 cases of substantiated abuse, an average of 23% are prosecuted, of which an average of 79% are convicted, of which and average of 80% are incarcerated, of which an average of 50% are incarcerated for more than a year (100 x .23 x .79 x .80 x .50 = 7.3).

represents a tiny percentage of the population of *unidentified* offenders. This is a grim analysis of a system designed to protect its young charges.

Unidentified Offenders: Random Retrospective Studies

The previous analysis suggested that the vast majority of offenders do not come to the attention of authorities. Thus, it is critical to understand how *identified* offenders compare to the much larger population of *unidentified* offenders. The purpose of this section is to present the minimal information available on *unidentified* offenders. To do so, retrospective surveys—which are the only studies that currently provide information on a representative sample of *unidentified* offenders—are reviewed. Even then, the focus of these studies is on the victims, and little information is available concerning the identity of the offenders. Nonetheless, the minimal available literature is reviewed next.

Gender: The first random studies suggested that 95% or more of offenders were male (Russell, 1983; Wyatt, 1985). In Russell's (1986) retrospective community prevalence study on females, only 2% of abusive parents and 5% of intrafamilial abusers were female. Overall, 2% of all offenders in her sample were female. Males, however, are at greater risk to be sexually abused by females. In the *Los Angeles Times* Poll's survey (Finkelhor, Hotaling, Lewis, & Smith, 1990), 17% of male victims, as compared to 1% of female victims, were abused by females.

Age of offender: The stereotypical image of a perpetrator is of an older man with a sexual attraction to younger children. The empirical literature, however, suggests that the stereotype about age is not supported empirically. Instead, juvenile offenders account for 20% to 50% of all reported offenders (Davis & Leitenberg, 1987; Fehrehbach, Smith, Monastersky, & Deisher, 1986). In Russell's (1983) sample, the one retrospective study in which approximate ages of unidentified offenders are available, 39% of all offenders were less than 20 years of age.[7]

Race of offender: Only two known random prevalence studies, those by Wyatt (1985) and Russell (1983), provide information on the race of the offender. Because Wyatt's (1985) study was stratified by race, however, her findings cannot be extrapolated to a larger population. Russell's study found that Caucasian offenders were over-represented.[8] Whereas 69% of offenders were Caucasian, 57% of the population in San Francisco in 1980 was Caucasian.

Education of offender: Russell's (1983) study also provides information concerning the education of the offender. Of the incidents in which the victim knew the educational history of the adult offender (i.e., an offender older than 21 years of age), which included 54% of incidents committed by adults, 32% of offenders had less than a high school education.

Relationship of offender to victim: Perhaps one of the most disconcerting findings concerning child sexual abuse is the pervasiveness of its threat. This pervasiveness is not only demonstrated by the sheer numbers of children who are sexually abused, but also by the threat to children by virtually all groups of males

---

[7] Computed by author.
[8] Computed by author.

with whom they come into contact. It would be encouraging if one group of offenders such as strangers or fathers were over-represented. If this were the case, prevention measures could target these high-risk groups.

Regretfully, random retrospective prevalence studies find that offenders have many different types of filial and nonfilial relationships with victims. Approximately 30% of child sexual abuse is intrafamilial (Tables 7-1 and 7-2). This abuse is divided rather equally into abuse by fathers, uncles, siblings, and cousins, with fathers and uncles accounting for slightly more of the abuse. Of the 70% of abuse that is extrafamilial, abuse by strangers accounts for only 11% to 21% of the abuse of females (Tables 6-1 and 6-2). The most prolific offender group is acquaintances, accounting for 28% to 33% of all abuse (Finkelhor et al., 1990; Russell, 1983). Indeed, 12% of all women in Russell's study were abused by acquaintances. Yet, friends of the family, personal friends, dates, and strangers also frequently abuse. In Russell's study, approximately 7% of all respondents were abused by strangers, 4% to 6% were abused by authority figures, family friends, and dates, and 3% were abused by friends. (Because the average victim suffered 1.8 assaults, victims could be abused in multiple categories.)

Finally, the relationship of the offender to the victim varies by the race, ethnicity, and age of the victim. Not surprisingly, younger children are at greater risk than older children of intrafamilial abuse.[9] Further, African American children may be at greater risk than Caucasian children of abuse by a stepfather, surrogate father, or cousin (Wyatt, 1985).

Comparison of Identified to Unidentified Perpetrators

Having discussed the minimal information available on *unidentified* perpetrators, this information is now compared to information available on *identified* perpetrators. First, there appear to be differences in gender when comparing these two bodies of literature. As mentioned earlier, random prevalence studies have consistently concluded that only about 5% of all offenders are female. Because this finding was so different than that of the 1980 National Incidence Study (NIS-1), in which 46% of reported offenders were mothers or mother substitutes, many professionals were skeptical of the findings of the prevalence studies (Finkelhor & Hotaling, 1984). The discrepancy in these figures, however, resulted from the unfortunate practice by child protective services of listing mothers as co-offenders in cases of father-daughter incest, perhaps because it was assumed that the mothers *should* have known and thus *should* have done something to protect their children.

While this collusion theory has now been refuted, this practice continued in the most recent NCANDS incidence study done in 1998 in which females were charged as offenders in 44% of all substantiated abuse cases and 53% of all parental abuse cases (U.S. Department of Health and Human Services, 2000). Because only 7% of all parental abuse was committed solely by a mother, however, the more likely scenario is that the mother was charged as a co-offender because of her perceived

---

[9] In Russell's (1983) study, victims of intrafamilial abuse were on average 11 years of age, as compared to 13 years of age for victims of extrafamilial abuse (computed by author).

inability to protect.[10] Thus, *identified* populations of offenders continue to vastly over-represent females and especially mothers.

Identified offenders are also grossly over-represented by intrafamilial abusers. As discussed previously, random prevalence studies suggest that approximately 70% of all abuse is committed by someone outside the family (Bolen, 2000a), and that only approximately 7% to 8% of all abuse is committed by fathers (Russell, 1986; Wyatt, 1985). In contrast, the NIS-3 (Sedlak & Broadhurst, 1996) found that 54% of substantiated abuse was committed by parents or parental substitutes. Thus, current policies also continue to lead to the identification of a disproportionate number of intrafamilial offenders, especially offenders of father-daughter incest.

Finally, Tzeng et al. (1999) assessed the demographic characteristics of 532 offenders whose cases had been prosecuted. They found that Caucasian offenders were under-represented (68% as compared to 78% of individuals in the general population) and that 53% of offenders had less than a high school education (as compared to 34% of individuals in the general population). In comparison, Russell (1983) found that Caucasian offenders were over-represented (69% as compared to 57% in the 1980 San Francisco census) and that only 32% of adult offenders whose educational history was known had less than a high school education. While her study is limited because it relies on the report of those victims who knew the educational history of the offender (thus eliminating strangers and some other known others), differences between these studies are stark enough to warrant some interest. Tzeng et al. conclude that "offenders were more likely to be from the socially 'disadvantaged' group—minorities, the poorly educated, labor workers, and the unemployed" (p. 74). Yet, findings from Russell's study suggest that the "disadvantaged" may simply be more likely to be prosecuted.

Models and Typologies of Identified Offenders

Even though there are important differences between *identified* and *unidentified* offenders, studies on *identified* offenders remain useful. One of the most important sets of literature on *identified* offenders is that which allows us to understand why they abuse, and especially to understand why certain individuals abuse, even though others with similar characteristics do not. Several models and typologies that conceptualize the motivations of offenders have been developed. Another similar set of literature has attempted to categorize offenders into discrete groups. The first well-known model to be developed divided offenders into those who were fixated (those with a primary sexual orientation towards children) and those who were regressed (those with a primary sexual orientation towards peers or adults) (Groth, 1978; Groth & Birnbaum, 1978). Another popular method of dividing offenders is by whether they are intrafamilial or extrafamilial offenders (i.e., incest offenders or child molesters) (Becker, 1994). The empirical literature, however, has found that neither of these models adequately distinguish groups of offenders (Becker, 1994; Simon, Sales, Kaszniak, & Kahn, 1992).

---

[10] 100% - 28% = 72%, and 87% - 72% = 15%. Thus, 15% of this abuse had to be committed by both mothers and fathers, whereas 13% (100% - 87%) had to be committed by mothers only.

Another early model of sexual offending—the four-preconditions model—was developed by Finkelhor (1984). This was a different type of model because it focused on four preconditions in child molesters that were hypothesized to precede the abuse. These preconditions are as follows: the potential offender has to (a) be motivated; (b) overcome internal inhibitions; (c) overcome external impediments; and (d) undermine or overcome the child's resistance. Motivations considered in this model are emotional congruence between the child and adult, sexual arousal to children, and blockages such as limited social skills that interfere with appropriate adult relationships. In this model, individuals abuse only when all preconditions are present. Of importance, this model was the first to consider motivating factors for the abuse. Another important contribution of this widely used model is that it recognized the importance of disinhibitors.

Two other models are more truly typologies (i.e., they classify offenders into discrete groups). The first, by Hall and Hirschman (1992), groups offenders by their primary motivation to offend. The second, by Knight, Carter, and Prentky (1989), is much more complex but also categorizes offenders based upon factors that at least partially reflect the offenders' motivations for abuse.

Quadripartite model: Hall and Hirschman's (1991, 1992) quadripartite model hypothesizes that sexual offenders, including both rapists and child molesters, can be grouped into one of four groups based upon their motivation for the abuse. These motivations are as follows.

(a) Offenders motivated by *physiological factors* offend primarily because they seek sexual gratification, although they may or may not exhibit high levels of sexual arousal to the targeted age group. There is a tendency for sexual arousal to become associated with aggressive behavior, with that aggressive behavior itself becoming sexually arousing. Violence is more likely to occur in offenders in which this pairing of aggression and sexual arousal occurs. Another characteristic of this subtype is multiple victims.

(b) The second motivator, *cognitive factors*, may be present in most abuse situations because the offender often appraises threats and benefits to determine whether the risk is worth the encounter. What distinguishes this group, however, is that the offender is motivated by cognitive distortions such as perceiving some type of justification for offending or having negative perceptions of women. Generally, this type of offender lacks sexual or general impulsivity.

(c) The third group, motivated by an *affective state,* tends to exhibit affective dyscontrol in which affective states such as depression become so powerful that they overcome other inhibitions to abuse. For this group, sexual aggression tends to be opportunistic, unplanned, violent, and predatory. Affect disinhibitors such as alcohol or stress are more likely to be determinants for offenders in this category.

(d) The final category, *personality factors*, contains offenders with chronic impairment affecting many functional domains, including intellectual impairment, family conflicts, poor social skills, chronic substance abuse, poor adult adjustment, significant impulse dyscontrol, and general antisocial activity. Early experiences may create lasting personality deficits that increase the likelihood of later sexual aggression. This group may also engage in other types of criminal activities. These offenders abuse violently and over the greatest length of time and have the poorest prognosis for rehabilitation.

Hall and Hirschman (1991) recognize that multiple motivations may exist for any given offender. The primary motivational theme (i.e., the most potent motivator) determines the category into which the offender is assigned. Motivational factors reflecting different categories may also combine to substantially increase the risk that the person will offend. An important advantage of this model is that it is multicausal. A disadvantage, however, is that it has not been empirically tested and does not recognize environmental issues such as the sociocultural context of sexual abuse. Another disadvantage is that it combines child molesters and rapists. Although there are often overlaps between child molesters and rapists, Knight and Prentky (1990) found that research does not support a single typology for both types of offenders.

Massachusetts Treatment Center—Child Molester Typology: One of the most sophisticated typologies of offenders is that by Knight, Carter, and Prentky (1989) of the Massachusetts Treatment Center. Using both inductive and deductive processes, they developed a classification system for sexual offenders over a 10- to 15-year period. This typology attempts "to find naturally occurring homogeneous groups on the basis of offenders' similarities and differences on a specific set of attributes" (Knight & Prentky, 1990, p. 27), that is, to find consistent theory-driven organizing structures underlying the characteristics of offenders of child sexual abuse. The typology is multidimensional and hierarchical, suggesting that multiple characteristics need to be considered and that characteristics might overlap among groups. Although fairly complex, it has been shown to be reliable.

Unlike other typologies, this method scores nonincestuous child molesters on two axes—the degree of sexual fixation to the child and the amount of contact the offender has with the child (Knight & Prentky, 1990). In turn, both high- and low-fixation offenders can be either high or low in social competence. Thus, Knight and Prentky found that social skills and sexual fixation towards children are some of the important discriminators among child molesters. The dimension measuring high and low contact is somewhat more complex. High contact offenders can have either an interpersonal or narcissistic orientation towards their victims. Low contact offenders, however, are first divided by the severity of physical injury and then by whether the offense is sadistic. Offenders are rated on both continua.

One advantage of this system lies in the rigor of its empirical analysis, which exceeds that of any other typology. Another advantage is that offender groups appear to have different developmental pathways. For example, Prentky et al. (1989) found that family-of-origin pathology was related to greater alcohol abuse and school-related acting out behavior, both of which were then related to higher levels of sexual fixation and contact. The most important disadvantage of the model lies in its complexity. Another significant drawback is that because it was developed using nonincestuous child molesters who were committed, its relevance to other offenders, especially juvenile and incest offenders, cannot be determined.

WHY OFFENDERS ABUSE

The previous section focused primarily on offenders' motivations for abuse. This section now examines certain of these motivations as well as other theories concerning offending behavior within an ecological context.

Exosystem and Macrosystem

In the previous chapter, the context of child sexual abuse within the greater society was established. It was suggested that child sexual abuse must first and foremost be considered a societal problem resulting from the following issues: power disparities between males and females and between adults and children; increased stressors as a result of oppression; socialization of traditional and stereotypical heterosexual scripts that are passed on through the major institutions within children's lives (i.e., families and schools); and a lack of connectedness to the greater community. Of these, it is suggested that the most powerful causal factors for child sexual abuse are power disparities and socialization of traditional heterosexual scripts that result in a sense of male entitlement to sex. Thus, sociocultural norms play a large role in setting the stage for child sexual abuse to thrive.

This chapter furthers the discussion by suggesting that these sociocultural norms may act either as inhibitors or disinhibitors of sexual abuse, depending on the ages of the offender and victim. For offenders who are close in age to their victims (i.e., peers), it is suggested that sociocultural norms act as *disinhibitors*. For offenders who are clearly older than their victims, it is suggested that sociocultural norms act primarily as *inhibitors*. Whether sociocultural factors act as inhibitors or disinhibitors may be an important difference between *identified* and *unidentified* offender populations.

Offender and Victim Age Disparity

The models and typologies presented in the previous section apply mostly to abuse in which offenders seek out much younger victims. These offenders probably experience sociocultural taboos about adult sex with children as *inhibitors*. This interpretation was forwarded by Finkelhor (1984), who argued that pedophiles had to overcome the *inhibiting* effect of sociocultural taboos against adult sex with children by employing some other type of *disinhibitor*. One *disinhibitor* they might employ is simply an inculcated sense of entitlement to and ownership over females and children within the offender's environment. In this situation, the sociocultural norm of entitlement—a *disinhibitor*—might act in competition with the *inhibiting* sociocultural norm of the taboo of adult sex with children. More likely, however, an additional *disinhibitor* may be needed. For example, the potential offender's level of sexual arousal to children may be so powerful that it acts to override cultural taboos. Another *disinhibitor* forwarded by Finkelhor (1984) is that the social ineptness of the potential offender may interfere with adult relationships, resulting in age-inappropriate advances. Cognitive distortions typical of offenders may also act as *disinhibitors* (Blumenthal, Gudjonsson, & Burns, 1999; Hartley, 1998; Ward, Fon, Hudson, & McCormack, 1998).

Age-Appropriate Victims (Peer Abuse)

For offenders who seek out age-appropriate victims (i.e., peers), it is suggested that sociocultural norms may be strong enough to act as the only *disinhibitor* necessary to precipitate a potential abusive act. Many males are socialized beginning at a very young age into traditional heterosexual scripts in which they are considered dominant to females and entitled to sex with age-appropriate partners. As such, younger males who abuse age-appropriate victims may not perceive the encounter as abusive, but may instead rationalize their behaviors as normative within the values endorsed by society. Because victims are age-appropriate, no other *disinhibitor* than inculcated sociocultural norms may be necessary to precipitate abuse. In this type of abuse, young men target appropriate sexual partners inappropriately.

In a recent case-by-case analysis of extrafamilial abuse cases in Russell's (1983) community prevalence study of female respondents (Bolen, 2000a), sociocultural norms acting as *disinhibitors* were evident among many of the younger offenders. These offenders often appeared to have no other motivation to abuse than simply to act out traditional heterosexual scripts. Because this study was based upon an *unidentified* random population of offenders, the findings resulting from this study are especially important.

One theme that emerged among this group of offenders was the abuse of the victim for sport. For example, one group of adolescents made sexual advances towards a group of girls at a swimming pool; in another incident a group of soldiers harassed and fondled an older adolescent in a bus lobby. One victim was continually harassed by male acquaintances as she walked home daily from school. Because she was the first in her class to wear a padded bra, another girl became the center of attention and abuse of a group of boys. Other situations were even more overt, such as the snipe hunt on which two boys forced the victim to undress and left her naked to walk home. In virtually every situation of abuse that appeared to be for sport, a group of males was involved and, in most situations, the males actively encouraged each other to perpetrate. (See *Our Guys* for an excellent case example of a rape "for sport."[11])

In another type of abuse, a single male abused the victim but then used the abuse incident to bolster his own reputation. The theme of this type of abuse could be classified as female conquest. This abuse occurred in one of two ways. In one, the victim was abused by a single male while other males watched. In another method, after the victim was abused and usually raped by a solitary male, who was most often a friend or date, he would then boast about it to his friends. The victims were often humiliated and degraded by the perpetrator's bragging behavior.

A final and similar theme was of male entitlement to sex, a theme that was most obvious when victims were abused by dates and lovers. The sense of entitlement was overt and clear for certain of these incidents. For example, one perpetrator told his victim to "either put out or get out;" another said, "you know what you came here for." Still another told his victim that she could not be his girlfriend if she could not "ease his pain."

These motivational themes—of abuse as sport, conquest, and entitlement—are probably similar in origin, as they all clearly represent the objectification of the female and the overriding concern of the male's reputation and right to sexual

---

[11] *Our Guys* (1997), authored by Lefkowitz, is an investigative report of a gang rape of a 17-year-old mentally challenged adolescent female by high school students, many of whom were considered leaders within the school.

access. In the themes of sport and conquest, the male's reputation was clearly at stake as he participated in the commission of the group abuse or, as a single perpetrator, used it to further his reputation among peers. In the theme of entitlement, especially in abuse by dates and lovers, the abuse possibly exemplified an unconscious mindset of the perpetrator—that sexual access to the victim was his right.

Thus, much of the abuse by the younger offenders in this study was an extension of socialization patterns between males and females. Dates who raped and friends and acquaintances who made sport of the female victim speak to socialization patterns gone awry. It is unlikely that these perpetrators would even have labeled their behaviors as illegal. Hence, it seems that the only or primary motivation and *disinhibitor* for this group of offenders was what they considered culturally normative behaviors for heterosexual encounters.

Finally, a study on an *unidentified* population of offenders has important implications. Briere and Runtz (1989), as mentioned earlier, found that 7% of male college students, knowing they would not get caught, might sexually abuse a child, whereas 21% admitted some level of sexual attraction to children. Significantly, many of the same factors found in men with a propensity to rape were found in this cohort of younger males, including an acceptance of interpersonal violence, self-reported masturbation to pornography, frequent sex partners, and a hypothetical likelihood of raping a woman. Thus, both studies are examples of sociocultural factors operating as *disinhibitors* of abuse.

Microsystem

Three factors at the level of the family have previously been hypothesized to place individuals at greater risk to offend. Two factors—dysfunction within the offender's family and a weak parent/child bond—relate primarily to incest. The third, insecure attachment, may be a general risk factor for all types of abuse. This section discusses only the latter two factors. Even though incest offenders often live within families with some level of dysfunction, offenders must still make the decision to offend. A discussion of family dynamics tends by nature to implicate members of the family other than just the offender. Given that offenders—and not their families—make the choice to abuse, this chapter does not discuss family dysfunction as a risk factor, although recognizing that it may coexist.

Parental bonding: The consideration of parental bonding as a risk factor derives from biosocial theory, which suggests that an innate biosocial mechanism that inhibits incest exists (Williams & Finkelhor, 1995). While early writings discussed the existence of this incest taboo, later writings hypothesized that this taboo was triggered by the environment, specifically by the strength of the bond between father and child. As such, it has been hypothesized that fathers with closer relations to their children are less likely to abuse them (Parker & Parker, 1986; Williams & Finkelhor, 1995).

Because these studies were discussed in detail in Chapter 7, "Intrafamilial Abuse," their findings are only briefly reviewed. While caretaking does appear to provide an inhibitory mechanism for incest, its effect is weakened when other predisposing factors are present (Parker & Parker, 1986; Williams & Finkelhor,

1995). Further, a small group of fathers actually use the early caregiving as a method of grooming the victim for later abuse. Finally, the mechanism of inhibition (i.e., decreased sexual arousal) is not supported.

Attachment: Another theory that is receiving an increasing amount of interest is the relationship of attachment to offending behaviors. While Alexander (1992) was the first to consider the relationship of attachment to families in which incest occurs, Ward, Hudson, and Marshall (1996) were among the first to consider whether attachment deficits were related to greater offending behavior. Specifically, they hypothesized that child molesters would be primarily dismissing or fearful in attachment style. Indeed, they found that not only were most child molesters (82%) insecurely attached, but they were slightly more likely to be fearful (38%) than to be preoccupied or dismissing (22% each), although mean scores were most elevated on the fearful and dismissing scales. An unpublished dissertation also found differences in attachment based upon whether offenders were preference (having a sexual orientation towards children) or situational (Gibeau, 1989). Preference offenders were more likely to display an absence of attachment (i.e., detachment), whereas situational offenders were more likely to be anxiously attached. These studies suggest that attachment status is related to the type of offending behavior.

It is also probable that offenders having different types of attachment deficits may act out their sexual deviance in distinct manners. For example, because anxious attachment is characterized by a greater neediness towards the attachment figure and a high level of anxiety (Bowlby, 1988), anxiously attached (preoccupied) offenders may be more likely to develop long-standing relationships with their victims and may exhibit a great need for being in contact with them. Detached (avoidant) offenders, who are more dismissing in their relationships and exhibit greater hostility, may be more aggressive with victims and may have lower needs for physical proximity. They may also be at greater risk to abuse multiple children. Finally, fearful offenders may exhibit components of both strategies. Although they may be more aggressive and violent, they may also exhibit high needs for proximity.

Ontogenic

At the level of the individual, five areas have been most often discussed and analyzed: sexual arousal to children, psychopathology, alcohol use, social incompetence, and a history of previous child sexual abuse. Obviously, these conditions may be a result of developmental or sociocultural factors. They are discussed, however, at the ontogenic level because they relate uniquely to the individual.

Sexual Arousal to Children

Historically it was thought that offenders abused primarily because they were sexually aroused to children. More specifically, it was thought that offenders could be divided by whether they had a primary preference to younger or older children and whether they preferred male or female children (Knight, 1992). Findings, however, are not as clear. Many studies have now used penile tumescence to measure sexual arousal of perpetrators to victims across age groups and gender. A review of such studies concluded that while many have methodological problems, there is considerable consistency among findings (O'Donohue & Letourneau, 1992). Studies have been able to distinguish fairly clearly between self-admitted child molesters (i.e., those offenders who abuse outside the family) and control groups, with child molesters showing more sexual arousal to children. These studies correctly identify between 80% and 96% of perpetrators. Differentiating nonadmitters (i.e., those who do not admit to the offense) from control groups, however, is more difficult, and success rates are no greater than chance alone. Findings are mixed when distinguishing child molesters from other types of sexual offenders such as rapists or exhibitionists. Penile tumescence measurements have also been less reliable in differentiating incest offenders from pedophiles.

The most important explanation for these varied findings may be that many perpetrators engage in multiple paraphilic acts across age groups, thus exhibiting more than one arousal pattern. In a sample of unidentified sex offenders who had assurances of confidentiality and immunity, Abel et al. (1988b) found that a wide range of sexually deviant behaviors was fairly normal. Of the 192 offenders against children or adolescents entering treatment, 45% targeted both male and female victims, 44% offended both intrafamilially and extrafamilially, and 59% abused both children and adolescents. Another study on this population found that 49% of incest offenders abused female children outside of the home, 12% abused male children outside of the home, and 19% raped adult women (Abel et al., 1988a). A significant minority were also involved in exhibitionism, voyeurism, sadism, and frottage (public rubbing against a nonconsenting person). Ballard et al.'s (1990) comparable findings for incest offenders indicate that half of these offenders had extrafamilial affairs, 80% used pornography, 47% visited prostitutes, and almost 20% engaged in bestiality. A final study of perpetrators of female children and normal controls found five groups of arousal patterns, including sexual arousal to adults only, to adults and teens, to children, to children and adults, or no discriminating pattern of arousal (Barbaree & Marshall, 1989). Only 35% of child molesters showed a sexual arousal pattern only to children. Those who did so had a greater number of victims, used more force in the act, were considered more dangerous than offenders in other categories, and were more often from a lower socioeconomic status. Other child molesters had a more heterogeneous pattern. Incest offenders were divided fairly equally among the adult and nondiscriminating groups. Those in the control group never showed a preference pattern for children.

This analysis suggests that only a minority of all offenders of child sexual abuse are true pedophiles who show a sexual arousal pattern only to children. Other offenders show a mixed pattern of responding and may also exhibit arousal to adults. Thus, multiple paraphilias and sexual arousal across age groups may be the norm within the population of both *identified* and *unidentified* offenders.

Psychopathology

An historical theory is that "men who commit sex crimes must be 'sick'" (Herman, 1990, p. 178). The empirical literature, however, has not been supportive of this theory. Across studies, only a small number of offenders have evidence of serious psychopathology. Indeed, in their review of studies on incestuous fathers, Williams and Finkelhor (1990) concluded that one-quarter to one-third of incest offenders seemed quite normal. This is a similar conclusion to that of Herman (1990), who concluded after reviewing studies for all types of sex offenders:

> The most striking characteristic of sex offenders, from a diagnostic standpoint, is their apparent normality....The great majority of convicted offenders do not suffer from psychiatric conditions that might be invoked to diminish criminal responsibility. (p. 180)

Although most perpetrators do not show significant psychopathology, many do have personality disorders that:

> involve a relative failure of human attachments and social relations—a preoccupation with one's own fantasies, wishes, and needs, a lack of empathy for others, and a desire to control and dominate others rather than to engage in mutual relationships. (Herman, 1990, p. 180)

Given that the studies conducted include primarily convicted or incarcerated perpetrators, it is perhaps surprising that more perpetrators do not have severe psychiatric disturbances. That these populations do not have high levels of serious psychopathology surely suggests that *unidentified* offenders may be even more "normal."

Substance Use

The use of alcohol or drugs as a *disinhibitor* has also received attention, and a number of studies have found evidence of alcohol use in perpetrators. In an early review, Araji and Finkelhor (1986) concluded, "alcohol plays a role in the commission of offenses by some groups of sex abusers" (p. 116). Later reviews conclude the same. Herman (1990), for example, found that as many as 25% to 50% of sex offenders (not specifically child molesters) were alcohol abusers. She suggested caution in the interpretation of these figures, however, citing a study by Vaillant (1983) in which 11% to 60% of working-class men could be classified as alcohol abusers, depending upon the definition employed. This author's case-by-case analysis of *unidentified* offenders in Russell's (1983) community prevalence study also suggested that although alcohol or drug use was present in some of the cases, it was either incidental to the abuse itself or was used as a weapon against the victim. For example, once incapacitated, the victim was then raped.

These reviews suggest that a substantial minority of offenders are probably substance users, although fewer offenders use substances during the commission of the crimes. Herman (1990) concludes:

> The role of alcohol can probably best be understood as a facilitating one; intoxication may serve as an aid to overcoming inhibitions in those already predisposed to commit sexual assaults, while those who have no desire will not do so—drunk or sober. (p. 185)

Williams and Finkelhor (1990) also conclude in their review of incest offenders:

> *Alcohol and drug abuse are related to so many social problems that it obviously belongs among any listing of correlates of incestuous abuse. On the other hand, many believe that its popularity as an explanatory factor stems primarily from the fact that offenders so often invoke it themselves to minimize the opprobrium directed toward their crime. (p. 247)*

Clearly, some perpetrators looking to excuse their behavior may conclude that they were less responsible for their acts because they were under the influence of the substance. The findings from Russell's data, however, suggest another conceptualization of substance abuse—as a weapon.

Social Incompetence

The social incompetence of the offender has been suggested and analyzed for a number of years, and both Finkelhor (1984) and Knight and Prentky (1990) consider it a major dimension of their models and typologies of offenders. In this theory, offenders are assumed to be socially incompetent and unable to achieve intimacy with adults and are therefore more likely to approach children (Marshall, 1989). Ward et al. (1996) extended the social incompetence construct even further by suggesting that it is directly related to the offenders' early attachments with parents. Although several studies have found that offenders do have social interaction problems (Araji & Finkelhor, 1986; Marshall, Hudson, & Hodkinson, 1993), Knight and Prentky (Knight, 1992) have also found that approximately a quarter of *identified* offenders are instead socially competent. That approximately one-third of all extrafamilial abuse in Russell's (1983) study of *unidentified* offenders was by dates, friends, and family friends also suggests that a number of offenders are socially competent.

Childhood History of Sexual Abuse

Several different theories have been advanced to explain the phenomenon of male victims who grow up to sexually abuse, although the themes "can be loosely categorized as either cognitive-behavioral or psychodynamic" (Garland & Dougher, 1990, p. 489). Cognitive-behavioral formulations suggest that conditioning or modeling processes are involved. Conditioning might occur through masturbatory fantasies in which early sexual experiences are paired with orgasm. Through processes such as memory distortion, these fantasies may evolve over time into sexual arousal of children through, for example, fantasizing oneself as the adult. This conditioning, in turn, may lead to sexual precociousness and increased sexual behavior. Modeling also occurs as the sexually abused child learns that adults can sexually interact with children and that the experience may be rewarding.

Psychodynamic formulations view the abused-abuser process as an attempt at mastery or as identification with the aggressor. By identifying with the older partner, the child may be predisposed to later becoming involved with a child. "Such an individual may identify with young males as the recipients of his affection and can therefore easily rationalize his behavior" (Garland & Dougher, 1990, p. 491). In turn, by identifying with the aggressor and becoming the active participant instead of the passive victim, the person attempts to gain mastery over the childhood experience. Of this abused-abuser hypothesis, Hanson and Slater (1988) state, "The intuitive appeal of such a relationship is so strong that many clinicians have accepted it as an article of faith" (p. 487).

A number of studies have analyzed the offender's history of child sexual abuse, yet few employ control groups and methodological difficulties abound. At least two reviews of these studies have been done (Garland & Dougher, 1990; Hanson & Slater, 1988). Hanson and Slater combined totals for all studies reviewed to determine overall levels of childhood victimization rates among different types of perpetrators. Because of their more rigorous methodology, only their study is reviewed.

Studies were included only if sexual offenses against children were clearly delineated, the number of offenders who had sexually abused children was reported, and sample size was reported (Hanson & Slater, 1988). Overall, 18 studies involving 1,717 perpetrators were found. Using a broad definition that included noncontact abuse, 33% of these perpetrators had been sexually abused as children; using a narrower definition of contact abuse, 23% were abused. Of the perpetrators who abused females, 18% had been abused as children; of the perpetrators who abused males, 35% had been abused as children. When perpetrators abused both males and females, 67% had been abused as children. Finally, 27% of incest perpetrators, 24% of extrafamilial perpetrators, and 31% of mixed (or unknown type) perpetrators were abused as children.

In another study, Bagley et al. (1994) randomly sampled a cohort of males ages 18 to 27. Males were divided into three groups: (a) no unwanted sexual contact during childhood; (b) one instance of unwanted contact; and (c) multiple events. Overall, 16% of males experienced at least one instance of unwanted sexual contact during childhood. These groups were then compared based upon current (i.e., after the age of 18) sexual interest in or contact with a child. Of those males who had not been victimized as children, 6% had some sexual contact with a child when they were adults. Of those with a single childhood victimization incident, 12% had sexual contact with a child. Of those with multiple childhood experiences, 37% had sexual contact with a child. Male victims of childhood sexual abuse were two times more likely to abuse a child if they were sexually abused once and six times more likely to abuse a child if they were abused multiple times. There were also differences in the gender of the victims to whom the males were attracted. Ninety-five percent of offenders (those who had sexual contact with a child) with no childhood victimization abused females, as compared to 75% of offenders with one incident in childhood, and 26% of offenders with multiple victimization episodes in childhood.

Taken as a group, these studies suggest that males sexually victimized as children are at somewhat increased risk to abuse a child. The risk may be greatest for those abused multiple times, and those males may be especially likely to target male victims or both male and female victims. As important, some men not abused in childhood do offend. Females appear to be at greater risk of abuse by males who were not abused or who were abused only one time during childhood, whereas males appear to be at greater risk for abuse by males who themselves were victimized multiple times during childhood. As concluded by others, however, a history of sexual abuse does not presuppose the offending behavior. Most victimized males do not grow up to offend. As Hanson and Slater (1988) conclude, "Child sexual victimization appears to be neither a necessary nor sufficient condition for becoming a child sexual abuser" (p. 496).

SUMMARY AND CONCLUSIONS

This chapter has made several important points about offenders. First and probably most important, a significant minority of all males profess some propensity to sexually abuse children. Of course, the studies are few in number, and methodological issues in the only random prevalence study preclude an exact interpretation. On the other hand, that the few studies done have such high numbers of offenders or potential offenders (4% to 21%) is of utmost concern.

Another important point, however, is that studies assessing sexual interest in children target only a portion of all potential offenders. Another significant population of potential offenders may be those who subscribe to traditional heterosexual scripts of dominance over and sexual entitlement to females. It was of great concern that a group of offenders emerged in the author's (Bolen, 2000a) review of the extrafamilial abuse cases in Russell's (1983) community prevalence study in which females were abused for sport, conquest, or entitlement. In these cases, males were almost always age-appropriate sexual partners who exceeded the limits of appropriate behavior, often by raping their victim. Thus, it is suggested that another perhaps larger group of potential male, youthful offenders exists in which traditional sociocultural heterosexual scripts act as *disinhibitors* to allow them to offend.

Finally, the literature suggests that *disinhibitors* other than sexual arousal to children or an acting out of traditional heterosexual scripts exist. A large body of literature on *identified* offenders now documents the link for at least some offenders to a history of their own childhood victimization. Other literature discusses the important role of social incompetence and attachment deficits. Because the literature on *unidentified* offenders is so sparse, it is impossible to know whether other important factors are being overlooked.

Given this literature, how many males are at risk to sexually offend? How many females? It is obvious that the literature cannot as yet support an estimate. Yet, what we do know is that vastly more men than women abuse, and the literature certainly suggests that a substantial minority of males may be at risk to purposefully sexually abuse a child. If other studies confirm the existence of another large group of mostly *unidentified* adolescent and young adult male offenders—who may not endorse sexual arousal to young children but who abuse as extremes of normative behavior—then the percentage of males at risk to offend may be even greater than the previous 4% to 21% estimate.

The literature presented in these last two chapters recognizes that child sexual abuse is a societal tragedy of epidemic proportions. The previous chapter suggested that child sexual abuse is not so much about factors within children or families that increase their risk of sexual abuse, but about sociocultural factors that allow child sexual abuse to thrive. The most important of these societal factors, it was suggested, are (a) power disparities between males and females, and between adults and children; and (b) the socialization of traditional heterosexual scripts that are transmitted through schools and family. Yet, child sexual abuse cannot survive without an aura of denial of the problem that continues to permeate society.

Finally, this chapter furthered the discussion in the previous chapter by recognizing that societal values act not only as *inhibitors* of abuse but also as *disinhibitors*. For adults, the taboo of adult sex with children acts as an *inhibitor* that must be overcome though the incorporation of some type of *disinhibitor* such as alcohol use, sexual arousal to children, and others. Sociocultural values may also act as *disinhibitors*, however, especially when the victim is an age-appropriate partner. In this case, sociocultural values of sexual entitlement and male dominance over females may act as the only *disinhibitors* necessary to provoke an abuse incident. Thus, sociocultural standards for heterosexual interactions taken to extremes may be all that is required to precipitate an abusive event. If this is the case, then many "normal" males may be at risk to sexually abuse, not as a result of perversity, but simply because they are acting out what they have been taught by society.

IMPLICATIONS AND RECOMMENDATIONS[12]

Taken together, these last two chapters suggest that a far different approach to the prevention of child sexual abuse is needed. Current school-based programs target children by teaching them skills to deflect the approaches of potential offenders. Yet, the literature presented in this book suggests that the current methods of prevention simply do not work. First, there is no evidence to support the notion that abuse prevalence has been reduced during the nearly 20-year history of the prevention programs (Bolen, in press). Second, the pervasiveness and omnipresence of the threat to children is so great that no amount of training can prepare them for the numerous approaches of both filial and nonfilial offenders in a multitude of locations.

The pervasiveness of the threat of sexual abuse suggests that only by targeting potential offenders and sociocultural norms that support an abuse-prone culture can the epidemic of child sexual abuse be reduced (Bolen, in press). Thus, preventing child sexual abuse requires a realignment of existing sociocultural structures that allow abuse to thrive. One of the most important of these is the male sex role. Indeed, ours is a society in which males are encouraged to have younger, less experienced partners. Our society is also one "that encourages predatory male sexuality, that sexualizes all intimacy, and that fosters male irresponsibility towards children" (Finkelhor, 1990b, p. 389). If effective programs can be developed that target the redefinition of the male sex role and thus the reduction of offending behavior, then for the first time in modern history we may be able to consider the possibility of significantly reducing the prevalence of child sexual abuse.

Promotion of Healthy Relationships

Programs that target the male sex role and the reduction of offending behavior require a very different paradigm than the current prevention model of introducing

---

[12] This section is taken in part from Bolen (in press).

occasional programs to children in which they are taught skills to deflect the approaches of offenders. Instead, a proposed paradigm that targets males as potential offenders is suggested. While there are various facets to this proposed paradigm, the one that is discussed here is the school-based component that infuses content throughout the curriculum and across age groups. (See Bolen, in press, for an expanded discussion of this proposed paradigm.) The content of this curriculum focuses on teaching healthy relationship behaviors to children and adolescents. The remainder of this chapter considers how the proposed prevention paradigm differs from the existing one, while offering far greater potential for reducing the prevalence of child sexual abuse. To develop this section, the existing paradigm for the prevention of child sexual abuse is compared to the proposed paradigm along four domains—basic assumptions, orientation, methods, and outcomes.

Assumptions: The current paradigm for the prevention of child sexual abuse targets children and teaches them methods for deflecting approaches of potential offenders. The goal of these programs is to prevent abuse by relatives, known others, and strangers by reducing the "vulnerability of children to abuse and exploitation" (Kohl, 1993, p. 139). Thus, these programs: (a) teach children the concept of sexual abuse, often described as bad touching in private places; (b) teach children that they can refuse such overtures and get away from the potential offender; and (c) encourage children to tell an adult about overtures that occur (Finkelhor & Strapko, 1992). At its core, then, the current prevention paradigm has a dire and hopeless assumption—because we cannot effectively target potential offenders, we must target potential victims. Thus, the best we can do is to thwart the attacks of offenders. This strategy is analogous to teaching self-defense strategies to all persons in the United States as the primary prevention strategy for lowering overall levels of violence.

The primary assumption of the proposed paradigm is that the problem behavior—the abuse itself—can be dramatically reduced. This more optimistic assumption provides hope for reducing the prevalence of child sexual abuse.

Orientation: Another important difference in these two paradigms is their general orientation. For the existing paradigm, the orientation is one of prevention. For the proposed paradigm, the orientation is one of promotion. Much like the Healthy Start program in Hawaii (Mansfield, 1997), this paradigm shift assumes that promoting healthy behaviors is an even better method for reducing problems. In this particular case, the problem behavior is the offending behavior itself. This orientation, then, assumes that male children can be presented alternative and more prosocial definitions of masculinity that allow them to express their masculinity in healthier ways than by choosing aggressive sexuality.

Method: The current method of prevention primarily targets young children, teaching them messages of empowerment and methods to thwart potential offenders. These specialized programs, presented to children on an occasional basis, do not consider differential abuse patterns over time and are typically not offered to preadolescents or adolescents.

The proposed paradigm, by addressing abuse through the promotion of healthy behaviors, instead infuses content throughout the school curriculum across age groups. Social learning theory suggests that those messages that are most likely to be internalized are those heard consistently over time. Thus, all classes could have some content that models and rewards prosocial behaviors. Further, health or similar classes could have consistent time devoted to this material.

While these messages of prosocial behavior should be interwoven throughout the curriculum, there are probably windows of particularly effective opportunity, including preschool and early adolescence. A developmental task of the preschool period is to come to some understanding of gender identity (Schuster & Ashburn, 1992). A developmental task of adolescence is to experience one's own sexuality and contemplate how to express it. As windows of opportunity, special courses or course content could be developed to target these developmental periods.

The focus of this program must also change over time. One of the pertinent findings from the author's (2000a) secondary analysis of Russell's (1983) community prevalence survey was that patterns of risk of abuse changed over the lifespan of the child. Approximately half of all abuse committed by juvenile offenders (i.e., under the age of 21) was perpetrated against a friend or date.[13] Another 30% of all abuse was perpetrated against an acquaintance. While most friend abuse was committed by offenders under the age of 14, most date abuse was committed by offenders between 14 and 21 years of age. These findings suggest that the program for younger age groups needs to focus on the promotion of healthy behaviors in friendship relations. For middle school and high school populations, however, the focus must include romantic relationships. For all ages, males must be taught better methods of expressing their masculinity than appropriating acquaintances for their sport or conquest. Further, adolescents must learn that sexual activity with younger children—indeed, any child at a younger developmental stage—is never appropriate and is instead harmful. These messages combat those societal messages that encourage males to have sex with younger, less experienced females.

Because most abuse is heterosexual, these programs should be especially sensitive to this type of abuse. Yet some abuse is not heterosexual. Some males abuse male children. Further, a few females also abuse male or female children. It is important that these populations are not overlooked. Therefore, broader messages that teach the bounds of appropriate contact in same-sex friendships or romantic relationships, as well as messages concerning the bounds of appropriate contact for younger children, are also necessary. Finally, even though this paradigm directly focuses on healthy relationship patterns that are taught through a guided curriculum, the promotion of healthy relationships can also be interwoven throughout the policies and philosophy of schools.

Goals: Outcomes for existing child sexual abuse prevention programs have been measured primarily by the retention of information by participants. The short-term goal for these prevention programs is that some children are able to thwart the attacks of offenders by using the information they are taught.

The short-term goal for the proposed paradigm is two-fold. The first short-term goal is that male children and adolescents exposed to this curriculum will internalize a healthier and more prosocial model of expressing their masculinity. The second short-term goal is that these same male children and adolescents will perpetrate less abuse. Of course, sexually aggressive females should also benefit from this curriculum. The long-term goal for the proposed paradigm is that these young males will also

---

[13] As computed by the author.

perpetrate less abuse as they come into their manhood. Thus, a realistic goal of this paradigm is that the prevalence of offending behavior can be reduced over time.

In summary, it is argued that the only effective method of reducing the prevalence of child sexual abuse is to target potential offending behaviors. To do so, a very different paradigm is needed. This paradigm targets one of the most critical causal roles in child sexual abuse—the societal definition of the male role—by promoting healthy relationship patterns. Framing the program in this manner moves the focus and rubric of the program away from methods of extinguishing negative behaviors—a deficit model and one that might be experienced by males as demoralizing—to that of promoting healthy behaviors, a strengths perspective. Further, the focus changes from prevention to promotion.

Programs for the promotion of healthy relationship patterns might be successful for the same reason that current prevention programs do not appear to be successful at reducing the prevalence of abuse. They target the reduction of offending behavior rather than the reduction of victimization. Further, they target what many experts consider to be one of the primary causal factors for the epidemic of child sexual abuse and the preponderance of male offenders—the social definition of the male sex role. Targeting one of the important causes of child sexual abuse while providing healthy alternatives for behavior has the potential to finally reduce the intolerable tragedy of child sexual abuse.

CHAPTER 10
NONOFFENDING GUARDIANS

INTRODUCTION

Position available: Hero/role model. Job description: Be perfect. Requirements: Some supernatural skills, nice smile....Hours: Forever. Pay: None....One would have to think twice before applying for this opening. And yet it's a job that is thrust upon all our [mothers], whether they've asked for it or not....We are continually let down by our [mothers]. It could hardly be otherwise, since our desire to have [women] fill these roles is so great and our scrutiny of them so intense...that failure is inevitable. (Telander, 1991, p. 108)

This article on sports stars appearing in *Sports Illustrated* could just as easily have been written about mothers. And this quote could very well be the message of this chapter—that mothers of sexually abused children have expectations thrust upon them for which they are ill prepared to cope. Inevitably, they sometimes fail. Is it the failure that is the problem or the expectations placed upon them that is the problem? This chapter addresses this essential question.

Mothers have typically taken almost the full weight of the burden for their children's physical and emotional wellbeing after disclosure of child sexual abuse. One reason that this occurs is simply because of the significant proportion of *investigated* abuse (although not abuse that *occurs*) that is committed by fathers. In these cases, the available nonoffending parent is almost always the mother. The second reason for a narrow focus on mothers can best be attributed to a gender bias. Regardless of whether the abuse is intrafamilial or extrafamilial, professionals consider the mother the primary protector and supporter of her child. This policy is exemplified by two statistics in the child sexual abuse literature. First, in a recent review of 16 studies on the guardian's support of the child after disclosure (Bolen, 2000b), at least 1,498 of the 1,518 guardians (99%) assessed were mothers. On the other hand, 92% to 93% of all abuse is committed by someone other than the father (Russell, 1983; Wyatt, 1985). Therefore, while a nonoffending father is a potential guardian of the child in 90% to 95% of all committed abuse, 99% of all guardians assessed in these studies were mothers. Further, not a single known paper on nonoffending fathers has been published, as compared to 50 or more with a primary focus on the nonoffending mother. Because of this substantial gender bias on nonoffending mothers, literature on guardian support in this chapter must necessarily concern itself with the mother's response to her child's sexual abuse. This is not, however, to ignore the importance of the father's response and support.

The purpose of this chapter is to review the extant knowledge base on nonoffending guardians, asses its historical roots, and consider whether current policies on nonoffending guardians are more reflective of the historical literature or the empirical knowledge base. It has been the thesis throughout this book that the current conceptualization of the problem of child sexual abuse has far more to do with its historical formulation than with the available empirical literature. It will be argued that this thesis is especially true for nonoffending guardians. A further purpose of this chapter is to consider the multiple stressors on nonoffending guardians and their families during and after the disclosure of abuse. It is also the contention of this chapter that expectations for nonoffending guardians after disclosure are idealistic, deriving from a system-defined conceptualization of guardian support. A final purpose of this chapter is to present an alternative method for conceptualizing expectations for nonoffending guardians after disclosure, while also forwarding recommendations for changes to existing policies.

HISTORICAL PERSPECTIVE

Early Theories on Nonoffending Mothers

Mothers of victims of sexual abuse, especially those of children abused by their fathers, have taken an historical beating in the clinical literature. As discussed in Chapters 2 and 3, mothers were long assumed to contribute to the initiation of the abuse and to collude in ongoing incest by not reporting the abuse and by maintaining dynamics in the family that would support the incest (Alexander, 1985; Frude, 1982). After analyzing this historical literature, various authors have categorized early hypotheses concerning mothers (Breckenridge & Baldry, 1997; Jacobs, 1990; McIntyre, 1981; Wattenberg, 1985). Groupings of hypotheses by these authors are similar and generally emphasize the mother as colluding in the incest, as withdrawing from her roles as mother and wife, as having personality defects, and as a victim herself.

Collusion and withdrawal of the mother: Literature that viewed the mother as colluding in father-daughter incest developed from early studies (1950 to 1980) done mostly by male physicians (Wattenberg, 1985). In this theory the mother was said to "derive unconscious pleasure from the sexual interaction [of the father and daughter] through the voyeuristic role she assumes" (Jacobs, 1990, p. 502). Often the assumption that the mother colluded was used in tandem with clinical literature in which the daughter was described as seducing her father (Frude, 1982) or in conjunction with the role reversal hypothesis, which stated that the mother relinquished her roles as mother and wife (Cohen, 1983). The mother was said to reject her role as a wife because of her inability to tolerate intimacy and ambivalence about her sexuality (James & MacKinnon, 1990). As a result, the mother was theorized to either consciously or unconsciously reject her own role in the family, instead promoting her oldest daughter into the role of fulfilling the physical, emotional, and sexual needs of the husband. By abandoning her role, the mother was then assumed to force the father into a position of having to seek the fulfillment of his sexual needs through his daughter (Cohen, 1983; Frude, 1982). Those mothers who tried to escape the enormous responsibilities in their home by taking care of themselves were viewed as deviants from a cultural norm of servicing everyone else's needs before their own. In what McIntyre (1981, p. 463), in an analysis of this literature labeled a "flight of responsibility," mothers who were unable or unwilling to satisfy their husbands sexually were labeled frigid or hostile. A striking paradox of this literature, however, was the definition of dysfunctional sexuality. Although the mother's alleged lack of interest in the sexual relationship was considered dysfunctional in early papers, the father's need for aberrant sex with children was considered functional and normal (James & MacKinnon, 1990).

This concept of collusion is also found in more recent work, but with slight alterations. Greenspun (1994) believes that "the collusive marital pattern" (p. 7) contributes to the family's vulnerability to incest. These "abuse-prone" (p. 7) families have a parentified child (the future victim) who was identified even "at an early age as being quite mature and capable" (p. 7). The introduction of any unusual or prolonged stress disrupts the marital relationship, at which time "the daughter is placed, both consciously and unconsciously into the wife's role" (p. 8). Thus, the "mother who encourages incest, passively or actively, strives toward achieving her own personal and ultimate goal of superiority" (Tinling, 1990, p. 295). Siblings may also collude in ongoing abuse by "unconsciously sacrificing their sister in order to protect themselves and keep their father happy" (p. 8). Here the assumption is that both mother and siblings at some level recognize the ongoing abuse. The concept of the "incestuous family" also continues in recent literature, a term that connotes a mother who, at the least, contributes to the abuse (Haugaard & Samwel, 1992; Hudson, 1996).

Personality defects: Alternately, mothers are conceptualized as weak, helpless, powerless, needy, and dependent upon their husbands to fulfill their great emotional needs (Abbott, 1995; Cohen, 1983). Zuelzer and Reposa (1983) suggested that "incestuous mothers" function at a "pregenital level" and "go to any length to satisfy their needs for affection, attention and support, even if at the cost of their own children" (p. 101). By labeling these mothers incestuous, Zuelzer and Reposa also elevate them to the level of an offender. The wives' dependence on their husbands then contributes to marital strain as well as to their inability to protect their daughters. It is interesting that the previous hypothesis of the withdrawal of the mother elevates her into a position of power, whereas this theory disempowers her.

Theory of mother as victim: The final conceptualization of mothers presented in the early clinical literature is one in which the mother is also considered a victim. Her own childhood sexual victimization is said to contribute to an atmosphere of denial and repression of the realities of both her family's dysfunction and her child's victimization (Jacobs, 1990). To recognize her child's victimization is also to recognize her own. Ignoring the plight of her child, she chooses instead to remain in the relationship with her husband (Frude, 1982).

In summary, mothers of victims of incest perpetrated by fathers were traditionally conceptualized as women who colluded either knowingly or unknowingly, obtaining vicarious pleasure from the abuse. By abdicating their roles as mother and wife, they placed their oldest daughters in those positions. Because of their own history of childhood sexual abuse or because they were weak and powerless women with great dependency needs, they were unable to protect their children from further abuse. Those mothers who did avoid the enormous responsibilities placed upon them by their families and who attempted to take care of themselves were considered deviant.

Empirical Support for Early Theories

These theories were harbingers of early formulations of family systems theory in which mothers were conceptualized as kingpins in the incestuous family (Machotka, Pittman,

& Flomenhaft, 1967). In Chapter 7, "Intrafamilial Abuse," it was shown that many of the hypotheses that derive from this historical conceptualization of family systems theory are unsupported by the empirical literature. This section continues that discussion by reviewing the empirical literature specific to the role of nonoffending mothers, most of which focuses on incest committed by the father.

Theory of collusion: Do mothers know about the ongoing abuse of their child? Findings are fairly convincing that most mothers are not aware of the ongoing abuse. In a study of sexual abuse by the mother's partner, only 5% of mothers knew about the ongoing abuse by the father but "felt powerless to stop it" (Faller, 1990, p. 67). Another study of abuse by grandfathers found that 87% of mothers were unaware of the ongoing abuse (Margolin, 1992). In those cases in which the mother had been sexually abused in childhood by this man (her father and the victim's grandfather), 79% were unaware of the ongoing abuse, as compared to 92% of mothers not involved in trigenerational abuse. Myer (1985) also found that at least 75% of mothers were unaware of the ongoing abuse by their partner.

Another indicator that mothers are unaware of their child's abuse is the literature indicating that a majority of child victims never disclose the abuse to anyone (Russell, 1983). Mothers cannot report what they do not know. Further, many mothers whose children are abused by the mothers' partners are responsible for the official disclosure (Elbow & Mayfield, 1991; Sirles & Lofberg, 1990). If collusion of mothers were widespread, they would not be reporting the abuse.

These studies challenge the theory of collusion. First, collusion implies knowledge, yet these studies suggest that most mothers report that they did not know about the ongoing abuse. Second, collusion requires equal access to power and information (Driver, 1989), something that does not appear to happen in most families in which incest by a father occurs.

Theory of withdrawal of the mother: In this theory, which often appears in tandem with that of collusion, mothers are said to withdraw from their roles as wife and mother (Cohen, 1983). There are conflicting findings for the dynamic of role reversal. In her retrospective study of 40 adults who had experienced father-daughter incest as children, Herman (1981) found that 45% of victims, as compared to 5% of nonabused control women, reported that they were in the role of a parental child. In a more recent study that contrasted narratives of completed story stems between maltreated and nonmaltreated preschool children, however, only physical abuse was associated with role reversal (Macfie et al., 1999).

Even if role reversal does occur, and there is as yet no consensus, two issues must be considered. First, why does the role reversal occur? Second, does this role reversal contribute to the abuse? First to be considered is why it occurs.

One of the most striking characteristics of families in which father-daughter incest occurs is their extreme stressors. These families often have a higher-than-average number of children (Groff & Hubble, 1984; Owen & Steele, 1991) and financial concerns (Gordon, 1989), among many other stressors. (See Chapter 7, "Intrafamilial Abuse," for further discussion.) These families also have traditional divisions of labor (Herman, 1981) with structured roles and responsibilities (Dadds, Smith, Webber, & Robinson, 1991; Herman, 1981). Families are often emotionally and socially isolated (Herman, 1981; Williams & Finkelhor, 1990), further decreasing available resources. Thus, one very good reason for the role reversal is that mothers are so burdened by the multiple stressors that they require extra assistance in meeting their obligations. Since traditional roles preclude assistance by their husbands, mothers may feel that they have to look to their children for assistance. Indeed, in those cases in which mothers were temporarily unable to fulfill their roles, Herman (1981) found that fathers did not step into that role but expected their daughters to do so.

Another concern is whether role reversal contributes to the onset of abuse. Early theories hypothesized that because these families were socially isolated, fathers turned to their (primarily oldest) daughters for their sexual needs (Frude, 1982). It is striking, therefore, that many incest offenders abuse children not only outside the family but also abuse multiple children within the family. For example, Abel et al. (1988a) found that 49% of incest offenders had abused nonrelated female children, 12% had abused nonrelated male children, 19% had committed rape, and 20% had committed exhibitionism. Other paraphilias were used less frequently. Another study found that incest offenders in Parents United abused 2.6 to 4.5 victims (depending on their childhood abuse history) both inside and outside the home (Ballard et al., 1990). In this study, 80% of incest offenders used pornography, 47% visited prostitutes, and almost 20% committed bestiality. Finally, Faller (1990) found that about 80% of biological fathers molested more than one child, one-third of whom were outside the home, whereas more than two-thirds of stepfathers abused multiple children within the home.

Further, it is not at all clear that offenders are being denied sexual access to their wives. Herman (1981) found that many offenders had sex upon demand with their wives. Another study found that marital satisfaction in couples in which the husband had committed incest was higher before treatment than even that of controls (Maddock, Larson, & Lally, 1991). Faller (1990) also found that significant sexual difficulties occurred in only 10% of couples with abusive biological fathers.

In summary, while role reversal might be more likely in families in which sexual abuse occurs, it may exist in combination with, and even as a result of increased stressors, traditional divisions of labor, and decreased resources. Further, the suggestion that incest offenders have no other method of fulfilling their sexual needs than through their parentified daughter is groundless.

Personality defects: In 1996, Nakhle Tamraz reviewed the available studies comparing personality and psychological characteristics in mothers of sexually abused children to those of mothers representing other populations. Three studies compared characteristics of mothers of victims of father-daughter incest to those of mothers of victims of nonincestuous abuse (Bennett, 1980; Harrer, 1981; Wald, Archer, & Winstead, 1990). These studies found that mothers of victims of father-daughter incest reported higher levels of depression and interpersonal guardedness, greater weaknesses in reality testing, and more separations and threats of separations from their children than controls. It is worth noting, however, that women who have lost their spouses or are concerned with the loss of their children might have good reasons to be depressed and guarded after disclosure.

In the five studies reviewed by Nakhle Tamraz (1996) that compared mothers of sexually abused victims to mothers in normal populations, more similarities than differences were noted (Friedrich, 1991; Groff, 1987; Muram, Rosenthal, & Beck, 1994; Peterson, Basta, & Dykstra, 1993). Indeed, only one of the five studies found that mothers of abused victims scored as more problematic on personality and psychological characteristics (Peterson et al., 1993). In this study, mothers of abused victims scored lower than mothers of nonabused children on an intelligence scale, and scored as having more problems on seven of the 12 scales assessing abnormal personality functioning. Conversely, one study found that mothers of victims were less impulsive than mothers of nonabused children (Muram et al., 1994). The remaining three studies found that mothers of sexually abused victims were all within the normal ranges on the characteristics assessed and did not differ significantly from samples of mothers of nonabused children. Another recent study also found that nonoffending mothers scored similarly on psychological characteristics to a community sample of mothers (Smith & Saunders, 1995).

While Nakhle Tamraz (1996) concludes from her findings that "data are inconsistent regarding psychological problems in nonoffending mothers" (p. 80), four of five studies in her review found that mothers of abused and nonabused children scored similarly on psychological tests, suggesting that a stronger statement can be made. Instead, the weight of the evidence suggests that mothers of sexually abused children are remarkably normal. Considering the incredible stressors facing mothers after disclosure, it is even more striking that these women do not stand out from mothers of nonabused children.

Mother as victim: Several studies have assessed the sexual abuse history of nonoffending mothers, although many early studies did not use a control group. In studies without control groups, the percentage of mothers of victims reporting a childhood history of sexual abuse ranged from 34% to 80%. The study with the highest percentage of mothers experiencing childhood sexual abuse was of abuse by grandfathers (Goodwin, Cormier, & Owen, 1983). In this small study, eight of ten grandfathers had also abused their own daughters. Interestingly, the study with the lowest percentage (34%) of abused mothers also assessed only for abuse by grandfathers (Margolin, 1992). In other studies, Salt et al. (1990) found that mothers had an abuse history in 55% of abuse perpetrated by a biological parent, 23% of abuse cases perpetrated by a parent figure, 5% of other intrafamilial abuse cases, and 50% of extrafamilial abuse cases. Finally, Myer (1985) found that 45% of mothers of incest victims were themselves abused by a relative in childhood.

In studies employing control groups, Goodwin et al. (1981) found that 24% of mothers of physically or sexually abused victims had experienced incest, as compared to 3% of women in the control group of mothers in the community. Sansonnet-Hayden et al. (1987) also found that 67% of mothers of sexually abused victims who were currently on an inpatient psychiatric unit had been sexually abused, as compared to 3% for the control group of mothers of nonabused children. Using a matched nonclinical control group, Reis and Heppner (1993) found that 53% of mothers of children abused by an adult male caretaker were sexually abused in childhood, as compared to 13% of control mothers. In the most recent study, Oates et al. (1998) found that 34% of mothers of sexually abused children reported a childhood history of sexual abuse, as compared to 12% of mothers in the control group.

These empirical data support an hypothesis that mothers of sexually abused victims are more likely to have a history of childhood sexual abuse than mothers of nonvictims. An equally important question, however, is whether their abuse history precludes their ability to support their victimized child after disclosure. Instead, in a review of guardian support, five of six studies found that a maternal history of childhood sexual abuse was not a predictor of the mother's level of support (Bolen, 2000b).

Summary: Overall, this review of the literature suggests that many mothers of sexually abused children may have been sexually abused during childhood, although their maternal history of childhood sexual abuse is not related to their ability to appropriately support their child after disclosure. Nonoffending mothers may react to their childhood deprivation, however, as well as to the many demands placed upon them and their social isolation by seeking assistance from their oldest daughters, although the findings remain mixed. Yet again, there is no evidence to suggest that this dynamic of role reversal is causal to the abuse. Indeed, instead of abusing just this parentified daughter, fathers often abuse multiple children both inside and outside the family. Finally, there is strong evidence to conclude that the vast majority of mothers do not collude in ongoing incest.

Impact of the Early Theories

The previous section suggested that the empirical literature is largely unsupportive of the assumptions and primary hypotheses of early theories of nonoffending mothers. Regretfully, however, the impact of this early literature has been profound and may continue to color the professional response to child sexual abuse. This section develops three areas in which this early literature may affect current professional responses to and conceptualizations of nonoffending guardians.

Perceived Culpability of the Mother

Even though the empirical data do not support the theory of collusion, mothers continue to be blamed at least in part for the abuse. As discussed in Chapter 3, "Theories of Child Sexual Abuse," studies on the attribution of blame for child sexual abuse continue to find that mothers are held at least partially responsible for the abuse. In studies published in the 1990s, 70% to 86% of the professional respondents attributed partial responsibility to the mother for both father-daughter incest and sexual abuse by a neighbor (Johnson, Owens, Dewey, & Eisenberg, 1990; Kelley, 1990; Reidy & Hochstadt, 1993). In studies that apportioned responsibility for the abuse, 11% to 21% of the blame was attributed to the mother (Kalichman, Craig, & Follingstad, 1990; Kelley, 1990). Even though this is not a large percentage, it still reflects a conceptualization of the mother as partially responsible and culpable for her child's abuse. Breckenridge and Baldry's (1997) Australian study confirms this belief in maternal culpability. They found that 10% of professionals felt that most mothers knew about the ongoing abuse, and another 61% felt that some mothers knew. Those who were most likely to hold this belief were professionally trained caseworkers as compared to post-disclosure counselors and other professionals.

Another indication that mothers are considered at least partially responsible for the abuse is that they have historically been charged as co-offenders of the abuse. As discussed in the previous chapter, "Offenders," mothers were listed as offenders in 46% of cases of child sexual abuse in the first National Incidence Study (NIS) conducted in 1981 (Finkelhor & Hotaling, 1984). Most mothers, however, did not actually commit the abuse but were charged for their alleged failure to protect. This mother-blaming trend continues, however. The third NIS conducted in 1993 found that 87% of abuse committed by parents involved a male and 28% involved a female (Sedlak & Broadhurst, 1996). This finding implies that 13% of all abuse was perpetrated solely by mothers and that another 15% of all abuse involved both a mother and father.[1] In the most recent national incident study done through the NCANDS in 1998, 51% of child sexual abuse cases identified by child protective services were committed by parents (U.S. Department of Health and Human Services, 2000c). In *more than half* of these cases, mothers were charged as the sole offender (4% of all abuse) or as co-offenders (23% of all abuse).

Yet in her random community prevalence study of 930 women, Russell (1983) found that only one respondent was abused by her mother, whereas 44 respondents were abused by their fathers. Thus, only 2% of all parental abuse was committed by mothers (or 0.2% of all abuse). Further, no mothers were reported as offenders in Wyatt's (1985) or Saunders et al.'s (1999) studies or the *Los Angeles Times* Poll survey (Finkelhor, Hotaling, Lewis, & Smith, 1990). Of the 7812 respondents across these combined studies, 1971 incidents of abuse were reported. Of these, 163 were cases of paternal abuse and one was a case of maternal abuse. Thus, the prevalence of maternal abuse for the combined samples was 0.01%. Further, mothers accounted for only 0.6% of all parental abuse and 0.05% of all abuse. Given the random nature of these retrospective studies and their community- or nation-wide focus, it is difficult to believe that the much larger percentage of abusive mothers in the NIS-3 (28%) and the NCANDS (27%) does not imply some type of bias.

A study utilizing child protective services case records of intrafamilial abuse also found specific evidence that caseworkers often assume that mothers are collusive. By the report of caseworkers, 81% of mothers were assessed to have known about the abuse *before* its report (Ryan, Warren, & Weincek, 1991), only 42% of whom were considered mostly or very protective. Given that the large majority of mothers across studies are *not* aware of ongoing abuse (Faller, 1990; Margolin, 1992; Myer, 1985) and are adequately supportive after disclosure (Bolen, 2000b), the findings by Ryan et al. more likely represent a profound bias against mothers by child protective services caseworkers.

Another indication that professionals consider the mother at least partially responsible for the abuse, if not outright collusive, is that some treatment models for incest require that mothers apologize to the child for their inability to protect the child (Giarretto, 1982, 1989). In Giarretto's model for reconstructing the family, the child is not even allowed to return home until the mother apologizes for her inability to protect, and evidence of treatment success is when mothers agree that they were very responsible for conditions leading to the incest. Bentovim also considers families doubtful for rehabilitation—as if it is also the family that needs rehabilitation—when "the mother, although accepting that the abuse has happened, cannot see that she had any role in being unavailable to her child" (1991, p. 194). In another striking finding, Conte, Fogarty, and Collins (1991) found that 59% of professionals agreed that mothers of incest victims should apologize to their child for their failure to protect.

Asking the mother to apologize for her inability to protect her child is a matter that has seldom been addressed in the literature, but appears to be a direct impact of the early clinical literature on nonoffending mothers. What is the rationale for having

---

[1] See footnote 10 in the previous chapter.

mothers apologize? Simply stated, it is that mothers *should have* protected their child from the abuse, thus implying that they *could have*. There are several important problems with this rationale. First, 92% to 93% of all abuse is committed by someone other than the father (Russell, 1983; Wyatt, 1985), suggesting that numerous fathers might also fail to protect their children. To the author's knowledge, however, no literature has ever suggested that nonoffending fathers routinely apologize to their children for their failure to protect, suggesting a profound gender bias in the literature.

The second and even more important issue is that the apology assumes that mothers *could have* protected their children. Yet findings presented in the previous chapter, "Offenders," suggest that most abuse situations cannot be prevented by the guardian. Sexual abuse occurs in too many locations by too many types of filial and nonfilial relations using too many different methods of approach for guardians to adequately protect their children. Further, 30% to 40% of females and 13% or more of males are sexually abused in childhood (Bolen & Scannapieco, 1999), suggesting that child sexual abuse is of epidemic proportions. That so many of our children are abused is a failure of our society—not of our mothers. Asking mothers to shoulder the responsibility for that failure by apologizing for their inability to protect simply fuels a system that desperately needs these mothers to protect the child because the system has not and cannot.

Another concern with asking mothers to apologize is that it *disempowers* them when instead they need to be *empowered*. Chapter 7, "Intrafamilial Abuse," presented a number of studies that suggested that fathers in these families wield great power. Asking mothers to take responsibility for a portion of the abuse (even if it is framed as their inability to protect) by apologizing to their child feeds into this power disparity. A more appropriate intervention would be to balance the power inequity in the family by *empowering* the mother and *disempowering* the father.

Finally, an important advantage of the apology session is the therapeutic value to the victimized child. Yet because the apology of the mother sustains the power imbalance within the family while maintaining the assumption that the mother *could have* prevented the abuse, the disadvantages outweigh the advantages. It is incumbent upon clinicians to develop new methods that have the advantages of the apology session without its disadvantages. A good alternative is the "abuse clarification process" (Lipovsky, Swenson, Ralston, & Saunders, 1998, p. 729). This process involves: clarifying the abusive behaviors; having the offender assume responsibility for the abuse; having the offender express his awareness of the impact of the abuse on the victim and family; and initiating a safety plan. Thus, the focus remains on the offender and the offender's actions.

Effect on the Definition of Guardian Support

Another important consequence of the early pejorative literature on nonoffending guardians is that it had an important effect on how guardian support came to be defined. The historical notion of mothers in these families was that they were dysfunctional, having their own histories of childhood victimization. These mothers were also assumed, at the least, to have inadequately protected their children, or worse, to have knowingly colluded in the abuse.

At the same time that these ideas were being forwarded, professionals were rushing to respond to the burgeoning problem of child sexual abuse. Children were being reported in ever-increasing numbers within a system not designed to accommodate them. Because this system prioritized intrafamilial abuse and especially father-daughter incest, problems immediately emerged. One of the most compelling of these problems was how to maintain the safety of children abused by a resident father figure. This problem developed because (a) the accused are presumed innocent until proven guilty, (b) child sexual abuse is so difficult to prove, and (c) child protective services has no jurisdiction over the offender.

Abuse is a hidden crime and often leaves little evidence. For example, in one study, only 17% of sexually abused children presenting for a medical examination had evidence of that abuse (e.g., hymenal tear or sexually transmitted disease) (Palusci et al., 1999). Thus, unless there is striking evidence of the abuse (and there usually is not), the offender cannot be forcibly removed from the home even in those cases in which the victim lives with the offender. Unless the offender is jailed or ordered by the court out of the home, then child protective services must consider how to maintain the protection of the child. One of the ways they do so is by making the nonoffending guardian (almost always the mother) responsible for the continued protection of the child. At the least, this requires that the nonoffending guardian either keep the offender out of the house or move away from the offender. If child protective services does not believe that the nonoffending guardian can do so, then their recourse is to remove the child from the home.

Given the available but pejorative literature on mothers in the 1980s, it is not surprising that child protective services workers were highly suspicious of the ability of mothers to protect their sexually abused children. Of course, once a worldview is created, it is intransigent to change. Therefore, these pejorative beliefs continued to some extent throughout the 1990s, resulting in a high percentage of removals of sexually abused children from their nonoffending mothers. For example, Jaudes and Morris (1990) found that 40% of sexually abused children experienced a court-ordered change of custody shortly after disclosure. Confirming these findings, other studies found that 42% to 59% of victims were removed shortly after disclosure (Everson, Hunter, Runyan, Edelsohn, & Coulter, 1989; Leifer, Shapiro, & Kassem, 1993; Pellegrin & Wagner, 1990; Ryan Warren, & Weincek, 1991). Further, Hunter et al. (1990) found that not only were half of all children removed shortly after disclosure, but that approximately 59% of all children had been removed at the 24-month follow-up evaluation. Other studies that followed children for some time after disclosure found that 62% to 66% of victims were eventually removed (Faller, 1991b; Ryan et al., 1991). Combined, the seven known studies presented in this section had a total of 783 cases. For the 725 cases for which disposition of the case was known after disclosure, 361 (50%) of the children were removed. Of the 435 cases that were followed for some period of time, 284 (65%) of the children were eventually removed.

These findings suggest that either mothers of sexually abused children are doing a very poor job of supporting their victimized child or that a significant systemic bias against nonoffending mothers continues, which then is manifested in biases held by child protective services workers. If mothers are doing a poor job of protecting their child, we would expect that a similarly high proportion of mothers would be scored as unsupportive after the disclosure of abuse. Instead, a review of 16 available studies on guardian support found that an average of 81% of mothers across studies responded with some or full support and 65% to 85% believed their child's disclosure (Bolen, 2000b). Another interesting study comparing maternal support of children sexually abused by someone other than a parent to maternal support of nonabused girls found that, after controlling for other stressful events, no significant differences were found (Esparza, 1993). Thus, whereas most mothers are appropriately supportive and are as supportive as mothers of nonabused children, large numbers of children continue to be removed from their homes.

To place these figures in context, roughly 30% of cases in which professionals suspect that abuse occurred is not reported (King, Reece, Bendel, & Patel, 1998), and child protective services only investigated 42% to 44% of all suspected sexual abuse reported to them in the latest NIS (Sedlak & Broadhurst, 1996). [2] Thus, mothers appear to be as capable as professionals at taking seriously a suspicion or report of abuse. While it is clear that protecting children is a complex problem, it appears most likely from this review that a significant bias against nonoffending mothers persists.

Minimization of the Role of the Father

Finally, early theories of nonoffending mothers led to the sad consequence of minimizing the role of the nonoffending father. Indeed, the nonoffending father has been almost completely ignored in the child sexual abuse literature, a bias that may have detrimental consequences. In a recently conducted study of children undergoing forensic sexual abuse exams in which only nonoffending mothers were routinely asked to accompany their child to the appointment, it is not surprising that far more nonoffending mothers than nonoffending fathers were at the appointment (Bolen, 1998a). What was striking, however, was that one of the most important predictors of the child's outcome was whether both parents accompanied the child to the hospital. Children accompanied by both parents had significantly lower child-reported posttraumatic symptoms and overall symptomatology scores, as well as lower parent-reported total problem behaviors. This study thus suggests that a narrow focus on the nonoffending mother may be detrimental to the welfare of the child.

Summary

Rushing to protect children from further sexual abuse, well-meaning professionals relied on the clinical literature available at the time to construct their expectations, views, and interventions for nonoffending mothers. That these expectations, views, and interventions became ingrained in the lexicon of professionals might be expected given the urgency with which professionals had to respond in the 1980s and the dearth of empirical literature available.

---

[2] Also see the section, "Decision to Report," in Chapter 11, "Professional Response to Child Sexual Abuse."

Once a policy is set in motion on a particular course, it is difficult to change. This pattern has dictated the course for nonoffending mothers. As a result, it is not surprising that mothers are still required to provide primary protection from the offender. Nor is it surprising that so many of them fail, given the historic and pejorative attitudes against them as they carry the full weight of society's failure for its inability to protect its young members. And still no known paper has suggested that this burden should instead fall upon law enforcement. The end result is a collection of professional literature and practices that inadvertently perpetuate the myth of the mother as all-knowing and therefore all-responsible.

DISCLOSURE AND POST-DISCLOSURE

Abuse From the Mother's Perspective

The literature to this point has been quantitative and from the perspective of the professional attempting to define the experience of nonoffending guardians. This section now shifts the focus to nonoffending mothers as they relate their experiences of finding out about the abuse and reacting to it. A qualitative study of 15 mothers done by Hooper (1992) is the basis for this section. This section focuses on three portions of her analysis: finding out about the abuse, reacting to the abuse, and the meaning of the abuse to the mothers.

Finding out about the abuse: Mothers in this study did not talk about disclosure but about finding out about the abuse (Hooper, 1992). While some mothers found out about the abuse because of a single incident, other mothers had suspected for a long time that abuse might be occurring. For these women, however, suspicions were not the same as knowing. Their suspicions were "characterised by the inaccessibility of clear information about events conducted in secrecy and uncertainty about the meaning of the information available...They were also often faced with multiple, conflicting and changing versions of events and their meaning, from the child, the abuser and others who became involved" (pp. 64–65). While offenders, when asked, most often denied the abuse, some children also did not acknowledge the abuse when asked or were too young to easily question. Another problem was discerning what was normal and what was not, especially when defining behaviors between a father and his daughter. Thus, finding out was a process of "'piecing the jigsaw together'" (p. 67), a process that evolved over time.

It may seem ludicrous to some that mothers can suspect abuse for so long without actually knowing. Yet, when the process is considered from the perspective of mothers, it is not so difficult to understand. When the mother has not actually observed the abuse, when there is no physical evidence, and when the offender or child denies the abuse, how is she to know for sure that the abuse is occurring? Another important consideration is what mothers should do when they suspect abuse but cannot confirm it. Perhaps some professionals would expect mothers to report their suspicions, something some of these mothers did. Yet what if child protective services refuses to consider the case without further evidence or does not substantiate the abuse? What if the abuse really did occur? In this case, as with some of the mothers in Hooper's (1992) study who reported their suspicions, the system fails in its responsibility.

Further, the ramifications to the victim and family of a failed report or investigation make it much more difficult to initiate a second report.

The other issue is what professionals consider appropriate action within the home by a mother who suspects without proof that her child is being abused by someone in the family. A first response might be to expect the mother to maintain heightened vigilance of the relationship between the offender and child, especially if the suspected offender is the father. Yet, marriages and families are built on trust. To be adequately protective of a child is to completely change the dynamics of the familial relationships. The mother could not allow the child to be alone with the suspected offender at any time, necessitating that the mother be home at all times when the suspected offender was home and that the suspected offender had no private moments with the child. And what happens if the mother is employed?

Protection of a child requires total effort, for leaving the child with the suspected offender only one time might create an opportunity for abuse. This is important if the child is being abused, but what if abuse is not occurring? How much damage will the protective actions of the mother do to the familial relationships? The point is that steps the mother must take to protect her child also do damage to family relationships. At what point are suspicions enough that the damage to the familial relationships is warranted? These are difficult questions with no clear answers. Given the lack of evidence and the difficult questions that arise from a suspected abuse situation, it is not surprising that mothers in Hooper's (1992) study talked about how confused and ambivalent they were during this long period of "finding out," a process that Hooper termed "ambiguous, limited, and/or conflicting" (p. 569).

Reacting to the abuse: Even after mothers found out about the abuse and the knowledge became public, confusion continued. Sometimes this confusion was because the mother was not given full information about the circumstances of the abuse. Offenders also sometimes continued to deny the abuse, as did some children. The desire to meet the needs of all family members also contributed to this confusion and ambivalence (Hooper, 1992). Hooper and Humphreys (1998) talk about how mothers responded to finally knowing about the abuse.

> *While previous research had tended to describe women as either knowing or not knowing, believing or disbelieving, protecting or not protecting, our research suggested that these states were frequently not either/or, but often both/and, and that women's position [sic] in relation to them was often not fixed and stable but fluctuating....*
> *Women spoke of a multi-layered state in which quite contradictory positions could be held simultaneously, and where the certainty of belief held one day could not be predictably held on to the next. Within this multi-layered experience there appeared to be both cognitive and emotional aspects to believing that a child had been sexually abused. Most mothers spoke of their initial responses in terms of belief and disbelief, with the latter occurring as a spontaneous, emotional reaction—a natural defence against traumatic news.....This complex state, characterized by fluctuation and change, occurred against a backdrop of intense and conflicting relationships involving the child, the offender and other members of the immediate and extended family, and of the major material, emotional and legal consequences which mothers had to tackle as part of the aftermath of discovery. Mothers frequently spoke of their isolation and of the immensely hostile environment. (pp. 568–570).*

Thus, reacting to the abuse disclosure is better described as a process that includes confusion and ambivalence, a process that professionals often fail to recognize as normative. Instead, professionals are more likely to consider confusion and ambivalence as indicators of an unsupportive response necessitating removal of the child (see Everson et al., 1989, for example).

Regretfully, mothers' interactions with agencies in Hooper's (1992) study were disappointing, and two themes stood out—the sense of not being heard, and "anger and disillusionment at the failures of agencies to provide help or to exercise authority at the appropriate time and with the appropriate person" (p. 132). Although these mothers wanted legal action or some other type of control imposed upon the offender, legal action was seldom taken and the mothers more often experienced the social control as being imposed upon them. Thus, mothers "often contested the degree of responsibility expected of them and resented the stigma and loss of control intervention could involve, usually in the absence of any effective control exercised against the abuser" (p. 132). For those cases in which legal action was not taken or when the child was removed, mothers were especially disillusioned. Mothers also felt blamed by most professionals and felt that the interventions focused on their inadequacies. On the other hand, a few professionals were supportive of the mothers and their attempts, and these professionals were especially meaningful to the mothers, who felt that they had been heard.

Meaning of the abuse: The meaning assigned by the women in Hooper's (1992) study to the sexual abuse was one of loss. Some of the losses were more intangible, such as the loss of trust in the offender and in a just world, the loss of control over their and their children's lives, as well as the loss of family unity and togetherness. There was also the loss of their sense of identity as a mother, and sometimes as a wife, which also brought with it a loss of a sense of femininity. In relationship with their child, there was the loss of trust in the relationship, a loss of feeling needed, and a lost sense of oneself as a protective parent, as well as the experience of secondary victimization. Mothers whose partners abused also often experienced primary sexual victimization by the offender. Overall, losses were multiple, ongoing, and unremitting, with a sense of their endlessness.

Effect of Disclosure on the Family

This section continues the discussion of the repercussions of the abuse, now concentrating on the deleterious consequences following abuse disclosure. In this section, however, studies are quantitative, and all focus on abuse by the father.

The most widely known effect on the family, and perhaps what the child fears most, is family breakup. In fact, there is good reason to fear this because it is a common effect of disclosure whether or not the abuse is intrafamilial or extrafamilial. As discussed earlier, 40% to 59% of children are removed from their homes after abuse is disclosed and up to two-thirds are eventually removed (Mast & Lundy, 1998; Faller, 1991b). When the child is abused by his or her father, marital dissolution also frequently occurs (Levitt, Owen, & Truchsess, 1991; Wright, 1991). Yet even victims of extrafamilial abuse often experience some change in parenting figures (Sauzier, 1989).

Financial changes are also prevalent after disclosure and may have a profound effect on the family (Levitt et al., 1991). Indeed, Massat and Lundy (1998) found that mean income for families in which intrafamilial abuse occurred dropped from $50,293 before disclosure to $29,600 after disclosure (and from $30,000 to $20,000 for median income). Half of all respondents also reported a change in residence, and 25% reported a job loss or having to get a new job. Wright (1991) also found that many of the families in which father-daughter incest was disclosed faced financial stress even before disclosure. This stress was then exacerbated by treatment costs, legal fees, and the cost of living expenses for two households. Both parents often had to take on extra jobs, and all within the family were affected by the financial strain. Some of these previously middle-class families were also forced onto welfare, a finding confirmed by Tyler and Brassard (1984), who found that 40% of families went on welfare following a report of incest.

Other changes are traumatic as well. In the study of intrafamilial sexual abuse by Tyler and Brassard (1984), 40% of the families had to cope with the humiliation of a public announcement of the abuse. Massat and Lundy (1998) also reported that 50% or more of nonoffending mothers reported worsening family relations or loss of intimacy with the perpetrator. At least 25% also reported declines in relationships with friends. Wright (1991) also found that 64% of the victims noted a decline in their relationships with their mothers and that relationships with their fathers usually became distant. These children reacted sometimes by "being out of control" (p. 144). Many children also had to take on a parental role. Nonabused siblings, however, seemed to become peripheral to this family drama.

Finally, Wright (1991) found that each family had an average of 2.9 crisis events with which to cope, whereas Massat and Lundy (1998) found that nonoffending guardians experienced three major costs with disclosure. Levitt et al. (1991) also found that 82% of families indicated that the sexual abuse and its aftermath was the single most stressful event in the last three years. Clearly, the effects of disclosure upon a family are profound.

There are also specific effects of the disclosure on the mother. In a study of children evaluated at a sexual assault center (De Jong, 1988), 55% of mothers who were supportive of their children after disclosure suffered emotional changes, including posttraumatic symptoms such as anger, anxiety, sleep disturbance, recurrent episodes of crying, and intrusive thoughts or dreams. Some mothers had somatic complaints as well, and symptoms were severe enough in some women to require hospitalization. In another study (Wagner, 1991), although mothers seeking treatment for their abused children had similar levels of depression to mothers seeking treatment for nonabused children, 9% were extremely depressed, and 59% were mildly to moderately depressed. Another study found that slightly more than half of mothers had clinical levels of symptomatology a few weeks after disclosure, and a third retained clinical levels at the one-year follow-up evaluation (Newberger, Gremy, Waternaux, & Newberger, 1993).

The primary theme of this section is that disclosure of incest has devastating effects on family members as they struggle to reconstitute after the disclosure. The most difficult changes with which to cope may be the removal of the child or offender from the home and the financial repercussions of the disclosure. Other major effects of the abuse are that families are often forced to move, mothers must often return to work, and the quality of relations among family members worsens. The psychological wellbeing of mothers of victims also frequently deteriorates.

WHERE DOES THE PROBLEM LIE?

Studies presented in this chapter suggest that most nonoffending mothers, although certainly not all, are appropriately supportive and appropriately believe their children's disclosures. This chapter has also shown that this support comes at exceptional cost to the nonoffending mother and her family. The stressors placed on these families are extreme, and many of these stressors are system-induced.

This chapter opened by posing the question: Is it the failure of nonoffending guardians that is the problem or the expectations placed upon them? The evidence presented in this chapter suggests that it is the expectations placed upon nonoffending guardians that is the problem. As Hooper and Humphreys (1998) state,

> *Maternal failure can be seen as almost inevitable against the idealized image of motherhood held both by society and by children...in whose fantasies mothers are all-powerful and all-knowing and to whom human limitation may seem deliberate betrayal. (p. 573)*

Given that the expectations placed upon nonoffending guardians are so burdensome, it is important to consider how these expectations can be modified. To do so, however, requires a different model for conceptualizing nonoffending guardians and their responses to the abuse disclosure that is more congruent with the empirical knowledge base. In the following sections, reconceptualizations are forwarded for two issues—the response of the guardian to the disclosure, and the definition of guardian support.

THE GUARDIAN'S RESPONSE TO DISCLOSURE

Feminist Conceptualization

Several papers have reframed the response of nonoffending mothers to the disclosure of their child's abuse using a feminist-oriented approach (Birns & Meyer, 1993; Cammaert, 1988; Hooper, 1989; McIntyre, 1981; Wattenberg, 1985). These and other writers presenting alternate views recognize that a power imbalance exists in families in which incest occurs. As such, mothers are often financially dependent upon the offender, which significantly increases the costs of disclosure to the mother. This problem may be worsened when mothers with physically abusive partners fear physical retribution against their children or themselves for reporting the abuse. Further, mothers, who receive no formal training in how to identify abuse, may recognize that their child is distressed but may not realize that the distress is related to sexual abuse.

Society also places expectations on mothers to stand by their partners in times of trouble, while placing the burden of responsibility on them for their family's wellbeing. As such, mothers may try to stop the abuse themselves or may seek out informal sources for help, perhaps not even considering that they can or should seek formal assistance. Conversely, the loss of support after disclosure by friends and family might exert pressure on mothers to believe their partner over the child. Finally, in today's climate in which false-memory syndrome stories make the headlines in newspapers across the country, guardians may be led to believe instead that the disclosure is false.

Conservation of Resources Theory: Reacting to an Extreme Stressor

Another method of considering the response of nonoffending guardians after disclosure is as a response to an extreme stressor. This premise is borrowed from Hobfoll's (1989, 1991) conservation of resources theory. The underlying tenet of the conservation of resources theory is that "individuals strive to obtain, retain, and protect that which they value" (Hobfoll, Freedy, Green, & Solomon, 1996, p. 323). Those valuables they wish to retain, as well as the means for protecting and preserving them, are labeled resources. These resources can then be used to build other resources. Conversely, stress occurs when resources are threatened or lost or when invested resources fail to achieve an adequate gain. Available resources become increasingly depleted when multiple losses occur. Because resources are used to combat further stressful circumstances, individuals become "decreasingly capable of meeting stress challenges" as stressors mount, "resulting in loss spirals" (p. 326).

Hobfoll et al. (1996) further consider a category of extreme stress in which the stressor (a) attacks the individual's basic values, (b) makes excessive demands, (c) often comes without warning, (d) is "outside the realm of which resource utilization strategies have been practiced and developed," and (e) leaves a "powerful mental image that is evoked by cues associated with the event" (p. 328). Extreme stressors not only result in more rapid resource loss but also may affect a broader band of resources. The availability of community, social or individual resources, however, can mediate reactions to extreme stress.

The conservation of resources theory offers an important framework for understanding the response of nonoffending guardians to their child's disclosure of sexual abuse. The original stressor, the abuse, results in a number of losses for both the victims and nonoffending guardians. Children experience a loss of innocence and often deteriorating wellbeing, whereas nonoffending guardians lose at the least their idealized, or wished for, childhood for their child. Many other major losses may also be associated with abuse disclosure. Intrafamilial abuse may threaten the sanctity of the nuclear and extended families, whereas abuse by the father may result in the loss of the marriage. Other potential major losses are the removal of the child, financial hardships, loss of familial and friendship relationships, and the psychological wellbeing of the nonoffending guardian, among others. The breadth and number of resource losses suggests that abuse and its disclosure are in most situations experienced by the child and family as an extreme stressor. Thus, the abuse often comes without warning and attacks one's basic values, whereas the disclosure of abuse makes excessive demands on nonoffending guardians who have not been trained to cope with such a problem. One of the effects of this disclosure on the child and nonoffending guardian may be posttraumatic (intrusive) symptoms.

These losses represent not only the loss of resources, but also the means for generating other resources. For example, the loss of real income that many families incur also eliminates or reduces the ability of families to use money to provide new resources such as legal or therapeutic support for family members. The loss of relationships with partners, family members, and friends also reduces the nonoffending guardian's sources upon which to draw for support, further isolating the nonoffending guardian. The loss of psychological wellbeing may also decrease the adaptive coping skills (Hobfoll et al., 1996) of nonoffending guardians. These spiraling losses are then compounded by additional stressors placed by professionals upon nonoffending guardians. The increased responsibility of nonoffending guardians for protecting the child from a known offender, the responsibility for providing transportation for family members to appointments, ongoing pressure from child protective services to be adequately supportive, the system's decision not to prosecute the offender, and pejorative and hostile attitudes of some professionals are all examples of how professionals can unwittingly escalate these loss spirals.

As these loss spirals escalate, nonoffending guardians may become less capable of utilizing problem-focused and active coping mechanisms, instead resorting increasingly on ineffectual coping mechanisms (Hobfoll et al., 1996). This less effective style of coping, which is indicative of the depletion of internal resources, then leads to even more difficulty obtaining resources, thus exacerbating the losses. Further, the community, which ideally is a resource, instead places further demands upon nonoffending guardians. Hobfoll et al. state that when community resources are depleted, "coping tends to take the form of emotion- and cognition-directed behaviors" (p. 343) that are self-defeating. "Consequently, those affected have difficulty emerging from a victim stance into a survivor role" (p. 345).

Conservation of resources theory (Hobfoll, 1989, 1991) appears to have important explanatory potential for understanding the reactions of nonoffending guardians to their child's disclosure of sexual abuse. Overall, this theory suggests that disclosure of abuse can be conceptualized as a devastating (extreme) stressor that results in numerous losses, which in turn decrease the abilities of nonoffending guardians to cope adaptively, which in turn leads to spiraling losses. Conceptualized in this manner, it is understandable that nonoffending guardians are often unable to meet the expectations placed upon them by professionals. Indeed, this conceptualization recognizes that interventions of professionals with nonoffending guardians may have the paradoxical effect of reducing resources while also increasing stressors, thus contributing to the spiraling losses and more ineffectual coping of nonoffending guardians. In response, child protective services workers may invoke the ultimate loss—removal of the child.

This model for nonoffending guardians and their responses to disclosure suggests a completely different strategy for working with nonoffending guardians. Instead of the current deficits-oriented model that contributes to resource loss, treatment models instead might need to be strengths-based, bringing needed resources to these nonoffending guardians and their families, reducing their losses, and empowering their use of problem-focused and active coping mechanisms. This treatment strategy may be far more effective at increasing the capability of nonoffending guardians to provide adequate support and protection to the victim than the current punitive model. This next section now turns to considering expectations placed on guardians after disclosure. These expectations are operationalized in the literature as maternal or guardian support.

GUARDIAN SUPPORT

Guardians are expected to be adequately protective of their children after disclosure, and their ability to be protective is assessed by professionals as their ability to provide guardian support. To consider how expectations for guardian support after disclosure can be reconceptualized, the first section closely examines how guardian support is currently defined while also considering important problems with its definition and conceptualization. Afterwards, a method for reconceptualizing guardian support that not only recognizes the extreme stressors that guardians face but also the strengths they bring to bear is presented. The final portion of this chapter then makes recommendations for changes in policies.

Definition and Criteria for Guardian Support

What are the criteria for adequate guardian support and who sets these criteria? There are probably two primary groups—child protective services and child sexual abuse researchers—that have contributed to establishing criteria for adequate guardian support. Child protective services' interest in establishing criteria for guardian support is because they must assess whether nonoffending guardians can provide adequate support for the child. While the actual policies vary, child protective services workers typically consider whether nonoffending guardians believe the child's disclosure, whether they are capable of keeping the offender away from the child, and whether they can provide a consistent protective and supportive environment for the victimized child. Researchers measuring guardian support also tend to assess one or more of these indicators, although some also consider whether nonoffending guardians are capable of utilizing professional services for themselves or their children (Bolen, 2000b). These criteria, in turn, have become the operationalized definition for guardian support.

   One important implication of the decision of most researchers to utilize the criteria for guardian support employed by child protective services is that the definition of guardian support in the empirical literature is largely a system-defined construct.[3] This is an important point because it suggests that most child sexual abuse researchers do not question the definition itself, but concur that guardian support should be defined based upon how child protective services assesses it. The problem with this approach, however, is that the construct of guardian support has

---

[3] A construct is simply a concept that is measured. Constructs are not concrete entities but become reified based upon the definition applied to them. For example, depression is a construct that can alternately be defined as major depressive disorder, dysthymia, or simply a despondent presentation, based upon how it is defined and assessed.

not been treated to the same rigorous scrutiny as other constructs. As discussed in Chapter 4, "Methodology," a series of steps are necessary to ensure the validity of the construct under question. Issues to be considered are both the theoretical and the operationalized definitions of the construct and whether the construct can be validly and reliably measured across populations. None of these issues have been addressed in the known professional literature on guardian support; yet these are the very questions that are critical to the development of valid measures.

Because researchers have not established validity for the construct of guardian support, some basic issues have never been debated. The first and most basic question is whether guardian support *should* be a system-defined construct. In other words, should the needs of child protective services drive the definition of guardian support? While it is clear that child protective services must assess nonoffending guardians within the current policies, it is not at all clear that what is being captured is guardian support. Thus, a fundamental question is: What is guardian support? How can it be conceptualized so that it captures the range of behaviors and emotions that nonoffending guardians experience after the disclosure of their child's sexual abuse? To consider this question requires an analysis of how guardian support is currently conceptualized.

Most studies currently conceptualize guardian support categorically, dividing nonoffending guardians into supportive, ambivalent, and unsupportive categories (Bolen, 2000b). This type of conceptualization matches the needs of child protective services workers, who are mandated to determine whether nonoffending guardians are supportive enough to retain custody of their children. Thus, it is not surprising that Everson et al. (1989) found that guardians deemed supportive were most likely to retain custody of their children. Children were most often removed and placed in a relative's home when guardians were scored as ambivalent in support and were most often placed in foster care when guardians were scored as unsupportive.

An important implication of these findings is that an ambivalent response appears to have negative ramifications, warranting removal of the child. Thus, even though an ambivalent response would seem to indicate neither a clearly supportive nor unsupportive stance, it is treated as an unsupportive stance necessitating removal by child protective services. This conceptualization of ambivalence as a negative response is also reflected in a study of guardian support by Leifer et al. (1993), who considered nonoffending guardians unsupportive if they did not score optimally on all three indicators of support. Therefore, nonoffending guardians with a total score of +3 or +4 on a scale of –5 to +5 could be considered unsupportive. In this study, any ambivalence or hesitation was construed negatively.

The Issue of Ambivalence

The difficulty with conceptualizing ambivalence in nonoffending guardians as a stance of nonsupport is that it neither takes into consideration normative nor traumatic responses to disclosure. Both are critical considerations.

First, ambivalence may be a normative response to the disclosure of abuse by a nonoffending guardian's loved one, who may have strong feelings towards both the victim and offender. This dual allegiance could result in vacillating emotions, thoughts, and behaviors that are expressed as ambivalence in support. An ambivalent response might also be normative if the costs associated with the disclosure are so great that the integrity of the family structure is threatened by acknowledging the abuse. Indeed, Hooper's (1992) qualitative analysis in an earlier section suggested that ambivalence was a normal response. This ambivalence could also reflect a breakdown of adaptive coping mechanisms brought on by spiraling losses. Having lost internal, social, and community resources, nonoffending guardians may then employ self-defeating coping mechanisms (Hobfoll et al., 1996) that may present as ambivalence. Regretfully, the cost to these mothers of appearing ambivalent, even if that ambivalence is normative, is that they most often lose their children.

Another consideration is that ambivalence may reflect a posttraumatic response to the abuse disclosure. Indeed, a large number of nonoffending guardians develop posttraumatic symptoms or posttraumatic stress disorder (De Jong, 1988; Wagner, 1991). One of the hallmarks of this symptom presentation is the alternation between avoidant and approaching symptoms and behaviors (American Psychiatric Association, 1994). These symptoms may present in nonoffending guardians as vacillations between belief and disbelief of the child's disclosure and even between supportive and nonsupportive behaviors. Considering that the disclosure has so many adverse and overwhelming meanings to nonoffending guardians, their ambivalence may be more keenly related to posttraumatic symptoms than to an unsupportive stance.

Regardless of whether an ambivalent response is normative or posttraumatic, an argument can be made that children remain in danger when allowed to stay with nonoffending guardians who are responding ambivalently to the abuse disclosure. This is certainly an important issue but one that retains prominence only because nonoffending mothers have primary responsibility for maintaining the safety of their child from the alleged offender and because successful treatment strategies have not yet been developed or widely implemented. By increasing supportive behaviors, well-designed intervention strategies might be successful in averting removal of the child. Further, if the burden for protection could be removed from mothers, or shared among others, then they would have greater freedom to work through their reactions to the abuse disclosure without such grave penalties. While it may seem implausible that our policies will change, we must still consider whether to so harshly penalize nonoffending guardians whose inability to cope adequately with the abuse disclosure may be normative or posttraumatic, or may even be exacerbated by the interventions of professionals.

The Issue of the Breadth of the Definition of Guardian Support

Another concern with the current definition of guardian support is that it does not take into consideration the more traditional indicators of a supportive environment or parenting behavior. There is now a large body of multidisciplinary literature that considers the support of either the environment or the parent, and many measures now capture these constructs. While different models exist, children and adults both tend to define support along four dimensions, including emotional support, information support, instrumental support, and companionship (Cauce, Reid, Landesman, & Gonzales, 1990). Literature that considers parental support also finds it to be multidimensional, encompassing parental sensitivity, predictability, and involvement in one study (Juang & Silbereisen, 1999), and promotion of independence, positive modeling/fairness, and love/support in another study (Nicholas & Bieber, 1997).

Although child protective services assesses guardian support for a very different reason, the question remains whether nonoffending guardians *should* be assessed using a different standard. If professionals agree on what sufficient support entails, why should child protective services assess nonoffending guardians using a different and more difficult standard? Again, the reason for this discrepancy is the policies in place. Perhaps, however, it is changes to the policies that need to be considered rather than changes to what professionals agree is sufficient support.

Summary

In summary, the traditional conceptualization of guardian support is system-defined and system-driven. As such, it is primarily concerned with the ability of the nonoffending guardian (almost always the mother) to provide a safe and supportive environment for the child. This type of environment is often operationalized as belief in the child's disclosure, protecting the child from the offender, and providing emotional support. Yet, this definition does not consider the breadth of support other professional bodies of literature utilize. Nor does it consider that effective and problem-focused coping skills deteriorate as stressors mount, stressors that are in part a result of the interventions of professionals. Ineffective coping may present as ambivalence, a presentation that most often leads to the removal of the child from the nonoffending guardian (Everson et al., 1989). Thus, interventions designed to promote the welfare of children instead may paradoxically bring harm if they are removed from nonoffending guardians experiencing normative ambivalence.

Reconceptualization of Guardian Support

This next section now considers how guardian support can be reconceptualized so that it considers the very real and sometimes overwhelming stressors impinging upon nonoffending guardians after disclosure as well as the effects of these stressors on guardian support. This section is a result of previous work by Bolen, Lamb, and Gradante (2000).

Believing that guardian support needed to be considered in a totally different manner, we introduced a humanistic model. Within this model, the clinical approach is genuine and empathic, and clients are approached with unconditional positive regard (Rogers, 1980). Humanists believe in the ability of individuals to self-actualize (Maslow, 1987) and to empower themselves (Rogers, 1980). While humanists strive to accept clients as they are and within a nonjudgmental framework, they also believe that individuals are responsible for acting on their own decisions (Payne, 1991).

While providing an important treatment framework for working with nonoffending guardians, humanism also offers a framework for redefining guardian support. One of humanism's basic premises is that the *client's* view of the world is paramount. Applied to nonoffending guardians, this premise would suggest that guardian support can only be understood within the context of the experiences of the guardians. Thus, definitions of guardian support must take into consideration their experience. Another basic premise forwarded by Maslow (1987) in his hierarchy of needs is that needs are hierarchical, with physiological needs reflecting the most basic needs, followed by safety needs, needs for love and belonging, esteem needs, and finally self-actualization. Maslow contends that lower-order needs must be met before higher-order needs can be satisfied. His hierarchy of needs is a fundamental model for understanding human motivation.

One method for conceptualizing nonoffending guardian support is as the provision of needs, or resources. Using this conceptualization, we posited that guardian support was also hierarchical, with progressively higher stages starting with meeting the physiological needs of the child, followed by safety needs, meeting the child's needs for love and belonging, and esteem needs. Recognizing that the definition of guardian support also had to consider the experiences of nonoffending guardians, we also hypothesized that resources available to guardians could be conceptualized hierarchically using similar stages. Further, we assumed that the resources available to guardians predicated those resources they could then make available to their children.

Using a humanistic model, we defined guardian support as the ability of nonoffending guardians to provide resources to their children to which they themselves have access. This definition is culturally sensitive by recognizing that resources are differentially allocated based upon race, ethnicity, class, and gender. This definition also works well with the conservation of resources theory (Hobfoll 1989, 1991) by recognizing that resources to guardian support may become increasingly limited as a result of the disclosure of sexual abuse and the interventions of professionals. By grounding this humanistic model of guardian support in the psychological literature, this model moves away from the more traditional categories of support, nonsupport, and ambivalence—a deficits model—to a needs-based assessment of guardian support. This latter model recognizes the strengths of the guardians who often overcome extreme stressors to provide for their children, while also recognizing the impact of the stressors on nonoffending guardians and their ability to cope effectively.

To operationalize the definition of guardian support, we hypothesized that it would fall within the four domains of the hierarchy of needs (i.e., physiological needs, safety, love and belonging, and esteem) (Maslow, 1987). Within each domain we then hypothesized that the measurement of guardian support would require two sets of information—the stage-specific resources available to the guardians and the stage-specific supportive behaviors exhibited by the guardian. The stage-specific operationalized definitions of guardian support are shown in Table 10-1.

As can be seen in this model, both the resources available to the nonoffending guardians and the supportive behaviors towards their children are arranged hierarchically. These hierarchical stages match, in content, those of Maslow's so that, for example, the resources available to the nonoffending guardian in stage one reflect physiological needs, and the supportive behaviors of the nonoffending guardian in stage three reflect those related to issues of love and belonging. Stages one through three are operationalized for both the guardian and child, whereas stage four is only

TABLE 10-1. Needs-based Assessment of Guardian Support

	Resources Available to Nonoffending Guardians	Supportive Behaviors Towards Child
Stage 1: Physiological	Food Housing Clothing No severe medical or mental health problems Medical or mental health insurance or access to reduced fee care Any means of transportation	Provides necessary food, shelter, and clothing Provides essential medical and mental health care
Stage 2: Safety	Safe home situation Affordable and safe child care Safe means of transportation Financial resources to provide safe alternative care for children when needed	Maintains safe environment for child Maintains adequate supervision of child When absent, places younger child with safe alternate caregiver When absent, provides older child or adolescent with resources in case of danger Provides safe means of transportation
Stage 3: Love and Belonging	Supportive network Feeling of embeddedness in immediate community (as defined by parent)	Makes consistent statements of belief and support to child Provides emotionally supportive environment Provides for nonessential medical and mental health concerns for child Appropriately focuses on own mental health issues Provides or helps to develop supportive network for child Treats child with love and concern
Stage 4: Esteem		Provides resources for esteem issues of child Treats child with dignity and respect

Note: See Bolen et al., 2000

operationalized for the child. We felt that guardians with adequate resources in stages one through three had sufficient resources to provide adequate support to their child.

After finalizing this theoretical model of guardian support, we developed a measure, the Needs-based Assessment of Parental Support (NAPS), that operationalized this model (Bolen et al., 2000). Clinicians scored guardians based upon their supportive behaviors, and guardians scored themselves on their level of concern about the resources available to them. For each stage, the guardian received scores reflecting both the guardian's resources at that stage and whether the guardian was meeting the support needs for the child.

We have now completed a preliminary study of this measure, which was administered to 183 guardians (Bolen et al., 2000). While both the guardian-assessed and clinician-assessed measures held up well under empirical scrutiny, the clinician's assessment of guardian support had especially strong psychometric properties, suggesting that the conceptual model of guardian support could be captured both validly and reliably. Of importance, guardian support did hold up to the hypothesis that it could be scored as stage-specific.

The hypothesis that guardian resources were related to guardian support was also upheld. As guardians were more concerned with meeting physiological needs for their family, they were scored by clinicians as less supportive. This important finding tested the underlying assumption of this model—that guardians cannot be as supportive when they do not have adequate resources. This finding also supports a definition of guardian support that requires information about both the supportive behaviors of the guardian and the resources available to them. Further, it suggests an intervention based on making resources available rather than removing the child.

Another interesting finding was that the traditional measure of guardian support used in this study to compare with the NAPS was most highly correlated with the stage-specific domain capturing love and belonging. This finding suggests that current methods of measuring guardian support, instead of assessing whether the safety needs of the child are being met, assess for a higher level of emotional support. This finding most likely suggests a major issue of validity with the current conceptualization of guardian support and also suggests that removals may be made even when guardians are appropriately providing for the safety needs of the child.

In sum, the conceptualization of guardian support as progressing along stages from meeting lower-level and more basic needs to meeting higher-level needs was strongly supported by this research, as was the contention that guardian support needs to be considered in combination with resources available. The measure was also sensitive to cultural issues. The positive results of this study suggest that guardian support can be reconceptualized in a much more humanistic manner that is more sensitive to the stressors facing nonoffending guardians.

RECOMMENDATIONS

Reiterating this chapter's important points: (a) Most nonoffending guardians are doing a good job responding to their child's disclosure of abuse even while contending with extreme stressors, and (b) Current policies make it difficult for nonoffending guardians to appear as if they are responding well and indeed may paradoxically contribute to poorer support in nonoffending guardians. Policies that require nonoffending guardians to provide primary protection to the victimized child from an offender who often remains in the child's environment create a situation in which expectations for nonoffending guardians soar unrealistically. The bar is raised so high that even those nonoffending guardians who respond in a normative fashion given the extreme stressors might lose custody of their children. It has been the contention throughout this chapter that the reactions of most nonoffending guardians are not the problem; it is rather the expectations placed upon these nonoffending guardians that are the problem.

If this is this case, and this chapter has presented much literature that suggests that it is indeed the case, then it is incumbent upon professionals to consider alternatives. One such alternative—reconceptualizing a framework for understanding the responses of guardians after disclosure—was discussed in the previous sections. Even such a reconceptualization will not have the needed impact, however, unless other policies change as well. The remainder of this chapter focuses on changes to current policies and methods for delivery of these policies.

Consider the Environment of the Child

The most basic and easiest recommendation is to expand the consideration of guardian support beyond that of the nonoffending mother. A sizable body of literature now recognizes the importance of multiple caregivers and supports in the child's environment. Even when children live with a single parent, they often form important attachments with other meaningful adults in their lives (Zimmerman, 1993). Further, at least one study now suggests that the presence of multiple caregivers after the child's disclosure of sexual abuse is related to better outcomes in the child (Bolen, 1998a). Other studies find that children who have supportive adults are more resilient (Hoffman, Ushpiz, & Levy-Schiff, 1988; Masten, Best, & Garmezy, 1990). Further, the conservation of resources theory recognizes the mediating influence of having a supportive network (Hobfoll, 1989, 1991).

Thus, it is important that we recognize the other significant attachment figures in the child's life as potential resources. Especially when the child lives with two or more nonoffending guardians, the combined abilities of these caregivers to provide a supportive environment is the more critical factor. Assessing the support of all significant adults will open up new avenues of support that are critical to the well-being of the victimized child, open up resources upon which the nonoffending guardian can rely, and reduce some of the intolerable burdens placed upon nonoffending guardians after the children's disclosure of sexual abuse.

Training of Child Protective Services Workers

One of the paradoxes presented in this chapter is that, while approximately 80% of guardians are somewhat or fully supportive of their child after disclosure (Bolen, 2000b), removals of children remain high. Indeed, some studies have found that approximately 50% of children are removed immediately after disclosure, and up to two-thirds of children are removed at some time (Faller, 1991b; Hunter et al., 1990; Ryan et al., 1991). These findings indicate that a bias concerning nonoffending guardians persists in child protective services, suggesting that training of child protective services workers is inadequate.

An essential recommendation is that current workers be retrained (and new workers be trained) so that the curriculum is reflective of the empirical literature. Prevailing myths about nonoffending guardians need to be debunked, and a new model that recognizes the many stressors facing these guardians along with their many strengths should be presented. Biases that workers might hold also need to be explored. As mental health professionals know well, personal biases affect professional delivery of services. Given the extreme iatrogenic trauma that occurs when children are removed from attachment figures, the inadequate training of child protective services workers is a problem that desperately needs resolution.

Consider Complexity of the Nonoffending Guardians' Responses

Hooper and Humphreys (1998) illustrate that the current method of dichotomizing support versus nonsupport and belief versus disbelief does an injustice to the complexity of the nonoffending guardians' responses to the disclosure of their child's sexual abuse, especially when the offender is a loved one. In "the immensely hostile environment" (p. 570) in which mothers are attempting to support their child, there is little room for fluctuations or ambivalence in thoughts and emotions. Yet, these fluctuations may be normative as guardians cope with multiple stressors and feel forced to choose between loved ones. That ambivalence in response continues to be pathologized and punished suggests that professionals have a long way to go before understanding and accepting the array of emotions, feelings, and actions that nonoffending guardians experience after disclosure. Yet, understanding these emotions and allowing room for them must become another essential priority for professionals. This work will not only improve our understanding of normative responses to disclosure, but will allow professionals to better serve the victims and their families.

Provide Treatment for Nonoffending Guardians

A developing body of literature recognizes the traumatic effects of the child's disclosure on many nonoffending guardians (De Jong, 1988; Wagner, 1991). Further, the conservation of resources theory (Hobfoll et al., 1996) suggests that the numerous losses incurred through the disclosure process may contribute to less effective coping mechanisms which then lead to further losses, and that even the interventions of professionals may paradoxically contribute to this spiral of losses.

As a result of the enormous stressors placed on nonoffending guardians and the centrality of these nonoffending guardians to the welfare of the child, it is recommended that all nonoffending guardians have access to their own treatment with a licensed graduate-level mental health professional. It is also strongly recommended that the provider not be employed by one of the agencies with which the nonoffending guardian must interface because of the conflict of interest presented by the agency. For example, because child protective services has the protection of the child as their principal concern, their primary interest in the nonoffending guardian is as a necessary resource for providing protection and support to the child. Because of their mandate, their ability to provide supportive treatment to the nonoffending guardian may be compromised. Further, nonoffending guardians may more easily move into a therapeutic alliance with someone outside these agencies. It is critical that this relationship be a resource for, instead of a stressor on, nonoffending guardians.

Another important and related concern is the worldview of the treatment provider. If the clinician simply reinforces the myth-bound perceptions of some of the dated clinical literature, then the guardian becomes a victim of iatrogenic (i.e., system-induced) trauma by that treatment provider, and the treatment becomes a stressor instead of a resource. Instead, the treatment provider needs to be familiar with the empirical literature and to maintain a strengths approach to treatment.

The central goal of treatment is to improve the nonoffending guardian's ability to provide support to the victimized child. Given the tenets of the conservation of resources theory (Hobfoll et al., 1996), it is suggested that one of the most basic goals of treatment is to reverse the spiraling losses experienced by nonoffending guardians and their families by reducing stressors and increasing available resources. This intervention, in turn, should increase the nonoffending guardian's ability to utilize problem-focused and active coping skills. Thus, the nonoffending guardian's treatment provider may need to interface with child protective services and other agencies to determine how stress associated with interventions can be reduced or ameliorated. The treatment provider may also need to actively advocate for the nonoffending guardian, providing access to real resources that can then mediate the effects of the disclosure.

Another method for increasing guardian support is to help guardians to separate their behaviors from their thoughts and feelings. For example, nonoffending guardians may have conflicting thoughts and emotions, especially when the offender is a partner or other valued relationship. While treatment providers can allow and respect the nonoffending guardian's normal ambivalence in feelings and thoughts, they can also stress the need to be concomitantly *behaviorally* supportive. In other words, treatment providers can work to strengthen the capability of nonoffending guardians to provide for their victimized child and to make the appropriate statements of belief while simultaneously honoring and providing a space for their evocative emotions and conflicting thoughts and feelings. Such a focus provides a working-through environment for nonoffending guardians while also recognizing and encouraging their supportive actions. This approach should lead to a reduction in symptoms while increasing supportive behaviors.

A final goal is to heal the relationship between the nonoffending guardian and victimized child. For various reasons, victims experience a complexity of feelings toward the nonoffending guardian (Hooper & Humphreys, 1998). Sometimes it is the naivete of childhood that allows children to experience their parents as all-knowing and thus as having failed to protect them. These feelings might also be influenced by societal expectations upon mothers. Problems within this relationship might even have been apparent before the disclosure or before the abuse began. Regardless, reparative work often needs to occur between the nonoffending guardian and victim.

Remove the Offender from the Victim's Home

Removing the offender instead of the victim from the home may be one of the most difficult policy changes because it conflicts with society's presumption that the accused is innocent until proven guilty. Only with sufficient evidence of abuse can an alleged offender be charged with a crime. Even then, alleged offenders can often post bond and return to the child's environment while awaiting trial. Further, most convicted offenders are either not jailed or serve only short sentences. All of these issues may quickly place the offender or alleged offender back into the child's environment.

How can victimized children be protected without requiring nonoffending guardians to be held responsible for their protection? The most logical response to this question is this: How can it *not* happen? Why do we think it reasonable to make mothers responsible for protecting the child from a known or alleged criminal? In what other felony are mothers held responsible for the protection of the victim?

Moving beyond this ideological issue, there is a more pressing concern. If the mother is not responsible for the protection of her child, who is responsible? There are two plausible answers to this question—law enforcement and the alleged offender. Perhaps the biggest issue of moving this responsibility under the purview of law enforcement is the difficulty in enforcing it. How would law enforcement know if the alleged or known offender was in contact with the child? Given our technological resources available today, it does not seem like a great stretch of the imagination to consider how law enforcement can bring these technological advances to bear in monitoring the location of a known or alleged offender. Surely it would not be difficult with existing universal locator systems such as the GPS (global positioning satellite) to track the whereabouts of a person, assuming a monitor was required. And if the offender did wear a monitor, then it seems that some other type of technological system could be utilized to monitor how close the known or alleged offender was to the child in question. While this might require some effort, the technology surely exists to monitor the location of one person in proximity to one or even a few children.

Employing technological advances in the service of monitoring alleged or known offenders would allow for several changes. First, it would place the burden of responsibility for contact with the child upon the alleged or known offender as opposed to the nonoffending guardian. Any contact could be punishable by immediate incarceration. Second, monitoring the whereabouts of known or alleged offenders would allow law enforcement to protect the child from revictimization from that offender. A third and important effect is that nonoffending guardians would then have the burden removed from their shoulders so that they had the time to work through all the ramifications of the abuse disclosure while not having to maintain such difficult vigilance of their victimized child. Further, they could devote their efforts to doing what they need to do—providing a supportive environment to their child—instead of having to also hold a policing function.

The final and perhaps most important effect is that the victimized child would have a much greater possibility of remaining in the home. Only those nonoffending guardians who were otherwise neglectful or abusive of their victimized child would lose custody. One of the most important ramifications of keeping the child in the home is that the child would not suffer the serious iatrogenic trauma of removal. Separation from an important attachment figure is traumatic under the best of circumstances. Under the stress of the child's disclosure, the iatrogenic trauma must be even more severe. Having a means of avoiding this trauma to an already victimized child is worth the effort that would be required to develop such a monitoring system.

Safe Houses

A final recommendation is to create safe houses that are made available to nonoffending guardians and their children for short-term housing when abuse disclosure occurs. These houses could serve two functions. First, they could provide transitional housing to nonoffending guardians who lose their houses as a consequence of the disclosure. The second important function is that victims and their families could be provided a safe area that is monitored to keep the offender away from the home. Houses are easily wired. If the known or alleged offender were also required to wear a device that was constantly monitored by law enforcement, then the child and guardian could live with greater assurance that the offender would not have access to the child. This type of safe house could be made available both in those instances in which law enforcement or child protective services was concerned that the child's safety might be compromised and in those situations in which the nonoffending guardian or child was particularly fearful of the offender. Again, the premise is that making use of available technology can increase the safety of victimized children.

Final Thoughts

These suggestions may appear to some to be outrageous. Others may wonder about the cost involved. Perhaps there are better options available. Regardless, we owe it to our victimized children to consider creative options that allow them the best chance of remaining in their homes. Given the scope of the problem of child sexual abuse, the sheer numbers of children that will come to the attention of authorities as we become better at identifying abuse will be so overwhelming that the cost of removing these children from their homes will be far greater than what society can bear. We need to bring our experts to the table to determine alternatives. Even while honoring the codes of our society, as expressed in our Constitution, we can develop alternatives that do not infringe upon the rights of alleged offenders while providing better protection to our victimized children. To do so, however, we as a society will have to shoulder *our* burden for protecting our young charges rather than placing this burden on the already overburdened nonoffending guardians.

PART III
AFTERMATH

CHAPTER 11
PROFESSIONAL RESPONSE
TO CHILD SEXUAL ABUSE

INTRODUCTION

This book has exposed a number of problems with society's response to the epidemic of child sexual abuse. While as many as 30% to 40% of girls and 13% or more of boys are sexually abused in childhood (Bolen & Scannapieco, 1999), only a small number of these children are identified each year. Victims of intrafamilial abuse, especially of abuse by a father figure, have the greatest access to professional resources, whereas the majority of victims—those abused by an extrafamilial offender—have little access to resources. Further, less than one in five identified offenders is convicted, and less than a third of those convicted spend more than a year in jail.[1] Conversely, 40% to 59% of sexually abused children are removed from their homes immediately after the disclosure, and as many as two-thirds are eventually removed (Faller, 1991b; Hunter, Coulter, Runyan, & Everson, 1990; Massat & Lundy, 1998), a rupture that may have devastating consequences. Thus, our system as it is currently designed and implemented tragically fails both the victims who are never identified and sometimes even those children who are identified.

Caught in this quandary are the many exceptional professionals working in this system. Some burn out quickly, perhaps the victims of their own passion to affect change and frustration with the slow-changing system; or perhaps they simply hear one too many stories of a shattered childhood. Others spend most of their professional careers working to improve the system, to improve the welfare of the children and families, or to treat the adult victims. Some dedicated professionals do the difficult work with offenders.

Yet these same professionals work in an environment in which their techniques are destined to be questioned, for the stakes are simply too high and the knowledge base too new. How many committed professionals in the 1980s responded to their clients' entreaties to finally know all that happened to them by using regressive techniques—only to find five years later that these techniques were susceptible to bias? These are not professionals who knowingly, maliciously mislead; they are well-meaning and mostly well-trained professionals for whom the problem remains better defined than the solution. And there are, unfortunately, those few unscrupulous professionals who instead purposefully do real harm to their clients.

The purpose of this chapter is to scrutinize the professional response to child sexual abuse. It is important to realize that, with few exceptions, problems with the professional response to child sexual abuse are not with the professional but with the limitations of the current knowledge base and with the structure of the systems within which professionals work. The number of studies available to guide interventions and

---

[1] See footnotes 5 and 6 in Chapter 9, "Offenders."

decisions increases each year, but there remains much to learn about how to better respond. Because the documented professional response to child sexual abuse is barely 20 years old, issues with this response will be identified and resolved with time and with a greater quantity of substantive research.

This chapter is organized chronologically by the interventions that take place after abuse is disclosed, including the interview of the child, decisions made by child protective services, the medical examination, and the court process. This first section sets the stage for this chapter by discussing how professionals apportion responsibility for the abuse among the victim, nonoffending mother, and offender, as well as the factors that predict how responsibility is apportioned.

ATTRIBUTIONS MADE BY PROFESSIONALS

The first area that is considered in this chapter is how professionals attribute blame and responsibility in incidents of child sexual abuse. Judgments that professionals make about who is to blame for the abuse are important to consider because they establish a framework within which to understand decisions about interventions made by these professionals. Studies assessing attribution of responsibility typically provide respondents with vignettes that vary on key characteristics (such as the age of the victim), from which they allocate responsibility for the abuse.

As discussed in Chapter 3, "Theories of Child Sexual Abuse," professionals assign the most responsibility to offenders and the least responsibility to victims (Johnson, Owens, Dewey, & Eisenberg, 1990; Kelley, 1990; Reidy & Hochstadt, 1993). This has been a recent change, however, as studies from the 1980s found that a significant portion of the responsibility for the abuse was also assigned to victims and nonoffending mothers. For example, Saunders (1988) found that mean scores for attribution of responsibility to victims and offenders made by professionals differed by only half a point. Similarly, Dietz and Craft (1980) also found that child protective services workers believed that the nonoffending mother was as responsible for the abuse as the father in father-daughter incest. Although attribution of responsibility apportioned to victims decreased substantially in the 1990s, attribution of responsibility for nonoffending mothers remained somewhat higher not only for intrafamilial abuse (Johnson et al., 1990; Reidy & Hochstadt, 1993), but also for extrafamilial abuse (Kelley, 1990). Further, many professionals continue to hold negative perceptions of nonoffending mothers. For example, a recent study found that 81% of mental health practitioners agreed with statements that mothers in families in which father-daughter incest occurred were emotionally immature, and 83% agreed that these mothers had feelings of worthlessness as a woman (Freet, Scalise, & Ginter, 1996). When these same questions were asked about other types of abuse, the percentages fell to 59% and 60%, respectively.

Some studies have also considered factors that predict levels of attribution. Three factors predict the perception of victim responsibility as assigned by professionals. First, professionals attribute more responsibility for the abuse to older children and adolescents than younger children (Johnson et al., 1990). Second, male professionals rate victims as having more responsibility for the abuse than do female professionals (Jackson & Sandberg, 1985; Reidy & Hochstadt, 1993). Third, victims described as encouraging (versus passive or resistant) during the abuse are attributed more responsibility (Johnson et al., 1990; Wagner, Aucoin, & Johnson, 1993). Therefore, while victim blame is low, it does remain. That attribution of responsibility increases for older children and for children described as encouraging also suggests that some professionals continue to endorse myths about victims.

Factors predicting professional attribution of responsibility to nonoffending mothers and offenders have not been scrutinized as closely. The only known factor related to attribution of responsibility for nonoffending mothers is gender of the professional, with male professionals attributing less responsibility to nonoffending mothers than female professionals (Reidy & Hochstadt, 1993). Hanson and Slater (1993) also found that attributions of offender culpability varied by the offenders' motivations for the abuse. In vignettes, offenders who stated that they were closer to their daughter than to their wife or who said that they had been sexually abused as a child were attributed the least responsibility of all abuse situations by professionals. In a related study, Kelley (1990) found that professionals were more tolerant of, and recommended less severe sentences for, an offender who was described as a prominent attorney versus an unemployed alcoholic.

Professionals also differentially believe hypothetical accounts of abuse. Jackson and Nutall (1993) found that female professionals were more likely than male professionals to believe a sexual abuse vignette and that clinical social workers were more likely than pediatricians, psychiatrists, and psychologists to believe that an incident was abuse. Other factors related to greater belief were the race of the perpetrator (with accounts of Caucasian offenders considered more believable than accounts of African American or Latino offenders) and race of the victim (with accounts involving nonCaucasian children considered more believable). When the child was younger or presented with negative affect or behavioral changes, or when the perpetrator had a history of substance abuse, the account of abuse was also more likely to be believed. Zellman (1992) found that cases were more likely to be considered abuse when the offender was a carpenter instead of a prominent attorney, the offender was a babysitter instead of an estranged father, the victim did not recant, and the child was young. Given that race, socioeconomic status, and presenting with negative affect are unrelated to abuse disclosure or even abuse prevalence, these findings are of concern. It is of further concern that older children and adolescents are considered less credible than younger children.

Other studies report beliefs of professionals that also warrant some concern. Hartman, Karlson, and Hibbard (1994) found that a fourth to a third of defense attorneys believed that digital or penile penetration of a 15- or 16-year-old by an adult was *not* sexual abuse, even if it had occurred multiple times. Another study found that abuse by female offenders was considered less serious than abuse by male offenders and that fewer recommendations for imprisonment were made (Hetherton & Beardsall, 1988). Still another study found that more than half of physicians surveyed believed that most allegations made during divorce proceedings were false (Marshall & Locke, 1997).[2] Given that false allegations filed maliciously are rare in divorce or custody disputes (Faller, 1991a; Jones & McGraw, 1987), this is a finding

---

[2] See the section, "Decisions to Screen In and Investigate," in this chapter for a more lengthy discussion on false allegations during custody or divorce disputes.

of great concern. Finally, one study found that female professionals said that they would be more likely to separate from the alleged perpetrator (their partner) if abuse were disclosed (Deblinger, Lippmann, Stauffer, & Finkel, 1994). When asked about what their clients (nonoffending mothers) should do, however, most believed that the nonoffending mother should utilize family counseling to maintain family unity. That female professionals believe that what is in their best interest is different than what is in their client's best interest is an issue for further consideration.

In sum, these studies highlight some areas for concern. First, the consistency of a victim-blame factor, even though minimal, suggests that some professionals still hold the victim partially responsible. That blame or belief varies based upon the age of the child—even when penetration occurs—also suggests that professionals do not yet fully agree upon the definition of an abuse event. It is of further concern that the type of behavior the child displays (i.e., whether the child is considered encouraging, passive, or resisting during the abuse) is related to attribution of responsibility. The continued existence of a stronger mother-blame factor and the finding that culpability varies based upon the offender's rationalization for the abuse also suggests that professionals do not as yet always place the blame fully on the offender. The differences of opinions between male and female professionals on basic issues of culpability and prosecution are also worrisome. Other issues are of even more concern—such as why socioeconomic status and race of the victim and perpetrator affect the way professionals assess abuse situations.

Overall, this variability is probably a reflection of the continued newness of the knowledge base surrounding child sexual abuse. While professionals working directly and closely with cases of child sexual abuse would be expected to stay abreast of the developing knowledge base, professionals more removed from it (such as pediatricians and mental health workers without a specific child sexual abuse practice) probably cannot do so. That some professionals would espouse outdated beliefs is thus somewhat understandable. These findings suggest that continued basic education of all professionals needs to remain a priority.

DECISION TO REPORT

Not all mandated reporters report known or suspected abuse. For example, fewer than half of all cases known to professionals were reported to child protective services in the second National Incidence Study (NIS) (Zellman & Faller, 1996).[3] Several studies have attempted to determine how many professionals fail to report suspected abuse and what accounts for the differences between reporters and nonreporters. These studies are in one of two formats, the most typical of which is when professionals read vignettes to determine whether they would report that case. More recently, studies have asked about professionals' previous histories of reporting and then compared reporting with nonreporting groups.

Several studies confirm the findings in the NIS-2 that some professionals would not report some instances of suspected abuse (Crenshaw, Lichtenberg, &

---

[3] Professionals may, however, report abuse that is then screened out by child protective services. These cases are not reflected in the statistics.

Bartell, 1993; Kalichman, Craig, & Follingstad, 1989). In the largest study, Zellman and Antler (1990) found that 40% of 1,196 professionals stated that they had at some time suspected abuse but failed to report it. Reporting behavior was divided into three groups—those who always reported suspected abuse (44%), never reported suspected abuse (6%), and discretionary reporters (33%). The remaining 17% had never had a case of suspected abuse. In another method of evaluating nonreporting behavior, King et al. (1998) computed the lifetime proportion of reported cases of abuse or neglect by dividing the lifetime number of cases reported by the lifetime number of cases suspected. The lifetime proportion of reported cases was 69%, and only 54% of professionals stated that child protective services would be their first point of contact for reporting suspicions about abuse.

Many reasons are cited for not reporting suspected child abuse, many of which reflect moral and ethical decisions that clinicians face, such as concerns about confidentiality (Schwartz, 1992) and even what constitutes a suspicion of abuse (Foreman & Bernet, 2000). These next sections review factors that researchers have identified as relating to decisions to report.

Characteristics of the abuse and disclosure: One of the most consistent findings across studies is that professionals are less likely to report suspected abuse when they are less sure of the reliability of the report (Crenshaw et al., 1993). Zellman and Faller (1996), for example, reported that the strongest factor predicting nonreporting behavior included the following items: the report lacked sufficient evidence that abuse had occurred; the abuse or neglect was not serious enough to warrant a report; the situation resolved itself; and someone had already reported the abuse. Another study found that a strong predictor of a professional's history of nonreporting behavior was a factor that combined lack of sufficient evidence with concerns that the report would harm the child or result in the child's removal from the family (King et al., 1998). More severe abuse including penetration is also related to increased likelihood of reporting (O'Toole, Webster, O'Toole, & Lucal, 1999; Zellman, 1992). Conversely, abuse is less likely to be reported when the child or teenager recants (Attias & Goodwin, 1985; Zellman, 1992). Given the frequency of recantations (Sorenson & Snow, 1991), this finding is of concern.

Characteristics of the child, offender, and family: Factors concerning the child, offender, and family are not related to reporting behavior (Kalichman et al., 1989; King et al., 1998), although Zellman (1992) found that cases involving younger children were more likely to be reported. Nor does the professional's attribution of responsibility in father-daughter incest affect reporting behavior (Kalichman, Craig, & Follingstad, 1990). One study, however, found that when the offender was the clinician's client, a report was more likely to be made if the offender was African American (93% versus 67% for Caucasian offenders) (Watson & Levine, 1989). Zellman and Antler (1990) also found that one of the most important reasons for failing to report suspected abuse was that doing so might worsen the child's condition, although Crenshaw et al. (1993) found that this concern was also expressed by reporters of abuse. Further, Zellman (1992) found that a case was more likely to be reported when the offender was a carpenter instead of a prominent attorney.

Characteristics of the professional: Characteristics of the professional are also related to propensity to report. One important variable is the professional's education and training, with those having more education (Kalichman, Craig, & Follingstad,

1988) and training (King et al., 1998) being more likely to report suspected abuse. Zellman and Faller (1996) also found that those who consistently failed to report cases of suspected abuse had little child abuse training and limited child abuse knowledge. A few professionals also endorsed concerns about the time a report took to complete as well as a fear of a lawsuit as reasons for not reporting. Those who both reported and did not report suspected abuse in the past (i.e., discretionary reporters), however, were quite knowledgeable and well-trained, expressed the greatest level of confidence in their ability to treat victims, and were often their agency's resource person for child abuse and neglect.

Issues concerning child protective services: One important predictor of reporting behavior is the professional's experience with child protective services. Zellman and Faller (1996), for example, found that professionals who had never reported a case of suspected abuse were more likely to endorse a factor that captured the professional's "negative opinion of the professionalism and capability of CPS staff and their beliefs that reports often had negative consequences for the children involved" (p. 368). Cases involving mild abuse, which professionals believed would not get adequate attention from overburdened caseworkers, were also seldom reported. Indeed, when Zellman and Antler (1990) made field visits to child protective services sites in six states to explore policies and procedures that affect mandated reporting, every agency stated that having inadequate resources was a serious problem. To regulate the workload, all states had either officially or informally limited the cases they accepted, sometimes by increasing the severity of abuse required to accept a case. Yet, prioritizing cases almost always meant that cases with the least ranking were not served. As Karski (1999) states, "within the current context of limited and competing resources, service rationing is now the norm" (p. 652).

Summary: The findings presented in this section focus on two issues. First is the issue of why professionals do not report suspected abuse. Perhaps Crenshaw et al. (1993) summarize this response best when they state:

> *These data suggest that both Reporters and Non-Reporters are doing what they believe to be in the best interest of their clients. The principal differences between the groups are the way in which they interpret their roles as professionals within a broader legal context and how they execute the treatment of their clients within this context. (p. 40)*

This is not the complete story, however, as some of the predictors of whether a case is reported reflect potential biases held by professionals. Watson and Levine's (1989) finding that African American offenders were more likely to be reported and the finding of others that recantation is related to nonreporting behavior (Attias & Goodwin, 1985; Zellman, 1992) are both worrisome. One reflects a racial bias, whereas the other reflects unfamiliarity with the abuse disclosure process. These findings again suggest a need for basic education for all mandated reporters.

The second important issue discussed in this section is the effect of funding problems for child protective services on decisions to report. Some mandated reporters make decisions not to report suspected abuse because of concerns that the case will not be investigated, handled properly, or will even be detrimental to the child. Most of these problems, however, are closely tied to funding problems. Were agencies funded based on need, they would not need to narrow the definition of child sexual abuse or further limit cases accepted for investigation. An obvious problem exists when a system is mandated a responsibility (that of investigating cases of suspected abuse) and is then inadequately funded to do so.

CHILD PROTECTIVE SERVICES DECISIONS

One of the interesting features of the professional literature on child sexual abuse is the dearth of studies on decision-making within child protective services. While a number of studies examine the child's disclosure and the mandated reporter's decision to report, few studies examine the process of investigation and substantiation. Thus, little information is available concerning some of the most critical stages of the disclosure process. This represents a critical oversight in the empirical literature. It is of equal concern that federal agencies have not mandated studies that assess for predictors of decisions such as screening out or substantiation made by child protective services. Having provided these caveats, the minimal empirical literature regarding the process of screening in, investigating, substantiating abuse, and deciding whether to remove the child is reviewed.

Decision to Screen In and Investigate

When a report is made to child protective services, the report is either screened in or out, but only those cases that are screened in are investigated. Child protective services cannot screen in and investigate all reported cases—nor should they. What is important to consider, however, is why cases are screened in or out.

In the latest NCANDS incidence study done in 1998, a third of all reports of suspected abuse or neglect were screened out (U.S. Department of Health and Human Services, 2000c). This is a higher estimate than even the NIS-3 done in 1993, in which only 42% to 44% of cases of suspected abuse or neglect known to professionals were investigated (and thus screened in) (Sedlak & Broadhurst, 1996). Neither study attempts to explain this discrepancy. Sexual abuse cases are more likely to be screened in and thus investigated (Karski, 1999; Sedlak & Broadhurst, 1996). Screening policies also vary across agencies (Downing, Wells, & Fluke, 1990) and are used at least partially "to reduce investigative caseloads to a point that at least approaches, if not matches, available resources" (Zellman & Faller, 1996, p. 371).

Only three known studies have examined reasons for screening cases in or out. First, Karski (1999) found that no reporting or case factors were associated with whether cases were screened in or out. This finding appears to be more related to the policies of that agency, however, as this agency had an unusually high percentage of sexual abuse cases (72%) that were screened in for investigation. In studies by Giovannoni (1991) and Downing et al. (1990), reasons child protective services employees cited most commonly for screening a suspected abuse case out were that the report fell out of the legislative mandate for that agency, the information given by the reporter was judged to be unreliable, the report was vague, and the reporter appeared to be motivated to make a false report. This latter reason for screening out was especially likely when the case was within a custody dispute.

There are several concerns about decisions to screen in or out. An historical concern is that race might be related to child protective services contacts. Although Karski (1999) found that race of the victim was not related to decisions to screen in or out, Sauzier (1989) instead found that child protective service contacts occurred in 36% of white families in which a child was a victim of sexual abuse as opposed to 68% of African American families. In addition, referral for services occurred in 25% of cases involving business or professional families versus 63% for unskilled labor families. Further, while the latest NIS found no significant differences in substantiated cases of child abuse and neglect by race (Sedlak & Broadhurst, 1996), the 1996 NCANDS national incidence study suggests that racial profiling may occur at least for sexual abuse cases (U.S. Department of Health & Human Services, 1998). In this study, 65% of victims of sexual abuse were Caucasian, 19% were African American, 14% were Latino, and 1% were Asian American. In national data, however, Caucasians constituted 73% of the population, African Americans constituted 12% of the population, Latinos constituted 11% of the population, and individuals of Asian descent constituted 4% of the population.[4] These findings suggest that African Americans and Latinos are somewhat over-represented in identified cases of child sexual abuse, whereas Caucasians and individuals of Asian descent are somewhat under-represented. Conversely, Russell's (1983) retrospective random community prevalence study found that the only difference in sexual abuse prevalence by race was that individuals of Asian decent were less likely to report a history of child sexual abuse. Thus, the over-representation of African Americans and Latinos in cases of identified child sexual abuse appears to be an artifact of the system of reporting, investigation, or substantiation.

Another concern about the screening process is that child protective services' mandate is primarily to protect children from caregivers who abuse them. Yet, only about 12% to 16% of all abuse in Russell's (1983) community prevalence study was committed by caregivers.[5] While cases of sexual abuse committed by individuals other than caregivers may be investigated by law enforcement, the over-representation of victims of father-daughter incest and other types of incest in identified populations suggests that children abused by someone other than a caregiver do not have the same access to treatment and other resources.

Still another concern about the screening process is that workers often screen out cases that occur within a custody dispute or divorce (Downing et al., 1990; Giovannoni, 1991). This has been an area of contentious and heated debate for a number of years. This debate originated because a few small clinical studies purported that 36% to 55% of allegations made by mothers against their partners during divorce or custody disputes were not only false, but maliciously filed (Benedek & Schetky, 1985; Green, 1986). More rigorous studies using larger samples have instead found that false disclosures within custody disputes remain rare (Jones & McGraw, 1987; Paradise, Rostain, & Nathanson, 1988). In the largest study done to date of 9,000 court cases of divorce or custody disputes (Thoennes & Tjaden, 1990), less than 2% involved allegations of sexual abuse, and only slightly less than half of those involved mothers making allegations of sexual abuse against fathers. In the

---

[4] *http://www.census.gov/population/estimates/nation/intfile3-1.txt*
[5] Computed by author

other half, fathers made allegations against the mother, stepfather, or mother's boyfriend, mothers made allegations against a third party, or allegations were made by someone other than a parental figure. The authors concluded that allegations made during a custody or divorce dispute were no more likely to be unfounded than other reports of child sexual abuse. The 1998 NCANDS (a yearly national incidence study) also tracked five states to record all intentionally false reports. Of 257,627 reports of child abuse or neglect filed in these states, 1,618 (or 0.7%) were intentionally false (U.S. Department of Health & Human Services, 2000c).

Another study by Faller (1991a) examined 136 reports of child sexual abuse made during custody or divorce disputes. The largest group of cases (38%) was of sexual abuse that began only after the parent's separation. In many of these cases the father was sexually attracted to the child even during the marriage. Eight percent of the allegations were filed in cases where the mother was seeking a divorce because her child had disclosed sexual abuse by the father while they were married, and 19% were of ongoing father-daughter incest that was only disclosed during the divorce proceedings. In only 2% of the total sample, however, were the allegations made by a parent who was consciously lying. In other cases in which abuse did not occur, the parent genuinely suspected abuse, and in some cases the child had been sexually abused, but by someone other than the mother's partner. In a similar but later study, Faller and DeVoe (1995) found that 5% of parents knowingly made false allegations.

A final study by Everson and Boat (1989) compared characteristics of child protective services workers with at least one false report of sexual abuse in their caseload to workers with no false reports. Groups differed on two important factors. First, the group with false reports had an overall substantiation rate of 45%, as compared to 63% for the group with no false reports. Second, whereas workers without false reports believed that about 5% of children lied about abuse allegations, workers with false reports believed that about 12% of children did so. Further, workers with false disclosures believed that 20% of adolescents' disclosures are false, and 13% of workers with false reports believed that more than half of all adolescents' reports are false. This study suggests that at least a subset of child protective services workers maintains extreme biases towards children and adolescents.

These studies suggest that malicious reports of sexual abuse made by parents during a custody or visitation dispute are rare. More importantly, the majority of allegations filed in custody or dispute cases are confirmed (Faller, 1991a). Yet, child protective services workers remain highly suspicious of these cases, resulting in a high level of cases screened out. The consequences of routinely screening out these cases is dramatized in a study of cases referred to an organization working with protective parents who had made formal allegations of sexual abuse against partners (Neustein & Goetting, 1999). In this self-selected sample, family court awarded 70% of the alleged offenders unsupervised access to the child either through joint custody or unsupervised visitation, and 20% of alleged offenders were awarded primary custody. While this study has a somewhat biased sample, its findings are still of great concern. Given the extraordinary cost to the child within a custody or divorce dispute whose valid case of sexual abuse is screened out, it seems more logical to always screen in these cases.

The final concern about the screening process is that it is partially a fiscal decision. Because budgets for child protective services have decreased significantly in recent years, agencies have had to restrict the cases they investigate. While not all reported cases need to be investigated, it is of great concern that some are screened out as a result of restricted definitions of abuse that have changed because of monetary considerations. Further, findings presented in this section suggest that child protective services is placing many children at risk for further abuse by failing to consider that allegations made in custody or divorce disputes are usually valid. Finally, child protective services' narrow jurisdiction of cases of suspected abuse by only a caretaker ensures that most victims of child sexual abuse are never officially identified and thus never receive treatment.

Decision to Find Abuse Substantiated

When abuse is investigated, child protective services workers then determine whether the abuse occurred. When enough evidence exists to conclude that abuse did occur, it is said to be substantiated. Overall, child protective services only substantiates about 34% of all investigated abuse and neglect (U.S. Department of Health and Human Services, 1998). One study of 293 randomly selected cases in a New York county, however, found that only 12% of child sexual abuse cases were substantiated, a rate lower than that of other types of abuse and neglect (Levine, Doueck, & Freeman, & Compaan, 1998).

Again, only a few studies have examined factors that predict whether abuse is substantiated. One predictor with mixed findings is the age of the child. While Eckenrode et al. (1988) and Freeman et al. (1996) both found that cases involving older children were more likely to be substantiated, another study found that age only approached significance after controlling for other significant predictors (Haskett, Wayland, Hutcheson, & Tavana, 1995). Dersch and Munsch (1999) also express concerns that cases involving male victims of sexual abuse are less likely to be substantiated, and this hypothesis was supported in their bivariate analysis. They also found, however, that male victims were significantly younger than female victims. These findings are consistent with those of Eckenrode et al. (1988), who found in bivariate analysis that males were less likely to have their cases substantiated. After controlling for the age of the child, however, gender was no longer significant. These findings suggest that any lower substantiation rate for male victims is most likely because of their younger age.

Another study asked 117 caseworkers about information that was more likely to lead to a valid report (Giovannoni, 1991). Items they mentioned were a specific allegation by the child, eye witnesses, allegations by the nonoffending parent, the reporter's firsthand knowledge, an admission by the perpetrator, medical reports, and physical evidence. Factors used in making their decisions to substantiate the abuse were the logical discourse of disclosure, its consistency with other reports and across interviews, and the presence of corroborating evidence. Offender access to the child was also a consideration in substantiating the abuse, as were the credibility of the child and how upset the child was during the interview.

Other factors have been studied less. Eckenrode et al. (1988) found that cases reported by professionals were more likely to be substantiated. Haskett et al. (1995) also found that while cases involving penetration were more likely to be substantiated, cases within a divorce or custody dispute were less likely to be substantiated. Only 15% of cases involving custody disputes were substantiated, as compared to 67% of all cases that were substantiated.

While most of the factors leading to substantiation are logical, even though not always desired (such as lower substantiation rates for younger victims), some are cause for concern. First, although the previous section found that most allegations of sexual abuse made within a custody or divorce dispute are valid, even the few cases that are screened in are usually not substantiated. Thus, many children are not adequately protected, especially considering that most of the alleged offenders may then have court-mandated, unsupervised access to the child. It is also of concern that the presentation of the child during the disclosure, especially whether or not the child is upset, is related to whether child protective services workers consider it a more valid case of abuse.

A final and lingering question is how many children whose cases are unsubstantiated are actually victims of sexual abuse. Most clinicians working with victims have probably had the experience of serving a child whose previous disclosure of abuse was not substantiated, only to have the child be revictimized. Until a rigorous study investigates cases of unsubstantiated abuse, this question cannot be answered. Yet, these false negative cases represent the failure of the system to protect identified victims of child sexual abuse. Even a few of these false negatives are cause for concern.

Decision to Remove a Child

Across studies, 49% to 59% of children are removed immediately after the official disclosure, and up to two-thirds of children are eventually removed (Faller, 1991b; Hunter et al., 1990; Massat & Lundy, 1998). Often these removals are lengthy or permanent. For example, Hunter et al. (1990) found that less than half of abused children were still residing with their original families 24 months after disclosure. Only 24% of the victims had not experienced a change in living situation following disclosure, and only 44% of the children who were not immediately removed experienced no placement change at the two-year follow-up evaluation. Although most children experienced only one move, 13% of the children experienced more than five moves. Children placed in foster care had the least overall stability, with an average of five different placements. Faller (1991b) also found that 62% of sexually abused children in her sample were placed out of the home between the initial report of abuse and the follow-up evaluation approximately one year later. Of those placed, 2% were placed with another parent, 17% were placed with another relative, 68% were placed in foster care, and 13% were institutionalized or placed in independent living. Another study of 277 cases of sexual abuse found that only 41% of children remained in their homes after disclosure (Ryan, Warren, & Weincek, 1991). Although 7% of all children were removed for less than one week, a further 18% were placed with relatives, and 34% were placed in foster care.

Several factors affect the decision of child protective service workers to place the child. One of the most consistently reported factors predicting removal is the support of the nonoffending mother (Hunter et al., 1990; Leifer, Shapiro, & Kassim,

1993). For example, Leifer et al. (1993) found that 74% of children were removed when the mother was deemed unsupportive, as compared to 15% of children who were removed when the mother was supportive.[6] Everson et al. (1989) also found that 80% of children were placed in foster or institutional care when the mother was deemed unsupportive, 100% were placed with relatives when mothers were scored as ambivalent in support, and 5% were placed when mothers were deemed supportive. Further, Pellegrin and Wagner (1990) found that children of more compliant mothers experienced fewer removals.

While these findings seem to support the relationship of guardian support to removals, there are indications that having a supportive guardian does not necessarily protect a child from removal. As mentioned previously, 40% to 59% of children are removed immediately after the official disclosure, and up to two-thirds of children are eventually removed. In the author's review of guardian support (2000b), however, 65% to 95% of mothers fully or partially believed the disclosure, and across studies, 81% of mothers responded to the abuse disclosure with some or full support. In other words, vastly more removals across studies occur than there are unsupportive guardians. Indeed, Ryan et al. (1991) found that 30% of children were removed from mothers assessed as very protective after disclosure, and 37% of children were removed from mostly protective mothers.

The study by Ryan et al. (1991) lends insight into why more removals occur than there are unsupportive guardians. These researchers categorized the mother's ability to protect the child *before the abuse was disclosed* as no protection (32%), little protection (16%), mostly protective (16%), and very protective (19%). Another 18% of mothers were considered to have no knowledge of the ongoing abuse. Yet across studies, 75% to 95% of mothers do not know about the ongoing abuse (Faller, 1990; Margolin, 1992; Myer, 1985). That child protective services workers considered that 82% of mothers knew about the abuse *before disclosure* appears to be a clear indication of systemic bias towards nonoffending mothers. Further, the mother's protective actions *before disclosure* was one of two factors that best explained the pattern of removals, the other being the mother's response after the abuse was disclosed. Removals were as follows for these categories: 89% for mothers offering no protection *before the report*; 47% for mothers offering little protection; 39% for mostly protective mothers; 28% for very protective mothers; and 44% for mothers who knew nothing about the ongoing abuse. These findings are striking examples that (a) an extraordinary systemic bias towards nonoffending guardians exists, and (b) some children are removed even when nonoffending mothers are deemed protective.

Another seemingly obvious factor relating to removal of the child is whether the offender resides in the same home with the victim. In one study, while fewer than 10% of children were removed initially when the offender did not reside in the home, more than half were removed when both the mother and father (who was the offender) were in the home, and 84% of children were removed when the offender was the only biological parent living in the home (Hunter et al., 1990). At the 24-month follow-up evaluation, approximately 50% of children had been removed when

---

[6] In the author's review of 16 studies assessing guardian support (Bolen, 2000b), this research group had the most stringent definition of guardian support. Indeed, their method of scoring could label a mother unsupportive if she scored +3 or +4 on a scale ranging from −5 to +5.

the offender was nonresident, about 75% had been removed when the offender was the mother's boyfriend, 80% had been removed when the offender was a resident father, and 100% had been removed when the offender was the resident father and no mother was present. Yet, the relationship of the offender to the victim was only significant in multivariate analysis for the initial placement. Another study also found no relationship between the decision to remove the child and the perpetrator's access to the child, the relationship of the perpetrator to the victim, or the identity of the perpetrator (Jaudes & Morris, 1990).

While this seemingly logical factor is generally unrelated to removals, other more illogical factors are related. Two different studies found that the most important variable relating to the decision to remove the child was whether the child made the initial outcry (Finkelhor, 1983; Jaudes & Morris, 1990). Those children who purposefully disclosed the abuse were removed from the home significantly more often. Other factors related to increased risk of removal are poverty, multiple children within the family, multiple types of abuse or other problems within the family, having the case referred for prosecution and then declined, and maternal employment (Cross, Martell, McDonald, & Ahl, 1999; Finkelhor, 1983; Pellegrin & Wagner, 1990). Mixed findings have been found for race and age of the child and severity of abuse (Cross et al., 1999; Finkelhor, 1983; Hunter et al., 1990). Factors not significantly related to removal are developmental delay of the child, presence of a sexually transmitted disease, presence of physical abuse, and the child's psychopathology scores (Hunter et al., 1990; Jaudes & Morris, 1990).

In summary, removals are closely related to perceived support of the nonoffending guardian (almost always the mother)—a logical relationship. The problem comes, however, with the perceived support. The study by Ryan et al. (1991) suggests that the perceptions about nonoffending guardians held by child protective services workers are extremely biased, most likely reflecting an institutionalized bias. If workers are trained to believe that most nonoffending guardians are unsupportive, then the close relationship between guardian support and removals would ensure that some children are needlessly removed. Indeed, this appears to be the case as far greater numbers of children are removed from their homes than there are unsupportive guardians. A similar concern with the literature is that compliance in nonoffending mothers is associated with fewer removals (Pellegrin & Wagner, 1990). Perhaps it is just the word *compliance,* but nonoffending guardians should instead be *empowered* by professionals to feel as if they can and do have the ability to protect their children. Compliance, on the other hand, suggests an acquiescent guardian. Perhaps we need to consider whether our interventions *disempower* guardians. Finally, it is always of concern when demographic and disclosure characteristics are related to decisions to remove.

THE DECISION-MAKING PROCESS

The Interview

In the early 1980s when sexual abuse began to be disclosed with increasing frequency, no guidelines for conducting interviews existed (Faller, 1996). Child protective services workers, who are required to have only a bachelor's level education and not necessarily one in a mental health field, were also those responsible for conducting these interviews. Because this agency was not prepared for the influx of reports, these early interviews of children "were conducted by professionals with little training, few skills, and not much time" (p. 84). Law enforcement officials, the other group most likely to interview the child, had training primarily in interrogating suspects, a skill that for obvious reasons did not lend itself to evaluating child victims. Even mental health workers involved in these initial efforts had no special training in determining whether an event did or did not occur.

This early environment of high-stakes interviewing—in a vacuum of guidelines—had two predictable results. First, research on issues surrounding the interviewing process became a priority, and second, a number of controversies erupted over the interviewing process. Indeed, by the mid-1980s, a backlash had begun that continues even today.

Faller (1996) categorizes the controversies relating to the interview process as four separate issues: (a) the ability of the interviewer to conduct a competent interview; (b) the structure and process of the interview; (c) the process of decision-making regarding whether sexual abuse occurred; and (d) the competence of the child to describe actual events. Within this last category, Faller also includes issues surrounding the child's reluctance to disclose, memory problems, vulnerability to suggestion, and whether children lie or fantasize about abuse incidents. Because this fourth category is beyond the scope of this book, it will not be discussed other than to note Gardner's recent and incredible comments that "children normally exhibit just about any kind of sexual behavior imaginable: heterosexual, homosexual, bisexual, and autosexual" (as cited in Faller, 1996, pp. 89-90). He also discusses how a four-year-old girl may "harbor, among her collection of polymorphous perverse fantasies, thoughts of some kinds of sexual encounters with her father" (p. 90). While his comments probably represent some of the more outlandish concerns, some of the issues being discussed today are salient, and research is now addressing these issues.

This next section focuses on Faller's (1996) first two issues: the ability of the interviewer to conduct a competent interview and the structure and process of the interview. The following section, "Factors Affecting Evaluation Decisions," then discusses Faller's third issue: the process of decision-making regarding whether sexual abuse occurred.

The Interviewer and the Process and Structure of the Interview

Properly conducted interviews with children are challenging and thus the interviewer requires extensive training. Because of these challenges, is not surprising that the few studies conducted have found that even with training, difficulties in the interviewing process occur. For example, one study examined 42 interview transcripts of child protective services workers in multiple counties from a single state (Warren, Woodall, Hunt, & Perry, 1996). Overall, the researchers found large discrepancies between interview guidelines and actual interviews within all phases of the interview.

Another study by Boat and Everson (1996) examined how child protective services workers used anatomical dolls in 96 videotaped interviews. The results of this study were more encouraging, as few concerning practices were noted when workers used the anatomical doll as a comforter, an icebreaker, or as an anatomical model. The number of concerning practices increased, however, when workers used the dolls as a method for allowing children to demonstrate what happened to them. Overall, concerning practices were evident in most of the interviews, although those with the greatest potential for shaping the outcome of the case were observed rarely. Even so, these studies suggest that training of child protective services workers can be improved. With structural problems such as high turnover rates and limited time for interviews, however, problematic interviewing techniques may continue even with better skills training.

Concerns have also been expressed about interviewers other than child protective services workers, many of whom are professional mental health workers with specialized training in interviewing techniques. Again the concern has been that poor practices might lead to false disclosures or partially confabulated responses. Some of the more outlandish allegations about these interviewers are again voiced by Gardner, who is summarized by Faller (1996):

> He calls interviewers "validators," a pejorative term, and says they are poorly educated, poorly trained, and involved in sexual abuse assessments for a variety of inappropriate motives. For example, Gardner suggests that they may be survivors of sexual abuse working out their own issues, sexually inhibited individuals ill at ease with their own pedophilia, sadists, paranoids, overzealous feminists, and hypocrites....Further, Gardner states that validators may experience sexual gratification when they imagine an act of sexual abuse and that this sexual problem apparently plays a key role in their need to foster false allegations. (p. 86)

It is worth mentioning that Gardner never provides support for these comments.

Even ignoring Gardner's outlandish comments, there are some concerns about interviewing practices. In an early study, Boat and Everson (1988) found that 67% of professionals responded that parents were sometimes present during the interview in which anatomical dolls were used, whereas the alleged perpetrator was present in about 6% of interviews. More recently, Lamb, Sternberg, and Esplin (1998) investigated 10 different types of utterances used by interviewers. The more focused of these utterances could potentially have some degree of suggestive influence, whereas the more open-ended utterances typically elicit better information. In their own studies as well as those of other researchers, they found that focused utterances were more common than open-ended utterances. Because of these findings, they designed a study in which one group of interviewers had a script that included many open-ended utterances during the rapport-building phase of the interview, whereas another group had a script that included more focused items. Children who had been "trained" through the use of open-ended utterances in the rapport-building phase gave more details throughout the remainder of the interview. The inclusion of open-ended questions in the rapport-building phase had no effect on interviewers, however, who quickly fell back into their pattern of asking more focused questions throughout the remainder of the interview.

In a more recent study, interviewers were trained in a NICHD "flexibly structured protocol incorporating a wide range of strategies believed to enhance retrieval" (Orbach et al., 2000, p. 734). Investigators trained in this procedure were able to establish superior retrieval conditions that led to elicited information from children of higher quality than before the interviewer was trained. The amount of information gathered, however, was similar. While this method requires extensive training, these findings suggest that interviewers can establish superior retrieval conditions that then elicit information from children that is of higher quality.

While few in number, these studies suggest that some problems in interviewing continue to occur. Because guidelines such as the American Professional Society for Abused Children's (APSAC) 1997 *Psychosocial Evaluation of Suspected Sexual Abuse in Children* and the NICHD protocol (Orbach et al., 2000) exist for how to conduct competent interviews, one important issue is the continued intensive education and training in skills for professionals conducting forensic interviews, while continuing research on how to improve techniques. Another important issue, however, is who should conduct the interviews. While child protective services workers are currently mandated to conduct these difficult interviews (Faller, 1996), they may not have a degree in a social services discipline nor a postgraduate degree. Their enormous time constraints and high turnover rates are other barriers to sufficient training. Given the time necessary to conduct multiple interviews (since disclosures often occur over multiple sessions with the child) (Sorenson & Snow, 1991), the extensive training required to conduct competent interviews, and the high stakes involved for both actual and false disclosures, it would appear that our most experienced, best-trained mental health professionals should instead have this difficult responsibility.

Factors Affecting Decisions on Evaluations

A variety of techniques and interventions are used to determine whether sexual abuse has occurred, including the medical evaluation, the child's interview (with or without anatomical dolls or projective techniques), and interviews with nonoffending guardians, alleged offenders, or others. Afterwards, professionals have the difficult task of determining whether the abuse occurred. Berliner and Conte (1993) discuss two different approaches used in the United States for evaluating child sexual abuse: the indicator approach and the standards approach.

In the indicator approach, professionals rely upon a number of behavioral or physical indicators of abuse that increase the professional's confidence in decisions regarding whether abuse occurred. When a child exhibits a number of these criteria, it would suggest that abuse had occurred; conversely, when a child does not exhibit these criteria, there would be less suggestion that abuse had occurred. While most professionals use these criteria simply to inform their judgments concerning whether abuse occurred (Berliner & Conte, 1993), this method has some pitfalls. First and foremost, sexually abused children have no generalized presentation, so that any given child not meeting the criteria might still have been sexually abused. For example, although a survey found that professionals attach the most importance to the existence of physical indicators (Conte, Sorenson, Fogarty, & Rosa, 1991), only a small minority of sexually abused children actually present with physical evidence (Palusci et al., 1999). Further, 90% of professionals in this survey believed that being the subject of a custody battle increased the likelihood of reporting distortions (Conte et al., 1991), a factor not supported in the empirical literature. Other factors that professionals endorsed as increasing the possibility of the child's distortion of the report were an early childhood fantasy remembered as reality (endorsed by 49% of professionals) or a wish to punish or torture a hated adult (endorsed by 78%).

Another concern of the indicator approach is that characteristics of the professional are related to their perceptions of indicators of sexual abuse. For example, Kendall-Tackett and Watson (1991) found that professionals who believed that children do not lie about sexual abuse were more convinced by behavioral indicators that sexual abuse had occurred. Further, law enforcement officials were more convinced than mental health professionals, and women were more convinced than men. Finally, this method has also been misused to establish criteria for discriminating true from false allegations. In Gardner's Sexual Abuse Legitimacy scale (as cited in Berliner & Conte, 1993), his 26 criteria purportedly discriminate between true and false allegations. Because the underlying criteria are based purely upon the author's personal observation and judgment and have not undergone empirical scrutiny, this method is fraught with both ethical and methodological issues. Since the indicator approach is susceptible to bias and to both false positives and false negatives, caution must be exercised in placing too much credence in the indicator approach. As mentioned previously, however, most professionals use it only to inform their judgments.

The other method—the standards approach—outlines the conduct of the professionals making the evaluations. One of the most well-known of these approaches is by APSAC, which now has a series of guidelines on psychosocial evaluation, the use of anatomical dolls, and photographic documentation, as well as more lengthy study guides.[7] These important resources contribute to increased validity of judgments as well as to continuity of interventions among professionals.

Overall, little work has yet been done to determine how characteristics of professionals affect their evaluations of sexual abuse. This is of concern because the literature on false disclosures suggests that clinicians' *a priori* beliefs can have an important influence on whether they are convinced by an abuse disclosure that abuse actually occurred. Because of the important role of the evaluator, studies that assess these factors are critical.

MEDICAL AND MENTAL HEALTH INTERVENTIONS

Medical Examination

The medical examination is important for at least four reasons: it reassures the victim and parents that the child is normal and healthy; it detects, treats, or prevents medical conditions as a result of the sexual contact; it provides evidence for the protection of the child; and it provides evidence to prosecute the offender (De Jong, 1998). Even though the medical examination is necessary in many (and some would argue all) cases of sexual abuse, "it is not unusual to hear physicians state that children are not

---

[7] See *http://www.apsac.org/public.html* for access to these guidelines.

upset by current sexual abuse evaluation procedures" (Berson, Herman-Giddens, & Frothingham, 1993, p. 42).

The few available studies instead indicate that the majority of children experience some distress. In a study of medically examined children, 57% described some pain associated with the exam and 50% described some fear (Lazebnik et al., 1994). A further 14% of children said that they experienced a lot of fear or pain, and 20% stated that they would be afraid to undergo a second exam. The intensity of fear of having to undergo a second (hypothetical) exam was related to a general fear of doctor visits, as well as fear and pain associated with the just completed examination. Waibel-Duncan and Sanger (1999) also found that 62% to 80% of children reported mild to moderate levels of examination distress, whereas 93% to 100% of guardians said that their children experienced it as distressing. Importantly, children receiving more information and more accurate information prior to the examination were scored by staff as less distressed during the examination. Finally, Berliner and Conte (1995) found that although children who had a medical examination had very positive views about the way they were treated by physicians, they were significantly more likely than those not undergoing an examination to report more symptoms an average of 3.5 years post-disclosure. It is likely, however, that this finding is because children undergoing medical examinations also suffered worse abuse.

These studies suggest that a significant minority of children experience this examination as extremely distressful and that half to three-fourths of children experience it as somewhat distressful. As such, researchers and clinicians must consider how to lower the levels of distress. Waibel-Duncan and Sanger (1999) found that one important method was by providing education to the children and their parents prior to the examination. Hogan (1996) also reports on the use of an oral dose of midazolam as a conscious sedative in children experiencing high levels of distress. These and other methods can be considered for lowering distress.

Mental Health Treatment

Another area of interest is the accessibility of treatment for sexually abused children and their families, as well as factors that predict entry into treatment. Only a few studies have examined either area. Kolko, Selelyo, and Brown (1999) investigated the treatment histories of 34 sexually abused children reported to a county children and youth services center. Approximately one-third of the children and parents received inpatient treatment, and another 21% of children received outpatient treatment. Just more than half of children's services were rated as helpful, whereas 60% of parents' services were rated as helpful. Sauzier (1989) also assessed a sample of 115 sexually abused children 18 months after the disclosure. A mental health treatment referral had been made for 78% of the families, and 35% had received psychiatric services. Of all agencies involved, parents reported that mental health treatment was the most helpful. Another study of 511 children evaluated by a multidisciplinary team found that 69% of children received therapy (Tingus, Heger, Foy, & Leskin, 1996).

A few factors are related to whether children receive treatment. One factor is the type of agency involved. Tingus et al. (1996) found that 96% of children involved with both child protective services and law enforcement entered therapy, as compared to 58% of children involved with only child protective services, and 13% of children involved with neither agency. Kolko et al. (1999) also found that greater service utilization at intake occurred when the child had less anxiety and when the parent had a history of childhood sexual abuse and heightened psychological distress. Sauzier (1989), however, found that referrals for psychiatric treatment were more likely to occur when the father was the offender and when the child had higher levels of psychopathology. Further, Caucasian children, children ages seven to 13, those suffering more severe abuse, and those placed outside the home were more likely to enter treatment (Kolko et al., 1999; Tingus et al., 1996).

Given that most children have some short-term effects of the abuse (Kendall-Tackett, Williams, & Finkelhor, 1993), mental health treatment might need to be made available to more children. Further, nonoffending guardians are often adversely affected by the abuse and might benefit from mental health treatment. Because few studies are available, however, more research is necessary to understand the availability of services to children and their families.

Legal Proceedings

Few sexually abused children appear in court as witnesses. For example, Martone, Jaudes, and Cavins (1996) found that only 7% of sexually abused children had to testify in court. Even though the number of children testifying in court is low, professionals have been concerned that the process of testifying and interfacing with the court is stressful. Indeed, this appears to be the case, as Saywitz (1989) found that approximately half of families reported that testifying at probable cause hearings and trials was too stressful. Runyan et al. (1988) also found that children involved in the criminal court process had greater distress, depression, and anxiety than those not involved in criminal court. Further, in a review of literature on the impact of court, Lipovsky (1994) concluded that many children found the court process distressing.

Some studies suggest that children involved in legal proceedings may remain symptomatic for long periods of time, although others disagree. In one study that compared sexually abused children who testified in criminal court to a matched control group of those who did not testify, children seven months after testifying had greater behavioral disturbances than nontestifiers (Goodman et al., 1992). Berliner and Conte (1995) also found that by both children's and parents' reports, having to go to court or having to talk with a prosecutor predicted more adverse outcome an average of 3.5 years after the abuse. Conversely, Lipovsky's (1994) review of the literature concluded that effects were not long-lasting and improved over time, although the pace at which the effects improved might be slower than for abused children who do not testify.

Several factors may be related to the distress children experience. King et al. (1988) found that children were subjected to processes traditionally viewed as stressful to victims, such as confrontation with the perpetrator, aggressive cross-examination, and failure to provide a supportive atmosphere. Conversely, Runyan et al. (1988) found that juvenile court settings were less difficult for children and the experience was even positive in some cases. Other factors are related to a decrease in stress over time, including greater maternal support, testifying fewer times, having a parent or loved one in the courtroom, and closing the courtroom to spectators (Goodman et al., 1992; Lipovsky, 1994).

Tentative conclusions can be drawn from these studies. Probably the conclusion of most importance is that criminal court involvement is stressful for at least a subgroup of victims. As Schwartz-Kenney et al. (1990) conclude, "The majority of literature supports the theory that the legal system as it currently exists is more likely, on average, to further exacerbate children's overall distress" (p. 307). On the other hand, some children may benefit from the legal proceedings, especially if they are conducted in juvenile court, perhaps because they have an opportunity to assert themselves and to feel a sense of self-efficacy and empowerment.

Many recommendations for how to reduce the stress experienced by children have been made, including reducing the number of interviewers and the children's courtroom exposure, possibly by videotaping (Schwartz-Kenney et al., 1990; Tedesco & Schnell, 1987). Indeed, Henry (1999) found that children whose interviews were taped experienced fewer interviews and testified less frequently than children whose interviews were not taped. Other suggestions for reducing stress are to educate attorneys and judges, prepare and support child victims and families, expedite cases, and to use courtroom orientations and victim advocates (King et al., 1988; Lipovsky & Stern, 1997; Schwartz-Kenney et al., 1990).

At least one study has now assessed the frequency with which special techniques are introduced in court to minimize stress on children. This survey of 227 state trial court judges found that, of 22 approaches listed, seven were used by half of the judges and 12 were used by at least a third of the judges (Hafemeister, 1996). Further, all were rated by at least half of the judges to be effective. No more than 40% of judges considered any technique unfair, though most items were scored by less than 20% of judges as being unfair. The simpler techniques, which could be instituted easily with available resources, tended to be used more widely and to be considered more effective and fairer. These techniques included: posing questions at the child's comprehension level, excluding the public during testimony, allowing an expert consultant, modifying the court schedule to meet the child's needs, and allowing the child to testify via a dialogue or monologue. Finally, judges who had attended educational programs (and most had) were most likely to institute these techniques. These findings suggest that most judges are aware of special issues associated with child witnesses, have attended specialized trainings, and are implementing stress-reduction techniques that are both fair and effective.

Prosecution

In Chapter 9, "Offenders," it was shown that across studies only 17% to 39% of substantiated cases of sexual abuse are submitted for prosecution and that only about 60% of cases submitted are actually prosecuted.[8] Because courts require more stringent levels of proof for prosecution than child protective services needs for substantiating abuse (Martone et al., 1996), it is not surprising that fewer cases are prosecuted than

---

[8]   See the section, "How Many Offenders are Identified?" in Chapter 9, "Offenders."

are substantiated. Because so few cases are prosecuted, however, it is important to understand those factors that predict a greater likelihood of prosecution.

While factors concerning the believability of the case are logical predictors of the decision to prosecute, the findings are not as clear. Both Bradshaw and Marks (1990) and Cross et al. (1994) found that a statement by the offender and the presence of medical evidence predicted whether a case was accepted for prosecution. Brewer et al. (1997), however, found that the relationship between medical evaluation and prosecution was more complex. Cases with medical evidence were more likely to be accepted for prosecution, but only in those cases in which the abuse was more severe. For cases involving less serious abuse, cases with medical evidence were less likely to be prosecuted. It is of note in this study that cases of sodomy and digital penetration were for some reason considered less serious abuse, along with indecent exposure and fondling. Finally, after reviewing the relationship between a medical evaluation and conviction, De Jong (1998) concluded that specific physical findings occur with a similar frequency in cases with and without confessions, as well as in cases with convictions and those with acquittals. These findings remain somewhat confusing, suggesting the need for further research.

Certain characteristics of the abuse may also predict the decision to prosecute. A few studies have found that cases of sexual abuse committed by biological parents or family members are less likely to be prosecuted (Brewer et al., 1997; Cross et al., 1994), although MacMurray (1989) found that stepfathers and uncles were most likely to be prosecuted, whereas brothers and day care workers were least likely to be prosecuted. Cases in which mothers are divorced, separated, or single are also less likely to be prosecuted (Brewer et al., 1997), possibly because of the general (although empirically unreasonable) fear that larger numbers of children in custody disputes are falsely led to disclose abuse. Another related finding is that cases are more likely to be prosecuted when mothers are considered more supportive of their child (Cross et al., 1994). Other factors related to an increased likelihood of prosecution are multiple victims (Brewer et al., 1997), lower levels of psychopathology in the child (Cross et al., 1994), abuse lasting from six months to two years, a male victim or male perpetrator, an older perpetrator (MacMurray, 1989), and older age of the child (Brewer et al., 1997; Cross et al., 1994), although another study did not find the latter relationship to be significant (Martone et al., 1996).

Regretfully, the stringency with which cases are chosen for prosecution means that many children remain at risk for removal long after disclosure. A study by Cross et al. (1999) highlights this problem. In this study, children were at almost three times greater risk to be removed when their cases were declined for prosecution, as compared to when their cases were accepted for prosecution, nor could these differences be explained by differences in maternal support. Indeed, rejecting the case for prosecution was the single strongest predictor of removal. While the reasons for this relationship cannot be clarified within the research design, the researchers "think it is likely that prosecution decisions influence child placement decisions" (p. 41) because the alleged perpetrator can no longer be prevented (through incarceration or other means) from approaching the child. To protect the child, they suggest, the child is removed. They conclude,

> *A reasonable inference is that the institutional response to child sexual abuse is not working well for most of these families, and child placement is the lesser of the two evils....When the two primary institutions designed to respond to child abuse reports both find it difficult to carry out their missions for a specific group of children, the tragedy of child abuse is compounded. (p. 42)*

When the legal system fails in its duty to protect the victim, it is insufficient to place that burden on the mother. The regrettable legacy of this practice is that many children are removed from their families. Professionals must develop other strategies for allowing children to remain in their homes so that they are not further traumatized by the system mandated to protect them.

SEXUAL ABUSE BY PROFESSIONALS

> *Who will protect us from those who would help us? (DeYoung, 1981, p. 92)*

This statement was made by one of three members in a 10-member adult incest support group who had been sexually abused by their therapists. This section addresses the frequency with which mental health professionals abuse their clients, especially when the victim has a previous history of childhood sexual abuse. First to be reviewed are studies that evaluate the prevalence of sexual abuse by clinicians, followed by the few studies discussing the sexual abuse of clients previously sexually abused.

Several studies now indicate that a significant minority of professionals have sex with a client. In a review of six studies using national samples of psychologists, Pope (1993) found that 1% to 12.1% (an average of 7%) of male and 0.4% to 3% (an average of 2%) of female psychologists and psychiatrists admitted to having had sex on at least one occasion with a client; 87% to 94% of the victims were female. Further, 44% to 65% of professionals across studies had worked with a client who was previously involved with a therapist. In the study with the largest percentage (65%) (Gartrell, Herman, Olarte, Feldstein, & Localio, 1987), only 8% of the psychiatrists had filed a report against the offending professional. Of the female offenders, none had sexual contact with more than one client, whereas 38% of the male offenders had done so. Interestingly, repeat offenders (psychiatrists having sex with more than one client) were most likely to have treated victims of previous abuse by a professional, and nonoffenders were least likely to have treated a previous victim. Repeat offenders were also significantly more likely to know colleagues who were sexually involved with their clients. The authors suggest that offending therapists might refer their abused patients only to colleagues known to be sympathetic. In another survey of 110 hospitals with inpatient psychiatric units, 36% of the units reported that a staff member had been accused of sexually abusing a patient between 1985 and 1990 (Berland & Guskin, 1994). More than 90% of the allegations accused a male staff member of being the offender, and 71% of the victims were female. Thirteen percent of all allegations occurred on an adolescent unit, and 25% of all victims were under the age of 20.

Other studies consider the issue of revictimization by therapists of sexual abuse survivors. Kluft (1990), who is known for his work with survivors of childhood abuse with dissociative identity disorder, published a study of all of his clients who were incest victims and who had been sexually exploited by their therapists. Of the 83 therapists these 12 patients had seen, 23 (28%) had initiated sexual contact with their patients, most of which culminated in intercourse. Of the 23 offenders, 22 (95%) were male. Although Kluft (1990) does not specify the ages of the clients, at least one was an adolescent when the revictimization occurred. Another study of female inpatients on a psychosomatic psychiatric inpatient unit in Austria found that four of nine patients who had previously undergone psychotherapy were sexually abused by their therapists (Kinzl & Biebl, 1992). In another study, three of 10 incest survivors currently in group therapy had been sexually involved or pressured to become involved with a professional (deYoung, 1981). This rate is similar to that of Armsworth (1989), who found that 23% of members in a support group for incest survivors had been sexually involved with their therapists. Seven percent of all helping professionals (i.e., counselors, ministers and support group leaders, and traditional clinicians) the clients had encountered initiated sexual contact, 77% of whom were spiritual or religious counselors. In Kluft's (1990) study, however, only 4% of offenders were pastoral counselors but 48% were psychiatrists.

Armsworth (1990) content analyzed interviews of six adult incest survivors who had been sexually abused by their therapists. The results portray the severity of these experiences. Only one of the six victims was able to terminate with the therapist after the first approach. The other five clients employed self-talk to cope with the trauma and to rationalize returning to therapy each week. Self-talk employed during the sexual interaction was in one of three categories: transference statements (e.g., "Did I make you happy, daddy?"; "Will you let me stay with you now?"); statements reflecting being trapped or helpless (e.g., "Just do it then you'll be free."; "I cannot escape—I have to stay."); or dissociative statements (e.g., "Look at the light—see only the light."; "Make your mind blank—hide until it's over.") (p. 547). To rationalize their weekly return, three types of self-talk were used that: reflected the trust or worthiness of the therapist (e.g., "Everyone I ask says he's the best."); their desperate need for help (e.g., "Unless I do what he wants, I'll never get any help."); or their feelings of being a nonperson (e.g., "This is your fate forever—so get used to it.") (p. 547). Therapist rationalizations for the abuse encompassed misrepresentations of moral or ethical standards. For example, one therapist told the client, "In therapy sexual intercourse is acceptable; outside of therapy this would be adultery" (p. 550).

How damaging is abuse by a therapist? All studies agree that this type of abuse is extremely harmful (Armsworth, 1990; DeYoung, 1981; Kluft, 1990). Indeed, one study of therapists working with clients sexually abused by another therapist found that the strongest predictor of impact on the client was a history of prior sexual victimization of the victim (adult or childhood) (Feldman-Summers & Jones, 1984). Victims in Armsworth's study also reported symptoms of posttraumatic stress disorder, deterioration in their lives, difficulty in interpersonal relationships, and problems in parenting. Of the four survivors seeking help for marriage-related problems, all marriages ended within the year. One survivor attempted suicide, and three others considered it.

In summary, studies suggest that sexual abuse by clinicians working with survivors of childhood sexual abuse is a real threat. In these studies, 23% to 44% of survivors of childhood sexual abuse were also sexually abused by clinicians from whom they sought treatment. Sample sizes were small in these studies (ranging in size from nine to 30), however, suggesting caution in interpreting these percentages. As with all sexual abuse, victimization of a client by a professional is damaging to clients, "especially if the client already has significant psychological problems" (Feldman-Summers & Jones, 1984, p. 1061).

It is a tragic consequence of our society that those who are supposed to help on occasion abuse instead. As Kluft (1990) says, "No matter how flagrant the temptation, it is the therapist's task to maintain a therapeutic atmosphere rather than to enter into a gross breach of ethics, however well rationalized" (p. 276). It is of great concern that so many clinicians abuse. It is of greater concern that they revictimize some of the more wounded members of society.

SUMMARY AND CONCLUSIONS

Professionals are doing many things very well, but there are some areas that can be improved. And, yes, there is some ugliness as well. Each of these categories is discussed next.

What professionals do well: The good news is that many committed professionals are working in this difficult field and doing an excellent job. The available research now appears to be widely read, and professionals are becoming more aware that practicing accountably means staying abreast of the latest research. Further, many evaluations of interventions are now being published. Organizations such as APSAC are also publishing guidelines for evaluations, and NICHD now has a protocol for interviewing. These guidelines and research are now substantive enough that clinicians can make sound decisions using the recommendations of experts. As such, interventions continue to improve and clinicians are increasingly capable of maintaining an empirically based practice.

What professionals can improve upon: The increased research on interventions has also suggested areas in which professionals could improve. First is a need for continued basic education. The historical and primarily clinical literature base in child sexual abuse has many myths, many of which continue to be expressed in policies and by a minority of professionals. Especially damaging myths that continue to be felt are the myth of the collusive mother, as well as the myth that intrafamilial abuse is more prevalent than extrafamilial abuse. These myths cause damage by restricting access to resources and sometimes even identification of the abuse, or alternately by removing children needlessly from their homes. The continued endorsement of myths indicates an ongoing need for basic education of professionals. While it is hoped that few professionals who frequently interact with child sexual abuse victims and their families maintain these myths, those who do so can cause real and significant damage. Because of the frequency with which they interface with victims and families, that damage becomes multiplied. Thus, basic education is still a necessity for child sexual abuse professionals as well as for those who interact with child sexual abuse cases less frequently.

Another area that applies to all professionals is self-examination. One of the disquieting findings throughout this chapter was that characteristics of professionals were related to the decisions they made. Further, characteristics of the child, family, and offender were related to decisions even when they should not have been.

Characteristics having an effect on intervention decisions and attributions of responsibility were the gender, race, socioeconomic status, and age of the victim and perpetrator, as well as beliefs that professionals held about adolescent victims and especially nonoffending guardians. When demographic characteristics are related to decisions, these usually reflect biases held by professionals or systemic biases. As clinicians know only too well, self-awareness is a critical feature for maintaining therapeutic integrity. To assist in this process, more rigorous research is needed. Further, trainings that assist professionals in examining biases they might hold can be utilized.

The final area that needs to be improved is the structure of child protective services. First, much more research is critical. The decisions and interventions of child protective services have rarely been investigated, whereas the techniques and interventions of other professionals have been more closely scrutinized. Thus, child protective services represents a black box in which information goes in but little comes out. Given the centrality of child protective services to child sexual abuse, this is a critical oversight in the literature. Much more research needs to be done on all phases of their interface, including factors that predict decisions to screen in and out, investigate abuse, substantiate abuse, and to remove the child. We know far too little about these interventions, but what little we know about them suggests that they are dramatically affected by funding limitations. Inconsistencies in these interventions are also probably a result of high turnover rates of child protective services workers, time pressures within which they must work, systemic biases, and the sometimes more limited education and training of workers. It is critical that these problems be brought to light and documented.

This chapter makes clear that the evaluation of a child and a decision of whether abuse has occurred is not only one of the most difficult decisions facing professionals, but is one that requires some of the most intensive training. Does the lack of a graduate degree or mental health education relate to decisions child protective services workers make? Why do some workers contend that large numbers of children make false allegations or that most nonoffending guardians know about the ongoing abuse? These are biases that those working closely with child sexual abuse should not maintain, as these biases have been unsupported in the literature for at least 10 years. How is it that some child protective services workers do not know these basic facts? These are grave concerns that require immediate and aggressive interventions.

And the ugly: There are three areas in the professional response that are ugly, only two of which were discussed earlier in this chapter. The one that was not discussed in this chapter was the backlash. This backlash is ugly to its core and has done an incredible disservice to many victims and their families, even as it has paradoxically led to an improved knowledge base.

Some of the issues that have been brought up during this 15-year backlash have been extremely important and have compelled professionals to find answers. Interviewing techniques today are far better because of the debate over suggestive techniques. Concerns about memory and recall have fostered a number of studies. While the debates contribute to the developing knowledge base, however, outlandish claims such as those by Gardner (cited in this chapter) and vituperative and vicious comments simply inflame. There is no place for these in the professional lexicon, nor even in the media. The issue of child sexual abuse is so serious and of such great consequence that while debates are essential for the development of the knowledge base, the contrived hysteria of the backlash simply slows the progress of the field and moves the focus to addressing the hysteria rather than working to relieve the suffering of the victims and their families.

The second ugly issue is the current system that responds to child sexual abuse. From the perspective of victims, the response must seem at times almost ludicrous, being brought into a system where they are sometimes not believed and where they must tell their story to various strange adults. If their stories are believed, they then face likely removal from their homes to live with strangers while the offender remains free. For many, their genitals are examined, photographed, and the pictures examined in detail, sometimes even being shown in court. If the offender is prosecuted, they may have to testify in court while often facing hostile cross-examination. This is if their abuse is identified and then substantiated. Otherwise, they often have to return to live with the offender or, in divorce cases, may even be given into the offender's custody. Needless to say, this is not a child-sensitive scenario, even though many professionals work to soften the effects of the interventions and even though most of the interventions are for the welfare of the child.

The final ugliness—perhaps the most ugly of all—is those professionals who sexually abuse their clients. While the numbers are few, those who do so should be sanctioned to the limits of the law. For those who sexually abuse underage clients, these professionals should be treated as the sexual offenders they are. There is no place in a helping profession for offenders, and they should be held fully accountable for their actions.

CHAPTER 12
CONCLUSIONS

INTRODUCTION

The premise of this book is that policies and programs depicting society's response to child sexual abuse are failing and that this failure is because their assumptions have far more to do with the historical conceptualization of child sexual abuse than with the empirical knowledge base. The purpose of this last chapter is to analyze whether this is the case by bringing together information developed in previous chapters. Having done so, recommendations are then made for moving forward.

To consider the premise of this book, the first section sets the stage by recapping how child sexual abuse eventually came to be recognized. This section briefly discusses Freud's influence on the developing knowledge base, how family systems theory reframed the psychoanalytic interpretation of child sexual abuse, followed later by the feminists' recognition that sociocultural factors are primary contributors to child sexual abuse. Concluding this section is a list of assumptions framing this historical understanding of child sexual abuse. The next section then considers a conceptualization of child sexual abuse based upon the available empirical knowledge base, also concluding with a list of its assumptions.

After these two views are presented, three areas of the systemic response to child sexual abuse—identification of victims, the professional response once the child is identified, and prevention—are considered. It is shown in this section that the systemic response to child sexual abuse is grossly biased. By reviewing the implicit assumptions underlying this systemic response, it is shown that the bias in the systemic response is because it is based upon the historical and often myth-bound conceptualization of child sexual abuse as opposed to the empirical knowledge base.

Having presented these arguments, the next section considers whether biases in the systemic response are a result of the statutes regarding child sexual abuse or the manner in which these statutes were implemented. It is argued that while both federal and state statutes are comprehensive, their implementation has been more targeted, thus limiting entry into the system for many victims. It is further argued that the implementation of these statutes was affected by the historical conceptualization of child sexual abuse.

The final section forwards recommendations for moving from this historically bound and limited systemic response to one that is commensurate with the empirical knowledge base. Recommendations are made for changes within the systemic response that improve the identification and assessment of abuse, as well as the prevention of further abuse. Recognizing the limitations of the current system, however, the final section joins with other professionals in calling for a complete overhaul of the system.

SUMMARY

Setting the Stage

A central premise of this book is that many policies and programs designed to protect, identify, and treat victims of child sexual abuse are failing because they are grounded in historical theories of child sexual abuse instead of the empirical knowledge base. As such, these policies and programs are invested with the values and beliefs brought forth from these earlier periods. Thus, to truly understand current policies and programs, we must first understand the historical formulation of the knowledge base.

As discussed in Chapter 2, Freud introduced the first theory of child sexual abuse in 1896, suggesting that hysterical symptoms in adult females were a result of childhood sexual abuse (Masson, 1984). Only a short time later and under immense professional pressure, he repudiated this seduction theory. In its place he forwarded the Oedipus complex, which posited that young female children, recognizing the inherent superiority of the male penis, fall victim to penis envy and choose their fathers as their preferred love objects.

Freud's repudiation of the seduction theory profoundly impacted the professional response to child sexual abuse. The first effect that reverberated for many years was that childhood sexual abuse was considered a nonevent. It simply did not exist. Those who reported histories of child sexual abuse were assumed to be hysterical females remembering their fantasized desire for the coveted sexual relationship with their father. Years later, when it became obvious that some child sexual abuse did occur, blame continued to be placed on the female victim. Now the victim was said to have seduced the offender, who fell within the victim's spell. This psychoanalytic interpretation was the prominent conceptualization of child sexual abuse well into the second half of the 20th Century.

The next major theory, introduced in the 1970s and 1980s, was family systems theory (Carper, 1979; Cohen, 1983). This theory evolved from general systems theory, which recognized the important interactions among parts of a system (Bronfenbrenner, 1977). Conceptualizing the family as a system allowed the theory to be adapted for use in understanding family dynamics, including dynamics of intrafamilial abuse.

One of the important premises of general systems theory is circular causation, which recognizes that all members or parts of a system contribute to its maintenance and evolution (Cohen, 1983). Applied to child sexual abuse, early theories thus considered that all members of the family, including victims and nonoffending mothers, contributed to the abuse. Victims were said to allow the abuse because of the secondary gratification they received, whereas mothers were conceptualized as central to the causal dynamics of these families. By withdrawing from their roles as mother and wife, they were said to force their daughter into these roles. Fathers were then said to turn without recourse to their daughters for sexual fulfillment, whereas the daughters were assumed to receive some secondary gratification from the abuse because of the power they gained (Cohen, 1983; Kadushin & Martin, 1988). Thus, like psychoanalytic theory, this early conceptualization of family systems theory retained a victim-blaming stance while also introducing a mother-blaming stance to a receptive audience.

The final important theory introduced prior to the 1980s was feminist theory, a new and important way of thinking about child sexual abuse (Brownmiller, 1975;

Rush, 1980). By recognizing that child sexual abuse was also a societal problem, this theory for the first time introduced a unit of analysis at the level of society. Feminist theory also suggested that sexual abuse was a natural derivative of a patriarchal society, thus legitimizing types of child sexual abuse other than those occurring just within the family. It also recognized that child sexual abuse might be endemic to a patriarchal society in which males were socialized to feel entitled to sexual access of females. Finally, it vociferously rejected the notion that the child and nonoffending mother contributed to the abuse, recognizing instead that responsibility for the abuse had to remain with only the offender.

Because feminist theory's focus was on society, as compared to the individual for psychoanalytic theory and the family for family systems theory, feminist theory has much to offer our understanding of child sexual abuse. Indeed, as is shown in the next section, many of its hypotheses have received support in the empirical literature. Even with this support, however, it had only a minor impact on the conceptualization of child sexual abuse by the early 1980s. While there are various reasons for why feminist theory was so slow to receive legitimacy (Armstrong, 1996), one important reason was that it implicated as causal to abuse dynamics the very structure of society—patriarchy.

Thus, the prevailing conceptualization of child sexual abuse in the early 1980s, deriving primarily from family systems theory and less so from psychoanalytic theory, had the following important assumptions.

- Intrafamilial abuse is far more prevalent than extrafamilial abuse, and father-daughter incest is far more prevalent than other types of intrafamilial abuse.
- Mothers actively contribute to the abuse, colluding to continue the abuse and failing in their duty to protect the child.
- Child sexual abuse is primarily a family problem.
- Many important dynamics contribute to the offender's propensity to abuse, including a previous history of victimization, sexual problems within the marital relationship, and dysfunctional dynamics within the current family. Thus, offenders have deficits at the level of the individual or family that explain their behavior.
- Victims receive some secondary gain from the abuse.

Current Conceptualization of Child Sexual Abuse

Moving forward to the current period, the empirical knowledge base presented in this book provides a very different perspective of child sexual abuse. Child sexual abuse is a sociological problem of immense proportions. Approximately one-third of girls are sexually abused before their 18th birthdays, as are approximately one-seventh of boys (Bolen & Scannapieco, 1999). While 95% of offenders are male, 70% of victims are female (Finkelhor, Hotaling, Lewis, & Smith, 1990; Russell, 1983; Wyatt, 1985), suggesting that child sexual abuse is primarily a gendered problem. Studies suggest that factors placing males at risk to abuse males are different than factors placing males at risk to abuse females. Males who abuse other males may do so at least in part because of their own childhood histories of sexual abuse, especially if they experienced multiple childhood victimizations. These findings are supported in retrospective studies of identified offenders (Hanson & Slater, 1988) as well as in populations of "normal" college students (Bagley, Wood, & Young, 1994).

Because seven girls are abused for every three boys, however, another explanation is required for why primarily male offenders, most of whom are not sexually abused in childhood (Bagley et al., 1994; Hanson & Slater, 1988), abuse primarily female victims. It was suggested in Chapter 8 that one of the primary reasons males sexually abuse children is because they are socialized within a patriarchal society to a sense of entitlement to the world around them, including entitlement to sex. Conversely, females develop a sense of their subordination to the more powerful male members of society. The primary mechanism for these worldviews is through socialization processes that occur within schools, homes, and communities. Once these worldviews become inculcated into the individual, however, they become largely unavailable to conscious thought. Instead, they are a part of what the individual considers normal, just as cultural values become inculcated into one's belief system. If the socialization of male entitlement is implicated in the abuse of females by males, then it would stand to reason that males are the primary offenders and females are the primary victims. It would also stand to reason that child sexual abuse is endemic to a patriarchal society. Thus, not only would a large number of girls be sexually abused, but a large number of males would also sexually abuse.

While hypotheses deriving from this conceptualization have not been evaluated directly, compelling support in the empirical knowledge base exists for them. As noted earlier, girls are indeed victimized more frequently, whereas males account for the vast majority of all offenders. Further, 6% to 21% of adult males self-report that they have either sexually abused a child or are sexually attracted to children (Bagley et al., 1994; Briere & Runtz, 1989; Finkelhor & Lewis, 1988). Thus, a significant minority of males self-identify as having risk factors that place them at risk to offend. Another group of males, however, may not necessarily self-identify as having a sexual attraction to younger children but might also be at increased risk to sexually offend, although for other reasons (Bolen, 2000a). These mostly adolescent and young adult males appear to be acting out sexual scripts of male dominance as they abuse their victims simply for sport, as conquests, or because of an enduring sense of entitlement to sexual access. This group may constitute as much as 25% of all extrafamilial abuse. Thus, not only is the risk of being sexually abused endemic within society, but the risk of abusing may be endemic for males.

Because child sexual abuse is endemic within society, it is far more than just a family problem. Indeed, approximately 70% of all abuse is extrafamilial (Table 6-1). These offenders approach their victims in numerous locations, most of which are considered safe (i.e., within the child's home or neighborhood) (Bolen, 2000a; Wyatt, 1985). Risk of abuse also varies by age of the child. Younger children are at greatest risk of abuse in their homes or neighborhoods, and are at greatest risk by strangers, neighbors, and friends of the family (Bolen, 2000a). Older children are at greatest risk of abuse by acquaintances, friends, or family friends, and are at greatest risk at the perpetrator's home or while walking. Adolescents are at greatest risk of abuse outside the neighborhood or in a car, and are at greatest risk of abuse by friends, family friends, or dates. Approaches of these offenders are also multifaceted, defying attempts at categorization. Thus, extrafamilial sexual abuse remains a generalized risk for all children in all locations by mostly male perpetrators using numerous methods of approach.

The remaining 30% of sexual abuse is intrafamilial (Table 7-1), and again more than 95% of this abuse is committed by males (Finkelhor et al., 1990; Russell, 1983; Wyatt, 1985). Of relatives who abuse, uncles abuse most frequently, although father figures and cousins abuse at close to the same levels (Tables 7-1 and 7-2). Intrafamilial abuse is similar to other types of abuse, with older males typically abusing younger females. Dynamics within these families also appear to express implicit societal values of power and control over women and children, including all types of gendered violence (Herman, 1981; Laviola, 1992; Wiehe, 1990).

One of the less frequent types of abuse is father-daughter incest, accounting for only 7% to 8% of all sexual abuse (Russell, 1984; Wyatt, 1985). While family dynamics are somewhat dysfunctional in families in which father-daughter incest or other types of intrafamilial abuse occur, these dynamics are not unique to families in which incest occurs and are found to a lesser extent in families with victims of extrafamilial abuse (Alexander & Lupfer, 1987; Ray, Jackson, & Townsley, 1991). Thus, family dynamics cannot be considered causal to this type of abuse. Instead, fathers may abuse the power they wield in these families by not only sexually abusing the child, but often victimizing the mother (Sirles & Franke, 1989; Finkelhor & Williams, 1990), other siblings (Phelan, 1986; Sirles, Smith, & Kusama, 1989), and even unrelated children (Ballard et al., 1990). Mothers in these families, while having higher rates of childhood sexual abuse, do not stand out on other psychological characteristics from mothers in normal populations (Nakhle Tamraz, 1996; Smith & Saunders, 1995). Further, 75% to 95% of mothers are unaware of the ongoing abuse by the father (Faller, 1990; Myer, 1985). When they find out about the abuse, 65% to 85% believe that the abuse is occurring, and 81% offer some or full support to their child (Bolen, 2000b).

The primary points of this empirically supported conceptualization of child sexual abuse are as follows.

- Child sexual abuse is endemic within society and may be a result of the unequal power of males over females. In support,
  - Females are at much greater risk of abuse than males.
  - Males are at much greater risk to offend than females.
  - Children are at high risk of abuse by filial and nonfilial males.
  - Child sexual abuse is primarily heterosexual, almost all of which is perpetrated by males against females.
- Extrafamilial abuse is more prevalent than intrafamilial abuse.
- Fathers abuse at approximately the same frequency as other intrafamilial abuse offenders, but less frequently than most extrafamilial abuse offenders.
- Neither intrafamilial abuse nor father-daughter incest is unique but instead shares many dynamics with extrafamilial abuse.
- Child sexual abuse is difficult to prevent because of the multiple types of offenders and their varied approaches in multiple locations.
- Most mothers react appropriately to the abuse of their child.

This conceptualization of child sexual abuse is very different than the one presented in the previous section. Differences between conceptualizations occur in the prevalence of father-daughter incest and its notions of causality, as well as in the focus on intrafamilial abuse instead of extrafamilial abuse. The most important difference between these two conceptualizations, however, is that the empirically supported conceptualization suggests that child sexual abuse is a sociocultural problem of immense proportions, whereas the historical and theoretical conceptualization suggests that sexual abuse is a problem unique to dysfunctional families. Thus, the primary unit of analysis supported in the empirical literature is at the level of society, whereas the primary unit of analysis supported in the historical conceptualization is at the level of the family and individual.

Finally, it is important to note that many of the tenets of the psychoanalytic interpretation of child sexual abuse and the early conceptualization of family systems theory are not supported in the empirical literature. Thus, these early theories presented a myth-based conceptualization of child sexual abuse.

SOCIETY'S RESPONSE TO CHILD SEXUAL ABUSE

This section now considers the basic premise of this book—that society's response to child sexual abuse has far more to do with the historical conceptualization of child sexual abuse than with the empirically supported conceptualization. Society's response to sexual abuse is analyzed along three domains—identification of abuse, professional response to abuse, and prevention.

Identification of Abuse

The first area considered is society's ability to identify child sexual abuse. Table 12-1 presents data on sexual abuse that occurs within the general population and compares the data to that reflecting society's ability to identify abuse. In other words, this table reflects society's ability to adequately identify and respond to the problem of child sexual abuse. To present this comparison, two data columns are provided. The first, entitled "Identified Abuse," presents data from national incidence studies. Because these studies capture all abuse coming to the attention of authorities, they represent the best information available concerning society's response to sexual abuse. The next data column, "Committed Abuse," reflects the best available estimates—deriving from random community, state, or national prevalence studies—of committed abuse known to occur in the general population. Data in this column were presented previously in Tables 5-1, 6-1, 6-2, 7-1, and 7-2.

Similarities in percentages between columns would suggest that society's ability to identify victims of child sexual abuse is commensurate with that abuse estimated to occur within the general population (or that abuse estimated to occur as reflected by the empirical knowledge base). As such, similarities between columns would also suggest that society's response to abuse is based upon assumptions brought forward from the empirical knowledge base. Conversely, discrepancies between columns would suggest that society's ability to identify child sexual abuse: (a) is not commensurate with that abuse estimated to occur in the general population; and (b) is not based upon the empirical knowledge base.

Table 12-1 provides convincing evidence that the identification of child sexual abuse is extraordinarily biased. Four compelling biases stand out in this table. First,

TABLE 12-1. Comparison of Identified Samples to Samples from Retrospective Studies

Perpetrator	Identified Abuse[1]	Committed Abuse[2]
Incidence of abuse yearly (females)[3]	6.8/1,000[4]	25/1,000 – 40/1,000[5]
Extrafamilial	21%[1] / 46%[4]	70%
Both parents	12%	0%
Father figure only	22%	7% – 8%[6]
Father figure and other	2%	0%
Mother only	4%	0.05%[7]
Mother and other	11%	0%
Father figure – total	36%	5%
Mother figure – total	27%	0.05%[7]
Parental abuse – total	51%	7% – 8%[6]
Other male relative – total	17%	16% – 21%[6]
Other female relative – total	1%	0% – 1%[6]
Female offender – total	44%[8]	5%
Male offender – total	81%[8]	95%

[1] Data were taken from the 1998 NCANDS incidence report (U.S. Department of Health and Human Services, 2000c). [2] Most figures in this column were compiled from Tables 6-1, 6-2, 7-1, and 7-2, which summarized data from random retrospective prevalence studies. [3] Regretfully, the incidence of abuse of male children cannot be estimated from retrospective studies so is not included. [4] This figure was taken from the NIS-3 (Sedlak & Broadhurst, 1996). [5] See Table 5-1 for how this incidence rate was estimated. [6] These percentages were computed from Wyatt's (1985) and Russell's (1984) studies because these two random prevalence surveys are the only ones providing information on all incidents of abuse. [7] This estimate combined information from all studies in Table 7-1 that specifically broke out maternal from paternal incest. See p. 194 for more information. [8] For 13% of all identified abuse, gender was not specified.

whereas 6.8/1,000 female children are identified yearly as having been sexually abused, it was estimated in Chapter 5 that between 25/1,000 and 40/1,000 female children are sexually abused yearly. Thus, only approximately 5% to 27% of all committed abuse is officially identified.[1]

Second, whereas 70% of all committed abuse is extrafamilial, only 21% of abuse identified by child protective services is extrafamilial. Further, the NIS-3 found that 46% of abuse was committed by offenders other than parents or parent substitutes (Sedlak & Broadhurst, 1996). Thus, the true percentage of identified extrafamilial abuse is at least 21% but less than 46%.

The third compelling bias in society's response to child sexual abuse is that 51% of all identified abuse is by a parental figure (Table 12-1), as compared to only 7% to 8% of committed abuse that is by a parental figure (Russell, 1984; Wyatt, 1985). Further, although abuse by an uncle is the most prevalent type of intrafamilial abuse committed (Table 7-2), the latest NCANDS incidence report does not even have a category for this type of perpetrator, suggesting that this type of intrafamilial abuse is infrequently identified (U.S. Department of Health and Human Services, 2000c). On the other hand, the only area in which the system's ability to identify abuse matches that of committed abuse is that by relatives (both male and female) other than parents.

---

[1] See Tables 5-1 and 5-2 for how these estimates were calculated.

The final and most incredible disparity between identified abuse and committed abuse is the number of mothers identified as offenders. First, females are listed as offenders in 44% of all cases of identified abuse, although only 5% of offenders in committed abuse are female. Second, whereas mothers account for 0.05% of all abuse committed, 27% of all identified abuse is by mothers (Table 12-1). Further, mothers are listed as primary offenders or co-offenders in *more than half* of all identified parental abuse (U.S. Department of Health and Human Services, 2000c), as compared to 0.6% of committed parental abuse in retrospective populations.[2] In other words, *mothers are being identified at 540 times their rate of committed abuse.*[3]

Professional Response

This section now considers professional responses to victims and nonoffending mothers once sexual abuse is identified. Again, these sections compare the profession's response in child sexual abuse to that information available in the empirical knowledge base. Studies presented in this section are more varied than in the previous section but typically reflect samples of professionals who are queried about their views concerning child sexual abuse and decisions they make regarding how to intervene. Studies presented in this section were reviewed in the previous chapter.

Views and practices concerning the child: Experts in the area of child sexual abuse concur that sexually abused children are victims and must be held blameless. Concomitantly, studies of apportioned blame in hypothetical abuse vignettes find that only a small proportion of that blame is allocated to victims. Of more concern, however, is the percentage of professionals who apportion any blame to the victim. In studies published in the 1990s, 12% to 45% of professionals continue to attribute some, even if minimal, blame to the victim (Kalichman, Craig, & Follingstad, 1990; Kelley, 1990; Reidy & Hochstadt, 1993). Further, older victims and those described as more encouraging are apportioned more responsibility for the abuse (Johnson, Owens, Dewey, & Eisenberg, 1990; Wagner, Aucoin, & Johnson, 1993). Some writers also continue to endorse outdated and fictitious views of preschool girls as sexually provocative (for example, see Gardner, as cited in Faller, 1996).

Another concern is that some professionals continue to believe that false allegations of abuse by children are a significant problem. For example, some child protective services workers consider that at least half of all disclosures by adolescents are false (Everson & Boat, 1989). Further, most professionals continue to believe that allegations made within a custody or divorce dispute are more likely to be false (Marshall & Locke, 1997). Indeed, child protective services routinely screens out reports of abuse made within these disputes, considering most of them to be maliciously filed (Downing, Wells, & Fluke, 1990; Giovannoni, 1991). When these cases are screened in and then investigated, only about 15% are substantiated (Haskett, Wayland, Hutcheson, & Tavona, 1995). These views by some professionals stand in stark contrast to the empirical knowledge base in which less than 1% of all abuse reports are intentionally false (U.S. Department of Health & Human Services,

---

[2]   Refer to page 194 for how the percentange of committed abuse was computed.

[3]   This figure was computed as follows: 27 / .05 = 540.

2000c), and in which 5% or less of all sexual abuse reports made within a custody or divorce dispute are intentionally false (Faller, 1991a; Faller & DeVoe, 1995).

Views and practices concerning the nonoffending mother: Regretfully, the response to nonoffending mothers is even more biased. First, because only 7% to 8% of all abuse is committed by a father (Russell, 1984; Wyatt, 1985), a nonoffending father is potentially available as a supportive guardian in approximately 92% to 93% of all abuse. A review of studies on guardian support, however, found that 99% of nonoffending guardians in cases of identified abuse were mothers (Bolen, 2000b).

Another concern is the views maintained by child protective services about nonoffending mothers. As previously discussed, whereas only 0.05% of all offenders of committed abuse are mothers, 27% of identified offenders are mothers (Table 12-1), suggesting that workers continue to maintain extraordinary biases. Further, whereas 0.6% of parental abuse is committed by mothers, they are charged as offenders in more than half of the cases of identified parental abuse. Thus, it is not surprising that in hypothetical vignettes, a significant proportion of nonoffending mothers continue to be blamed for the abuse. In studies published in the 1990s, 70% to 86% of professional respondents attributed some responsibility to the mother for the abuse (Johnson et al., 1990; Kelley, 1990; Reidy & Hochstadt, 1993), and 59% of professionals in one study agreed that mothers should apologize to the victim for their failure to protect (Conte, Fogarty, & Collins, 1990). Indeed, some treatment centers require that mothers apologize before the victim is returned home (Giarretto, 1982, 1989). Most mental health workers also believe that these mothers are emotionally immature (Freet, Scalise, & Ginter, 1996).

Extraordinary biases also continue in the literature regarding the mother's response during and after the abuse. For example, even though 75% to 95% of mothers across studies are unaware of ongoing abuse (Faller, 1990; Meyer, 1985), one study found that child protective services workers considered that more than 80% of mothers were aware of the ongoing abuse (Ryan, Warren, & Weincek, 1991). Further, whereas 81% of mothers across studies are partially or fully supportive of their children after disclosure (Bolen, 2000b), other studies find that 40% to 59% of children are immediately removed from their homes, and up to two-thirds are eventually removed for some period of time (Faller, 1991b; Hunter, Coulter, Runyan, & Everson, 1990; Ryan et al., 1991). The disparity between the number of children removed and the number of supportive mothers again suggests that biases against nonoffending mothers continue.

Prevention

The final area to be considered is prevention. The empirical literature indicates that child sexual abuse is endemic within society and that all children are at risk of abuse in virtually any location by virtually any filial or nonfilial relations (almost all of whom are male). Methods of approach are also widely divergent. Conversely, because socialization patterns inculcate males into beliefs of superiority and entitlement to sexual access of females, males appear to be at increased risk to offend. Thus, 4% to 21% of males have either sexually abused a child or profess some likelihood to abuse (Bagley et al., 1994; Briere & Runtz, 1989; Finkelhor & Lewis, 1988). Another group of young males also appears to be at risk to abuse as extremes of socialized conduct, abusing for sport, as a conquest, or because of a sense of male entitlement (Bolen, 2000a). In contrast, society's primary method (and almost the only method) of preventing child sexual abuse is teaching children how to deflect the approaches of potential offenders. These programs are taught to children in elementary schools and are held on an occasional basis.

In a previous paper (Bolen, in press), it was argued that this prevention paradigm has not worked and cannot work. First, there is no indication that child sexual abuse prevalence has been reduced over the 15- to 20-year history of these programs. Second, the problem of child sexual abuse is too varied—with too many locations, types of perpetrators, and methods of approach—for children to be effectively targeted. Indeed, the current prevention strategy is analogous to teaching self-defense strategies to all persons in the United States as the primary prevention strategy for lowering overall levels of violence. Needless to say, such a strategy in which victims rather than offenders are targeted is destined to fail.

Summary

This section has presented data to suggest that society's ability to identify abuse estimated to occur in the general population is grossly inadequate. Not only does the vast majority of abuse estimated to occur in the general population remain unidentified, but abuse that is identified is grossly disproportionate from that abuse estimated to occur. Societal systems that respond are most capable of identifying abuse by fathers, although it appears that their ability to identify fathers is at the expense of identifying extrafamilial offenders. The other gross distortion between identified abuse and abuse estimated to occur is that mothers are identified as offenders at 540 times their rate of actual abuse.

Further, some professionals, especially child protective services workers, continue to maintain biases concerning victims and nonoffending mothers. The worst of these biases are the falsely held beliefs that: (a) up to half of all reports made by adolescents are false; (b) most allegations made within a divorce or custody dispute are maliciously and falsely filed, most often by mothers; and (c) nonoffending mothers often collude in ongoing abuse. None of these beliefs are supported in the empirical literature. Other concerns are that a small number of professionals continue to endorse a view that children are partially (although minimally) responsible for the abuse and that many more professionals continue to believe that mothers are partially responsible.

Given society's response to child sexual abuse, certain assumptions appear to underlie society's response to child sexual abuse. These assumptions, deriving from samples of identified victims, are as follows.

- Children are abused most frequently by parents, followed by other intrafamilial offenders and caregivers.
- Mothers co-offend in most parental abuse, and less frequently they are the sole perpetrators.
- When mothers do not actually commit the abuse, they most likely knew that it was occurring.

- Child sexual abuse is primarily a family problem, and both mothers and fathers contribute to and must be held responsible for the abuse.
- Even though mothers must be held responsible for the protection of their children after abuse, most cannot adequately do so, necessitating removal of the child.
- Some abuse is committed by offenders unrelated to the victim.

When comparing these assumptions with those deriving from the historical conceptualization of child sexual abuse, it is clear that the systemic response to child sexual abuse is closely associated with early theories, especially family systems theory. This theory focuses primarily on intrafamilial abuse and especially father-daughter incest while also considering mothers with high levels of suspicion. Indeed, these are some of the primary underlying assumptions of the systemic response to child sexual abuse. Thus, the professional response to child sexual abuse is grounded in its historical conceptualization. Regretfully, however, most of the tenets of this historical conceptualization are not supported empirically. It is no wonder that our society is doing such a poor job of responding to the problem of child sexual abuse.

HOW THESE BIASES ORIGINATED AND THEIR IMPACT

Child Sexual Abuse Statutes

The premise of this book is that policies, programs, and statutes of child sexual abuse (or society's response to child sexual abuse) are grounded within the historical and often myth-bound conceptualization of child sexual abuse. The purpose of the previous section was to show that the outcomes of these policies, programs, and statutes are indeed bound within assumptions of this historical conceptualization of child sexual abuse. The purpose of this section is to consider how these policies, programs, and statutes reflect these biases. The specific question asked in this section is whether biases are reflected in the actual statutes regarding child sexual abuse or whether they occur in the implementation of these statutes.

Both federal and state laws are in place for the identification of child sexual abuse. At the federal level, the most pertinent statute is the Child Abuse Prevention and Treatment Act (CAPTA), originally passed by Congress in 1974 and most recently amended in 1996 (U.S. Department of Health and Human Services, 1996). Among its many provisions, it provides grants "for purposes of assisting the States in improving the child protective services system of each State" (42 U.S.C. § 5106a). To be eligible for these grants, states have a number of eligibility requirements, including established procedures for: reporting known instances of child abuse and neglect; screening, safety assessment, and prompt investigation of reports; and protecting the safety of children. Importantly, only one of these eligibility requirements even tangentially recognizes abuse by caregivers. This requirement requires "procedures for immediate steps to be taken to ensure and protect the safety of the abused or neglected child and of any other child under the same care who may also be in danger" (42 U.S.C. § 5106a). Thus, CAPTA reflects criteria for protecting children of *all* types of abuse or neglect. The other important contribution at the federal level is found embedded within specific court cases. In several cases, federal courts have ruled that "parents and children have a 'right' to family autonomy, privacy, or integrity," a right that can only be usurped with "'compelling state interest,' such as the need to protect children from significant harm" (Bulkley, Feller, Stern, & Roe, 1996, p. 272). Thus, the federal government: (a) requires states to adequately identify, assess, and protect children; and (b) recognizes the rights of families.

At the level of the state, two types of laws have been enacted. First, all states have laws that make sexual abuse a crime, although the definition of abuse varies by state (U.S. Department of Health and Human Services, 2000a). In addition, 47 states have laws specifically prohibiting incest (National Victim Center, 1995). Thus, most states view incest (often including abuse by any related or unrelated caregiver) as qualitatively different than abuse by a noncaregiver. Second, states have laws requiring individuals to report suspected cases of child sexual abuse. In all states, reporting laws apply to both intrafamilial and extrafamilial abuse (U.S. Department of Health and Human Services, 2000b), although states differ on who is considered a mandated reporter (Bulkley et al., 1996). Further, states differ on whether child protective services is mandated to investigate all types of abuse or only abuse by caregivers. A review of state statutes indicates that about 80% of states have laws charging their child protective services agencies with investigating all types of abuse (U.S. Department of Health and Human Services, 2000a). In the other states, law enforcement is charged with the responsibility of investigating abuse by noncaregivers.

Two points can be made regarding reporting statutes. First, while CAPTA requires all states to have procedures for protecting children, about 20% of states have enacted not only differential, but probably unequal, access to resources based upon the type of abuse. Even though states are currently overwhelmed with reports of suspected abuse, many state budgets for child protection have been cut in recent years, suggesting scarce resources. In those states that route only abuse by caregivers through child protective services, it seems likely that victims of other types of abuse do not have equal access to screening, safety assessment, prompt investigation of reports, and procedures for protecting the safety of children. Yet all are stipulations of CAPTA. Second, child protective services agencies in states requiring all types of abuse to be reported to child protective services also likely prioritize abuse by caregivers. If victims of abuse by noncaregivers did have equal access to resources, the columns in Table 12-1 regarding the proportion of intrafamilial abuse to extrafamilial abuse would have more similarities than differences. The sharp discrepancies between data in these columns instead suggest unequal access to resources. Thus, reports of extrafamilial abuse, which are not prioritized, are also more easily overlooked.

In summary, all states have laws making both intrafamilial and extrafamilial abuse a crime and require mandated reporters to report all types of suspected abuse. Further, approximately 80% of states have laws that do not limit the type of abuse child protective services is mandated to investigate. Yet, national incidence studies suggest that intrafamilial abuse is disproportionately represented in populations of identified victims, leading to the conclusion that state laws are not being properly implemented. Thus, while statutes are in accordance with CAPTA guidelines, their implementation across states is not in accordance.

Issues in Implementing Statutes

This section now considers some of the more serious issues arising from the manner in which child sexual abuse statutes are implemented. Specifically, this section considers issues related to the prioritization of abuse by caregivers and the tension that exists between victims' rights and offenders' rights.

Prioritization of Abuse by Caregivers

The previous section indicated that although CAPTA guidelines and state statutes afford protection to victims of all types of child sexual abuse, the implementation of these statutes has resulted in a system of unequal access to protection and resources based upon the identity of the offender. As a result, cases of abuse by noncaregivers easily fall through the many cracks in the system, as evidenced by the stark data in Table 12-1 indicating that victims of extrafamilial abuse remain disproportionately unidentified. Given that approximately 84% to 88% of abuse is by nonguardians, this is a tragic consequence of the prioritization of abuse by caregivers over noncaregivers.[4]

While this issue has not seemed to arouse much concern historically (as evidenced by the dearth of professional literature), there are extremely important and negative ramifications to this prioritization of abuse by caregivers. First, because victims of extrafamilial abuse are more likely than victims of intrafamilial abuse to disclose their abuse (Finkelhor, 1984; Sauzier, 1989), the voices of these children are more easily ignored, and thus silenced. Second, even though extrafamilial abuse is less likely than intrafamilial abuse to occur only a single time, more than one-fourth of all extrafamilial abuse occurs multiple times. Further, extrafamilial abuse is perpetrated at a more severe level than intrafamilial abuse and is more likely to involve multiple perpetrators (Bolen, 1996). Thus, even though the risk of revictimization for extrafamilial abuse is less than that for intrafamilial abuse, it still occurs with enough frequency and with the threat of serious enough abuse to warrant great concern. Finally, even victims of extrafamilial abuse who are identified are at a disadvantage because they may not have the same resources available to them as do victims of intrafamilial abuse. One piece of compelling evidence is studies indicating that although victims of extrafamilial abuse suffer significant deleterious effects from the abuse (Gregory-Bills & Rhodeback, 1995), they remain significantly under-represented in treatment populations of children (Bolen, 1998a; English & Tosti-Lane, 1988). Thus, most states have failed to implement strategies that provide adequate access to protection and treatment for victims of extrafamilial abuse, as required by CAPTA.

Tension between Children's and Offender's Rights

Child protective services is mandated to protect the rights of children, whereas the criminal justice system is mandated to protect the rights of the accused. Within the current system, the rights of the accused appear to take precedence. While there are

---

[4] As computed by author from Russell's (1983) survey.

various reasons to make this statement, the most compelling is that almost all offenders are allowed to stay within the child's environment, whereas the majority of children are removed from their homes (Faller, 1991b; Hunter et al., 1990). An analysis presented in Chapter 9, "Offenders," found that offenders are convicted in less than 2% of all abuse suspected by authorities. Of substantiated abuse, only approximately 7% of offenders spend more than one year in jail. Given that an estimated three-fourths or more of all abuse that occurs is never identified and substantiated (Tables 5-1 and 5-2), it is probably safe to say that less than 1% percent of victims of abuse are adequately protected by the system. Further, considering that most offenders abuse multiple victims (Abel et al., 1987, 1988a; Ballard et al., 1990), other children are also unprotected by this failure of the system.

Because 93% or more of all offenders are allowed to remain within the child's environment or to return within the year, child protective services has the enormous responsibility of providing adequate protection to victims whose offenders remain free. How this problem has been resolved may be one of the most critical factors related to certain systemic biases, including the high number of mothers charged as offenders (Table 12-1), the high number of mothers assumed to be collusive or unsupportive (Ryan et al., 1991), and the high number of children removed from their homes (Faller, 1991b; Hunter et al., 1990). Yet, to fully understand this relationship requires an understanding of how some of the myth-bound tenets of early family systems theory influenced the thinking of professionals.

Probably in no area has the historical conceptualization of child sexual abuse done so much harm as in the manner in which nonoffending mothers are conceptualized and treated. As discussed in an earlier section of this chapter, most professionals continue to assume that mothers are partially culpable for the abuse (Kelley, 1990; Reidy & Hochstadt, 1993), probably knew about the ongoing abuse (Breckenridge & Baldry, 1997), and have emotional and personality deficits (Freet et al., 1996). These findings contradict the empirical literature, which indicates that most mothers do not know about the ongoing abuse (Faller, 1990; Margolin, 1992; Myer, 1985), are partially or fully supportive when they do find out (Bolen, 2000b), and have personality characteristics that fall within the normal range (Muram, Rosenthal, & Beck, 1994; Peterson, Basta, & Dykstra, 1993). Yet, the consequences of these biased beliefs have been devastating for nonoffending mothers. In one of the most graphic examples, one study found that child protective services workers considered that 81% of mothers of children whose cases were substantiated knew about the ongoing abuse, and most of these mothers were considered unsupportive (Ryan et al., 1991). This factor—the perception that the mother knew about the ongoing abuse—was one of two important factors predicting removal of the child. Thus, the mere *perception* that mothers know about the ongoing abuse substantially increased their risk of losing their child. As such, the falsely held belief that mothers collude in ongoing abuse is probably directly related to increased removals of children. If this is the case, then this false belief held by child protective services workers may explain why one set of studies indicates that most mothers are somewhat or fully supportive after abuse disclosure (Bolen, 2000b), whereas another set of studies indicates that most mothers experience the removal of their child (Faller, 1991b; Hunter et al., 1990).

Another issue, however, looms large. Although child protective services is mandated to protect children, the system fails to remove all but a few offenders from the child's environment. Thus, because law enforcement fails in its responsibility, child protective services is burdened with the responsibility of protecting children whose offenders remain free. Further, in an era of high-profile media exposure and general negativity directed towards child protective services, the stakes are high. How can child protective services *guarantee* the protection of the child? The only way to do so is to remove the victim. A study by Cross et al. (1999) provides a stark example of this dilemma. More than 40% of children whose cases of sexual abuse were referred for prosecution and then denied were removed from their homes. Why were these children removed at this point? While the design of the study precludes definitive answers, it may be that this was the only way that child protective services felt that they could adequately protect the child.[1]

It is suggested that the current implementation of child sexual abuse statutes provides an extraordinary quandary to child protective services, a quandary that is best resolved by considering mothers collusive and unprotective. If child protective services is charged with protecting the child when the offender remains in the child's environment, who is to say that the child cannot be sexually abused again by the same offender? And surely child protective services is acutely aware of its failures, as they are so often sensationalized by the media. With such intense pressure on child protective services to protect the victims, it is not unreasonable to suggest that the pressure to remove children is also intense, even though this pressure is probably implicit and even though foster care homes may be scarce. Yet, court cases have consistently upheld the rights of family unity except in extreme circumstances (Bulkley et al., 1996). Because children can only be removed from nonoffending guardians who are not adequately protective, the historical conceptualization of nonoffending mothers as collusive has provided a solution. Child protective services can resolve their dilemma by maintaining a false belief that most mothers are collusive. By charging mothers as co-offenders or with failure to protect their children, their extraordinary dilemma is solved. Believing that the best interests of the children are being served, workers can then remove them from their homes.

This analysis is not in any way to suggest that child protective services workers or supervisors purposefully or knowingly falsely accuse mothers of colluding in ongoing abuse or of not being adequately supportive. It is instead to suggest that, over time, biases have become institutionalized within child protective services because these biases offer one of the few methods for successfully accomplishing their mandates. Thus, new child protective services workers are inculcated into a system that believes that most mothers are collusive and unsupportive. Having a preconception about what to expect of these mothers and needing some leverage to adequately protect the child, child protective services may have institutionalized a method of charging mothers as unfit parents or even as co-offenders. Compelling evidence for this supposition is found in the 1998 NCANDS national incidence study in which more than half of mothers in cases of parental abuse were identified as offenders (U.S. Department of Health and Human Services, 2000c).

Thus, a tragic set of circumstances may have predestined the response to mothers. Our fundamental rights as citizens of the United States have resulted in the paradoxical consequence that almost no offenders are removed from the victims'

---

[1] Of course, some removed children are also abused while in foster care or other settings.

environments. Yet realizing its responsibility, the federal government has charged states, and specifically child protective services, with the responsibility of protecting its children. Because the federal government has laws that protect the rights of the alleged offender and the sanctity of the family, these laws place child protective services in the unique position of having to destroy family sanctity to maintain its mandate to protect victims. These systemic challenges have thus prioritized the rights of the offender over those of the victim and family. The eventual scapegoat has become the nonoffending mother, the one person whose rights are not protected. By charging her as unfit, unsupportive, or even a co-offender, as the historical conceptualization of child sexual abuse suggests, child protective services can then meet its mandated function of protecting children.

In summary, the tension between the rights of the victim and offender and the influence of a myth-laden historical conceptualization of child sexual abuse have coalesced at enormous cost to the victims and their nonoffending guardians. The pejorative assumptions of nonoffending guardians have virtually guaranteed their abuse and misuse within a system designed to eye them with deep suspicion. Thus, nonoffending mothers are routinely charged as co-offenders even when they do not commit the abuse. Many other mothers are labeled unfit, and their children are removed. The system thus blames nonoffending mothers with the failure for the protection of these children. The reality, however, is that the profound failure to protect identified victims lies instead with the system. And this failure is beyond imagination, for only 5% to 26% of all abuse within the general population is identified (Table 5-2). Of the abuse that is identified, only approximately 7% of offenders are incarcerated for more than a year. On the other hand, the large majority of individuals who could provide the greatest protection to the child—nonoffending mothers and other nonoffending guardians—are at greatest risk either to be ignored by the system, falsely charged as co-offenders, or presumed to be unsupportive. As a result, the majority of identified children live their nightmare—that disclosure of the abuse will dissolve the family structure. This is an unconscionable failure by a system designed to protect abused children and to maintain family unity.

RECOMMENDATIONS FOR MOVING FORWARD

Having considered some of the profound failures of the systemic response to child sexual abuse, this section makes recommendations for moving forward with a more child-centered, appropriate, and empirically grounded response to the problem. In 1990, the U.S. Advisory Board on Child Abuse and Neglect referred to child abuse as a "national emergency," requiring the "replacement of the existing child protection system" (Schene, 1996, p. 386). While many of the problems within the current system necessitate structural change, the implementation of such changes will require time. In the meantime, it is essential that society make some immediate changes that improve its ability to adequately and appropriately respond to the scope of the problem of child sexual abuse. The purpose of this section is to forward suggestions that can be implemented within the current system for improving society's response. A later section considers a future response to child sexual abuse.

Identification of Victims

Statutes at both the state and federal levels are largely sufficient to provide for the identification of victims of child sexual abuse. The problem is primarily in the implementation of these statutes. Therefore, only two suggested changes to existing statutes are made. First, it is suggested that CAPTA be amended to explicitly require equal access to resources for victims of both intrafamilial and extrafamilial abuse. Second, it is recommended that all states amend their statutes so that equal access to resources is guaranteed for victims of both intrafamilial and extrafamilial abuse. It is further recommended that the federal government provide heightened supervision so that states are denied funds if they cannot implement equal access to resources for victims. Such a strategy would also require increased funding by the federal government so that states had budgets necessary to implement equal access.

It is further recommended that an appeal system be developed so that parents who believe their child was inaccurately assessed as not having been abused have adequate recourse to provide for their child's safety. Appeals could be considered by a multidisciplinary specialty team outside child protective services. This type of appeal would be especially beneficial to parents involved in custody and divorce disputes who had reason to suspect that their child was abused but whose request for investigation was denied.

Protection of Victims

Changes for Victims

While state and federal statutes are sufficient for identifying victims (assuming proper implementation), they are insufficient for providing ongoing protection. Instead, the rights of the accused have precedence over the rights of the victims. As a result, far too many children are needlessly removed from their homes, thus introducing iatrogenic (system-induced) trauma by the system designed to protect the children. To move towards a resolution of this very difficult problem, it is recommended that state and federal laws be enacted that protect the rights of children, as follows.

- All children and adolescents have the right not to be sexually abused.
- All children and adolescents have the right to be protected by society from all known offenders who physically perpetrate sexual abuse.
- All sexually abused children and adolescents have the right to remain in their own homes with their nonoffending guardians after abuse disclosure (i.e., with those who did not physically perpetrate the sexual abuse) unless the guardians are charged with perpetrating another type of child maltreatment unrelated to the sexual abuse.

The first right ensures that society is responsible for developing prevention programs that effectively and substantially reduce the prevalence of child sexual abuse. Thus, the sexual abuse of any child is recognized as a failure of society to protect that child. The second right—that children and adolescents have the right to be protected from know sexual offenders—has two important components. The most important component is that it establishes that children have the right to be protected from all known offenders. Because the word *offender* has been interpreted to include mothers living with perpetrators, however, a second component was added that defined offenders as only those individuals who physically perpetrate sexual abuse, removing the temptation to use mothers as scapegoats. The final right also recognizes that children have the right to remain in their homes with their nonoffending guardians after abuse disclosure, assuming the guardian is not perpetrating another type of maltreatment not associated with the sexual abuse. Defining this maltreatment as unrelated to the sexual abuse again removes the tendency to charge mothers with emotional neglect for purportedly not protecting the child from the sexual abuse.

The proposed rights of children are simple—the rights to be protected and to remain in their homes with their nonoffending guardians after disclosure. Given the hostile environment towards nonoffending guardians, however, caveats have to be added to these basic rights so that there is no misinterpretation. By establishing these as the rights of children, a tension between the legal system's mandate to protect the rights of the accused and the child welfare system's mandate to protect the rights of children will be created. Moving beyond this tension will require creative solutions in working with both nonoffending guardians and alleged offenders.

Changes in Working with Nonoffending Guardians

The two most important recommendations regarding nonoffending guardians are: (a) to stop charging mothers as co-offenders when they do not physically perpetrate the sexual abuse; and (b) to remove the burden of protection for abused children from their shoulders. First to be discussed is the need to consider guardians as nonoffenders rather than co-offenders.

Because nonoffending mothers continue to be charged at an astounding rate for a crime they did not commit, nonoffending guardians may require legal intervention. First, it is recommended that the legal definition of an offender be clarified so that only those who *physically perpetrate* the sexual abuse can be labeled or charged as offenders, and thus potential felons. This definition should apply not only to the legal system but also to child protective services. Second, it is recommended that failure to protect be redefined so that it can only be applied when there is *court-admissible evidence* that the nonoffending guardian knew about the abuse before it was officially disclosed and did nothing *formally or informally* to stop it. Evidence of formal or informal protective measures could be waived if guardians feared that initiating such measures would jeopardize their or their children's safety, such as for victims of domestic violence. Third, nonoffending guardians should be provided the right to legal representation and to appeal to a body independent of child protective services if they believe they are falsely charged as a co-offender or with failure to protect. If these rights were enacted within CAPTA, all states would be obliged to enact them as well. Fourth, it is recommended that all child protective services staff receive basic training or retraining to dispel the myths concerning nonoffending mothers and to provide them with a view consistent with the empirical literature. This retraining should be initiated will all due haste. Finally, it is recommended that all cases in which mothers were charged as co-offenders within at least the last five years be reviewed by independent panels of experts so that reparation can be made to mothers who were wrongly charged and who suffered grievously from this practice. Children of mothers falsely accused also need to be returned to their mothers unless convincing evidence of further danger to the child exists.

These measures may seem harsh, but falsely charging mothers with a crime they did not commit is also harsh. Finkelhor and Hotaling first documented this horrendous problem in 1984, at which time they noted that 46% of offenders in the NIS-1 (done in 1981) were listed as females (mostly mothers and mother figures). In 1993 the rate for abuse by females had dropped to 28% (Sedlak & Broadhurst, 1996). Conversely, 0.5% of all abuse is actually committed by females, and only 0.05% is committed by mothers (Table 12-1). As a result, within the 18-year period between 1981 and 1998, *more than 500,000 women* have been falsely charged as offenders.[1] Most of these women have been mothers of the child. This is an extraordinarily large population of females suffering exceptional losses because of institutionalized biases. At this rate, it will take many years before the rates of identified abuse by mothers and females are comparable to the rates of abuse committed by mothers and females.

Other than immediately targeting the reduction of false allegations against nonoffending mothers made by child protective services workers, another important recommendation is that the burden for the protection of the child be removed from nonoffending guardians. First, doing so will reduce the temptation by child protective services to make the mother the scapegoat. As importantly, however, by no longer having the burden for providing physical protection, these nonoffending guardians can then focus their efforts on providing a more emotionally supportive environment to the child. Methods for removing the burden of protection from the nonoffending mother are discussed in the next section.

Other recommendations, while important, do not have such a great sense of urgency. First, we need to consider moving the focus from the nonoffending mother to the supportiveness of all nonoffending guardians, for the supportiveness of the environment is surely more important than that of any single person. Allowing other nonoffending guardians, especially nonoffending fathers, to share in this responsibility will ease some of the discriminatory behaviors against nonoffending mothers, while providing a richer and broader environment of support for the children and recognizing the important role of nonoffending fathers.

Another recommendation is to create safe houses supported by communities that can provide further protection to children and their families on a temporary basis. Alternately, shelters that have separate living quarters for families can be created for those families needing either further protection or more time to reconstitute. Shelters such as these can be designed after state-of-the-art shelters used in domestic violence cases such as that at The Family Place in Dallas, Texas.[2]

---

[1] This computation was made based upon data available in the three National Incidence Studies and the 1998 NCANDS incidence study. It assumed that: (a) identified cases increased proportionally between 1981 and 1993, with a decrease of 29% between 1993 and 1998, and a proportionate decrease thereafter; (b) approximately 1% of all committed abuse is by mothers and 5% is by females; and (c) the rate of charging females as co-offenders decreased proportionally from 46% in 1981 to 12% in 1993 and then remained constant.

[2] The Family Place completed construction in 2000 on a state-of-the-art shelter for victims of domestic violence. They can be reached at Box 7999, Dallas, TX 75209.

Next, we need to make more physical resources available to nonoffending guardians after disclosure. It is highly likely that some of their diminished coping strategies after disclosure are a result of the stress of the disclosure and even the systemic interventions. Bringing needed resources to these nonoffending guardians can increase their coping capabilities and allow them to be more emotionally supportive to their victimized child.

Finally, many nonoffending guardians are also traumatized by the abuse, or perhaps have problems before the disclosure that decrease their ability to adequately support their children. It is important that these guardians have access to strengths-oriented treatment provided by clinicians specializing in this type of treatment and who endorse no serious biases about nonoffending guardians. The treating clinician also needs to be employed outside child protective services. As discussed in Chapter 10, goals of this treatment are to increase resources, decrease stressors, increase guardian support, and provide a working-through environment in which guardians are allowed to access their evocative and confusing emotions concerning the abuse. With this more strengths-oriented approach, perhaps the phrases *collusive mother, incestuous mother or family,* and *mothers who fail to protect* will disappear from our professional lexicon.

Identification and Control of the Offender

If children are allowed to remain in their homes with their nonoffending guardians, then the manner in which offenders are handled by the system must also change. The most important change is that offenders need to be removed from the child's environment or, if allowed to stay, need to be monitored closely by law enforcement so that the victim can be protected. Because this is such a complex issue, it is recommended that a panel of legal and child sexual abuse experts be brought together to consider methods for protecting children while allowing them to remain in their homes. Two issues need to be addressed. The first issue is how to get offenders out of the immediate environment of the child and second is how to make law enforcement (instead of the mother) responsible for protecting the victim. Both require the commitment of local and state governments for their success.

The first issue—how to remove the offender instead of the child from the home—is fraught with legal considerations. Because it is primarily a legal issue, it is beyond the scope of this book. It does seem logical to suggest, however, that if there is enough evidence to conclude that abuse likely occurred, then there should be enough evidence to conclude that the alleged offender is a potentially serious threat to the child. Just as victims of domestic violence can seek protection through a restraining order, it seems that courts, acting to protect the child, could issue orders requiring offenders (even if they were only alleged offenders) to maintain adequate distance from the victim. If punishment were to include automatic incarceration or other severe penalties, then alleged and convicted offenders would be less inclined to violate the order.

The second issue is how law enforcement can enforce these orders. Here it seems that the likely solution is the implementation of sophisticated monitoring such as the global positioning system. This method has already been partially implemented in at least four states to monitor violent felons and sex offenders (Leinknecht, 1997). If such a monitoring system were implemented in all states, then law enforcement would be able to enforce the court orders. It might also be possible that victims and their families could temporarily be moved to safe houses that were constantly monitored, thus ensuring the safety of the victim. Alternately, alleged or known offenders could be moved to temporary residents so that the victims could remain with their nonoffending guardians within their own homes.

Summary

Even within current laws, children are afforded the right to remain with their families except for extenuating circumstances. Yet because the criminal justice system has failed in its responsibility to remove offenders from the child's environment, this law has been grossly abused. Without other recourse, the primary method that child protective services has used to protect the victim is to remove the child. Regretfully, however, this has meant that the nonoffending guardians, almost always considered the mother, had to be charged as either co-offenders or as unfit parents by failing to protect their child. As a result, the right of the children to remain with their family has been denied them. The denial of this right has also potentially induced iatrogenic trauma for the victim, nonoffending guardian, and family.

   If children are to be allowed the right to remain with their families, major changes are required. First, responsibility for the protection of victims needs to be moved from nonoffending guardians to law enforcement. Second, law enforcement needs the means for protecting the victims. The best method for doing so may be making sure that the offender is removed from the child's environment, after which sophisticated monitoring can be used to ensure the child's safety.

   While these changes are complex, they are also central to reforms of the child protective system. The alternative—blaming mothers for a crime they did not commit and removing children from their homes—is anathema to a compassionate society.

Prevention

To adequately prevent child sexual abuse requires that we target the offending behavior. To do so, we need to design and fund programs that test innovative prevention approaches. While the causal research to fully understand risk factors for offending has not yet been done, enough research is available to suggest that sexual abuse is often an extension of the socialization patterns of males. Thus, prevention programs that target sociocultural factors need to be given priority. We also need to consider programs that teach the bounds of appropriate behavior to children and adolescents (Bolen, in press). These age-specific programs could be integrated into the curriculum of all elementary, middle, and high schools. These programs should especially focus on the bounds of behavior between males and females, although same-sex relationships should not be ignored. Funding could also be earmarked for longitudinal studies that follow sexually aggressive children exposed to these programs.

   Programs should also consider how to target the greater society. How can messages about appropriate conduct with children be heard? How can the media be utilized to give messages about appropriate conduct with children? Another important prevention program is the basic education of the layperson, which should become a priority so that parents become aware of the threat of sexual abuse to their children. While basic education should continue to inform the layperson about the threat of sexual abuse by nonrelated but known others, we also need to continue the emphasis on the threat of intrafamilial abuse. Professionals have fought long and hard to educate an unwilling public that relatives also pose a threat of sexual abuse to children. Thus, educating the public that both relatives and nonrelatives, and especially individuals the child already knows, pose a real threat is the logical course of action.

Basic education should also target the erroneous and sometimes outlandish messages of the backlash. Parents, teachers, and all individuals coming into contact with children should be made aware that false disclosures are rare, even in custody or divorce disputes. The public should also be aware that a significant number of traumatized individuals do forget and later remember incidents of abuse. In other words, the public should have the information available to allow them to make informed judgments. This basic information will not only contribute to the prevention of child sexual abuse, but will also defuse the power of the backlash.

Other Considerations

Identification and Treatment of Juvenile Offenders

In Chapter 6, "Extrafamilial Abuse," it was shown that approximately 25% of all extrafamilial abuse is committed by young offenders whose abuse represents the extremes of socialization standards. These young men appeared to abuse for sport, as a means of conquest, and through a sense of entitlement. Because of their youth, the more punitive model of labeling them as sex offenders, with all the stigma attached, seems in some ways too harsh. While in no way wanting to diminish their responsibility for their crimes, a method that allows them to maintain responsibility for their crime while also allowing them the potential to move beyond their offender status seems more humanistic.

A model that can be used to accomplish both is restorative justice. In this model, offenders are held accountable to their victims and community members for their crime, while also allowing for opportunities for dialogue, problem solving, and negotiation among the victim, community members, and offender (Center for Restorative Justice & Peacemaking, 1997). Thus, offenders often meet with their victims and community members in settings that are mediated by a professional. While this model is most appropriate to adult victims, who might receive some sense of empowerment from confronting their offender, this process could be modified to make it appropriate for youthful sex offenders. Hearing about the impact of their crime from representatives for the victim and having to make reparation to the victim or community allows offenders to be held more personally accountable for their behavior. Such a direct intervention might provide enough of an impact to youthful offenders that they might modify future behavior. Such a method might also allow first-time youthful offenders to avoid the lifetime stigmatization of being labeled a sex offender.

Research

In 1997, the General Accounting Office (GAO) concluded that "focuses on such topics as the causes and effects of child sexual abuse" are mostly irrelevant to "most local agencies' attempts to reform their services" ("GAO Calls For," p. 132). Instead, this book has demonstrated conclusively that this basic research *must* underlie reforms, for its current services are so far removed from the reality of child sexual abuse as to be almost absurd. Thus, calls for ongoing basic research are absolutely critical to effectively respond to the problem of child sexual abuse. Research that is needed for developing and extending the empirical knowledge base is as follows.

Scope of the problem of child sexual abuse: Many gaps in the knowledge base concerning the scope of the problem remain. First, national random prevalence studies with rigorous methodology sensitive to eliciting disclosures of abuse should be funded. While some rigorous random surveys have been conducted, they are either dated, are community-based samples, or have such small sample sizes that their findings cannot be generalized with confidence. Of the few available national surveys, limitations of the studies preclude reliable estimates. Thus, we still cannot reliably estimate the national prevalence of child sexual abuse for males and females. Complementary studies assessing the prevalence of offenders within community populations and the likelihood to abuse are also needed. Because juvenile offenders account for 20% to 50% of all offenders (Davis & Leitenberg, 1987; Fehrenbach, Smith, Monastersky, & Deisher, 1986), studies should also assess juvenile populations. These studies need to have a broad enough definition of child sexual abuse that it captures all types of motivations for sexual abuse, including children or adolescents who abuse for sport or conquest, or simply out of a sense of entitlement.

Factors contributing to the risk of abuse or risk to offend: This type of research should move beyond a focus on factors within the family related to greater risk of abuse, and instead focus on sociocultural factors related to risk. Studies can be at both the macro and micro level. Macro-level studies can assess factors at a societal level that covary with differences in fluctuations of identified abuse. Studies such as these can also take into account the backlash and how it has affected the reporting and identification of abuse. The obvious caveat to this research is that it is limited by the biases of child protective services in identifying abuse. Micro-level studies can also consider sociocultural factors by capturing their effect upon the individual. For example, factors such as hostility towards women can be measured at the level of the individual, but stand as proxies for stereotypical and sociocultural messages. Studies such as these can be designed to identify factors that predict greater risk of abuse as well as greater risk to offend. Factors that place primarily males at risk to offend as extremes of socialized behaviors (i.e., for sport, as a conquest, and as a result of entitlement) should also be considered. How do these offenders differ from other normative populations of males and other sexual offender groups?

Extrafamilial abuse: Basic research on all types of extrafamilial abuse is also needed. While many studies of pedophiles or child molesters exist, they are more typically concerned with the characteristics of the offender than the characteristics of the abuse. As a result, the empirical knowledge base on different types of extrafamilial abuse is extremely limited, especially for the most common types of extrafamilial abuse. Prioritization by funding agencies of this type of research would help to fill the significant gaps in this knowledge base.

Nonoffending guardians: Studies have traditionally defined expectations for nonoffending guardians as those placed on them by the system, regardless of whether they were realistic, and then determined whether nonoffending guardians could meet those expectations. As such, quantitative studies on normative responses to abuse disclosure for nonoffending guardians are sorely needed. Funding also should be made available for studies that analyze constructs such as guardian support and ambivalence. What do these constructs mean? When we remove the expectations of the system from our guiding framework, how can these constructs be conceptualized that is in keeping with the normative responses of nonoffending guardians? Much work also remains to be done on developing models of nonoffending guardians that (a) are strengths-oriented rather than punitive; (b) focus on all nonoffending guardians rather than just nonoffending mothers; (c) recognize the multiple stressors these nonoffending guardians are facing; and (d) develop criteria for guardian support that are no harsher than those by which other parents are judged. Thus, much research remains on filling the numerous gaps in the literature on the responses of nonoffending guardians, including nonoffending mothers, nonoffending fathers, and other legal nonoffending guardians.

Professional response to child sexual abuse: Findings throughout the previous chapter suggest that the beliefs and value systems of professionals might critically impact how they make decisions. Because most of these studies use hypothetical vignettes, we need more specific information about how the values and beliefs of professionals actually impact decisions about interventions. Another important consideration is why these biases occur. For example, why do male professionals reach different conclusions about a given case than female professionals?

Decision-making process within child protective services: A corollary concern is how child protective services makes decisions. While certain studies suggest that child protective services workers maintain beliefs that are not empirically supported (Downing et al., 1990; Ryan et al., 1991), we have no information concerning why child protective services workers maintain these beliefs and how the beliefs are maintained by the system. Another area of research is the costs to the system and individuals associated with falsely charging mothers as co-offenders and removing so many children needlessly. Still another area of compelling research is whether the qualifications of child protective services workers are related to decision-making capacities. Do workers with bachelor degrees assess cases differently than those with graduate degrees? Do workers with mental health degrees assess cases differently than those with other degrees, and is the type or level of education related to biases workers maintain? Is training within child protective services related to their ability to more correctly endorse items that assess knowledge and myths about child sexual abuse? As yet, no known research has considered these issues.

Child protective services workers also make critical decisions about whether to screen in or out a case, substantiate a case, and remove the child. Again, research is extremely limited, even though these are all critical to the welfare of the child and family. There are some indications that unsupported beliefs about child sexual abuse that are maintained by child protective services workers are related not only to decisions to screen a case in or out (Downing et al., 1990; Giovannoni, 1991), but also to decisions to substantiate abuse (Haskett et al., 1995). Thus, we need much more research on case and worker characteristics predicting decisions made by child protective services workers.

A final consideration is how funding affects decisions. Are funding fluctuations of child protective services agencies related to rates of substantiation and removals? How is the time a case worker spends on an average case related to decisions made in that case, and how does funding affect the average time allocated to cases? Finally, it is suggested that the federal government mandate annual federal studies that assess decision-making in child protective services. This black box called child protective services should be opened to greater empirical examination, and one important method of doing so is to have large federally mandated studies.

Education and Training for Professionals

Another area for consideration is the education and training for professionals working in the area of child sexual abuse, including child protective services workers. While licensing and continuing education have already been implemented in many areas, some consideration needs to be given to the minimum requirements necessary for professionals in a decision-making capacity. For example, individuals without a graduate degree in a medical or mental health field could be (a) required to work under the supervision of a professional with that training; (b) limited in the interventions they are allowed to do; and (c) restricted from making decisions about cases. Given the number of child protective services workers that maintain institutionalized biases, workers with decision-making capacities should also be screened to determine whether they have an adequate knowledge base and whether they maintain biases detrimental to the victims or their families. Those who do maintain serious biases should be screened out of positions that place them in contact with the families or in positions to make decisions.

For all professionals, trainings should be developed or continued that allow self-examination. Because studies suggest that personal biases influence decisions and frame beliefs, self-examination is an important function for clinicians. Basic education programs for mandated reporters should also be developed, as too many continue to hold false beliefs about child sexual abuse.

Cultural Sensitivity

By choice, this book has included little on cultural sensitivity. This decision was made because child sexual abuse is primarily a gendered problem that crosses all races and ethnicities, as well as all socioeconomic strata. On the other hand, once victims become known to the system, they are subject to institutionalized biases that exist. That professionals react to hypothetical vignettes differently based upon the gender, age, socioeconomic status, and race of the victim or offender (Jackson & Nutall, 1993; Watson & Levine, 1989; Zellman, 1992), and sometimes even the professional, suggests that institutionalized biases continue. The previous chapter also presented data suggesting that some minorities appear to be over-represented in identified populations. It is thus critical that all interventions be culturally sensitive and that all children, regardless of race, ethnicity, gender, or socioeconomic status, have equal access to all resources offered by the system. It is also important to ensure that no cohort receives more preferential or punitive treatment. A panel with expertise in both child sexual abuse and cultural sensitivity could be convened to assess all systemic interventions with sexually abused victims, families, and offenders for their cultural sensitivity. This panel could then make recommendations for change or for further research to assess and address these issues.

Summary

Many recommendations have been made along a number of domains. Most require that funding be made available for innovative programs or essential research. As such, many must wait until funding agencies prioritize these efforts. Others, however, require less funding or can be done within current budgets. While all recommendations seem critical for a reformed system that adequately targets the problem of child sexual abuse, some seem more critical than others. One of the most critical of these is the retraining of child protective services workers to address the extraordinary biases inculcated within that system. These biases do real and extensive damage. Other urgent concerns are to develop procedures or to enact laws so that victims can remain in their homes with their nonoffending guardians after disclosure and so that nonoffending guardians are not charged for a crime they did not commit.

LONG-TERM GOALS

The vision of the children and family service system of the future is quite different from what it is today. (Schene, 1996, p. 395)

All recommendations in the previous section related to changes that could be made within the child protection system. On the other hand, it is generally acknowledged that an effective response to child sexual abuse will require major structural change. As noted earlier, the U.S. Advisory Board on Child Abuse and Neglect recommended the "replacement of the existing child protection system" (Schene, 1996, p. 386).

One of the most essential steps needed for moving toward an effective future response to child sexual abuse is to form a task force or think tank whose task it is to consider how the problem of child sexual abuse can be effectively targeted. This task force should have the lassitude to think creatively and independently, for confined to the current structure, such an endeavor would be doomed. As its primary goal, this task force should reach a consensus on the future response to the problem of child sexual abuse. Questions that might need to be answered to reform the child protection system are as follows.

- How can *all* victims of child sexual abuse be effectively identified?
- How can investigation be sensitive both in cases in which abuse has occurred and in those in which the suspicion was not founded?

- How can we respond sensitively to the victims and their families, collaborating with the nonoffending guardians instead of considering them adversaries?
- How can we remove the burden for protection from nonoffending guardians and place it on law enforcement and the offenders?
- How can we maintain and protect children in their homes after disclosure?
- How can we bring resources to nonoffending guardians and their families that reduce stressors, thus increasing their ability to cope effectively and to be more supportive of their child?
- How can we provide access to treatment for all family members who need it?
- How can we develop strengths-based treatment modalities for nonoffending guardians?
- How can we ensure access of the nonoffending guardians to their removed children?
- How can we maintain the safety and wellbeing of the removed children?
- How can necessary interventions reduce anxiety experienced by victims?
- How can we intervene with all identified offenders?
- How can the courts protect the rights of the victims and their families with the same vigor that they protect the rights of the accused?
- How can we effectively identify and treat sexually aggressive children and adolescents?
- How can we effectively target some of the sociocultural factors that create an environment in which child sexual abuse thrives?
- How can we effectively target the reduction of offending behaviors?

Because of the many questions that need to be addressed, members of this task force should represent many different disciplines, philosophies, and orientations. There are many outstanding professionals in this field working towards a better future for our children. Some work inside the system, whereas others work outside the system, yet both offer essential views for this forward-thinking task. As a young field, many of its leaders have worked in it since the early 1980s and sometimes earlier. They would bring the history and the voice of experience to this task force. We should also not forget those new thinkers who have come into the field more recently and who perhaps have a different view. They also have much to offer.

There are also the many different perspectives that should have a voice within this task force. One of the most important groups may be the feminists with their essential understanding of sociocultural effects of living within a patriarchal world. Theirs is a voice that cannot be diminished at this table. Other voices that should be heard are the empiricists, the developmentalists, the sociologists who understand the trends within society, the policy analysts, and the legal experts who can offer guidance on the bounds of the law. Bringing together the voices of the protagonists and antagonists is also important. There are so many who should be at this table, including those who represent the different cultures and socioeconomic groups. Their special task is to ensure that the ideas brought forward from this group are sensitive to the needs of all families and all children.

Perhaps the most essential voice at this table, however, is that of the survivors. The backlash has gone far to silence their voices, returning in many ways to the days of psychoanalytic thought in which victims who dared to disclose were considered to be as guilty as—indeed more guilty than—the offender. Yet, their perspective and experience with the system are critical to developing an effective response. Adult survivors of childhood sexual abuse who were never identified as victims, as well as those who were identified, offer critical perspectives. Nonoffending guardians can also speak for youthful victims identified by the system. Their often harsh experiences within the system offer important lessons. Thus, the voices of the victims and their loved ones must be lifted up within this task force.

With this task force comprised of some of the best minds in the country and focused on the task of developing a future response to the problem of child sexual abuse, we will then have a model with which to move forward. The next task of this or an equivalent task force is then to determine steps for making the transition from the current system to the new system. Needless to say, this is as critical as the forward-thinking task of the previous group. While this is a process that will take time, it is a necessary process for ensuring a system that works.

CONCLUSION

In Chapter 1 of this book, an analogy of a jigsaw puzzle was used to describe the differences between the empirical knowledge base and the system's policies and programs. The jigsaw puzzle representing the system's policies and programs was incomplete, with many of the exterior pieces still missing and large gaps in the interior. The many pieces missing from this puzzle represented the numerous victims that go unrecognized by the current system. Further, pieces were still so poorly placed inside this puzzle that the picture itself remained almost unrecognizable. The jigsaw puzzle representing the empirical knowledge base, however, was much better constructed. While a number of pieces were still missing, the emergent pattern had coherence and continuity. Yet, the emerging picture of the empirical knowledge base in this puzzle bore little resemblance to the picture of the existing policies and programs in the previous puzzle.

This is the message of this book: Our current approach to targeting the problem of child sexual abuse is doomed. It fails because it tries to solve a problem whose scope is different from the problem of child sexual abuse as defined by the empirical knowledge base. Thus, our system identifies far too few victims of abuse, reports far too few case of suspected abuse, substantiates far too few cases of identified abuse, convicts far too few identified offenders, charges far too many nonoffending mothers as offenders or as unfit, removes far too many children, and allows far too many offenders to retain access to the victim. This is a system that has failed in its entirety.

To move forward requires that we destroy the jigsaw puzzle representing our programs and policies and begin anew. The good news is that the picture representing our empirical knowledge base can act as a mirror for our reconstructed puzzle. The bad news is that little of the puzzle representing our programs and policies can be salvaged. To reconstruct our programs and policies will require our best minds and our best efforts. We have far to go, but our empirical knowledge base provides us with a roadmap. Now we must define the steps for getting from here to there. To do so, however, will require the efforts of not only our professionals, but also our politicians, our media, our communities, and those who live within these communities.

Thus, changes will be hard and will occur only over a long period of time. Yet, changes can come and they must come. It is our children's futures and their children's futures with which we are gambling. It is time to provide what the youth of our nation deserve—a society committed and impelled to take action for their safety and protection.

EPILOGUE
IT TAKES A VILLAGE

With one of this book's primary purposes being to explicate the incredible scope of the problem of child sexual abuse, I found myself again and again struggling with its magnitude. As both a professional and parent, I often despaired at the enormity of this societally imposed calamity and at the threat it poses to my children and the children of our nation. To cope, I would detach emotionally as I did my work. Yet, even with this protection, two portions of this book recently broke through my defensive detachment, overwhelming me with the sheer tragedy and immensity of the problem.

First, as I worked on the chapter on offenders (Chapter 9), I needed to know how many offenders were actually identified, convicted, and prosecuted. Gathering the applicable studies, I made the necessary computations. Yet, I simply was not ready for the answer. How can our society allow more than 90% of offenders to remain within the child's environment or to return within the year? It seems incredible. And even as I write these words, a case of child sexual abuse was recently reported in the media in which the offender picked the child up off the street and molested him while brandishing a weapon. The presiding judge, however, believing that the case was not severe enough to warrant incarceration, placed the offender on probation. Thus, until evicted by the housing authority, the offender continued to live in a complex, within the victim's environment, that housed many other young children. Not surprisingly, the reaction of the public and media to this event was outrage. How could this judge possibly allow this offender to go free? And yet my calculations suggest that the vast majority of identified offenders are allowed to remain within the child's environment or to return within the year. How can this be?

The second finding for which I was simply unprepared was the number of nonoffending mothers who continue to be charged as co-offenders. While the only previous study reporting this information found that an extraordinarily high percentage of mothers were charged as co-offenders, this study was done in 1981 (Finkelhor & Hotaling, 1984). Surely, a society moving into the 21st Century had given up this barbaric practice. Then, just within the last few months, the latest NCANDS national incidence study reported information not published in its previous annual studies (U.S. Department of Health and Human Services, 2000c). This report found that mothers were charged as either offenders or co-offenders by child protective services in 53% of all abuse by parents. It is difficult to find the emotional detachment necessary to distance myself from this knowledge.

In my work with other professionals, however, and while writing the chapter on the professional response to child sexual abuse, I was struck many times by the intent and purpose of exceptional professionals who have devoted their professional careers to the problem of child sexual abuse. Indeed, this book is only possible because researchers have worked to develop a professional body of empirical literature on child sexual abuse that is now extensive. These researchers, as well as clinicians, lawyers, law enforcement agents, and others move me to hope that the scope of the problem of child sexual abuse will someday be so diminished that it will not require an army of professionals to respond to it.

As such, this epilogue acknowledges both my despair and my hope. The first section, by discussing prerequisites that may be necessary for effectively responding to the problem, pays tribute to the despair. The second section, by providing one perspective for what an effective response to child sexual abuse might be within our future society, pays tribute to the hope.

PREREQUISITES FOR TARGETING CHILD SEXUAL ABUSE

To effectively target an epidemic often requires changes on the part of all members of society, who must buy in to the need for addressing the epidemic. Yet, today's social milieu is not one in which most Americans will willingly commit to some of the changes in socialization patterns or the power structure that will be necessary for substantially reducing the problem of child sexual abuse. Thus, this section considers possible prerequisites for a receptive society. These prerequisites represent roadblocks to reaching a goal of the drastic reduction of child sexual abuse.

The first proposed prerequisite may be that the level of violence within society must become intolerable. We remain a nation of more than 200 million guns, nearly one gun for every adult and child. We are not only the most violent industrialized society in the world, but our homicide rates are two to 10 times higher than rates in other developed countries.[1] To reduce the level of violence will require the nation, the media, the institutions within society, and most Americans to embrace the belief that we have the right, and even demand the right, to live in a violence-free nation. Because sexual abuse is in many ways a violent act and one that is endorsed more frequently by those who also endorse interpersonal violence (Briere & Runtz, 1989), the prevalence of sexual abuse may not decrease until Americans commit to living within a safer society.

The second prerequisite may be that society must become more child-centered. While our words and the words of our leaders often suggest that we are child-centered, it is difficult to concur when a fifth or more of all children live in poverty (Betson & Michael, 1997). And with our mainly puritan backgrounds, we are still a country that endorses the ownership of children and the parental right and privilege to use corporal punishment. As long as we are a country that believes in the ownership of children, they will remain at risk for abuses of power over them.

The third prerequisite may be a far less patriarchal society. Sexual abuse remains primarily a gendered abuse of females by males. While not wishing to ignore the unfortunate male victims nor the few female offenders, the beliefs and value systems of male privilege and domination remain probably the single most important causal factors for child sexual abuse. Until males are willing to cede some of that power and to take responsibility for their abuses of that power, and until these abuses of power are recognized as violent actions, child sexual abuse may remain a significant problem.

The final prerequisite for decreasing the prevalence of child sexual abuse may be a public so outraged about the problem that our nation becomes intolerant of the

---

[1] *www.soros.org/crime/gunreport.htm.*

sexual abuse of any child. With this level of public outrage, the media may finally be influenced to stop highlighting sexual victimization, sensationalizing male privilege, and sexualizing children.

If these are the prerequisites, then we are many years away from being able to substantially reduce the problem of child sexual abuse, for we are still too violence-prone and violence-proud. It may take years of violent deaths of our children and youth for society to become fed up with its self-induced calamity. The violence will also likely have to move into the middle-class and affluent sections with as much ferocity as it plagues some of the lives of those without before those with power add their voices to the fight for change. It will also take time for us to adopt our nation's children as our own so that we become intolerant of the harm not only to our own children, but to our neighbor's, and even those children who represent our differences instead of our similarities. And surely it will take time for the powerful to cede their power for the good of the people. Thus, major change is probably many years away. Yet, we must hope that the time will come when simply being a child, or worse being a girl, will not be a significant risk factor for child sexual abuse.

A LOOK INTO THE FUTURE

And when we have arrived—when we live in a society that is fully focused on reducing the tragedy of child sexual abuse—what would that response be? This section suggests one possibility. As such, it represents the ever-present hope for a better future.

First, the people in this future society would lead the battle, for mothers and fathers, as well as their schools and communities, would demand protection for their children. Most individuals would have a working knowledge of the prevalence and risk factors associated with child sexual abuse, as well as its effects. Armed with that knowledge, survivor-led grassroots organizations would advocate for the protection of children. Knowing that they must represent the people to stay in office, politicians would also trumpet the cause. Mothers and fathers would also take responsibility for socializing their children differently, especially their boys, conscientiously parenting them in ways that would not perpetuate messages that provide children with implicit permission to be sexually aggressive.

Curriculum-based prevention programs would be in all schools for all grade levels. Not only would these programs teach young children about the rights they have over their bodies, but they would also teach children about the boundaries of appropriate behavior with others. These programs would be neither harsh nor punitive, but would simply be another focal point for moving society's young from childhood to adulthood. The media would support these programs, and male domination, the sexualization of children, and sexual aggressiveness would no longer be premium fare for prime-time viewing. Many other community-based programs would also be in place to prevent child sexual abuse, including regular screening for previous or ongoing sexual abuse.

Offenders would also be treated very differently. While a dominantly punitive model such as exists today would remain in place for repeat offenders, mandated treatment or reparative justice programs would be required for all first-time offenders in addition to any other type of punishment. Recognizing, however, that male children and adolescents have been socialized into sexually aggressive behaviors, specialized programs would be in place to identify and treat young offenders. Treatment would be especially sensitive to young sexually abused offenders. Further, recognizing the important sociocultural context of their abusive behaviors, the criminal justice system would treat youthful offenders very differently. Thus, a two-tiered system, based upon the age of the offender and circumstances of the abuse, would be in place for offenders.

The system of protecting children from known offenders would also be more sophisticated. Reports of suspected intrafamilial and extrafamilial abuse would be made to community-based, multidisciplinary advocacy sites where teams comprised of highly trained, licensed professionals with graduate-level degrees would be assigned to each case. The decision to investigate would be made jointly by team members, based at least in part on probability data. For example, reports of abuse made within custody or divorce disputes would almost certainly be investigated because of their probability of occurrence and the high costs associated with false negatives (i.e., determining that abuse did not occur when it actually did). Investigations, conducted by this same team of professionals, would also be more sophisticated. A central goal of this investigative phase would be to determine whether abuse was occurring, while also protecting the rights of the accused. More sophisticated techniques might also ensure less invasion of privacy during the investigation.

When children making disclosures identified specific offenders or abuse was strongly suspected but had not yet been proven conclusively, individuals suspected of committing the abuse would be asked to remove themselves from the children's premises for the length of the investigation. Temporary living quarters would be provided for them if needed. If they refused, then the victim's family would be moved into a safe house for the length of the investigation. Once abuse was determined to have occurred, the case would immediately be brought before a special court to determine whether enough evidence existed to order the alleged offender to be removed from the child's environment and to be monitored. This court would not have the power to convict—only to protect the victim.

Technological advances might also allow much more effective monitoring. Future systems might monitor proximity between individuals, thus providing victims with more protection against repeated abuse by an offender. Future monitoring systems might also be designed such that they (a) would not infringe upon the rights of the accused unless they violated court orders; (b) would offer protection to the victim; and (c) would eliminate the need to make nonoffending guardians responsible for the protection of the victim, while providing law enforcement with the technology necessary to enforce this protection. Thus, for example, location sensor devices might only note the location of offenders who were within a certain proximity of the victim or near an area with many children, such as schools or parks. In this way, the rights of both the victims and offenders could be protected.

Removals would be rare, but when necessary, the child would be placed in a therapeutic foster home in which the foster parent was a specially trained para-professional whose sole job was the caretaking of a single child (or children if multiple children were removed from a single family) for as long as that child was out of the home. Even when children were removed, nonoffending guardians would have ongoing supervised access to their children. In the even rarer cases in which nonoffending guardians were deemed unfit for parenting, the children would remain with this foster parent until they were adopted. Sexually aggressive children would also be placed by themselves in therapeutic foster homes with paraprofessionals where one-on-one attention was available.

In the many more instances in which children were not removed from the home, their treatment team would be comprised of the interdisciplinary professionals plus all significant nonoffending legal guardians. Together, this team would consider the unique concerns for the child and family in planning the treatment strategy. Treatment might utilize traditional modes of treatment, resource acquisition, advocacy, or any of a variety of more creative strategies such as live-in assistance. Nonoffending guardians would be consulted about all options, and decisions would be made about the child's welfare only in consultation with them. All victims and their nonoffending guardians and siblings would have access to necessary treatment.

These ideas are projections about what an effective response to child sexual abuse might be when society is fully committed to protecting all children and ending child sexual abuse. Two statements can be made with more certainty, however. First, the future effective response to child sexual abuse will be far different than the current response. Second, technological advances that we might only dream of today may change the way that child sexual abuse is identified and prevented.

IT TAKES A VILLAGE

There are reasons to hope, but there are also reasons to despair. Far too few children are adequately identified within the current system, whereas far too many offenders go free. Consequently, far too many nonoffending mothers are considered co-offenders, and far too many children are removed from their homes. The current backlash has also succeeded in silencing far too many victims, suggesting, as did Freud, that they are hysterically recounting fabrications of abuse. Thus, there are many reasons to despair not only of the tragedy of child sexual abuse, but also of the problems within the current system, society's reception to the victims, and the slowness with which change comes.

Yet, there are reasons to hope. Because society's response to child sexual abuse has been cyclical (Olafson, Corwin, & Summit, 1993), there should come a time when society is more willing to consider its shadow side and to make changes for the protection of its children. When that occurs, however, the army of professionals currently in place will probably not be sufficient to mount and maintain lasting changes. Instead, it may take a village of professionals, the media, politicians, and even communities. The battle may even be led by citizens, for until they become sufficiently informed about the problem, they may not be sufficiently outraged to demand changes. Thus, child sexual abuse may only be reduced when parents react with such outrage over the loss or threat of loss of their children's innocence that they demand changes—when mothers and fathers, as well as schools, churches, and communities, are willing to socialize their young males differently. Lasting change may require the media to become responsible to the communities it serves and the power structure to yield its power over the less empowered and to share its power. Then, and only then, may there be enough momentum to adequately target the epidemic of child sexual abuse.

Thus, change will only come slowly, so slowly that our children's generation will probably not reap the benefits. Perhaps, though, their children—or surely their children's children—can live in a society in which child sexual abuse prevention programs are no longer common fare in school; in which we do not have to instruct our children to be wary of strangers or even of loved ones; when we can safely allow our children to go to their friend's houses or to walk to and from school; when we do not have to hear the anguished narratives of adult survivors or those heartrending stories of small victims.

It is with this hope that this book concludes—that we can someday provide a nation for our youth that is free of sexual violence. It cannot come soon enough.

REFERENCES

Abbott, B. R. (1995). Some family considerations in assessment and case management of intrafamilial child sexual abuse. In T. Ney (Ed.), *True and false allegations of child sexual abuse: Assessment and case management* (pp. 260-274). New York: Brunner/Mazel.

Abel, G. G., Becker, J. V., Cunningham-Rathner, J., Mittleman, M., & Rouleau, J. L. (1988a). Multiple paraphilic diagnoses among sex offender. *Bulletin of the American Academy of Psychiatry and Law, 16*, 153-168.

Abel, G. G., Becker, J. V., Mittleman, M., Cunningham-Rathner, J., Rouleau, J. L., & Murphy, W. D. (1987). Self-reported sex crimes of non-incarcerated paraphiliacs. *Journal of Interpersonal Violence, 2*(1), 3-25.

Abel, G. G., Mittelman, M., Becker, J. V., Rathner, J., & Rouleau, J. L. (1988b). Predicting child molesters' response to treatment. In R. A. Prentky & V. L. Quinsey (Eds.), *Human sexual aggression: Current perspectives* (pp. 223-234). New York: New York Academy of Sciences.

Abma, J. C., Chandra, A., Mosher, W. D., Peterson, L. S., & Piccinino, L. J. (1997). *Fertility, family planning, and women's health: New data from the 1995 National Survey of Family Growth* (Series 23 , No. 19). Hyattsville, MD: U.S. Department of Health and Human Services.

Adler, N. A., & Schutz, J. (1995). Sibling incest offenders. *Child Abuse & Neglect, 19*(7), 811-819.

Ageton, S. S. (1983). *Sexual assault among adolescents.* Lexington, MA: Lexington Books.

Ageton, S. S. (1988). Vulnerability to sexual assault. In A. W. Burgess (Ed.), *Rape and sexual assault: III. A research handbook* (Vol. 3, pp. 221-243). New York: Garland Publishing.

Alexander, P. C. (1985). A systems theory conceptualization of incest. *Family Process, 24*, 79-88.

Alexander, P. C. (1992). Application of attachment theory to the study of sexual abuse. *Journal of Consulting and Clinical Psychology, 60*, 185-195.

Alexander, P. C., & Anderson, C. L. (1998). Incest, attachment, and developmental psychopathology. In D. Cicchetti, & S. L. Toth (Eds.), *Developmental perspectives on trauma: Theory, research, and intervention: Vol. 8. Rochester Symposium on Developmental Psychopathology* (pp. 348-378). Rochester, NY: University of Rochester Press.

Alexander, P. C., & Lupfer, S. L. (1987). Family characteristics and long-term consequences associated with sexual abuse. *Archives of Sexual Behavior, 16*(3), 235-245.

Alexander, P. C., & Schaeffer, C. M. (1994). A typology of incestuous families based on cluster analysis. *Journal of Family Psychology, 8*(4), 458-470.

American Association of University Women (1991). *Shortchanging girls, shortchanging America.* Washington, DC: Author.

American Professional Society on the Abuse of Children (1997). Psychosocial evaluation of suspected sexual abuse in children (2nd ed.). Author.

American Psychiatric Association (1994). *Diagnostic and statistical manual of mental disorders* (4th ed.). Washington, DC: Author.

American Psychological Association (1985). *Standards for educational and psychological testing.* Washington, DC: Author.

Anderson, E. M., & Levine, M. (1999). Concerns about allegations of child sexual abuse against teachers and the teaching environment. *Child Abuse & Neglect, 23*(8), 833-843.

Anderson, L. M., & Shafer, G. (1979). The character-disordered family: A community treatment model for family sexual abuse. *American Journal of Orthopsychiatry, 49*(3), 436-445.

Araji, S., & Finkelhor, D. A. (1986). Abusers: A review of the research. In D. Finkelhor (Ed.), *A sourcebook on child sexual abuse.* Beverly Hills, CA: Sage.

Armstrong, L. (1996). In the footsteps of Doctor Freud and down the proverbial garden path. *Feminism & Psychology, 6*(2), 298-303.

Armsworth, M. W. (1989). Therapy of incest survivors: Abuse or support? *Child Abuse & Neglect, 13*, 549-562.

Armsworth, M. W. (1990). A qualitative analysis of adult incest survivors' responses to sexual involvement with therapists. *Child Abuse and Neglect, 14*, 541-554.

Arroyo, J. A., Simpson, T. L., & Aragon, A. S. (1997). Childhood sexual abuse among Hispanic and non-Hispanic White college women. *Hispanic Journal of Behavioral Sciences, 19*(1), 57-68.

Attias, R., & Goodwin, J. (1985). Knowledge and management strategies in incest cases: A survey of physicians, psychologists and family counselors. *Child Abuse & Neglect, 9*, 527-533.

Attridge, M., & Berscheid, E. (1994). Entitlement in romantic relationships in the United States: A social-exchange perspective. In M. J. Lerner & G. Mikula (Eds.), *Entitlement and the affectional bond: Justice in close relationships. Critical issues in social justice* (pp. 117-147). New York: Plenum Press.

Bagley, C., & Ramsay, R. (1986). Sexual abuse in childhood: Psychosocial outcomes and implications for social work practice. *Journal of Social Work & Human Sexuality, 4*, 33-47.

Bagley, C., Wood, M., & Young, L. (1994). Victim to abuser: Mental health and behavioral sequels of child sexual abuse in a community survey of young adult males. *Child Abuse & Neglect, 18*(8), 683-697.

Baldwin, A. L., Baldwin, C., & Cole, R. E. (1990). Stress-resistant families and stress-resistant children. In J. Rolf, A. S. Masten, D. Cicchetti, K. H. Neuchterlein, & S. Weintraub (Eds.), *Risk and protective factors in the development of psychopathology* (pp. 257-280). New York: Cambridge University Press.

Ballard, D. T., Blair, G. D., Devereaux, S., Valentine, L. K., Horton, A. L., & Johnson, B. L. (1990). A comparative profile of the incest perpetrator: Background characteristics, abuse history, and use of social skills. In A. L. Horton., B. L. Johnson, L. M. Roundy, & D. Williams (Eds.), *The incest perpetrator: A family member no one wants to trust* (pp. 43-64). Newbury Park, CA: Sage.

Barbaree, H. E., & Marshall, W. L. (1989). Erectile responses among heterosexual child molesters, father-daughter incest offenders, and matched non-offenders: Five distinct age preference profiles. *Canadian Journal of Behavioral Sciences, 21*(1), 70-82.

Bartholomew, K., & Horowitz, L. M. (1991). Attachment styles among young adults: A test of a four-category model. *Journal of Personality and Social Psychology, 61*, 236-244.

Beck, J. C., & van der Kolk, B. (1987). Reports of childhood incest and current behavior of chronically hospitalized psychotic women. *American Journal of Psychiatry, 144*(11), 1474-1476.

Becker, J. V. (1994). Offenders: Characteristics and treatment. *The Future of Children, 4*(2), 176-197.

Beckett, K. (1996). Culture and the politics of signification: The case of child sexual abuse. *Social Problems, 43*(1), 57-76.

Belsky, J. (1980). Child maltreatment: An ecological integration. *American Psychologist, 35*, 320-335.

Bender, L., & Blau, A. (1937). The reaction of children to sexual relations with adults. *American Journal of Orthopsychiatry, 7*, 500-518.

Bender, L., & Grugett, A. E. (1952). A follow-up report on children who had atypical sexual experience. *American Journal of Orthopsychiatry, 22*, 825-837.

Benedek, E. P., & Schetky, D. H. (1985). Allegations of sexual abuse in child custody and visitation disputes. In D. H. Schetky & E. P. Benedek (Eds.), *Emerging issues in child psychiatry and the law* (pp. 145-156). New York: Brunner/Mazel.

Bentovim, A. (1991). Clinical work with families in which sexual abuse has occurred. In C. R. Hollin & K. Howells (Eds.), *Clinical approaches to sex offenders and their victims* (pp. 179-208). New York: John Wiley & Sons.

Berland, D. I., & Guskin, K. (1994). Patient allegations of sexual abuse against psychiatric hospital staff. *General Hospital Psychiatry, 16*, 335-339.

Berliner, L., & Conte, J. R. (1993). Sexual abuse evaluations: Conceptual and empirical obstacles. *Child Abuse & Neglect, 17*, 111-125.

Berliner, L., & Conte, J. R. (1995). The effects of disclosure and intervention on sexually abused children. *Child Abuse & Neglect, 19*(3), 371-384.

Berliner, L., & Saunders, B. E. (1996). Treating fear and anxiety in sexually abused children: Results of a controlled 2-year follow-up study. *Child Maltreatment, 1*(4), 294-309.

Berson, N. L. Herman-Giddens, M. E., & Frothingham, T. E. (1993). Children's perceptions of genital examinations during sexual abuse evaluations. *Child Welfare, 72*(1), 41-49.

Betson, D. M., & Michael, R. T. (1997). Why so many children are poor. *The Future of Children, 7*(2).

Birns, B., & Meyer, S. L. (1993). Mothers' role in incest: Dysfunctional women or dysfunctional theories? *Journal of Child Sexual Abuse, 2*(3), 127-135.

Blauner, R. (1972). *Racial oppression in America*: New York: Harper & Row.

Blumenthal, S., Gudjonsson, G., & Burns, J. (1999). Cognitive distortions and blame attribution in sex offenders against adults and children. *Child Abuse & Neglect, 23*(2), 129-143.

Boat, B. W., & Everson, M. D. (1988). Use of the anatomical dolls among professionals in sexual abuse allegations. *Child Abuse & Neglect, 12*, 171-179.

Boat, B. W., & Everson, M. D. (1996). Concerning practices of interviewers when using anotomical dolls in child protective services investigations. *Child Maltreatment, 1*(2), 96-104.

Bolen, B. (1996). *Secondary analysis of Russell's community prevalence study of child sexual abuse*. Final report. Submitted to National Center for Child Abuse and Neglect. (Grant no. 90CA1537).

Bolen, R. M. (1998a). *Development of an ecological/transactional model of sexual abuse victimization and analysis of its nomological classification system*. Dissertation Abstracts International, 59(9), 3645. (University Microfilms No. 9904160).

Bolen, R. M. (1998b). Predicting risk to be sexually abused: A comparison of logistic regression to event history analysis. *Child Maltreatment, 3*(2), 157-170.

Bolen, R. M. (2000a). Extrafamilial child sexual abuse: A study of perpetrator characteristics and implications for prevention. *Violence Against Women, 6*(10), 1137-1169.

Bolen, R. M. (2000b). *Support of nonoffending guardians of sexually abused children: A review*. Manuscript submitted for publication.

Bolen, R. M. (2000c). Validity of attachment theory. *Trauma, Violence, & Abuse, 1*(2), 128-153.

Bolen, R. M. (in press). Child sexual abuse: Prevention or promotion. *Social Work.*

Bolen, R. M., Lamb, J. L., & Grandante, J. (2000). *The Needs-based Assessment of Parental (Guardian) Support: A test of its validity and reliability*. Manuscript submitted for publication.

Bolen, R. M., & Scannapieco, M. (1999). Prevalence of child sexual abuse: A corrective metanalysis. *Social Service Review, 73*(3), 281-313.

Bowlby, J. (1969). *Attachment*. New York: Basic Books.

Bowlby, J. (1973). *Separation*. New York: Basic Books.

Bowlby, J. (1980). *Loss*. New York: Basic Books.

Bowlby, J. (1988). *A secure base: Parent-child attachment and healthy human development*. New York: Basic Books.

Bradshaw, T. L., & Marks, A. E. (1990). Beyond a reasonable doubt: Factors that influence the legal disposition of child sexual abuse cases. *Crime and Delinquency, 36*(2), 276-285.

Brandcraft, B., & Stolorow, R. D. (1984). A current perspective on difficult patients. In P. E. Stepansky & A. Goldberg (Eds.), *Kohut's legacy: Contributions to self psychology* (pp. 93-115). Hillsdale, NJ: Analytic Press.

Breckenridge, J., & Baldry, E. (1997). Workers dealing with mother blame in child sexual assault cases. *Journal of Child Sexual Abuse, 6*(1), 65-80.

Brewer, K. D., Rowe, D. M., & Brewer, D. D. (1997). Factors related to prosecution of child sexual abuse cases. *Journal of Child Sexual Abuse, 6*(1), 91-111.

Briere, J. (1992). Methodological issues in the study of sexual abuse effects. *Journal of Consulting and Clinical Psychology, 60*(2), 196-203.

Briere, J., & Conte, J. R. (1993). Self-reported amnesia for abuse in adults molested as children. *Journal of Traumatic Stress, 6*(1), 21-31.

Briere, J., & Elliot, D. M. (1993). Sexual abuse, family environment, and psychological symptoms: On the validity of statistical control. *Journal of Consulting and Clinical Psychology, 61*, 284-288.

Briere, J., & Runtz, M. (1989). University males' sexual interest in children: Predicting potential indices of "pedophilia" in a nonforensic sample. *Child Abuse & Neglect, 13*, 65-75.

Briere, J., & Zaidi, L. Y. (1989). Sexual abuse histories and sequelae in female psychiatric emergency room patients. *American Journal of Psychiatry, 146*(12), 1602-1606.

Bronfenbrenner, U. (1977). Toward an experimental ecology of human development. *American Psychologist, 32*, 513-31.

Brownmiller, S. (1975). *Against our will*. New York: Simon & Schuster.

Bryer, J. B., Nelson, B. A., Miller, J. B., & Krol, P. A. (1987). Childhood sexual and physical abuse as factors in adult psychiatric illness. *American Journal of Psychiatry, 144*(11), 1426-1430.

Budin, L. E., & Johnson, C. F. (1989). Sex abuse prevention programs: Offenders' attitudes about their efficacy. *Child Abuse & Neglect, 13*, 77-87.

Bulkley, J. A., Feller, J. N., Stern, P., & Roe, R. (1996). Child abuse and neglect laws and legal proceedings. In J. Briere, L. Berliner, J. A. Bulkley, C. Jenny, & T. Reid (Eds.), *The APSAC handbook on child maltreatment* (pp. 271-296). Thousand Oaks, CA: Sage.

Bureau of Justice (1994). *Uniform Crime Reports for the United States*. Washington, DC: U.S. Department of Justice.

Cantwell, H. B. (1981). Sexual abuse of children in Denver, 1979: Reviewed with implications for pediatric intervention and possible prevention. *Child Abuse & Neglect, 5*, 75-85.

Carlson, V., Cicchetti, D., Barnett, D., & Braunwald, K. (1989). Disorganized/ disoriented attachment relationships in maltreatment infants. *Developmental Psychology, 25*, 525-531.

Carmen, E. H., Rieker, P. P., & Mills, T. (1984). Victims of violence and psychiatric illness. *American Journal of Psychiatry, 141*(3), 378-383.

Carper, J. M. (1979). Emergencies in adolescents: Runaways and father-daughter incest. *Pediatric Clinics of North America, 26*(4), 883-894.

Carson, D. K., Gertz, L. M., Donaldson, M. A., & Wonderlich, S. A. (1990). Family-of-origin characteristics and current family relationships of female adult incest victims. *Journal of Family Violence, 5*(2), 153-171.

Carter, B., Papp, P., Silverstein, O., & Walters, M. (1986). The procrustean bed. *Family Process, 2*, 301-304.

Cauce, A.M., Reid, M., Landesman, S., & Gonzales, N. (1990). Social support in young children: Measurement, structure, and behavioral impact. In B.R. Sarason, I. G. Sarason, & G. R. Pierce (Eds.), *Social support: An interactional view* (pp. 64-94). New York: John Wiley & Sons.

Cicchetti, D., & Lynch, M. (1993). Toward an ecological/transactional model of community violence and child maltreatment: Consequences for children's development. *Psychiatry, 56*, 96-118.

Cicchetti, D., & Rizley, R. (1981). Developmental perspectives on the etiology, intergenerational transmission, and sequelae of child maltreatment. *New Directions for Child Development, 11*, 31-55.

Cluff, R. B., Hicks, M. W., & Madsen, C. H. (1994). Beyond the circumplex model: I: A moratorium on curvilinearity. *Family Process, 33*, 455-470.

Cohen, J., & Cohen, P. (1983). *Applied multiple regression/correlation analysis for the behavioral science.* (2nd ed.). Hillsdale, NJ: Lawrence Erlbaum.

Cohen, T. (1983). The incestuous family revisited. *Social Casework, 64*, 154-161.

Cole, E. (1982). Sibling incest: The myth of benign sibling incest. *Women in Therapy,* 1(3), 79-89.

Cole, P. M., Woolger, C., Power, T. G., & Smith, K. D. (1992). Parenting difficulties among adult survivors of father-daughter incest. *Child Abuse & Neglect, 16*, 239-249.

Cole, P. M., & Putnam, F. W. (1992). Effect of incest on self and social functioning: A developmental psychopathology perspective. *Journal of Consulting and Clinical Psychology,* 60(2), 174-184.

Coleman, H., & Collins, D. (1990). Treatment trilogy of father-daughter incest. *Child & Adolescent Social Work, 7*(4), 339-355.

Conte, J. R. (1991). Child sexual abuse: Looking forward and backward. In M. C. Patton (Ed.), *Family sexual abuse: Frontline research and evaluation* (pp. 3-22). Newbury Park, CA: Sage.

Conte, J. R., Fogarty, L., & Collins, M. E. (1991). National survey of professional practice in child sexual abuse. *Journal of Family Violence, 6*(2), 149-166.

Conte, J. R., Sorenson, E., Fogarty, L., & Rosa, J. D. (1991). Evaluating children's reports of sexual abuse: Results from a survey of professionals. *American Journal of Orthopsychiatry, 61*(3), 428-437.

Conte, J. R., Wolf, S., & Smith, T. (1989). What sexual offenders tell us about prevention strategies. *Child Abuse & Neglect, 13*, 293-301.

Cook, T. D., & Campbell, D. T. (1976). The design and conduct of quasi-experiments and true experiments in field settings, *Handbook of industrial and organizational psychology* (pp. 223-325). Chicago: Rand McNally.

Craine, L. S., Henson, C. E., Colliver, J. A., & MacLean, D. G. (1988). Prevalence of a history of sexual abuse among female psychiatric patients in a state hospital system. *Hospital and Community Psychiatry, 39*(3), 300-304.

Crenshaw, W. B., Lichtenberg, J. W., & Bartell, P. A. (1993). Mental health providers and child sexual abuse: A multivariate analysis of the decision to report. *Journal of Child Sexual Abuse, 2*(4), 19-42.

Cross, T. P., De Vos, E., & Whitcomb, D. (1994). Prosecution of child sexual abuse: Which cases are accepted? *Child Abuse & Neglect, 18*(8), 663-667.

Cross, T. P., Martell, D., McDonald, E., & Ahl, M. (1999). The criminal justice system and child placement in child sexual abuse cases. *Child Maltreatment, 4*(1), 32-44.

Cross, T. P., Whitcomb, D., & De Vos, E. (1995). Criminal justice outcomes of prosecution of child sexual abuse: A case flow analysis. *Child Abuse & Neglect, 19*(12), 1431-1442.

Cunningham, J. (1988). Contributions to the history of psychology: l. French historical views on the acceptability of evidence regarding child sexual abuse. *Psychological Reports, 63*, 343-53.

Cupoli, J. M., & Sewell, P. M. (1988). One thousand fifty-nine children with a chief complaint of sexual abuse. *Child Abuse & Neglect, 12*, 151-162.

Dadds, M., Smith, M., Webber, Y., & Robinson, A. (1991). An exploration of family and individual profiles following father-daughter incest. *Child Abuse & Neglect, 15*, 575-586.

Davis, G. E., & Leitenberg, H. (1987). Adolescent sex offenders. *Psychological Bulletin, 101*, 417-427.

Deblinger, E., Lippmann, J., Stauffer, L., & Finkel, M. (1994). Personal versus professional responses to child sexual abuse allegations. *Child Abuse & Neglect, 18*(8), 679-682.

De Jong, A. R. (1988). Maternal responses to the sexual abuse of their children. *Pediatrics, 81*(1), 14-21.

De Jong, A. R. (1989). Sexual interactions among siblings and cousins: Experimentation or exploitation? *Child Abuse & Neglect, 13*, 271-279.

De Jong, A. R. (1998). Impact of child sexual abuse medical examinations on the dependency and criminal systems. *Child Abuse & Neglect, 22*(6), 645-652.

deMause, L. (1974). The evolution of childhood. In L. deMause (Ed.), *The history of childhood*. New York: Psychohistory Press.

deMause, L. (1988). On writing childhood history. *The Journal of Psychohistory, 16*(2), 135-171.

Dempster, H. L., & Roberts, J. (1991). Child sexual abuse research: A methodological quagmire. *Child Abuse and Neglect, 15*(4), 593-595.

Dersch, C. A., & Munsch, J. (1999). Male victims of sexual abuse: An analysis of substantiation of Child Protective Services reports. *Journal of Child Sexual Abuse, 8*(1), 27-48.

DeYoung, M. (1981). Case reports: The sexual exploitation of incest victims by helping professionals. *Victimology, 6*(1-4), 92-101.

Dietz, C. A., & Craft, J. L. (1980). Family dynamics of incest: A new perspective. *Social Casework, 61*(10), 602-609.

Dill, D. L., Chu, J. A., Grob, M. C., & Eisen, S. V. (1991). The reliability of abuse history reports: A comparison of two inquiry formats. *Comprehensive Psychiatry, 32*(2), 166-169.

Dinsmore, C. (1991). *From surviving to thriving: Incest, feminism, and recovery.* New York: State University of New York Press.

Dolmage, W. R. (1995). Accusations of teacher sexual abuse of students in Ontario schools: Some preliminary findings. *The Alberta Journal of Educational Research, 56*(2), 127-144.

Dominelli, L. (1989). Betrayal of trust: A feminist analysis of power relationships in incest abuse and its relevance for social work practice. *British Social Work Journal, 19*, 291-307.

Downing, J. D., Wells, S. J., & Fluke, J. (1990). Gatekeeping in child protective services: A survey of screening policies. *Child Welfare, 69*(4), 357-369.

Draucker, C. B. (1996). Family-of-origin variables and adult female survivors of childhood sexual abuse: A review of the research. *Journal of Child Sexual Abuse, 5*(4), 35-63.

Driver, E. (1989). Introduction. In E. Driver & A. Droisen (Eds.), *Child sexual abuse: A feminist reader* (pp. 1-68). New York: New York University Press.

Dube, R., & Hebert, M. (1988). Sexual abuse of children under 12 years of age: A review of 511 cases. *Child Abuse & Neglect, 12*(3), 321-330.

Duvall, E. M. (1985). *Marriage and family development* (6th ed.). New York: Harper and Row.

Eckenrode, J., Powers, J., Doris, J., Munsch, J., & Bolger, N. (1988). Substantiation of child abuse and neglect reports. *Journal of Consulting and Clinical Psychology, 56*(1), 9-16.

Eisenberg, N., Owens, R. G., & Dewey, M. E. (1987). Attitudes of health professionals to child sexual abuse and incest. *Child Abuse & Neglect, 11*, 109-116.

Elbow, M., & Mayfield, J. (1991). Mothers of incest victims: Villians, victims, or protectors? *Families in Society, 72*, 78-85.

Elliott, D. M., & Briere, J. (1992). Sexual abuse trauma among professional women: Validating the Trauma Symptom Checklist-40 (TSC-40). *Child Abuse and Neglect, 16*, 391-398.

Elliott, M., Browne, K., & Kilcoyne, J. (1995). Child sexual abuse prevention: What offenders tell us. *Child Abuse & Neglect, 19*(5), 579-594.

English, D. J., & Tosti-Lane, L. G. (1988). Child protective service workers' ratings of likely emotional trauma to child sexual abuse victims. *Journal of Social Work & Human Sexuality, 7*, 109-124.

Erickson, M. T. (1993). Rethinking Oedipus: An evolutionary perspective of incest avoidance. *American Journal of Psychiatry, 150*(3), 411-416.

Erickson, P. I., & Rapkin, A. J. (1991). Unwanted sexual experiences among middle and high school youth. *Journal of Adolescent Health, 12*, 319-25.

Esparza, D. (1993). Maternal support and stress response in sexually abused girls ages 6–12. *Issues in Mental Health Nursing, 14*, 85-107.

Essock-Vitale, S. M., & McGuire, M. T. (1985). Women's lives viewed from an evolutionary perspective. I. Sexual histories, reproductive success, and demographic characteristics of a random sample of American women. *Ethology and Sociobiology, 6*, 137-154.

Everson, M. D., & Boat, B. W. (1989). False allegations of sexual abuse by children and adolescents. *Journal of the American Academy of Child and Adolescent Psychiatry, 28*(2), 230-235.

Everson, M. D., Hunter, W. M., Runyan, D. K., Edelsohn, G. A., & Coulter, M. L. (1989). Maternal support following disclosure of incest. *American Journal of Orthopsychiatry, 59*(2), 197-207.

Faller, K. C. (1988). The spectrum of sexual abuse in daycare: An exploratory study. *Journal of Family Violence, 3*(4), 283-298.

Faller, K. C. (1990). Sexual abuse by paternal caretakers: A comparison of abusers who are biological fathers in intact families, stepfathers and noncustodial fathers. In A. L. Horton, B. L. Johnson, L. M. Roundy, & D. Williams (Eds.), *The incest perpetrator: A family member no one wants to treat* (pp. 65-73). Newbury Park, CA: Sage.

Faller, K. C. (1991a). Possible explanations for child sexual abuse allegations in divorce. *American Journal of Orthopsychiatry, 61*(1), 86-91.

Faller, K. C. (1991b). What happens to sexually abused children identified by Child Protective Services? *Children and Youth Services Review, 13*, 101-111.

Faller, K. C. (1994). Extrafamilial sexual abuse. *Child and Adolescent Psychiatric Clinics of North America, 3*(4), 713-727.

Faller, K. C. (1996). Interviewing children who may have been abused: A historical perspective and overview of controversies. *Child Maltreatment, 1*(2), 83-95.

Faller, K. C., & DeVoe, E. (1995). Allegations of sexual abuse in divorce. *Journal of Child Sexual Abuse, 4*(4), 1-25.

Fehrenbach, P. A., Smith, W., Monastersky, C., & Deisher, R. W. (1986). Adolescent sex offenders: Offender and offense characteristics. *American Journal of Orthopsychiatry, 56*(2), 225-233.

Feinauer, L. L. (1988). Relationship of long term effects of childhood sexual abuse to identity of the offender: Family, friend, or stranger. *Women & Therapy, 7*, 89-107.

Feldman-Summers, S., & Jones, G. (1984). Psychological impacts of sexual contact between therapists or other health care practitioners and their clients. *Journal of Counseling and Clinical Psychology, 52*, 1054-1061.

Finkelhor, D. (1979). *Sexually victimized children.* New York: Free Press.

Finkelhor, D. (1980). Sex among siblings: A survey on prevalence, variety and effects. *Archives of Sexual Behavior, 9*(3), 171-194.

Finkelhor, D. (1983). Removing the child—prosecuting the offender in cases of child sexual abuse: Evidence from the national reporting system for child abuse and neglect. *Child Abuse & Neglect, 7,* 195-205.

Finkelhor, D. (1984). *Child sexual abuse: New theory and research.* New York: Free Press.

Finkelhor, D. (1987). The sexual abuse of children: Current research reviewed. *Psychiatric Annals, 17*(4), 233-241.

Finkelhor, D. (1990a). Is child abuse overreported? *Public Welfare, Winter,* 22-29.

Finkelhor, D. (1990b). New ideas for sexual abuse prevention. In R. K. Oates (Ed.), *Understanding and managing child sexual abuse* (pp. 385-396): Sydney, Australia: W. B. Saunders.

Finkelhor, D. (1994). Current information on the scope and nature of child sexual abuse. *The Future of Children, 4*(2), 31-53.

Finkelhor, D. (1998). A comparison of the responses of preadolescents and adolescents in a national victimization survey. *Journal of Interpersonal Violence, 13*(3), 362-382.

Finkelhor, D., & Baron, L. (1986). Risk factors for child sexual abuse. *Journal of Interpersonal Violence, 1*(1), 43-71.

Finkelhor, D., & Hotaling, G. T. (1984). Sexual abuse in the National Incidence Study of Child Abuse and Neglect: An appraisal. *Child Abuse & Neglect, 8,* 22-33.

Finkelhor, D., Hotaling, G., Lewis, I. A., & Smith, C. (1990). Sexual abuse in a national survey of adult men and women: Prevalence, characteristics, and risk factors. *Child Abuse & Neglect, 14*(9), 19-28.

Finkelhor, D., & Lewis, I. A. (1988). An epidemiological approach to the study of child molestation. In R. A. Prentky & V. L. Quinsey (Eds.), *Human sexual aggression: Current perspectives* (Vol. 528, pp. 64-78). New York: New York Academy of Sciences.

Finkelhor, D. & Strapko, N. (1992). Sexual abuse prevention education: A review of evaluation studies. In D. J. Willis, E. W. Holden, & M. Rosenburg (Eds.), *Prevention of child maltreatment: Developmental and ecological perspectives* (pp. 150-167). New York: John Wiley & Sons.

Finkelhor, D., Williams, L. M., & Burns, N. (1988). *Nursery crimes: Sexual abuse in day care.* Newbury Park, CA: Sage.

Foreman, T., & Bernet, W. (2000). A misunderstanding regarding the duty to report suspected abuse. *Child Maltreatment, 5*(2), 190-196.

Fox, N. A., Kimmerly, N. L., & Schafer, W. D. (1991). Attachment to mother/attachment to father: A meta-analysis. *Child Development, 62,* 210-225.

Freeman, J. B., Levine, M., & Doueck, H. J. (1996). Child age and caseworker attention in child protective services investigations. *Child Abuse & Neglect, 20*(10), 907-920.

Freet, M. A., Scalise, J. J., & Ginter, E. J. (1996). Sexual abuse, incest, and sexual exploitation: Mental health practitioners' perspective. *Journal of Mental Health Counseling, 18,* 263-274.

Frenzel, R. R., & Lang, R. A. (1989). Identifying sexual preferences in intrafamilial and extrafamilial child sexual abusers. *Annals of Sex Research, 2*(3), 255-275.

Freund, K., McKnight, C. K., Langevin, R., & Cibiri, S. (1972). The female child as a surrogate object. *Archives of Sexual Behavior, 2*(2), 119-133.

Friedrich, W. N. (1991). Mothers of sexually abused children: An MMPI study. *Journal of Clinical Psychology, 47*(6), 778-783.

Frude, N. (1982). The sexual nature of sexual abuse: A review of the literature. *Child Abuse & Neglect, 6*, 211-223.

Gagnon, J. (1965). Female child victims of sex offenses. *Social Problems, 13*, 176-192.

Galdston, R. (1978). Sexual survey #12: Current thinking on sexual abuse of children. *Medical Aspects of Human Sexuality, 12*, 44-47.

Gallup Poll (1995). *Disciplining children in America.* Princeton, NJ: The Gallup Organization.

GAO calls for an enlarged federal-local partnership. (1997, August 7). *Child Protection Report, 23*(16), 136.

Garbarino, J. (1977). The human ecology of child maltreatment: A conceptual model for research. *Journal of Marriage and the Family, 39*, 721-732.

Garland, R. J., & Dougher, M. J. (1990). The abused/abuser hypothesis of child sexual abuse: A critical review of theory and research. In J. R. Feierman (Ed.), *Pedophilia: Biosocial dimensions* (pp. 488-509). New York: Springer-Verlag.

Gartrell, N., Herman, J., Olarte, S., Feldstein, M., & Localio, R. (1987). Reporting practices of psychiatrists who knew of sexual misconduct by colleagues. *American Journal of Orthopsychiatry, 57*(2), 287-295.

Gavey, N., Florence, J., Pezaro, S., & Tan, J. (1990). Mother-blaming, the perfect alibi: Family therapy and the mothers of incest survivors. *Journal of Feminist Family Therapy, 2*(1), 1-25.

Gelinas, D. J. (1983). The persisting negative effects of incest. *Psychiatry, 46, 312-332.*

George, L., & Winfield-Laird, I. (1986). *Sexual assault: Prevalence and mental health consequences:* Unpublished final report submitted to the National Institute of Mental Health.

Giarretto, H. (1982). A comprehensive child sexual abuse treatment program. *Child Abuse & Neglect, 6*, 263-278.

Giarretto, H. (1989). Community-based treatment of the incest family. *Psychiatric Clinics of North America, 12*(2), 351-361.

Gibeau, D. (1989). Secure attachment, types of discipline, separation threat and the quality of peer affectional systems in two types of child sexual offenders: An application of Bowlby's attachment theory. *Dissertation Abstracts International, 49*(11), 5020.

Gilbert, N. (1992). Social constraints on primary prevention: The case of child sexual abuse policy. In H. U. Otto & G. Flosser (Eds.), *How to organize prevention: Political, organizational, and professional challenges to social services.* Berlin: Walter de Gruyter.

Giovannoni, J. M. (1991). Unsubstantiated reports: Perspectives of child protection workers. *Children and Youth Services, 15*(2), 51-62.

Goff, D. C., Brotman, A. W., Kindlon, D., Waites, M., & Amico, E. (1991). Self-report of childhood abuse in chronically psychotic patients. *Psychiatric Research, 37*(1), 73-80.

Goldwert, M. (1986). Childhood seduction and the spiritualization of psychology: The case of Jung and Rank. *Child Abuse & Neglect, 10*, 555-57.

Gomes-Schwartz, B., Horowitz, J. M., & Cardarelli, A. P. (1990). *Child sexual abuse: The initial effects.* Newbury Park, CA: Sage.

Goodman, G. S., Pyle-Taub, E. P., Jones, D.P.H., England, P., Port, L. K., & Prado, L. (1992). The effects of criminal court testimony on child sexual assault victims. *Monographs of the Society for Research in Child Development, 57*, 1-163.

Goodwin, J., Attias, R., McCarty, T., Chandler, S., & Romanik, R. (1988). Reporting by adult psychiatric patients of childhood sexual abuse. *American Journal of Psychiatry, 145*, 1183.

Goodwin, J., Cormier, L., & Owen, J. (1983). Grandfather-granddaughter incest: A trigenerational view. *Child Abuse & Neglect, 7*, 163-170.

Goodwin, J., McCarthy, T., & DiVasto, P. (1981). Prior incest in mothers of abused children. *Child Abuse & Neglect, 5*, 87-95.

Gordon, M. (1989). The family environment of sexual abuse: A comparison of natal and stepfather abuse. *Child Abuse & Neglect, 13,* 121-130.

Gordon, M., & Creighton, S. J. (1988). Natal and non-natal fathers as sexual abusers in the United Kingdom: A comparative analysis. *Journal of Marriage and the Family, 50,* 99-105.

Gorey, K. M., & Leslie, D. R. (1997). The prevalence of child sexual abuse: Integrative review adjustment for potential response and measurement biases. *Child Abuse & Neglect, 21*(4), 391-398.

Gray-Fow, M. (1987). Child abuse, historiography and ethics: The historian as moral philosopher. *The Journal of Psychohistory, 15*(1), 455-465.

Green, M. G. (1986). True and false allegations in child custody disputes. *Journal of the American Academy of Child Psychiatry, 25,* 449-456.

Greenberger, S. S. (2000, August 30). SAT math scores best since 1969. *Boston Globe,* pp. A1, A4.

Greendlinger, V., & Byrne, D. (1987). Coercive sexual fantasies of college men as predictors of self-reported likelihood to rape and overt sexual aggression. *Journal of Sex Research, 23*(1), 1-11.

Greenspun, W. S. (1994). Internal and interpersonal: The family transmission of father-daughter incest. *Journal of Child Sexual Abuse, 3*(2), 1-14.

Gregory-Bills, T., & Rhodeback, M. (1995). Comparative psychopathology of women who experienced intra-familial versus extra-familial sexual abuse. *Child Abuse & Neglect, 19*(2), 177-189.

Groff, M. G. (1987). Characteristics of incest offenders' wives. *Journal of Sex Research, 23,* 91-96.

Groff, M. G. & Hubble, L. M. (1984). A comparison of father-daughter and stepfather-stepdaughter incest. *Criminal Justice and Behavior, 11*(4), 461-475.

Groth, A. N. (1978). Patterns of sexual assault against children and adolescents. In A. Burgess, A. N. Groth, L. Holstrom, & S. Sgroi (Eds.), *Sexual assault of children and adolescents.* Lexington, MA: Lexington Books.

Groth, A. N. (1982). The incest offender. In S. M. Sgroi (Ed.), *Handbook of clinical intervention in child sexual abuse* (pp. 215-240). Lexington, MA: Lexington Books.

Groth, A. N., & Birnbaum, H. J. (1978). Adult sexual orientation and attraction to underage persons. *Archives of Sexual Behavior, 7*(3), 175-181.

Groth, A. N., Longo, R. E., & McFadin, J. B. (1982). Undetected recidivism among rapists and child molesters. *Crime and Delinquency, 28*(3), 450-458.

Hadley, J. A., Holloway, E. L., & Mallinckrodt, B. (1993). Common aspects of object relations and self-representations in offspring from disparate dysfunctional families. *Journal of Counseling Psychology, 40*(3), 348-356.

Hafemeister, T. L. (1996). Protecting child witnesses: Judicial efforts to minimize trauma and reduce evidentiary barriers. *Violence & Victims, 11*(1), 71-91.

Hall, C. S. (1954). *A primer of Freudian psychology.* New York: New American Library.

Hall, E. R., & Flannery, P. J. (1984). Prevalence and correlates of sexual assault experiences in adolescents. *Victimology, 9*(3-4), 398-406.

Hall, G.C.N., & Hirschman, R. (1991). Towards a theory of sexual aggression: A quadripartite model. *Journal of Consulting and Clinical Psychology, 59*(5), 662-669.

Hall, G.C.N., & Hirschman, R. (1992). Sexual aggression against children: A conceptual perspective of etiology. *Criminal Justice & Behavior, 19*(1), 8-23.

Hanson, R. K., & Slater, S. (1988). Sexual victimization in the history of sexual abusers: A review. *Annals of Sex Research, 1,* 485-499.

Hanson, R. K., & Slater, S. (1993). Reactions to motivational accounts of child molesters. *Journal of Child Sexual Abuse, 2*(4), 43-57.

Hare-Mustin, R. (1987). The problem of gender in family therapy. *Family Process, 26,* 15-27.

Harter, S., Alexander, P. C., & Neimeyer, R. A. (1988). Long-term effects of incestuous child abuse in college women: Social adjustment, social cognition, and family characteristics. *Journal of Consulting and Clinical Psychology, 56*(1), 5-8.

Hartley, C. C. (1998). How incest offenders overcome internal inhibitions through the use of cognitions and cognitive distortions. *Journal of Interpersonal Violence, 13*(1), 25-39.

Hartman, G. L., Karlson, H., & Hibbard, R. A. (1994). Attorney attitudes regarding behaviors associated with child sexual abuse. *Child Abuse & Neglect, 18*(8), 657-662.

Haskett, M. E., Wayland, K., Hutcheson, J. S., & Tavana, T. (1995). Substantiation of sexual abuse allegations: Factors involved in the decision-making process. *Journal of Child Sexual Abuse, 4*(2), 19-47.

Haugaard, J. J., & Emery, R. E. (1989). Methodological issues in child sexual abuse research. *Child Abuse & Neglect, 13,* 89-100.

Haugaard, J., & Samwel, C. (1992). Legal and therapeutic interventions with incestuous families. *Medicine and Law, 11*(5-6), 469-484.

Haugaard, J. J., & Tilly, C. (1988). Characteristics predicting children's responses to sexual encounters with other children. *Child Abuse & Neglect, 12,* 209-218.

Henry, J. (1997). System intervention trauma to child sexual abuse victims following disclosure. *Journal of Interpersonal Violence, 12*(4), 499-512.

Herman, J. L. (1981). *Father-daughter incest.* Cambridge, MA: Harvard University Press.

Herman, J. L. (1990). Sex offenders: A feminist perspective. In W. L. Marshall, D. R. Laws, & H. E. Barbaree (Eds.), *Handbook of sexual assault: Issues, theories, and treatment of the offender* (pp. 177-193). New York: Plenum Press.

Herman, J. L., & Schatzow, E. (1987). Recovery and verification of memories of childhood sexual trauma. *Psychoanalytic Psychology, 4*(1)7, 1-14.

Hernandez, J. T. (1992). Substance abuse among sexually abused adolescents and their families. *Journal of Adolescent Health, 13,* 658-662.

Hetherton, J., & Beardsall, L. (1988). Decisions and attitudes concerning child sexual abuse: Does the gender of the perpetrator make a difference to child protection professionals? *Child Abuse & Neglect, 22*(12), 1265-1283.

Hibbard, R. A., Ingersoll, G. M., & Orr, D. P. (1990). Behavioral risk, emotional risk, and child abuse among adolescents in a nonclinical setting. *Pediatrics, 86*(6), 896-901.

Hobfoll, S. E. (1989). Conservation of resources: A new attempt at conceptualizing stress. *The American Psychologist, 44,* 513-524.

Hobfoll, S. E. (1991). Traumatic stress: A theory based on rapid loss of resources. *Anxiety Research, 4*(3), 187-197.

Hobfoll, S. E., Freedy, J. R., Green, B. L., & Solomon, S. D. (1996). Coping in reaction to extreme stress: The roles of resource loss and resource availability. In M. Zeidner & N. S. Endler (Eds.), *Handbook of coping: Theory, research, applications* (pp. 322-349). New York: John Wiley & Sons.

Hoffman, M. A., Ushpiz, V., & Levy-Shiff, R. (1988). Social support and self-esteem in adolescence. *Journal of Youth & Adolescence, 17,* 307-316.

Hogan, M. (1996). Oral midazolam for pediatric nonacute sexual abuse examinations. *Child Maltreatment, 1*(4), 361-363.

Hooper, C. (1989). Alternatives to collusion: The response of mothers to child sexual abuse in the family. *Educational & Child Psychology, 6,* 22-30.

Hooper, C. (1992). *Mothers surviving child sexual abuse.* London: Tavistock.

Hooper, C., & Humphreys, C. (1998). Women whose children have been sexually abused: Reflections of a debate. *British Journal of Social Work, 28,* 565-580.

Hoorwitz, A. N. (1983). Guidelines for treating father-daughter incest. *Social Casework, 64*, 515-524.

Hudson, J. J. (1996). Characteristics of the incestuous family. In C. C. Kroeger & J. R. Beck (Eds.), *Women, abuse, and the Bible. How Scripture can be used to hurt or to heal* (pp. 70-85). Grand Rapids, MI: Baker Books.

Hunter, W. M., Coulter, M. L., Runyan, D. K., & Everson, M. D. (1990). Determinants of placement for sexually abused children. *Child Abuse & Neglect, 14*, 407-417.

Hyland, K. Z., Tsujimoto, R. N., & Hamilton, M. (1993). A new comparison group for research on child sexual abuse. *Child Abuse & Neglect, 17*, 367-370.

Jackson, H., & Nuttall, R. (1993). Clinician responses to sexual abuse allegations. *Child Abuse & Neglect, 17*, 127-143.

Jackson, J. L., Calhoun, K. S., Amick, A. E., Maddever, H. M., & Habif, V. L. (1990). Young adult women who report childhood intrafamilial sexual abuse: Subsequent adjustment. *Archives of Sexual Behavior, 19*(3), 211-221.

Jackson, T. L., & Sandberg, G. (1985). Attribution of incest blame among rural attorneys and judges. *Women & Therapy, 4*(3), 39-56.

Jacobs, L. L. (1990). Reassessing mother blame in incest. *Signs: Journal of Women in Culture and Society, 15*, 500-514.

Jacobsen, A., Koehler, J. E., & Jones-Brown, C. (1987). The failure of routine assessment to detect histories of assault experienced by psychiatric patients. *Hospital and Community Psychiatry, 38*, 386-389.

James, B., & Nasjleti, M. (1983). *Treating sexually abused children and their families.* Palo Alto, CA: Consulting Psychologists Press.

James, K., & MacKinnon, L. (1990). The "incestuous family" revisted: A critical analysis of family therapy myths. *Journal of Marital & Family Therapy, 16*(1), 71-88.

Jaudes, P. K., & Morris, M. (1990). Child sexual abuse: Who goes home. *Child Abuse & Neglect, 14*, 61-68.

Johnson, P. A., Owens, R. G., Dewey, M. E., & Eisenberg, N. E. (1990). Professionals' attributions of censure in father-daughter incest. *Child Abuse & Neglect, 14*, 419-428.

Jones, D.P.H., & McGraw, J. M. (1987). Reliable and fictitious accounts of sexual abuse to children. *Journal of Interpersonal Violence, 2*(1), 27-45.

Joyce, P.A. (1995). Psychoanalytic theory, child sexual abuse and clinical social work. *Clinical Social Work Journal, 23*(2), 199-214.

Juang, L. P., & Silbereisen, R. K. (1999). Supportive parenting and adolescent adjustment across time in former East and West Germany. *Journal of Adolescence, 22*(6), 719-736.

Kadushin, A., & Martin, J. A. (1988). *Child welfare services* (4th ed.). New York: Macmillan.

Kalichman, S. C., Craig, M. E., & Follingstad, D. R. (1988). Mental health professionals and suspected cases of child abuse: An investigation of factors influencing reporting. *Community Mental Health Journal, 24*, 43-51.

Kalichman, S. C., Craig, M. E., & Follingstad, D. R. (1989). Factors influencing the reporting of father-child sexual abuse: Study of licensed practicing psychologists. *Professional Psychology: Research & Practice, 20*(2), 84-89.

Kalichman, S. C., Craig, M. E., Follingstad, D. R. (1990). Professionals' adherence to mandatory child abuse reporting laws: Effects of responsibility attribution, confidence ratings, and situational factors. *Child Abuse & Neglect, 14*, 69-77.

Karski, R. L. (1999). Key decisions in child protective services: Report investigation and court referral. *Children and Youth Services Review, 21*(8), 643-656.

Keckley Market Research (1983). *Sexual abuse in Nashville: A report on incidence and long term effects.* Unpublished paper prepared for WSM-TV, Nashville.

Kelley, S. J. (1990). Responsibility and management strategies in child sexual abuse: A comparison of child protective workers, nurses, and police officers. *Child Welfare, 69*(1), 43-51.

Kelly, L. (1988). What's in a name? Defining child sexual abuse. *Feminist Review, 28,* 65-71.

Kendall-Tackett, K. A., & Watson, M. W. (1991). Factors that influence professionals' perceptions of behavioral indicators of child sexual abuse. *Journal of Interpersonal Violence, 6*(3), 385-395.

Kendall-Tackett, K. A., Williams, L.M., & Finkelhor, D. (1993). Impact of sexual abuse on children: A review and synthesis of recent empirical studies. *Psychological Bulletin, 113,* 164-180.

Kercher, G. A., & McShane, M. (1984). The prevalence of child sexual abuse victimization in an adult sample of Texas residents. *Child Abuse & Neglect, 8,* 495-501.

Kilpatrick, A. C., & Lockhart, L. L. (1991). Studying sensitive family issues: Problems and possibilities for practitioners. *Families in Society, 72,* 610-617.

Kinard, E. M. (1994). Methodological issues and practical problems in conducting research on maltreated children. *Child Abuse & Neglect, 18*(8), 645-656.

King, G., Reece, R., Bendel, R., & Patel, V. (1998). The effects of sociodemographic variables, training, and attitudes on the lifetime reporting practices of mandated reporters. *Child Maltreatment, 3*(3), 276-283.

King, N.M.P., Hunter, W. M., & Runyan, D. K. (1988). Going to court: The experience of child victims of intrafamilial sexual abuse. *Journal of Health Politics, Policy & Law, 13*(4), 705-721.

Kinnear, K. (1995). *Childhood sexual abuse: A reference handbook.* Santa Barbara, CA: ABC-CLIO.

Kinsey, A.C., Pomeroy, W., Martin, C., & Gebhard, P. (1953). *Sexual behavior in the human female.* Philadelphia, PA: W.B. Saunders.

Kinzl, J., & Biebl, W. (1992). Long-term effects of incest: Life events triggering mental disorders in female patients with sexual abuse in childhood. *Child Abuse & Neglect, 16*(4), 567-573.

Kirkland, K. D., & Bauer, C. A. (1982). MMPI traits of incestuous fathers. *Journal of Clinical Psychology, 389*(3), 645-649.

Kluft, R. P. (1990). Incest and subsequent revictimization: The case of therapist-patient exploitation, with a description of the sitting duck syndrome. In R. P. Kluft (Ed.), *Incest-related syndromes of adult psychopathology* (pp. 263-287). Washington, DC: American Psychiatric Press.

Knight, R. A. (1992). The generation and corroboration of a taxonomic model for child molesters. In W. O'Donohue & J. H. Geer (Eds.), *The sexual abuse of children: Theory and research,* (Vol. 2, pp.24-70). Hillsdale, NJ: Lawrence Erlbaum.

Knight, R. A., Carter, D. L., & Prentky, R. A. (1989). A system for the classification of child molesters: Reliability and application. *Journal of Interpersonal Violence, 4*(1), 3-23.

Knight, R. A., & Prentky, R. A. (1990). Classifying sexual offenders: The development and corroboration of taxonomic models. In W. L. Marshall, D. R. Laws, & H. E. Barbaree (Eds.), *Handbook of sexual assault: Issues, theories, and treatment on the offender* (pp. 23-52). New York: Plenum Press.

Kohl, J. (1993). School-based child sexual abuse prevention programs. *Journal of Family Violence, 8*(2), 137-150.

Kolko, D. J., Selelyo, J., & Brown, E. J. (1999). The treatment histories and service involvement of physically and sexually abusive families: Description, correspondence, and clinical correlates. *Child Abuse & Neglect, 23*(5), 459-476.

Koss, M. P. (1993). Detecting the scope of rape: A review of prevalence research methods. *Journal of Interpersonal Violence, 8*(2), 198-222.

Krieger, M. J., Rosenfeld, A. A., Gordon, A., & Bennett, M. (1980). Problems in the psychotherapy of children with histories of incest. *American Journal of Psychotherapy, 34*(1), 81-88.

Kuhn, T.S. (1970). *The structure of scientific revolutions* (2nd ed.). Chicago, IL: University of Chicago Press.

Lacey, J. H. (1990). Incest, incestuous fantasy & indecency: A clinical catchment area study of normal-weight bulimicwomen. *British Journal of Psychiatry, 157*, 399-403.

Lamb, M. E., Sternberg, K. J., & Esplin, P. W. (1998). Conducting investigative interviews of alleged sexual abuse victims. *Child Abuse & Neglect, 22*(8), 813-823.

Landis, C. (1940). *Sex in development*. New York: Harper & Brothers.

Landis, J. (1956). Experiences of 500 children with adult sexual deviance. *Psychiatric Quarerly Supplement 30*, 91-109.

Langan, P. A., & Harlow, C. W. (1994). *Child rape victims, 1992*. Washington, DC: Bureau of Justice.

Larson, L. R. (1993). Betrayal and repetition: Understanding aggression in sexually abused girls. *Clinical Social Work Journal, 21*(2), 137-150.

Larson, N. R., & Maddock, J. W. (1986). Structural and functional variables in incestuous family systems: Implications for assessment and treatment. In T. S. Trepper & M. J. Barrett (Eds.), *Treating incest: A multimodal systems perspective* (pp. 27-44). New York: Haworth Press.

Laviola, M. (1992). Effects of older brother—younger sister incest: A study of the dynamics of 17 cases. *Child Abuse & Neglect, 16*, 409-421.

Laws, D. R., Marshall, W. L. (1990). A conditioning theory of the etiology and maintenance of deviant sexual preference and behavior. In W. L. Marshall, D. R. Laws, & H. E. Barbaree (Eds.), *Handbook of sexual assault: Issues, theories, and treatment of the offender* (pp. 177-194). New York: Plenum Press.

Lazebnik, R., Zimet, G. D., Ebert, J., Anglin, T. M., Williams, P., Bunch, D. L., & Krowchuk, D. P. (1994). How children perceive the medical evaluation for suspected sexual abuse. *Child Abuse & Neglect, 18*(9), 739-745.

Lefkowitz, B. (1997). *Our guys*. New York: Vintage Books.

Leifer, M., Shapiro, J. P., & Kassem, L. (1993). The impact of maternal history and behavior upon foster placement and adjustment in sexually abused girls. *Child Abuse & Neglect, 17*, 755-766.

Leinknecht, W. (1997, Nov. 27). Global positioning technology can monitor criminals 24 hours a day. *The San Francisco Examiner*.

Lerman, H. (1988). The psychoanalytic legacy: From whence we come. In L.E.A. Walker (Ed.), *Handbook on sexual abuse of children: Assessment and treatment* (pp. 37-52). New York: Springer.

Levang, C. A. (1989). Father-daughter incest families: A theoretical perspective from balance theory and general systems theory. *Contemporary Family Therapy, 11*, 28-43.

Leventhal, J. M. (1988). Have there been changes in the epidemiology of sexual abuse of children during the 20th century? *Pediatrics, 82*(5), 766-773.

Levine, M., Doueck, H. J., Freeman, J. B., & Compaan, C. (1998). Rush to judgment? Child protective services and allegations of sexual abuse. *American Journal of Orthopsychiatry, 68*(1), 101-107.

Levitt, C. J., Owen, G., & Truchsess, J. (1991). Families after sexual abuse. What helps? What is needed? In M. Q. Patton (Ed.), *Family sexual abuse: Frontline research and evaluation* (pp. 39-56). Newbury Park, CA: Sage.

Lexington Herald-Leader. (January, 1992). Survey of state dispels myths of child sexual abuse, pp. 1, 14.

Lipovsky, J. A. (1994). The impact of court on children: Research findings and practical recommendations. *Journal of Interpersonal Violence, 9*(2), 238-257.

Lipovsky, J., & Stern, P. (1997). Preparing children for court: An interdisciplinary view. *Child Maltreatment, 2*(2), 150-163.

Lipovsky, J. A., Swenson, C. C., Ralston, M. E., & Saunders, B. E. (1998). The abuse clarification process in the treatment of intrafamilial child abuse. *Child Abuse & Neglect, 22*(7), 729-741.

Longo, R. E. (1982). Sexual learning and experience among adolescent sex offenders. *International Journal of Offender Therapy & Comparative Criminology, 21*, 249-254.

Macfie, J., Toth, S. L., Rogosch, F. A., Robinson, J., Emde, R. N., & Cicchetti, D. (1999). Effects of maltreatment on preschoolers' narrative representations of responses to relieve distress and of role reversal. *Developmental Psychology, 35*(2), 460-465.

Machotka, P., Pittman, F. S., & Flomenhaft, K. (1967). Incest as a family affair. *Family Process, 6*, 98-116.

MacMurray, B. K. (1989). Criminal determination for child sexual abuse: Prosecutor case-screening judgments. *Journal of Interpersonal Violence, 4*(2), 233-244.

Maddock, J. W., Larson, P. R., & Lally, C. F. (1991). An evaluation protocol for incest family functioning. In M. Q. Patton (Ed.), *Family sexual abuse: Frontline research and evaluation* (pp. 162-177). Newbury Park, CA: Sage Publications.

Madonna, P. G., Van Scoyk, S., & Jones, D. P. H. (1991). Family interactions within incest and nonincest families. *American Journal of Psychiatry, 148*(1), 46-49.

Main, M., Kaplan, N., & Cassidy, J. (1985). Security in infancy, childhood and adulthood: A move to the level of representation. *Monographs of the Society for Research in Child Development, 50*, 66-104.

Major, B. (1987). Gender, justice, and the psychology of entitlement. In P. Shaver & C. Hendrick (Eds.), *Sex and gender* (pp. 124-148). Newbury Park, CA: Sage.

Major, B. (1993). Gender, entitlement, and the distribution of family labor. *Journal of Social Issues, 49*(3), 141-159.

Mansfield, H. (1997). Hawaii's Hana Like home visitor program, a healthy start program. *Journal of Psychohistory, 24*(4), 332-338.

Mannarino, A. P., & Cohen, J. A. (1986). A clinical-demographic study of sexually abused children. *Child Abuse & Neglect, 10*, 17-23.

Margolin, L. (1991). Child sexual abuse by nonrelated caregivers. *Child Abuse & Neglect, 15*, 213-221.

Margolin, L. (1992). Sexual abuse by grandparents. *Child Abuse & Neglect, 16*, 735-741.

Margolin, L. (1994). Child sexual abuse by uncles: A risk assessment. *Child Abuse & Neglect, 18*(3), 215-224.

Margolin, L., & Craft, J. L. (1989). Child sexual abuse by caretakers. *Family Relations, 38*, 450-455.

Margolin, L., & Craft, J. L. (1990). Child abuse by adolescent caregivers. *Child Abuse & Neglect, 14*, 365-373.

Marshall, W. L. (1989). Intimacy, loneliness and sexual offenders. *Behaviour Research and Therapy, 27*(5), 491-503.

Marshall, W. L., Hudson, S. M., & Hodkinson, S. (1993). The importance of attachment bonds in the development of juvenile sex offending. In H. E. Barbaree, W. L. Marshall, & S. M. Hudson (Eds.), *The juvenile sex offender* (pp. 164-181). New York: Guilford Press.

Marshall, W. N., & Locke, C. (1997). Statewide survey of physician attitudes. Controversies about child abuse. *Child Abuse & Neglect, 21*(2), 171-179.

Martin, J., Anderson, J., Romans, S., Mullen, P., & O'Shea, M. (1993). Asking about child sexual abuse: Methodological implications of a two stage survey. *Child Abuse and Neglect, 17*, 383-392.

Martone, J., Jaudes, P. K., & Cavins, M. K. (1996). Criminal proseictuionof child sexual abuse cases. *Child Abuse & Neglect, 20*(5), 457-464.

Maslow, A. H. (1987). *Motivation and personality* (3rd ed.). New York: Harper & Row.

Massat, C. R., & Lundy, M. (1998). "Reporting costs" to nonoffending parents in cases of intrafamilial child sexual abuse. *Child Welfare, 77*(4), 371-388.

Masson, J. M. (1984). *The assault on truth: Freud's suppression of the seduction theory.* New York: Farrar, Straus & Giroux.

Masson, J. M. (1985). *The complete letters of Sigmund Freud to Wilhelm Fliess: 1887 – 1904.* Cambridge, MA: Belknap Press.

Masten, A. S., Best, K. M., & Garmezy, N. (1990). Resilience and development: Contributions from the study of children who overcome adversity. *Development and Psychopathology, 2,* 425-444.

McIntyre, K. (1981). Role of mothers in father-daughter incest: A feminist analysis. *Social Work, 26*(6), 462-466.

Metcalfe, M., Oppenheimer, R., Dignon, A., & Palmer, R. L. (1990). Childhood sexual experiences reported by male psychiatric patients. *Psychological Medicine, 20*(4), 925-929.

Milner, J. S., & Robertson, K. R. (1990). Comparison of physical child abusers, intrafamilial sexual child abusers, and child neglecters. *Journal of Interpersonal Violence, 5*(1), 37-48.

Moore, D. (1994). Entitlement as an epistemic problem: Do women think like men. *Journal of Social Behavior and Personality, 9*(4), 665-684.

Moore, K. A., Nord, C. W., & Peterson, J. L. (1989). Nonvoluntary sexual activity among adolescents. *Family Planning Perspectives, 21*(3), 110-114.

Mosher, D. L., & Anderson, R. D. (1986). Macho personality, sexual aggression, and reactions to guided imagery of realistic rape. *Journal of Research in Personality, 20*(1), 77-94.

Muehlenhard, C. L., & Linton, M. A. (1987). Date rape and sexual aggression in dating situations: Incidence and risk factors. *Journal of Counseling Psychology, 34*(2), 186-196.

Muram, D., Rosenthal, T. L., & Beck, K. W. (1994). Personality profiles of mothers of sexual abuse victims and their daughters. *Child Abuse & Neglect, 18,* 419-423.

Murphy, J. (1987). *Prevalence of child sexual abuse and consequent victimization in the general population.* Paper presented at the Third National Family Violence Research Conference, Durham, NH: University of New Hampshire.

Murphy, J. E. (1991). An investigation of child sexual abuse and consequent victimization: Some implications of telephone surveys. In D. D. Knudsen & J. L. Miller (Eds.), *Abused and battered: Social and legal responses to family violence* (pp. 79-87). New York: Aldine de Gruyter.

Myer, M. H. (1985). A new look at mothers of incest victims. *Journal of Social Work and Human Sexuality, 3,* 47-58.

Nakhle Tamraz, D. (1996). Nonoffending mothers of sexually abused children: Comparison of opinions and research. *Journal of Child Sexual Abuse, 5*(4), 75-104.

Nance, K. (1992, January). Survey of state dispels myths of child sexual abuse. *Lexington Herald Leader (special reprint),* pp. 1, 14.

National Victim Center (1995). *National Victim Center Legislative Database search printout: Incest laws by state.* Author.

Neustein, A., & Goetting, A. (1999). Judicial responses to the protective parent's complaint of child sexual abuse. *Journal of Child Sexual Abuse, 8*(4), 103-122.

Newberger, C. M., Gremy, I. M., Waternaux, C. M., & Newberger, E. H. (1993). Mothers of sexually abused children: Trauma and repair in longitudinal perspective. *American Journal of Orthopsychiatry, 63*(1), 92-102.

Nicholas, K. B., & Bieber, S. L. (1997). Assessment of perceived parenting behaviors: The Exposure to Abusive Environments Parenting Inventory (EASE-P). *Journal of Family Violence, 12*(3), 275-291.

Oates, R. K., Tebbutt, J., Swanston, H., Lynch, D. L., & O'Toole, B. I. (1998). Prior childhood sexual abuse in mothers of sexually abused children. *Child Abuse & Neglect, 22*(11), 1113-1118.

Oberlander, L. B. (1995). Psycholegal issues in child sexual abuse evaluations: A survey of forensic mental health professionals. *Child Abuse & Neglect, 19*(4), 475-490.

O'Brien, M. J. (1991). Taking sibling incest seriously. In M. Q. Patton (Ed.), *Family sexual abuse: Frontline research and evaluation* (pp. 75-92). Newbury Park, CA: Sage.

O'Donohue, W., & Letourneau, E. (1992). The psychometric properties of the penile tumescence assessment of child molesters. *Journal of Psychopathology and Behavioral Assessment, 14*(2), 123-174.

O'Grady, D., & Metz, J. R. (1987). Resilience in children at high risk for psychological disorder. *Journal of Pediatric Psychology, 12*, 3-23.

Olafson, E., Corwin, D. L., & Summit, R. C. (1993). Modern history of child sexual abuse awareness: Cycles of discovery and suppression. *Child Abuse and Neglect, 17*, 7-24.

Olson, D. H., Russell, C. S., & Sprenkle, D. H. (1983). Circumplex model of marital and family systems: VI. Theoretical update. *Family Process, 22*, 69-83.

Olson, D. H., Sprenkle, D. H., & Russell, C. S. (1979). Circumplex model of marital and family systems: I. Cohesion and adaptability dimensions, family types, and clinical applications. *Family Process, 16*, 3-28.

Orbach, Y., Hershkowitz, I., Lamb, M. E., Sternberg, K. J., Esplin P. W., & Horowitz, D. (2000). Assessing the value of structured protocols for forensic interviews of alleged child abuse victims. *Child Abuse & Neglect, 24*, 733-752.

Orenstein, P. (1994). *School girls: Young women, self-esteem, and the confidence gap.* New York: Anchor Books.

O'Toole, R., Webster, S. W., O'Toole, A.W., & Lucal, B. (1999). Teachers' recognition and reporting of child abuse: A factorial survey. *Child Abuse & Neglect, 23*(11), 1083-1101.

Owen, G., & Steele, N. M. (1991). Incest offenders after treatment. In M. Q. Patton (Ed.), *Family sexual abuse: Frontline research and evaluation* (pp. 178-198). Newbury Park, CA: Sage.

Palusci, V. J., Cox, E. O., Cyrus, T. A., Heartwell, S. W., Vandervort, F. E., & Pott, E. S. (1999). Medical assessment and legal outcome in child sexual abuse. *Archives of Pediatric and Adolescent Medicine, 153*, 388-392.

Panton, J. H. (1978). Personality differences appearing between rapists of adults, rapists of children and non-violent sexual molesters of female children. *Research Communications in Psychology, Psychiatry and Behavior, 3*(4), 385-391.

Panton, J. H. (1979). MMPI profile configurations associated with incestuous and non-incestuous child molesting. *Psychological Reports, 45*, 335-338.

Paradise, J. E., Rostain, A. L., & Nathanson, M. (1988). Substantiation of sexual abuse charges when parents dispute custody or visitation. *Pediatrics, 81*(6), 835-839.

Parker, H., & Parker, S. (1986). Father-daughter sexual abuse: An emerging perspective. *American Journal of Orthopsychiatry, 56*(4), 531-549.

Parker, S., & Parker, H. (1991). Female victims of child sexual abuse: Adult adjustment. *Journal of Family Violence, 6*(2), 183-197.

Paterson, R. J., & Moran, G. (1988). Attachment theory, personality development, and psychotherapy. *Clinical Psychology Review, 8*, 611-636.

Paveza, G. J. (1988). Risk factors in father-daughter child sexual abuse: A case-controlled study. *Journal of Interpersonal Violence, 3*(3), 290-306.

Payne, M. (1991). *Modern social work theory: A critical introduction.* Chicago, IL: Lyceum Books.

Pedhazur, E. J., & Schmelkin, L. P. (1991). *Measurement, design, and analysis: An integrated approach.* Hillsdale, NJ: Lawrence Erlbaum.

Pellegrin, A., & Wagner, W. G. (1990). Child sexual abuse: Factors affecting victims' removal from home. *Child Abuse & Neglect, 14*, 53-60.

Pence, D. M., & Wilson, C. A. (1994). Reporting and investigating child sexual abuse. *The Future of Children, 4*(2), 70-83.

Peters, S. D., Wyatt, G. E., & Finkelhor, D. (1986). Prevalence. In D. Finkelhor (Ed.), *A sourcebook on child sexual abuse* (pp. 15-59). Beverly Hills, CA: Sage.

Peterson, R. F., Basta, S. M., & Dykstra, T. A. (1993). Mothers of molested children: Some comparisons of personality characteristics. *Child Abuse & Neglect, 17,* 409-418.

Phelan, P. (1986). The process of incest: Biologic father and stepfather families. *Child Abuse & Neglect, 10,* 531-539.

Pierce, L. H., & Pierce, R. L. (1987). Incestuous victimization by juvenile sex offenders. *Journal of Family Violence, 2*(4), 351-364.

Pierce, L. H., & Pierce, R. L. (1990). Adolescent/sibling incest perpetrators. In A. L. Horton, B. L. Johnson, L. M. Roundy, & D. Williams (Eds.), *The incest perpetrator: A family member no on wants to treat* (pp. 99-107). Newbury Park, CA: Sage.

Pleck, J. H., Sonenstein, F. L., & Ku, L. C. (1993). Masculinity ideology: Its impact on adolescent males' heterosexual relationships. *Journal of Social Issues, 49*(3), 11-29.

Pope, K. S. (1993). Licensing disciplinary actions for psychologists who have been sexually involved with a client: Some information about offenders. *Professional Psychology: Research and Practice, 24*(3), 374-377.

Powell, R.A., & Boer, D.P. (1994). Did Freud mislead patients to confabulate memories of abuse? *Psychological Reports, 74,* 1283-1298.

Prentky, R. A., Knight, R. A., Sims-Knight, J. E., Straus, H., Rokous, F., & Cerce, D. (1989). Developmental antecedents of sexual aggression. *Development and Psychopathology, 1,* 153-169.

Ray, K. C., Jackson, J. L., & Townsley, R. M. (1991). Family environments of victims of intrafamilial and extrafamilial child sexual abuse. *Journal of Family Violence, 6*(4), 365-374.

Reidy, T. J., & Hochstadt, N. J. (1993). Attribution of blame in incest cases: A comparison of mental health professionals. *Child Abuse & Neglect, 17,* 371-381.

Reis, S. D., & Heppner, P. P. (1993). Examination of coping resources and family adaptation in mothers and daughters of incestuous versus nonclinical families. *Journal of Counseling Psychology, 40*(1), 100-108.

Reiss, D. (1981). *The family's construction of reality.* Boston, MA: Harvard University Press.

Renken, B., Egeland, B., Marvinney, D., Mangelsdorf, S., & Sroufe, L. A. (1989). Early childhood antecedents of aggression and passive-withdrawal in early elementary school. *Journal of Personality, 57,* 257-281.

Resnick, H. S., Kilpatrick, D. G., Dansky, B. S., Saunders, B. E., & Best, C. L. (1993). Prevalence of civilian trauma and posttraumatic stress disorder in a representative national sample of women. *Journal of Consulting and Clinical Psychology, 61*(6), 984-991.

Rogers, C. R. (1980). *A way of being.* Boston: Houghton Mifflin.

Rosenfeld, A. (1987). Freud, psychodynamics, and incest. *Child Welfare, 66*(6), 485-496.

Rosenthal, J. A., Motz, J. K., Edmonson, D. A., & Groze, V. (1991). A descriptive study of abuse and neglect in out-of-home-placement. *Child Abuse & Neglect, 15,* 249-260.

Rouse, L. P. (1988). Abuse in dating relationships: Comparison of Blacks, whites, and Hispanics. *Journal of College Student Development, 29,* 312-319.

Rudd, J. M., & Herzberger, S. D. (1999). Brother-sister incest—father-daughter incest: A comparison of characteristics and consequences. *Child Abuse & Neglect, 23*(9), 915-928.

Runyan, D. K., Everson, M. D., Edelsohn, G. A., Hunter, W. M., & Coulter, M. L. (1988). Impact of legal intervention on sexually abused children. *The Journal of Pediatrics, 113,* 647-653.

Rush, F. (1980). *The best kept secret: Sexual abuse of children.* New York: McGraw-Hill.

Rush, F. (1996). The Freudian coverup. *Feminism & Psychology, 6*(2), 261-276.

Russell, D.E.H. (1983). The incidence and prevalence of intrafamilial and extrafamilial sexual abuse. *Child Abuse and Neglect, 7,* 133-146.

Russell, D.E.H. (1984). *Sexual exploitation: Rape, child sexual abuse, and workplace harassment.* Beverly Hills, CA: Sage.

Russell, D.E.H. (1986). *The secret trauma: Incest in the lives of girls and women.* New York: Basic Books.

Russell, D.E.H., & Bolen, R. M. (2000). *The epidemic of rape and child sexual abuse in the United States.* Thousand Oaks, CA: Sage.

Rutter, M. (1979). Protective factors in children's responses to stress and disadvantage. In M. W. Kent & J. Rolf (Eds.), *Primary prevention for psychopathology* (Vol. III. Social competence in children,). Hanover, NH: University Press of New England.

Rutter, M. (1987). Psychosocial resilience and protective mechanisms. *American Journal of Orthopsychiatry, 57,* 316-331.

Rutter, M., Cox, A., Tupling, C., Berger, M., & Yule, W. (1975). Attainment and adjustment in two geographical areas—The prevalence of psychiatric disorder. *British Journal of Psychiatry, 126,* 493-509.

Ryan, P., Warren, B. L., & Weincek, P. (1991). Removal of the perpetrator versus removal of the victim in cases of intrafamilial child sexual abuse. In D. D. Knudsen & J. L. Miller (Eds.), *Abused and battered: Social and legal responses to family violence* (pp. 123-133). New York: Aldine De Gruyter.

Sagatun, I. J., & Prince, L. (1989). Incest family dynamics: Family members' perceptions before and after therapy. *Journal of Social Work and Human Sexuality,* 69-87.

Salt, P., Myer, M., Coleman, L., & Sauzier, M. (1990). *The myth of the mother as "accomplice" to child sexual abuse.* Newbury Park, CA: Sage.

Salter, A. C. (1992). Epidemiology of child sexual abuse. In W. O'Donohue & J. H. Geer (Eds.), *The sexual abuse of children: Theory and research* (Vol. 1, pp. 108-138). Hillsdale, NJ: Lawrence Erlbaum.

Sansonnet-Hayden, H., Haley, G., Marriage, K., & Fine, S. (1987). Sexual abuse and psychopathology in hospitalized adolescents. *Jouurnal of the American Academy of Child and Adolescent Psychiatry, 26*(5), 753-757.

Saunders, B. E., & Kilpatrick, D. G., Hanson, R. F., Resnick, H. S., & Walker, M. E. (1999). Prevalence, case characteristics, and long-term psychological correlates of child rape among women: A national survey. *Child Maltreatment, 4*(3), 187-200.

Saunders, B. E., Villeponteaux, L. A., Lipovsky, J. A., Kilpatrick, D. G., & Veronen, L. J. (1992). Child sexual assault as a risk factor for mental disorders among women. *Journal of Interpersonal Violence, 7*(2), 189-204.

Saunders, E. J. (1987). Police officers' attitudes toward child sexual abuse: An exploratory study. *Journal of Police Science and Administration, 15*(3), 186-191.

Saunders, E. J. (1988). A comparative study of attitudes toward child sexual abuse among social work and judicial system professionals. *Child Abuse & Neglect, 12,* 83-90.

Sauzier, M. (1989). Disclosure of child sexual abuse: For better or for worse. *Psychiatric Clinics of North America, 12*(2), 455-469.

Saywitz, K. (1989). Children's conception of the legal system: Court is a place to play basketball. In S. Ceci, D. Ross, & M. Toglia (Eds.), *Perspectives on children's testimony* (pp. 131-157). New York: Springer-Verlag.

Schene, P. (1996). Child abuse and neglect policy: History, models, and future directions. In J. Briere, J. A. Bulkley, C. Jenny, & T. Reid (Eds.), *The APSAC handbook on child maltreatment* (pp. 385-397). Thousand Oaks, CA: Sage.

Schuster, C. W., & Ashburn, S. S. (1992). *The process of human development: A holistic life-span approach* (3rd ed.). Philadelphia, PA: J. B. Lippincott.

Schwartz, C. E. (1992). Involuntary intervention: Does the benefit exceed the cost [Letter]. *American Journal of Psychiatry, 149*(4), 424.

Schwartz-Kenney, B. M., Wilson, M. E., & Goodman, G. S. (1990). An examination of child witness accuracy and the emotional effects on children of testifying in court. In R. K. Oates (Ed.), *Understanding and managing child sexual abuse* (pp. 293-311). Sydney, Australia: Harcourt, Brace Jovanovich.

Sedlak, A. (1991). *National Incidence and Prevalence of Child Abuse and Neglect: 1988 Revised report*. Rockville, MD: Westat.

Sedlak, A. J., & Broadhurst, D. D. (1996). *Third National Incidence Study of Child Abuse and Neglect: Final report*. Washington, DC: U.S. Department of Health and Human Services.

Server, J. C., & Janzen, C. (1982). Contradictions to reconstitution of sexually abusive families. *Child Welfare, 61*(5), 279-288.

Siegel, J. M., Sorenson, S. B., Golding, J. M., Burnam, M. A., & Stein, J. A. (1987). The prevalence of childhood sexual assault. *American Journal of Epidemiology, 126*(6), 1141-1153.

Simon, L.M.H., Sales, B., Kaszniak, A., & Kahn, M. (1992). Characteristics of child molesters. Implications for the fixated-regressed dichotomy. *Journal of Interpersonal Violence, 7*(2), 211-225.

Sirkin, R. M. (1995). *Statistics for the social sciences*. Thousand Oaks, CA: Sage.

Sirles, E. A., & Franke, P. J. (1989). Factors influencing mothers' reactions to intrafamilial sexual abuse. *Child Abuse and Neglect, 13*(1), 131-139.

Sirles, E. A., & Lofberg, C. E. (1990). Factors associated with divorce in intrafamily child sexual abuse cases. *Child Abuse and Neglect, 14*(2), 165-170.

Sirles, E. A., Smith, J. A., & Kusama, H. (1989). Psychiatric status of intrafamilial child sexual abuse victims. *Journal of the American Academy of Child and Adolescent Psychiatry, 28*(2), 225-229.

Smith, D. W., & Saunders, B. E. (1995). Personality characteristics of father/perpetrators and nonoffending mothers in incest families: Individual and dyadic analyses. *Child Abuse & Neglect, 19*(5), 607-617.

Smith, H., & Israel, E. (1987). Sibling incest: A study of the dynamics of 25 cases. *Child Abuse & Neglect, 11*, 101-108.

Sorenson, T., & Snow, B. (1991). How children tell: The process of disclosure in child sexual abuse. *Child Welfare, 70*(1), 3-15.

Springs, F. E., & Friedrich, W. N. (1992). Health risk behaviors and medical sequelae of childhood sexual abuse. *Mayo Clinic Proceedings, 67*, 527-532.

Sroufe, L. A., & Fleeson, J. (1986). Attachment and the construction of relationships. In W. W. Hartup & Z. Rubin (Eds.), *Relationships and development* (pp. 51-71). Hillsdale, NJ: Lawrence Erlbaum.

Steil, J. M. (1994). Equality and entitlement in marriage: Benefits and barriers. In M. J. Lerner & G. Mikula (Eds.), *Entitlement and the affectional bond* (pp. 229-257). New York: Plenum Press.

Summit, R. C. (1989). The centrality of victimization: Regaining the focal point of recovery for survivors of child sexual abuse. *Psychiatric Clinics of North America, 12*, 413I(2)-430.

Swan, R. W. (1985). The child as active participant in sexual abuse. *Clinical Social Work Journal, 13*(1), 62-77.

Tabin, J. K. (1993). Freud's shift from the seduction theory: Some overlooked reality factors. *Psychoanalytic Psychology, 10*, 291-297.

Taubman, S. (1984). Incest in context. *Social Work, 29*, 35-40.

Tedesco, J. F., & Schnell, S. V. (1987). Children's reaction to sex abuse investigation and litigation. *Child Abuse & Neglect, 11*, 267-272.

Telander, R. (1991). The wrong people for the job. *Sports Illustrated, 75*, 108.

Thoennes, N., & Tjaden, P. G. (1990). The extent, nature, and validity of sexual abuse allegations in custody/visitation disputes. *Child Abuse & Neglect, 14*, 151-163.

Timnick, L. (1985, August 26). Children's abuse reports reliable, most believe. *Los Angeles Times.*

Tingus, K. D., Heger, A. H., Foy, D. W., & Leskin, G. A. (1996). Factors associated with entry into therapy in children evaluated for sexual abuse. *Child Abuse & Neglect, 20*, 63-68.

Tinling, L. (1990). Perpetuation of incest by significant others: Mothers who do not want to see. *Individual Psychology, 46*(3), 280-297.

Tjaden, P. G., & Thoennes, N. (1992). Predictors of legal intervention in child maltreatment cases. *Child Abuse & Neglect, 16*, 807-821.

Trepper, T. S., & Niedner, D. M. (1996). Intrafamily child sexual abuse. In F. W. Kaslow (Ed.), *Handbook of relational diagnosis and dysfunctional family patterns* (pp. 394-419). New York: John Wiley & Sons.

Troy, M., & Sroufe, L. A. (1987). Victimization among preschoolers: Role of attachment relationship history. *Child and Adolescent Psychiatry, 26*, 166-172.

Trute, B., Adkins, E., & MacDonald, G. (1996). Professional attitudes regarding treatment and punishment of incest: Comparing police, child welfare, and community mental health. *Journal of Family Violence, 11*(3), 237-249.

Tyler, A. H., & Brassard, M. R. (1984). Abuse in the investigation and treatment of intrafamilial child sexual abuse. *Child Abuse & Neglect, 8*, 47-53.

Tzeng, O.C.S., Robinson, R. L., & Karlson, H. C. (1999). Demographic correlates and judicial determinations of child sexual abuse offenses. *Journal of Social Distress and the Homeless, 8*(2), 55-77.

U.S. Department of Health and Human Services, National Center on Child Abuse and Neglect (1996). *Child Abuse Prevention and Treatment Act, as amended October 3, 1996.* Washington, DC: U.S. Department of Health and Human Services.

U.S. Department of Health and Human Services, National Center on Child Abuse and Neglect (1997). *Child maltreatment 1995: Reports from the States to the National Child Abuse and Neglect Data System.* Washington, DC: U.S. Department of Health and Human Services.

U.S. Department of Health and Human Services, National Center on Child Abuse and Neglect (1998). *Child maltreatment 1996: Reports from the States to the National Child Abuse and Neglect Data System.* Washington, DC: U.S. Department of Health and Human Services.

U.S. Department of Health and Human Services, National Center on Child Abuse and Neglect (1999). *Child maltreatment 1997: Reports from the States to the National Child Abuse and Neglect Data System.* Washington, DC: U.S. Department of Health and Human Services.

U.S. Department of Health and Human Services, National Clearinghouse on Child Abuse and Neglect Information (2000a). *Child abuse and neglect state statutes elements* (Reporting laws No. 6: Reporting procedures). Washington, DC: U.S. Department of Health and Human Services.

U.S. Department of Health and Human Services, National Center on Child Abuse and Neglect (2000b). *Child abuse and neglect state statutes elements* (Reporting laws No. 2: Mandatory reporters of child abuse and neglect). Washington, DC: U.S. Department of Health and Human Services.

U.S. Department of Health and Human Services, National Center on Child Abuse and Neglect (2000c). *Child maltreatment 1998: Reports from the States to the National Child Abuse and Neglect Data System.* Washington, DC: U.S. Department of Health and Human Services.

Vander Mey, B. J., & Neff, R. L. (1986). *Incest as child abuse: Research and applications.* New York: Praeger.

Violato, C., & Genuis, M. (1993). Problems of research in male child sexual abuse: A review. *Journal of Child Sexual Abuse, 2*(3), 33-54.

Vogeltanz, N. D., Wilsnack, S. C., Harris, T. R., Wilsnack, R. W., Wonderlich, S. A., & Kristjanson, A. F. (1999). Prevalence and risk factors for childhood sexual abuse in women: National survey findings. *Child Abuse & Neglect, 23*(6), 579-592.

Wagner, W. G. (1991). Depression in mothers of sexually abused vs. mothers of nonabused children. *Child Abuse & Neglect, 15*, 99-104.

Wagner, W. G., Aucoin, R., & Johnson, J. T. (1993). Psychologists' attitudes concerning child sexual abuse: The impact of sex of perpetrator, sex of victim, age of victim, and victim response. *Journal of Child Sexual Abuse, 2*(2), 61-74.

Waibel-Duncan, M. K., & Sanger, M. (1999). Understanding and reacting to the anogenital exam: Implications for patient preparation. *Child Abuse & Neglect, 23*(3), 281-286.

Wald, B. K., Archer, R. P., & Winstead, B. A. (1990). Rorschach characteristics of mothers of incest victims. *Journal of Personality Assessment, 55*(3 & 4), 417-425.

Waldby, C., Clancy, A., Emetchi, J., & Summerfield, C. (1989). Theoretical perspectives on father-daughter incest. In E. Driver & A. Droisen (Eds.), *Child sexual abuse: A feminist reader* (pp. 88-106). New York: New York University Press.

Wang, C. T., & Daro, D. (1997). *Current trends in chld abuse reporting and fatalities: The results of the 1996 annual Fifty State Survey* (Working Paper No. 808). Chicago, IL: Center on Child Abuse Prevention Research.

Ward, T., Fon, C., Hudson, S. M., & McCormack, J. (1998). A descriptive model of dysfunctional cognitions in child molesters. *Journal of Interpersonal Violence, 13*(1), 129-155.

Ward, T., Hudson, S. M., & Marshall, W. L. (1996). Attachment style in sex offenders: A preliminary study. *Journal of Sex Research, 33*(1), 17-26.

Warren, A. R., Woodall, C. E., Hunt, J. S., & Perry, N. W. (1996). "It sounds good in theory, but...": Do investigative interviewers follow guidelines based on memory research? *Child Maltreatment, 1*(3), 231-245.

Watson, H., & Levine, M. (1989). Psychotherapy and mandated reporting of child abuse. *American Journal of Orthopsychiatry, 59*(2), 246-256.

Wattenberg, E. (1985). In a different light: A feminist perspective on the role of mothers in father-daughter incest. *Child Welfare, 64*, 203-211.

West, M. M. (1998). Meta-analysis of studies assessing the efficacy of projective techniques in discriminating child sexual abuse. *Child Abuse & Neglect, 22*(11), 1151-1166.

Westerlund, E. (1986). Freud on sexual trauma: An historical review of seduction and betrayal. *Psychology of Women Quarterly, 10*, 297-310.

White, J. W., & Farmer, R. (1992). Research methods: How they shape views of sexual violence. *Journal of Social Issues, 48*(1), 45-59.

Widom, C. S. (1988). Sampling biases and implications for child abuse research. *American Journal of Orthopsychiatry, 58*,I(2) 260-270.

Wiehe, V. R. (1990). *Sibling abuse: Hidden physical, emotional, and sexual trauma.* Lexington, MA: Lexington Books.

Wilk, R. J., & McCarthy, C. R. (1986). Interventions in child sexual abuse: A survey of attitudes. *Social Casework, 67*, 20-26.

Williams, L. M. (1994). Recall of childhood trauma: A prospective study of women's memories of child sexual abuse. *Journal of Consulting and Clinical Psychology, 62*, 1167-1176.

Williams, L. M., & Finkelhor, D. (1990). The characteristics of incestuous fathers: A review of recent studies. In W. L. Marshall, D. R. Laws, & H. E. Barbaree (Eds.), *Handbook of sexual assault: Issues, theories and the treatment of the offender* (pp. 231-255). New York: Plenum Press.

Williams, L. M., & Finkelhor, D. (1995). Paternal caregiving and incest: Test of a biosocial model. *American Journal of Orthopsychiatry, 65*(1), 101-113.

Williams, L. M., Siegel, J. A., & Jackson Pomeroy, J. (2000). Validity of women's self-reports of documented child sexual abuse, *The science of self-report: Implications for research and practice.* Mahwah, NJ: Lawrence Earlbaum.

Winfield, I., George, L. K., Swartz, M., & Blazer, D. G. (1990). Sexual assault and psychiatric disorders among a community sample of women. *American Journal of Psychiatry, 147*(3), 335-341.

Wolf, A.P. (1993). Westermarck recidivus. *Annual Review of Anthropology, 22,* 157-175.

Wolf, J. (1992). *Adult reports of sexual abuse during childhood: Results of a statewide telephone survey in Kentucky.* Paper presented at the 47th Annual Conference of the American Association for Public Opinion Research, St. Petersburg Beach, FL.

Worling, J. R. (1995). Adolescent sibling-incest offenders: Differences in family and individual functioning when compared to adolescent nonsibling sex offenders. *Child Abuse & Neglect, 19*(5), 633-643.

Wright, S. (1991). Family effects of offender removal from the home. In M. Q. Patton (Ed.), *Family sexual abuse: Frontline research and evaluation* (pp. 135-146). Newbury Park, CA: Sage Publications.

Wyatt, G. E. (1985). The sexual abuse of Afro-American and White-American women in childhood. *Child Abuse & Neglect, 9,* 507-519.

Wyatt, G. E., Loeb, T. B., Solis, B., Carmona, J. V., & Romero, G. (1999). The prevalence and circumstances of child sexual abuse: Changes across a decade. *Child Abuse & Neglect, 23*(1), 45-60.

Wyatt, G. E., & Peters, S. D. (1986). Issues in the definition of child sexual abuse in prevalence research. *Child Abuse & Neglect, 10,* 231-240.

Yates, A. (1982). Children eroticized by incest. *American Journal of Psychiatry, 139*(4), 482-485.

Zellman, G. L. (1992). The impact of case characteristics on child abuse reporting decisions. *Child Abuse & Neglect, 16,* 57-74.

Zellman, G. L., & Antler, S. (1990). Mandated reporters and CPS: A study in frustration. *Public Welfare, Winter,* 30-47.

Zellman, G. L., & Faller, K. C. (1996). Reporting of child maltreatment. In J. Briere, L. Berliner, J. A. Bulkley, C. Jenny, & T. Reid (Eds.), *The APSAC handbook of child maltreatment* (pp. 359-381). Thousand Oaks, CA: Sage.

Zimmerman, L. (1993). *Multiple caregivers and the development of infants' sense of self and other.* Paper presented at the Annual Meeting of the American Journal of Orthopsychiatric Association. San Francisco, CA.

Zuelzer, M. B., & Reposa, R. E. (1983). Mothers in incestuous families. *International Journal of Family Therapy, 5*(2), 98-109.

Zuravin, S. J., Benedict, M., & Somerfield, M. (1993). Child maltreatment in family foster care. *American Journal of Orthopsychiatry, 63*(4), 589-596.

INDEX